Building Social Web Applications

Building Social Web Applications

Gavin Bell

O'REILLY®

Beijing · Cambridge · Farnham · Köln · Sebastopol · Taipei · Tokyo

Building Social Web Applications
by Gavin Bell

Copyright © 2009 Gavin Bell. All rights reserved.
Printed in the United States of America.

Published by O'Reilly Media, Inc., 1005 Gravenstein Highway North, Sebastopol, CA 95472.

O'Reilly books may be purchased for educational, business, or sales promotional use. Online editions are also available for most titles (*http://my.safaribooksonline.com*). For more information, contact our corporate/institutional sales department: (800) 998-9938 or *corporate@oreilly.com*.

Editor: Simon St.Laurent
Production Editor: Loranah Dimant
Copyeditor: Audrey Doyle
Proofreader: Loranah Dimant

Indexer: Lucie Haskins
Cover Designer: Karen Montgomery
Interior Designer: David Futato
Illustrator: Robert Romano

Printing History:

September 2009:   First Edition.

ISBN: 978-0-596-51875-2

[M]

1252955496

To Lucy:

Thank you for your support, encouragement,
and love.

To Oscar and Max:

The "Daddy go work" days can stop now.

Table of Contents

Preface

Over the past decade, the Web has become an increasingly social place. Social activity has moved beyond message boards to become a wider part of the Internet. Most people have heard of Facebook, MySpace, and Twitter; indeed, many people now have a profile on a social network. The term *social media* is part of our lives for better or for worse, and expressions such as *citizen journalism* are commonplace. Facebook alone has more than 200 million registered people.* What is different in this new world? People will come to you with a prior existence; they are on the Web already.

You need to recognize and incorporate this change into your design and development processes. Your website needs to offer something genuinely useful and become a home away from home for your community; the people coming to your site need to feel comfortable talking to other people there and keen to come back for more.

This book is about making applications in this new Web, frequently referred to as Web 2.0. Much heat and light (and a lot of hot air) have been spent on defining exactly what Web 2.0 is, but this book will focus on the social web. Over these 18 chapters, we'll look at designing systems that support social human behaviors. I'll be using terms such as *social software* and *community* to describe what we are building and to reinforce the idea that there are people out there, beyond the servers.

Design As the Primary Approach

This is primarily a "design is how it works" book, based on my experience as an interaction designer and product manager. The hardest part of creating a social application happens before any code is written. Understanding human behavior and creating something that fits in and perhaps changes current behavior is a tough nut to crack. There will be plenty of technical discussion later in the book, too. This book will show you how the Web is changing, as well as some emerging patterns for widespread social interaction, where individuals act as a composite person across dozens of sites on the social web.

---

* *http://radar.oreilly.com/2009/04/active-facebook-users-by-country-200904.html*

Who This Book Is For

The book is aimed primarily at developers and designers (of all kinds: product, inter-action, and visual), as well as project managers and editorial staff members. These are the people who will be implementing and running the actual product. If you are already running a web community, perhaps as a community manager or a developer evangelist, this book will help you figure out how to extend the functionality of your site to make the most of your community. If you have one of the many other roles involved in making a web company tick—business owner, web producer, marketing, or editorial—this book will help you understand the issues involved in bringing people to your website.

Who This Book Is Not For

I hope this book has something to offer most people who are considering building a social web application. However, I should give you an idea of what you will not find in these pages. If you are looking for detailed code examples of how to implement the various features in social web applications, this book is not for you; it is deliberately light on code samples. Languages and frameworks rise and fall in popularity, and I'm not a regular software developer. So, rather than include a load of code I didn't write, I spoke to a range of active software developers and included their thoughts throughout the book.

What You'll Learn

There are dozens of decisions you will need to make before you can launch your new feature or site. This book aims to help with the ones that fall between project management, design, and development. These are the decisions that derive the essence of the product you are making, but there is no single group of people that makes them.

The title of this book deliberately focuses on the application side of building things for the Web. Websites are gaining application programming interfaces (APIs) and a means of data exchange, so they are becoming more application-like and less a collection of pages.

The Web is important, but it is not all-encompassing (for most people). You need to see your website in the context of people's lives, not the other way around. Building social software focuses mainly on human behavior and expectations and less on technical issues, so there is not a lot of code in this book. Reading this book will challenge you with a wide range of questions about the site that you have or are planning. Answering these questions will enable you to build an appropriate product that fits well into people's lives. This book will help you articulate and quantify some critical things:

- How to go about creating the product—the vital initial planning phase
- How to figure out what to make first and what you are actually making
- How to model the relationships between yourself and the people on your site, as well as their independent relationships to one another
- How to represent these relationships in ways that feel right for your audience
- Understanding how your website interacts with the rest of the Web, how to make these connections stronger, and why this is a good idea
- How to implement these ideas in code, and the issues you will need to deal with when iterating your site after launch
- Why having an API is important for your site
- Why simple feature-for-feature copying of another site often fails

You must know how to do the following things in order to encourage a devoted community:

- Build something that people will use
- Make them feel at home
- Give them ownership
- Track them
- Let them follow what is happening on the site
- Know what to build next

I can't guarantee that reading this book will allow you to create the next Flickr or Facebook, but you will understand what made those sites a success, as well as how to apply those ideas and nuances to your own area.

How This Book Is Organized

Chapters 1 through 8 set out a series of questions for you to answer so that you can plan and build a good website. Chapters 9 through 18 are more practical, exploring how social software works and how to create and manage your own social application.

Typographical Conventions Used in This Book

The following typographical conventions are used in this book:

Italic
    Indicates new terms, URLs, email addresses, filenames, file extensions, pathnames, and directories

Constant width

Indicates code, text output from executing scripts, XML tags, HTML tags, and the contents of files

 This icon signifies a tip, suggestion, or general note.

 This icon signifies a warning or caution.

Safari® Books Online

 Safari Books Online is an on-demand digital library that lets you easily search over 7,500 technology and creative reference books and videos to find the answers you need quickly.

With a subscription, you can read any page and watch any video from our library online. Read books on your cell phone and mobile devices. Access new titles before they are available for print, and get exclusive access to manuscripts in development and post feedback for the authors. Copy and paste code samples, organize your favorites, download chapters, bookmark key sections, create notes, print out pages, and benefit from tons of other time-saving features.

O'Reilly Media has uploaded this book to the Safari Books Online service. To have full digital access to this book and others on similar topics from O'Reilly and other publishers, sign up for free at *http://my.safaribooksonline.com*.

We'd Like to Hear from You

Please address comments and questions concerning this book to the publisher:

O'Reilly Media, Inc.
1005 Gravenstein Highway North
Sebastopol, CA 95472
800-998-9938 (in the United States or Canada)
707-829-0515 (international or local)
707-829-0104 (fax)

We have a web page for this book, where we list errata, examples, and any additional information. You can access this page at:

http://www.oreilly.com/catalog/9780596518752

Supplementary materials are also available, including a bibliography, at:

    http://www.gavinbell.com/bswa/

To comment or ask technical questions about this book, send email to:

    bookquestions@oreilly.com

For more information about our books, conferences, Resource Centers, and the O'Reilly Network, see our website at:

    http://www.oreilly.com

How This Book Came About

This book came into being thanks to Simon St.Laurent. He approached me after I spoke at the O'Reilly Tools of Change 2007 conference in San Jose, California. The following weekend at Foo Camp '07, over a couple of glasses of wine, we decided that the presentation should grow into a proper book. From there through the book proposal and on into the writing, he has been a great help. There were lots of books that described the technology side of creating products for the Web, but a lack of books on making social products. I hope this book goes some way toward addressing that need.

I worked in many places while I wrote this book: The British Library, my home, on the London Underground, on various Virgin Atlantic flights, in hotel rooms in San Francisco, Austin, Boston, and New York, and in a number of London cafés.

There is a lot of Gavin Bell in this book. This book is about social applications, which includes personal profiles and information. Rather than impinge on my friends, I've used a lot of examples from my own usage of social applications. I hope you'll understand.

Acknowledgments

Thanks to all the speakers whose talks I've sat in on and the authors whose books I've read. I'm sure you will find some of your ideas in here. Forgive me if I've not credited you directly.

Thanks to the many people with whom I discussed the ideas in this book. You all influenced the shape and scope of this book in many ways: Matt Biddulph, Matt Jones, Tom Coates, Ben Cerveny, Matt Webb, Simon Willison, Tom Armitage, Chris Heathcote, Adam Greenfield, Tim O'Reilly, Dan Saffer, Meg Pickard, Jeremy Keith, Gavin Starks, Edd Dumbill, Kevin Anderson, Leah Culver, Steve Ganz, Adrian Holovaty, Larry Halff, Simon Wardley, Leslie Chicoine, James Governer, Lane Becker, Kevin Marks, Paul Hammond, Artur Bergman, David Recordon, Chris Thorpe, Kathy Sierra, Blaine Cook, rabble, Kellan Elliot-McCrea, Chris Messina, Jyri Engeström, and James Duncan Davidson.

Thanks also to Derek Powazek, Matt Haughey, Leisa Reichelt, danah boyd and Clay Shirky, Mark Earls, Steve Souders, Toby Segaran, Jesse James Garrett, Micheal Lopp, Tim Berners-Lee, and Steven Pemberton for helpful presentations. I'd also like to thank the authors of the books I've referenced; there is a bibliography on my website.

Additional thanks go to Timo Hannay and my colleagues at Nature: Louise Morton, Mat Miehle, Ian Mulvany, Euan Adie, and Alf Eaton. Matt Jankowski from ThoughtBot has been an excellent development partner. Timo let me take time off one day a week to work on the early part of the book; the book is much better for it. Thanks also to Timo for giving me freedom to explore my ideas at Nature.

Thanks to the many people who commented on the public chapter outlines on my blog, *http://takeoneonion.org*, and via Twitter—in particular, Terry Jones, Paul Mison, and Brendan Quinn. I'd also like to thank Simon Batistoni, Joshua Porter, and Elizabeth Churchill in particular for excellent feedback on drafts.

I'd like to thank my editor, Simon St.Laurent; my development editor, Robyn Thomas; and my technical editor, Matthew Rothenberg. They have caught and corrected many errors and stray thoughts. Any that remain are my own responsibility.

My production team: Audrey Doyle, copyeditor, and Loranah Dimant, production editor and proofreader; Karen Montgomery, who designed the cover; David Futato, the interior designer; Robert Romano, the illustrator; and Lucie Haskins, who created the index. They all deserve my thanks; there is a lot of work that goes into making a book, as I've learned.

My parents, Arthur and Doreen, gave me the support and encouragement to explore what I've wanted to do in my life, which I've really appreciated. My wife's parents, Tom and Vivienne, have been really supportive and helpful throughout.

Finally, thanks to my wife, Lucy, and my sons, Oscar and Max, who put up with my regular absences while I was writing this book. I could not have written it without the love and support of Lucy, nor the smiles and encouragement of my two boys.

CHAPTER 1

Building a Social Application

"Why are you building a community?"

If you cannot answer this question after a few seconds of thought, the odds are good that no one coming to your site will be able to, either. The elevator pitch should be about value for them, not for you. What will make them stay around?

Social applications come in three main types: those that focus on products, those that focus on content, and those that focus on activity. You need to decide what will be a good fit for your community or the community you want to attract, as well as understand what is happening in related communities and sites.

There are many ways to visualize this. As an example, Figure 1-1 shows the areas of photography captured by various imaginary websites. The lefthand side represents the act of taking pictures, and the righthand side represents the act of viewing photos. Different sites sit at different places in this process. A–D represent companies that each have a single and different product aimed at this market. Perhaps B is more focused on technical advice about taking photos, while C and D are more focused on viewing pictures.

A new company might want to offer something different—perhaps E positioned as shown in Figure 1-2. At one level, noting where the other products are in the market in relation to you is simple competitor analysis—finding places that aren't already occupied—but there is more to it than that. To build a good application, you need to understand the flow of activity and how your project might fit into this flow.

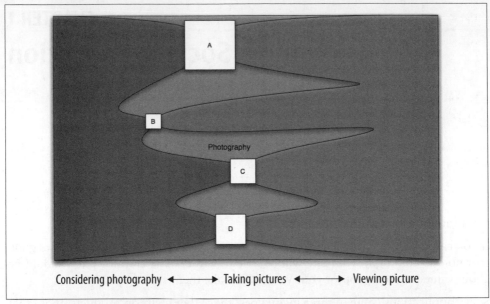

Figure 1-1. Flow of activity and corresponding web applications; each box represents a potential social application for photography

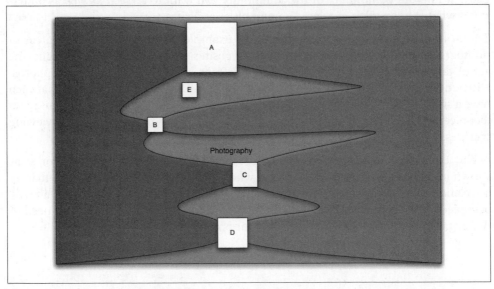

Figure 1-2. How your product (E) might fit into the flow of activity

A large part of this decision making draws on psychology as well as marketing or advertising approaches. Mark Earls' book *Herd* (Wiley) provides an excellent description of how mass audiences behave. Despite the frequent focus on individuals in social software, it is important to understand group activity, too.

Building Applications

Applications are based on the activities and behaviors of your community, but you can also borrow ideas from some of the great social applications on the Internet. I reference about 40 to 50 different sites in this book, but I focus on only a small number of well-known ones: Twitter, Last.fm, Flickr, and Dopplr. I chose these because they are popular, I use them, and they represent different types of sites. Roughly speaking, Twitter is a general conversation site; Last.fm is for listening to and recommending music; Flickr is for talking about photography and (personally) significant events; and Dopplr, the newest of the four sites, is a service for travelers.

Your site needs to make sense to an individual for him to use it—he needs to gain something from his solo interaction with the tools on your site, or at least see the sense in using the application. Community then happens almost as a by-product of the user's interaction with others. You cannot set out with the goal of creating a community. You can start with something that makes sense if lots of people use it, but you need to offer a core tool that makes sense when it's used alone. This acts as the scaffolding to support users returning to the site, where they will hopefully start to become part of a community for themselves.

Modern web applications need to be social by default. The Web no longer places site owners in a position above those who use their sites. No longer is it enough to see your site as a destination and to bolt on a message board as a small token toward interactivity. There has been a shift from issuing a persistent identity, which started with webmail (Hotmail, Gmail), to recognizing the external identities of the people using your products.

Many people now have a place on the Internet that they call home, and they are just visiting you. Integrating the preexisting lives of these individuals with your site gives them a richer and deeper connection to it. Bear in mind that you are likely to be drawing together an existing community, as it is hard to create a new community online completely from scratch. The groups you draw in will behave in a similar manner to real-world groups of people; after all, they are still human beings. Imagining that you are face to face with your users is an important technique to get your site behaving appropriately.

Genuineness and authenticity are key values in community management. You cannot make a community, you can only encourage one. If your community efforts are shallow and commercial, you are likely to provoke rather than encourage a community. Large commercial brands can work well with community, but they tend to play more of a supporting role. You have to be careful, however, not to try to take the easy route to building something that looks like—but really isn't—what you want. There is even a name for attempting to create community by faking it: *astroturfing*, which means trying to create fake grassroots support.

 Creating applications presents different challenges for startups and big companies. Small companies might lack the money and the staff to do big things, but they can be flexible in terms of approach and have plenty of commitment. Larger companies might have more resources and an established name, but they will have existing working practices and many other products to look after.

The Distributed Nature of Seemingly Everything

One surprising aspect of the Internet is the ease of information flow. The now former Domino's Pizza employees who posted a video of themselves doing unpleasant things to customers' pizzas on YouTube didn't realize how small the world has become.* Privacy is slowly evaporating, but you should make sure user expectations for privacy are clear within your application.

The Internet moves information quickly, but it also encourages distributed services. The traditional model for a website is a centralized server and software. More services are becoming distributed, such as music and video file distribution via peer-to-peer (P2P) services such as BitTorrent. Source code storage using tools such as Git and Mercurial has become increasingly popular for open source software. This same model can be applied to people. My music tastes are on Last.fm, my traveling habits are on Dopplr, my longer thoughts are on my blog, and my shorter ones are on Twitter.

Several services, such as FriendFeed (*http://friendfeed.com/*) and the Activity Streams (*http://activitystrea.ms/*) project, are trying to aggregate these fragments, recognizing this distributed nature can be turned into a strength. If you see the Internet as a place where people come to you, you will lose out. If you see the Internet as something that you integrate with and propagate your content and services through, you can take advantage of its distributed nature.

Real-Time Services

In addition to the social web, users are making a slow move toward a real-time Web. Real-time services are one of the main themes emerging on the Web in 2009. There are still blog posts, photographs, and longer writing, but being able to deliver content as it happens is becoming an important service. Twitter leads in this area, but news services

---

* *http://mashable.com/2009/04/15/youtube-fired/*

and similar businesses are also involved. Building a real-time service doesn't suit everyone and can be an enormous endeavor.

APIs and Their Importance

To effectively create services on the Internet, you need to create an API—a means of distributing your content and system behaviors across the Web. APIs let users connect to your application without working through your web interface, allowing them to build new applications on your work. Some companies fear people not coming to their site, resulting in lost ad banner revenue, but it is far better to reach out via an API and create long-term active users than to make transient income from a few click-through ads. The more someone uses your services, the more you can learn about him. Making this work demands good infrastructure planning and sound web operations—otherwise, your company will not thrive.

Collective Intelligence: The New Artificial Intelligence

Many of the newer web applications start out with community at their core, acting as collective intelligence gatherers. Built on an architecture of participation, they encourage individuals to enrich the site for themselves, and through this, engender a network effect that shows the richness available to all. A classic example of this is tagging—adding a tag helps an individual find information again, but it also labels the item for someone else to find. Community is a core part of these collective intelligence applications. The design process to make these work well covers much of the same ground as discussion-led community sites.

Summary

Designing your application and its role on the Internet is a start. Successful applications gather data, make it useful, and offer services based on it to the rest of the Web (as well as offering a fun place to hang out). A successful application is a combination of a small number of useful tools and a mechanism for social exchange among friends.

CHAPTER 2

Analyzing, Creating, and Managing Community Relationships

Building any sort of community site entails creating and managing many kinds of social relationships that are tightly bound to the context of their creation. In this chapter, we'll explore how individuals develop into communities and how this affects the kinds of relationships we can create. We'll also look at how companies and markets have changed such that now we need a new approach to managing and interacting with the people who form our communities, an approach that brings us closer to these individuals and creates less of an "us versus them" situation between customer and supplier.

Analyzing Your Users' Relationships

Perhaps you do not already have a space on your site for the people you interact with, but whether they are customers, readers, or viewers, they probably feel some sort of relationship with you. Developing social software will help you to deepen this relationship and allow these people to interact on a one-to-one basis with your company. Their relationship with your company is only the beginning: enabling the people who come to you to form relationships independently should also be a goal. If you already have a community space, you are probably thinking about updating it and also need to consider these possibilities.

The realization that there are several different types of people you can interact with is important and, perhaps, obvious. It has a definite impact on the types of communities you can foster. Age is a strong factor; younger people have a more immediate and personal relationship to technology than older people (I'll expand on this topic later in this chapter). However, this does not mean that older people are never going to become active members of your site—you just need to approach them differently.

Relationships with Baby Boomers to Gen-C'ers

Over the past 20 years, we have seen rapid changes in terms of what people can create. However, unlike the turn of the 20th century when the gentleman scientists were the only people who had the knowledge and financial means to experiment, today these abilities are open to many more groups of people, and cost is much less of an issue. This newest cohort is sometimes referred to as *Generation C*. The *C* represents content, creation, creativity, control, and celebrity, as defined by *http://www.trendwatching .com*, a large consumer trends firm—with a network of 8,000 trend watchers—that issues monthly reports on new trends. Generation C is not defined by a particular birth date, though most were born in the 1980s and later and are considered to be *digitally native*. They have been immersed in technology since at least their teenage years and so have very different expectations from people born in the 1960s and 1970s. For instance, rather than wishing a broadcaster would make a documentary on the plight of some group, they are likely to grab a video camera and make the documentary themselves. This urge has always been present, but it is now much more in the mainstream than it was in the days of analog tape and cameras.

People's expectations are often set by what was possible while they were growing up. For example, if you were born in 1971, you saw the arrival of music CDs. If you were born in 1985, by the time you were thinking about buying music in the late 1990s, iTunes had arrived and you were downloading music through the Internet. The music industry's plan to migrate from CDs to DVD-Audio or Super Audio CD wasn't a great success. Both of these higher-resolution physical disc formats languished in player and disc sales. Consumers started to demand individual tracks as opposed to entire CDs, and they wanted music that was free of digital rights management (DRM) schemes (not what the music industry hoped would happen when the CD was launched). Digital access to music encouraged people to think about reusing music and to break out of the album model for listening to it. People wanted to be able to listen to songs on the device of their choosing and in the order they preferred. This was possible in the 1980s with mix tapes, but with digital music, the record companies tried to lock the formats down tightly. Over the past decade, Generation C has won, as most music is now sold "DRM free."

Generation C is making a profound impact on how companies forge relationships with their customers. Until the late 1980s, other than a few people on the edge, consumers took a more passive role in society. Even the term *consumer* describes this "sit back" mentality. The process of creating content and even of forming opinions, as well as the distribution of the content and opinions, was in the hands of large organizations running television or print media. Now, with access to the Internet, increased computing power, and digitization of the media capture and production processes, consumers are taking a more active role.

Apple and others have been quick to recognize this new type of individual, sometimes called the *prosumer* (coined by Alvin Toffler in 1980) or the *pro-am movement* (coined in 2004 by Demos, the UK-based think tank). Products such as GarageBand (see Figure 2-1) are a good example of the fruits of this recognition. GarageBand offers a simple means for creating music, and allows people to create professional-sounding demos for hundreds of dollars, rather than the thousands a music studio might charge. GarageBand is also very useful for putting together (video) podcasts. These media changes are perhaps not directly relevant to traditional community software, but purely text-based communication is no longer the sole means for interacting online. Larger companies are not the only groups that can create an audience. Any motivated group of individuals can create quality content and attract an audience.

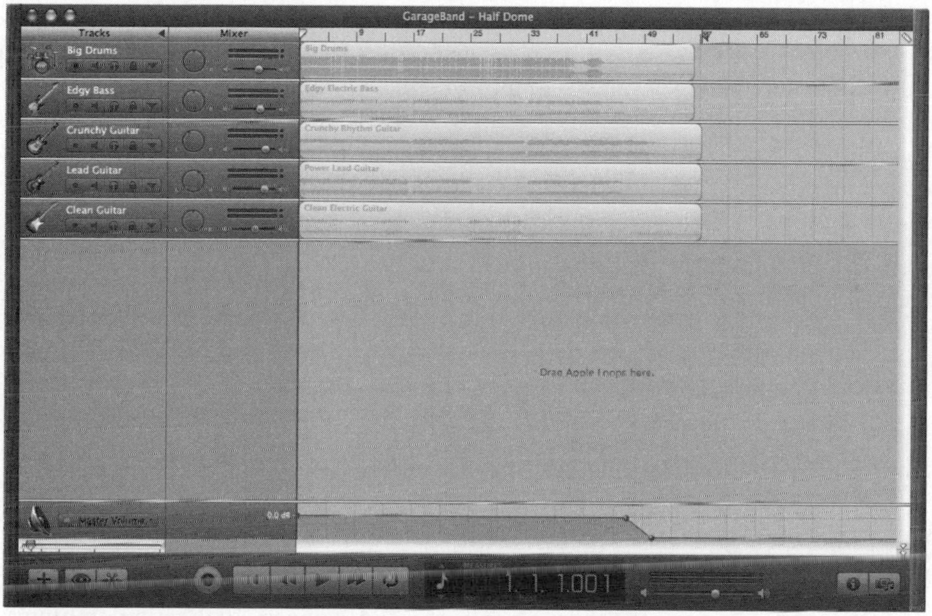

Figure 2-1. GarageBand, which enables both amateur and professional musicians to create high-quality music recordings

Behavior and Interaction-Based Relationships

The media landscape has changed with the rise of the *citizen journalist*. The derivation of this term is hazy, but it was popularized in the 2004 book *We the Media (http://oreilly .com/catalog/9780596007331/)* by Dan Gillmor (O'Reilly). The term refers to the idea that anyone can set up a blog, or shoot video and post it to YouTube. Media production is no longer the preserve of the large newspaper group or broadcaster. What relevance does this have if you are not in the media business? Your customers are now less likely to passively wait for you to respond to their desires. *The Cluetrain Manifesto*, by Rick Levine et al. (Basic Books), describes this change succinctly: "The end of business as usual."

Looking back over the past nine years, we saw a surge in web development, and then a crash. After the dot-com bust, a new approach evolved that focuses on fewer, leaner, smarter websites that value their relationships with people as individuals. However, for every Flickr or YouTube, there are thousands of failed startups. Getting the right mix of people and technology is difficult. Scaling for high-volume web traffic is also difficult, and every new technology raises concerns about it. However, scaling for community interactions is also a difficult social problem. While the scaling problems caused by growth generally mean that your product is doing well, scaling to support social growth needs earlier planning. The move to a social relationship means we are no longer simply concerned with the technical implementation of the website: "Does it function? Is it reliable?" We are now setting up systems that closely integrate with people's lives, and therefore these systems also need to solve problems of a sociological or psychological nature. Many interaction designers—among them Dan Saffer in his book *Designing for Interaction* (Peachpit Press)—argue that this was always the case, but the representation of people on our websites makes this explicit. It is no longer enough to make software that merely functions; we now have to create online spaces to host human behaviors and interactions.

Several common types of relationships can exist between an organization and its customers. I'll discuss these in the following subsections. Figures 2-2 through 2-5 show some examples.

 Choosing the right collective noun for people is tricky. Not every organization is a business, and not every organization has customers. So, I'll use a variety of terms, and let you insert the one that works best for you.

Customer-service-driven

Customer service is one of the more obvious reasons to engage with your community. This splits into two rough groupings: customer service based on the company generating the product or service, and customer service in a more retail-based setup in which the company is selling branded goods coming from another company. If you run an organization such as these, usually in retail, there is the secondary relationship with the manufacturer to handle. Customer service forums, such as the one shown in Figure 2-2, are often spaces for gaining help from the manufacturer or for helping other users of the same product.

Publisher-driven

The second group of community sites operate in response to some editorially produced material. This can range from a magazine or a newspaper to TV and radio. Generally, a strong voice at the center of the organization, usually the publisher, directs the opinions and views of the organization, and the viewers, readers, and listeners react. There

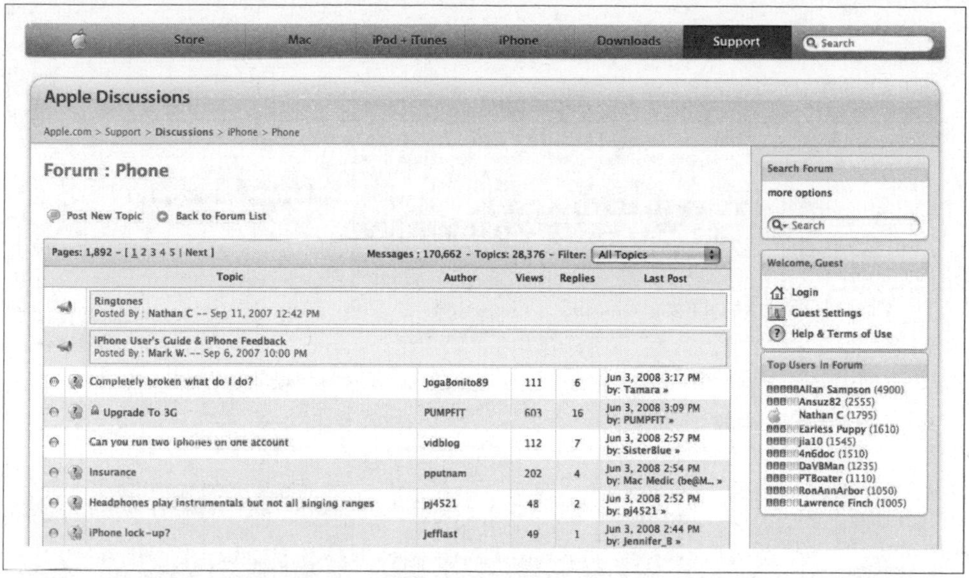

Figure 2-2. Apple customer-led discussion support website

is little opportunity for the individual to initiate conversation, though plenty of chances for him to respond and discuss, as shown in Figure 2-3.

Member-driven

The third group comprises people who want to host a conversation where anyone can initiate a new topic. This is the common message or bulletin board system, deriving from systems when dial-up was the main means of access. Jason Scott produced a documentary covering this early period of community, largely pre-Web (*http://www.bbsdocumentary.com/*). I'm making a distinction between these message boards and those support forums coming from a manufacturer. In the case of the generic message board, there is no direct support coming from a single company. The site will likely cover a hobby, an issue, and products from multiple companies, as shown in Figure 2-4. The contributors on the site do not have a financial arrangement with the people who run the site in terms of purchased product—by this I mean it is not a shopping site. These open, subject-led message boards represent a huge area of activity on the Internet.

Contributor-driven

The fourth group consists of community or social networking sites that allow postings of more complex content, such as Flickr (shown in Figure 2-5) and YouTube. Here, a more direct relationship exists between the site and the individual than in the other three types of relationships. The language people use to describe their relationship is

Figure 2-3. New York Times community comments on a blog post

different, too., i.e., people refer to their "profile page" or just their "page." In addition, they feel a stronger sense of attachment to these sites, and they will talk about their photos or videos with a sense of ownership. Often, this is because the sites help them manage some aspect of their lives, from trips to photos to events they are attending. These sites form part of their connected lives on the Internet. A major difference between these and the other types is that the entry to the site is often via a personal profile page and not a topic or the front page of the site. People visit to look at Tom's photos or to see which events Matt is planning to attend. This lack of a front door is significant and a positive.

Pros and Cons of Different Relationship Types

In the first three types of relationships—customer-service-driven, publisher-driven, and member-driven—the emphasis is on the site as a whole and the conversations that occur within it. For many types of companies, this seems to be the right model of interaction—the conversations are, after all, about their products, stories, or shared hobbies.

Figure 2-4. UK sports discussion forum (OUTDOORSmagic) showing community-generated reviews

However, these three types of relationships can start to feel a bit like islands; they tend to look inward for reference and there are few tools to connect the conversation to the outside world. The fourth social network type—contributor-driven—tends to be more open, allowing hosted content to be displayed off-site by embedding tools that allow for redisplay; e.g., YouTube videos or SlideShare presentations. There are many reasons for this. For one, the content tends to work better in isolation. In addition, it also works well as marketing for the hosting site: many people have seen a YouTube clip, even if they have not been to the YouTube site.

Contributor-led sites sound like the perfect model, but they can lead to a situation in which the same discussions occur again and again, as new people ask questions that have already been answered. Furthermore, some communities can suffer if there is too much focus on initiation of conversations. A representation of who contributes to the community and their level of experience can help. For example, a useful feature can be to show who has been on the forum for a while. However, if you simply count the number of posts, as many bulletin boards do, you can end up just tracking those who have free time on their hands, which might not be what you want. Additionally, you want to help new users find answers to questions that have already been asked. This is analogous to turning a training book into a reference book—archiving the previous discussions for both new visitors and regulars is a boon. Features such as the question profiling service on Get Satisfaction, a multiproduct customer support service, are

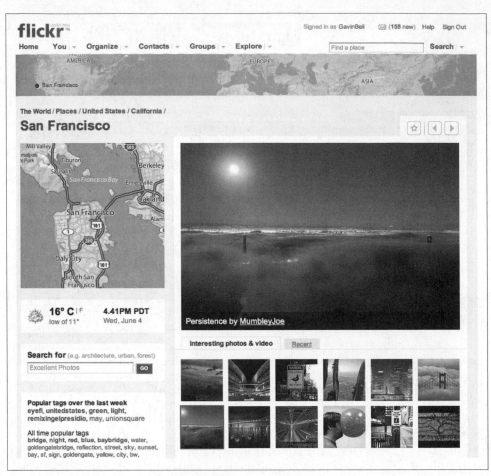

Figure 2-5. Flickr page showing aggregated content for San Francisco

invaluable for this reason. Essentially, this service tries to find questions that have already been answered that match the question being asked (see *http://getsatisfaction .com/*).

Analyzing the Essence of Your Community's Needs

Before you have people on your site, you need to have things for them to interact with. You need to identify the primary objects in your world that you can let your customers or readers own or give to you. It may be something more complex than just words on a screen, perhaps something such as pictures or video. You need to determine the essence of the interaction between people in your community, be it restaurant meals, books, pictures, or quality of plane travel. Table 2-1 shows some popular sites and the social objects around which they are designed.

Table 2-1. Social objects for popular sites

Site	URL	Social object
Flickr	http://www.flickr.com	Conversations about photographs (plus video and places)
Seesmic	http://seesmic.com	Video conversations
FFFFOUND!	http://www.ffffound.com	Pictures
Dopplr	http://www.dopplr.com	Trips (and meeting up with friends)
Twitter	http://twitter.com	Short text messages
FriendFeed	http://friendfeed.com	Aggregated flow of content and responses from a person
Delicious	http://delicious.com	URLs
Upcoming	http://upcoming.yahoo.com	Events and who is attending
SlideShare	http://www.slideshare.net	Presentations and the people who gave them
Last.fm	http://www.last.fm	Music listened to
YouTube	http://www.youtube.com	Videos

In the examples in Table 2-1, the obvious object is not always the one the community pivots around. At first glance, most people would say Flickr is about photographs, but more frequently it is your friends' reactions to those pictures that make Flickr work. Dopplr is about the trip and the potential for social interaction that the trip might engender. Last.fm is about the music on one level, but about social relationships and music discovery on another. For each of these cases, the site provides an initial means of data capture; more complex behavior can be layered on top.

This might seem a bit abstract, but bear with me. I have been designing social software for scientists for the past few years, so let's look at some of the analysis that resulted in the products for *Nature*, the science journal.

When examining what scientists do, you might say the primary things in their world are the experiments they conduct. Certainly, they spend a lot of time running experiments, and you might determine that they would like a community in which to discuss them. However, experiments are usually confidential. So, while the experiment is probably the most likely topic to engage a scientist in conversation, that conversation will happen only within the scientist's lab. Another approach might be to look at what scientists use, which might result in a product database site listing reagents or equipment. Interesting, but not really compelling.

Scientists are rated on their publications, so this is a good place to look next. They gain or lose grants on the basis of where they are published, so the conversation needs to be about papers that have been published, instead of papers about to be published (which would, of course, betray those secret experiments).

Stepping back from the life of a scientist for a moment, you can see the kind of analysis you might want to do for the people on your site. For each case, you need to consider what people might talk about and whether they are free to talk about these things. Then you need to create a framework to facilitate these discussions.

Photography is a different kind of field. People might discuss photographs and their merits, or lenses and cameras and their quality. However, how to actually take a picture is hard to discuss, as it is a more practical skill. So, you tend to see equipment and photo-critique conversations online, whereas illustration techniques are usually covered in books or on DVDs.

Essentially, you need to get down to the things that people care about, not the mundane details or the purely abstract. There is, however, great mileage in the "chewing the fat" conversations. So, there are many sites that discuss what Apple might do next, alongside forums for hardware and software products on hundreds of sites.

Now you have an idea that a simple message board might not be enough for compelling, long-term engagement with your readers. You'll want your site to reflect the products you create or the stories you generate. This leads to a challenging decision. Do you let people write what they want, or do you pick and choose what appears on your site? Sadly, the answer to this is not a simple yes or no, and there are legal ramifications underlying this decision. I'll return to this in Chapter 8, but I wanted to flag the possibility of an editorially managed community versus an open discussion space here. Each has strengths and weaknesses, so keep this in mind as you read on.

Alongside these different possible community arrangements are many types organizations. Even within the same industry, there are different kinds of companies. Each can create different types of relationships depending on its position in the market or the type of product it creates or trades. Some companies need to present multiple views of themselves to the world.

Apple and Its Many Communities

Apple is a good example of a multiview company that has embraced community. Apple chose to do it in different ways for each of its three audiences: journalists, consumers, and developers. (In reality, Apple has many other audiences, but for the sake of simplicity, I'm ignoring the retail community.) Apple has a different means of communication with each of these communities. For the people who buy its products, Apple has discussion forums on *http://discussions.apple.com*, where unofficial user-to-user support happens, under the oversight of Apple employees. For official support, you are still encouraged to contact Apple directly or use the support website.

Apple seems to take a dim view of negative threads on its products, and even locks or deletes such conversations on occasion. An article on a third-party site, Tom's Hardware (*http://www.tomshardware.com/re views/apple-display-update,1747.html*), covers the deletion of some conversations regarding LCD panel bit depth. The title of the linked-to article is "Apple Censorship." Many companies use this practice, though it does not make conversations go away. It is important to realize that the Internet is *one* network; you can push conversations such as these off your own site, but you cannot silence them.

For developers, Apple has a set of mailing lists hosted on *http://lists.apple.com* (again, it offers informal support). Apple also has a bug-tracking system and a ticket-based help system for developers.

For journalists, Apple has a press release website and mailing list. It also hosts invite-only briefings and events for the media and investors.

Each of these means of communication is a good fit for its audience. Mailing lists for developers is a good choice, as developers are good at using and finding technical information. It is also an ongoing conversation, one which the developer will perhaps be part of for years. Plus, the conversations can be archived locally on the developer's computer. For the more general discussion aimed at users of Apple's products, the public forums work because they are in an easy-to-discover place that many people will go to when they have a problem. (Visibility is more important than long-term involvement.) Finally, for journalists, Apple publishes press releases and runs press conferences; in this case, it fits its message to the working practices of journalists.

Determining Your Site's Purpose

To create a purposeful engagement with your (potential) community you first need to have a clear idea of who you are and the purpose of your company. For, say, fiction publishing, this might be entertainment. Once you know this, you can create something of value beyond an incremental extension of your core business. Moving from books to book reviews is social, but there are other areas to explore. For example, Penguin took this bolder approach and created We Tell Stories with the development company Six to Start (*http://sixtostart.com/we-tell-stories/*). The result was a set of stories that can be told only on the Internet.

Taking a wider view, book reviews are a popular idea. Another possibility might be fan fiction or sharecropping stories where community members write stories using the same worlds (settings, characters, etc.) as published authors. Neither of these is that satisfying for the hosting company, and to some degree it competes directly with the business of publishing books. So, moving onward, if books are about entertainment, then what about game playing that allows readers to continue experiencing the settings and characters in the worlds they've enjoyed when reading the books? This extension can work in many situations, and in Chapter 9, we'll explore some techniques to get beyond a simple message board.

 The term *sharecropping* comes from shared fields, which are common in agricultural communities, though the word has negative connotations in the United States because of past abuses. Some authors permit others to write stories in the worlds they have created, while others try to forbid it. For a good overview across different genres, see *http://home pages.paradise.net.nz/triffid/trimmings/volume1/art41.htm*.

If you create content for your site, try to avoid competition with the voice of your users. You need to make sure you do not create a platform that gives the impression that you have taken on the role of official "publisher" for your community. Clarity between what is your content and what is your users' content is important. Also, if the community individuals are commenting on your published content, it is important to have your staff interact with the community, to avoid a "you versus them" situation.

Creating and Nurturing Relationships

If the community is the focus of what you do—perhaps you run a hobby site or you are selling a product—you can concentrate on managing the relationship within your community. However, in any situation, there is a community host, and one of your most important decisions is who will represent your side of the community. As discussed in "Community Managers" on page 75, I suggest it should be a consistent person or group of people, and preferably not employees in marketing or sales. You need people who understand how the Internet works; they should be the digitally native people I mentioned earlier.

When Flickr launched, the hosting staff was present on the site for hours at a time, meeting and getting to know their new community of photographers. This early launch phase was intense, but it created a strong sense that the creators of Flickr cared about establishing a friendly community:

> George Oates (an early Flickr employee) and I would spend 24 hours, seven days a week, greeting every single person who came to the site. We introduced them to people, we chatted with them. This is a social product. People are putting things they love—photographs of their whole lives—into it. All of these people are your potential evangelists. You need to show those people love.[*]

This discussion on content leads nicely to a term I dislike: *user-generated content*. It implies faceless entities making valueless stuff. Kevin Anderson, blogs editor at the *Guardian*, a popular UK newspaper, renamed it *community-generated content*, which is better, in my opinion. Flickr's Heather Champ, along with her husband, author Derek

---

[*] From *Inc.*, "How We Did It: Stewart Butterfield and Caterina Fake, Co-founders, Flickr," December 2006; *http://www.inc.com/magazine/20061201/hidi-butterfield-fake_pagen_2.html*.

Powazek, uses the term *authentic media*,[†] which also indicates the right sense of community you want to encourage. However, if you can use more concrete terms, such as *photographers put photos and conversations on Flickr*, it is better than saying *users* or *user-generated content*.

Communities can also drive your own behavior. "The Archers," a long-running radio serial on the BBC, is a lovely example of giving the people something to do. The message boards used to close at 10:00 p.m. In the United Kingdom, bars close at 11:00 p.m., so the community set up a Yahoo! group to host the conversation until 11:00 p.m. This mimicked the natural lives of the characters in the radio program, so when time was called at 11:00 p.m., people would say good night and head to bed. ("The Archers" message board now operates all the time; the community encouraged the BBC to allow longer opening hours.)

Your company brand can work both for and against you when creating relationships. You need to determine the value your brand adds to your site. Will users react positively to it? Also, companies often operate in cost-constrained markets, so there might not be money to spend on community development. In this case, perhaps sponsoring another site would be a better choice than a company- (brand-) supported community site. If you don't have the resources to manage a community, it may make sense to support another site that does.

 If you have a prestigious brand, it can draw people to you, but it can also make them hesitant to contribute to your site. They may not wish to say something *lightweight* in the presence of senior peers. In situations such as this, you can operate moderated conversations like *The Economist* does with its Oxford-style debates. The Oxford Union hosts regular forthright debates, which encourage audience participation.[‡]

Chris Anderson, editor-in-chief of *Wired* and author of the book *The Long Tail* (Hyperion), notes that social networking is a feature, not a destination.[§] So you need to have a means for people to do something more than peruse through a "Rolodex of contacts," as Om Malik, a senior writer for *Business 2.0*, describes it.[‖] The social exchange around trips, photos, or music must be possible for there to be a reason to return.

The Flickr example showed the amount of work that launching a site can entail. Do not underestimate this. Whether you have an existing community or are starting from scratch, you will have a cold start in terms of community. The likelihood is that people

---

† *http://www.powazek.com/2006/04/000576.html*

‡ *http://www.oxford-union.org/debates*

§ *http://www.longtail.com/the_long_tail/2007/09/social-networki.html*

‖ *http://gigaom.com/2007/02/05/are-social-networks-just-a-feature/*

will come and kick the tires and then most of them will leave. If that happens, you need to look hard at what you are offering to and expecting of your community. They will not hang around to help you out for long; growing a community-led site beyond the first few hundred friends of friends is an arduous, but rewarding, task.

Summary

The aim of this chapter was to get you thinking about the kind of relationship you want to have with your community. What will the conversations focus on in your world? Who will go to your site? What will make them tell someone else about it? Why will they stay? Who will they interact with? Take some time to answer these questions before moving on to later chapters. This early understanding of why and for whom you are creating your community is vital.

CHAPTER 3

Planning Your Initial Site

When you're in your little room and
You're working on something good,
But if it is really good
You're gonna need a bigger room,
And when you're in the bigger room
You might not know what to do
You might have to think of
How you got started sittin' in your little room.
—"Little Room" by the White Stripes

The needs of the people using your site should drive its features and direction. You are no longer presenting a set of pages, but rather you are creating a place where people can talk and build relationships with one another and around your products.

This kind of software development draws on both desktop application design and website design approaches, but it takes a different shape from developing systems where users interact with an application rather than with each other.

Deciding What You Need

Creating a place for a community to hang out ultimately requires some software development, whether it's a small piece of integration work or a larger piece of system development. Why do you need to write software?

For relatively simple situations—when you are making something that is just for and about the community—you can tailor one of the many existing community products, such as message board systems or blogging software. However, if you want to have a blog *and* a message board, it can be difficult to integrate two different systems. Similar issues arise when you try to integrate content and social software. One way or another, you'll likely end up writing some software if what you're doing uses more than a simple post-and-respond model.

On the more ambitious side, building something fresh means you can get the right fit for your audience. You can build something that is tailored to their world, something *bespoke* rather than *off the peg (rack)*. Ensuring a close fit between the language and behavior of your existing audience and your new website will make the space feel natural to people. Creating a unique service costs more, but users will be happier.

 For an interesting description of the differences between the terms *bespoke* and *off the peg* from the point of view of tailoring a suit, see English Cut (*http://www.englishcut.com/archives/000016.html*), the blog of a *bespoke* Savile Row tailor.

Community software comes in a variety of different types. Assembling a site involves much more than just combining components, but these are the basic pieces:

Blogs
> Sites that host articles, usually offering a means of replying on the same page. The articles are listed on the front page of the blog in reverse chronological order. Articles may be written by an individual or a group, and may be long or short.

Comments
> Offer the ability to engage in a discussion about an article. While comments are an aspect of blogging, they can also be used in other contexts, typically in content that is published or broadcast in other media. The author of the article is usually less prominent than the author of a blog, and the interaction is usually less personal.

Wikis
> Collaboratively created and edited documents, usually heavily interlinked to form a deeply cross-referenced site. They are commonly used as project management or documentation tools.

Message boards
> Let users post short articles that invite responses, often question-based. Anyone on the message board can initiate a new topic, which is where message boards differ from blogs and commenting.

Social networks
> Sites that let people catalog and express themselves through objects that are hosted on the site—a photograph, for example.

Social applications
> Applications such as Drupal and Ning (also known as *white label social software*), which offer a range of the functionality in this list on top of being core social networking products.

Integrating these pieces and linking together separate pieces of software from different providers is hard to do well and often results in a poor user experience.

For example, you might use Movable Type for your blog, and then add MediaWiki as a wiki and phpBB for a message board. However, each of these applications expects to be the center of its own world. This means that it is difficult to get these applications to share the idea of a common registration database for the people on the site (registration databases are pretty much the foundation of a social software application). However, hope is in sight, as initiatives such as *OpenID*, a new mechanism for identity management, are showing that every application does not need to be the sole identity provider for its own registration database. ("Implementing User Management and Open Single Sign-On" on page 336 explores some of these possibilities.)

These integration issues mean that creating a social web application is not like creating a building or other construction project. When you start to create sites that are more like an application than a static set of pages, you need to take a different approach to development. If you are certain that you need only one means of interaction with your community, using off-the-shelf software can be a quick route.

Building a Web Application

Coming up with ideas for web applications is easy—creating the applications is the hard part.

Creating for the Web is very different from, say, television or radio production, or even book writing. In these areas, the means of delivery are well understood. For instance, fundamentally, the process of making television shows hasn't changed in decades— the special effects have become fancier and the crews have become smaller, but the process of making a program is the same. Time and money are invested in new program concepts, and copycat programs then take this new formula and apply it to other subject areas.

On the Web, the cycle has a different shape. You might start with ideas about online pet food delivery or photo-sharing sites or selling books or promoting charities. You could come up with 20 different ideas for websites on your next commute if you tried. There are no barriers, such as available channel space, so there are also dozens of people trying to do the same thing. So, what makes one particular site work and another that is seemingly the same disappear without a trace? The quality of the execution has a lot to do with it.

Let's step back from web application development and look at something that most people have experience with: cooking. Whereas I love to cook, you may not, but the setup is the same for all of us: we buy ingredients from the market and then prepare them at home. The meals can be simple or complex, but the process is the same. Good restaurants take a similar approach, but they have a large staff and more specific tools and processes. But regardless of how extensive the restaurants' menus may be, they all start with the same ingredients.

Like all analogies, this one collapses if you work it too hard (just like *whipped cream*). However, the level of preparation a good restaurant aspires to is the level you want to be thinking about when developing a new application. Good food is not only about the ingredients, or even their quality; it is about the overall process. Good ingredients, good hygiene, good preparation, and a good cook will generally result in a good meal. Skip any one of them, though, and the meal will suffer.

Translating the cooking analogy to web application development equates to hiring good people, starting with a good idea, doing the proper research, and then taking that research and ensuring that there is adequate time for all elements to be worked on. Website implementation breaks down into four main elements, the first three of which are "standard" web design practice:

Backend code
> Data storage and overall application behavior

Frontend HTML (including templates)
> Application interaction with the user

Visual design
> Look and feel of the application

Text
> Interface and communication

The fourth element—and the one that is often passed over—is the *copy*; the words that make up your application. This last piece is critical, as the language you use to communicate with your audience needs to reflect how they think and speak. Using corporate language or overtly technical terms such as *OAuth* (a means of allowing external applications access to content on a website, which we'll talk more about in Chapters 12, 14, and 16) will make it hard for users to enjoy your site. Simple, clear language describing purpose and intent is usually better (see Figure 3-1).

Choosing Who You Need

Addressing the elements discussed in the previous section requires selecting a development team and delegating tasks. I'll refer to a lot of basic job roles throughout this book, but there is a lack of consensus regarding precisely what tasks each role should perform. Following are my definitions of each role's responsibilities. Feel free to disagree with me, but this set of roles covers most of what needs to happen on a project:

Product manager
> This person defines what the product should do and who it is for; often this role is held by the main decision maker on the team. Ideally, product management is a single person who consults others, rather than a committee. It helps to have one

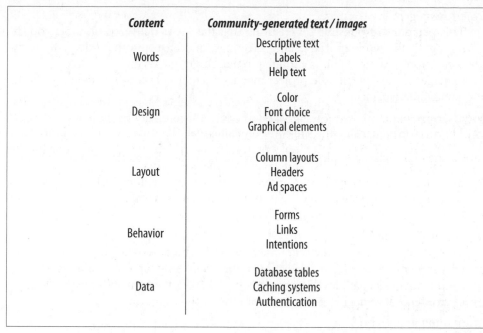

Content	Community-generated text / images
Words	Descriptive text Labels Help text
Design	Color Font choice Graphical elements
Layout	Column layouts Headers Ad spaces
Behavior	Forms Links Intentions
Data	Database tables Caching systems Authentication

Figure 3-1. The different layers in a website; in practice, each layer blurs into the one above and below it

person look after the product's long-term direction (at least the three- to six-month outlook).

Developer

This person writes the code that sits on the server and makes the application run. The developer will also define the database structure and set up the server infrastructure. As your company grows, you might also have a separate database administrator, perhaps a consultant. Having more than one person in the developer role helps a lot. In small companies, the developer often performs the operations role, too.

Frontend developer

This person is responsible for writing the code that generates the HTML, and often writes the CSS and JavaScript as well. This role blurs into the developer role to some degree when a framework such as Ruby on Rails or PHP is used.

Editorial

These are the people who are directly responsible for the company-provided written content on the site. In publishing or media companies, these people will probably think they are in charge, and that might be true according to the organizational chart, but you have to make sure they have experience developing web applications. Ideally, their role eventually morphs into that of community manager. Generally, they have the most direct contact with the people who use the site.

Project manager

This person is responsible for ensuring that the site is delivered on time, coordinating all the work efforts, calling meetings, and ensuring that adequate documentation is written. This is a tough job that sometimes is included in the product manager's role. Usually the project manager is focused on timely delivery and financial management.

Visual designer

This person makes sure the site communicates well. This involves much more than merely ensuring that the site looks pretty. Visual designers are responsible for the typography, color palettes, and layout of the site. This role overlaps with the frontend developer role and the interaction designer role. Ideally, these three roles cooperate on page layout, and their duties entail more than a simple handover of Photoshop or wireframe files.

Interaction designer

This person determines the potential flows of interaction through the application. Larger teams usually have a dedicated interaction designer. On smaller teams, the product manager handles these responsibilities, with the help of the visual designer or frontend developer and support from the rest of the team.

Information architect (IA)

This is often a freelance role. The IA defines the structure of the information on the site, and is heavily involved prior to launch and potentially during major changes.

Copywriter

Having a single person responsible for the words on the site will help to give the site a consistent voice and will aid in communicating what the site is about. However, often the interaction designer, the editorial staff, or the product person will take on this role.

Business manager

This person is financially responsible for the site and its advertisement. The business manager might be the editorial or product person, or a senior stakeholder outside the main product team.

Community managers

Ideally, any editorial staff members become the community managers. This role is responsible for contact with the audience, channeling feedback, moderating the site, and generally being the face of the site. Community managers can also act internally as the advocate for your site's users.

Small teams can work really well when launching a site. If you can manage to have a product person capable of handling the interaction design and information architecture tasks working with a developer who is sensitive to user experience issues, you will progress very rapidly. Adding a community manager, a server-side developer, and a visual designer will create a solid team. Once your team grows to more than five people (four people can sit together easily, six at a pinch), communication consumes much more overhead, and you will need to figure out more explicit processes for communication.

Planning the Life Cycle

Good products have a life cycle that evolves and responds to changes. Web applications in particular are not static services that are delivered once and then left in *maintenance mode* until no one uses them anymore. They need to evolve in response to the needs of the people using the site.

Web applications are alive in a sense; they change and alter their focus in response to the direction in which their communities are headed. Picking the right technology is only part of creating an application; picking the right problem is the key. Einstein once said that if he were given 20 days to solve a problem, he would spend 19 days defining the problem. When planning the life cycle, you are addressing the issues we discussed in Chapter 2: who are you making the site for and why will they bother to return to it? This is not a one-off capture of requirements—rather, it is a continuous process of listening and collaborating.

Expecting to Evolve with the Community

A pair of well-known examples will help to demonstrate how the evolutionary process works. It is important that you continue to evolve your application after launch. Communities and your subject are not static; new behaviors and better ideas will surface. If you stop improving your site, you cannot take on these opportunities, and people will leave. A social application in maintenance mode may as well be switched off.

Twitter

Twitter created a new type of communications medium that bridged email, instant messaging, mobile phones, and the Internet into a common messaging bus, one that operates at Internet scale. Twitter consists of 140-character messages sent from individuals to generally public profile pages, to which other people can subscribe. Twitter refers to the subscribers as *followers*, and messages can be sent by means of a Short Message Service (SMS) or text message from a mobile (cell) phone. You can also send a message from your Instant Messaging client application or via the web interface at *http://twitter.com*. Lastly, you can send a message via numerous client applications on the desktop or as web applications.

Twitter's main issues have been rapid growth and ensuing stability issues (*http://blog .twitter.com/2008/09/trimming-sails.html*). Twitter has also been watching how its product is evolving through usage. For instance, the syntax of using "@" and your screen name within a Twitter message comes from message boards and Internet Relay Chat (IRC). People started using "@" on Twitter to mark a comment for someone's attention. Initially, Twitter ignored this usage—the text was just displayed as plain text—but it subsequently adopted this syntax so that typing **@zzgavin** as the first thing in a message or *tweet* (a common expression for a message sent on Twitter) would do three things. First, it would make @zzgavin in a message become a link to the profile page *http://twitter.com/zzgavin*. Second, text would be added to the message displayed on the website saying that this was "in reply to" a message from @zzgavin; the "in reply to" text would then become a link to the most recently uttered tweet from the person who was being "@replied to." And third, there was a personal @replies view for these types of messages on the website as part of your own Twitter account.

The @reply syntax is supported in a number of external products, among them Twitterific, as it is supported in the API. This @reply functionality evolved again in early 2009 to find any mention of @zzgavin in a tweet. Figure 3-2 shows an early version of Twitter with a Replies tab.

Figure 3-2. An early screenshot of Twitter, showing the Replies tab, now reimplemented

Through clever use of the @reply approach, some of Twitter's early adopters encouraged the product team to add features it had not originally planned to. However, the team did not initially react to similar encouragement to incorporate *hashtags* (e.g.,

#oreilly is a hashtag for *O'Reilly*). Extracting hashtags required too much detailed parsing of the tweet, whereas the @reply just needed to check whether the first character was "@". Summize, a company that Twitter bought, provided a solution for hashtags by offering a comprehensive search product.

There is a balance between adding features that have evolved through use and maintaining your site. In early 2009, Twitter changed the @reply syntax to become *mentions*. Twitter now finds a mention of @zzgavin anywhere in the message. The feature has been renamed to *mentions*, too. Gradual evolution of functionality is the aim, which Twitter continues to do successfully.

Flickr

Flickr's initial product was a chat application with photo-sharing capability, as Jesse James Garrett discusses in his interview with Eric Costello (*http://adaptivepath.com/ideas/essays/archives/000519.php*). But Flickr added a huge range of functionality in response to how the application was being used. Flickr moved from being a real-time Flash-based chat product to a slower-paced but more useful web product with unique URLs for photos and persistent conversations. The real-time chat product, then called FlickrLive, was retired in favor of the purely HTML version.

The site enjoyed widespread usage of the web-based product, and maintaining both the Flash and the web-based tools was too much of a stretch for the development team. Removing functionality such as FlickrLive was a difficult decision, but it gave time back to the developers and allowed them to focus their efforts on the core features. And although some fans of FlickrLive were dismayed by its retirement, dealing with short-term unpopularity for the good of the whole site is sometimes necessary. The more popular solution would have been to try to maintain both products, but that may have resulted in weaker delivery of both. Focusing on specific features and stopping work on features that are no longer core is the right thing to do.

Keeping Your Application Simple

Thinking too far ahead can result in launching an application that is unable to evolve. It is very common to think that an application is not ready for launch. In fact, most people add too much functionality to their applications prior to launch. Keeping applications small and simple aids adoption, as such applications are easier for your community to understand.

Saying no to added functionality is really hard to do, but it is an important duty. To quote Steve Jobs in a *Fortune* interview, "I'm actually as proud of many of the things we haven't done as the things we have done."* Certainly, I've launched sites that had too much functionality present on day one. The problem with building too much is

---

* *http://money.cnn.com/galleries/2008/fortune/0803/gallery.jobsqna.fortune/6.html*

that you are hedging a big bet that you know what your target audience wants more than they do. As a result, you can end up with a site that has loads of ignored features and yet people who are clamoring for additional functionality. On the other hand, you want a site at launch to feel like a place where people can hang out with friends; you don't want it to feel empty. There are ways to mitigate this and to produce something that is big enough so that there is enough to do, but not so big that there is a seeming lack of focus. The starting stance for "Let's add this" should be "No"; the case must be made for each proposed feature. The book *Getting Real*, written and published by 37signals, has a good chapter on these ideas, which are neatly summarized in this quote from Clay Shirky:

> A brutally simple mental model of the software that's shared by all users turns out to be a better predictor of adoption and value than a completely crazy collection of features that ends up being slightly different for every user.[†]

Bigger companies can end up in this *too big an application* trap all too easily (it is less common for smaller startups, as they have less money). The scenario runs something like this. The company sets up the project and hires a product designer, usually someone with interaction design and information architecture skills. The product designer races forward, sketching out the possible layers of interaction and the types of information to be represented. However, the developers and designers for the project are busy elsewhere and arrive on the scene later than planned. In the meantime, the product designer has become committed to the functionality she has dreamed up and has moved on to some of the less frequently occurring areas (*edge cases*) in the environment, or maybe the more advanced functionality. Now, instead of launching a simple, clean product, your team and management are talking about the clever, cool stuff that could be made, and the launch date slips to make time to build "killer feature F." Sound familiar? This trap is seductive, and it is difficult to realize you have fallen prey to it. Figuring out what is essential early on, and then building small components, is one way to deal with this trap. Virtually everything in an application is disposable, as the Flickr example shows. So, if a team is arguing strongly for or against some piece of functionality, it might be time to step back and reassess. An 80% solution is optimal; explore your product space and focus on the core functionality and ignore the edge cases.

Avoiding the Line Item Approach

The opposite trap to the *too big an application* approach is the *line item* approach. Usually this comes from the project management side. A busy project manager wants to see the product described in terms that fit in a spreadsheet so that he can keep track of and tick them off easily. So, in the translation, much of the richness and interconnection inherent in social software is ditched or ill-described in a terse one-liner. This can result in an application with no cohesion or flow, as each element is dealt with in

[†] *http://blogs.wsj.com/buzzwatch/2008/05/05/wisdom-on-crowds-what-ceos-need-to-know-about-the -social-web/*

isolation. The best way to mitigate this is to use lightweight prototypes or simple user interface mockups showing each state in an interaction. To regain the flow, you need to be able to experience how the application will work before all the code is finished.

The line item approach can kill a good project and drive away good people, as it takes all the fun and passion out of building the application. Deadlines and delivery are important, but making a great product is more important. A line item approach can also lead to an inward-looking development approach, as the focus is on new features and not on the community you are trying to encourage. I'll expand on this in Chapter 7, when I address user-centered design and other approaches.

Building with Passion

It is worth discussing how to get to the nub of what your potential customers might want to do with your product. Most social software falls into the discretionary category. No one makes people use it. It doesn't file your tax return, nor does it run your business. Your site is competing with other fun or productive things to do, such as hanging out with friends, playing with your child, or watching a film. This suggests that your product should be fun or enjoyable, and people's interactions with it should be positive and engaging. Given a free hand, the best people to engender this feeling are those who are passionate about the subject. Hopefully, you work with some of them. If you can transfer their energy into the emotional aspects of the site, you will attract similar enthusiasts in your early adopters.

This community of enthusiasts is capable of articulating what they want, as they embody the hobby, interest, or recreation touted on your site. I'm basically saying that if you are building a site about mountain bikes, hiring some developers and designers who go mountain biking will result in a better product. However, not everyone works in a tight, focused startup company. Hence, the tools in Chapter 7 allow you to get inside the needs of the community for which you are building your product. You must feel a passion for the project. Any shortage of engagement on your part will come through clearly in your application's lack of focus.

Getting to the Core Quickly

What is the smallest possible problem you can solve for your audience? Often, there will be half a dozen closely related ideas to the main thing you will be making, but you want to build the main one first and not get distracted by nice-to-haves. You might want to get authors to tag their posts on a blogging system, allow readers to tag them, allow readers to mark a post as a favorite, allow comments, and then generate aggregate pages for each activity. However, unless you have a good system for creating the blog posts in the first place, the other things are a wasted effort. A similar case can be made for most pieces of feature development: get to the nub quickly. Also, adding features is more fun than making sure something works well, but bug fixing should come before adding features.

Taking Time to Plan

Once you've got the core idea, you need to plan, plan, and plan again.

Iterating

The 10-3-1 approach that Apple uses for its product designs is time-intensive,‡ but at least it allows for plenty of exploration of interface possibilities. Apple designers take 10 fully fleshed-out versions of the interface, created in Photoshop, with real example text. They choose the strongest features of those 10 and produce 3 new versions, and then they choose the strongest of those 3 and from them create a final interface design. The team at 37signals takes a user-interface-first approach, too, as discussed in *Getting Real*. Giving an idea this much time is very valuable, as it allows the real problem to be found and solved, rather than focusing on a surface feature. Ideally, the entire team contributes to this work. The product management, editorial, and design and development staff should participate in these iterations, although obviously the designers should do the design work. This allows everyone on the team to get deeply involved early on in the project.

Showing it off

At some point prior to completion, you will probably need to explain the project to people outside the project team. Typically, they will expect to see a home page, a sitemap, and some wireframes. Avoid giving them this, if at all possible.

In particular, I'm wary of sitemaps for web applications. They tend to trivialize the activity in favor of the page content. Once you have a highly interlinked system, one that has links from both people pages and tag pages to items of content, then the sitemap stops making sense. Ideally, you should offer these people a walkthrough of the visual created in the design iterations for the site. You can use linked PDFs or OmniGraffle files as a means of showing the site's functionality. A mockup in HTML with pretend content will provide a more web-like experience of the application. Create web pages with dummy content and mimic the behavior of the application.

In Chapter 7, I'll explain more formal means of defining the activity people will engage in on your site, how they will set goals, and how to document the structure of the information on your site. These interaction design and information architecture overviews are important reading for everyone on the team. I encourage you to use HTML prototypes as much as possible.

Figuring out the verbs

A good high-level task is to look at the verbs that represent the actions your audience wants and can perform with your content or product. Doing this will give you the main

‡ *http://www.businessweek.com/the_thread/techbeat/archives/2008/03/apples_design_p.html*

sections or areas of your web application. Of course, you'll need to verify this with your audience. For example, imagine you are creating a community site about outdoor cookery. What actions do people perform when they cook outside?

They prepare food, clean the barbeque, cook the food, open a beer, and perhaps take photographs. Your community might want to share the type of grill they own or their favorite recipes. In a few moments, you can list the activities a person might engage in. Note that none of this is about a particular choice of technology or even mode of interaction yet; it is purely about understanding what someone might do in this context. Then you need to look at what they might want to share regarding this topic, and you can then get to more concrete tasks such as uploading photographs or rating recipes.

"Figuring out the verbs" is key. It helps ensure that the visual, editorial, and development teams be in early agreement about who the site is for and what it is meant to do. This is not a software-based listing of the functions that need to be written. It is a level above that: it is identifying the significant actions that the people using your site will perform. Yet it is also not the high-level feature list of blogs and a community forum in bullet-point form. It is the shared middle ground in between these three areas that is trying to answer why they are using your site, and how. In Chapter 7, we'll look at some document formats and approaches that help communicate these ideas.

Communicating During Development

Good communication is important when developing web applications. The physical proximity of the development, design, and editorial teams is really important. Startup companies can usually achieve this fairly easily, but in larger companies it gets harder. One recommendation is to try to get everyone on the same floor, ideally within glancing distance of one another. If this is not possible, everyone should at least meet on a regular basis to sense-check the development cycle. If you are located in multiple buildings or in different countries, gather for the major product meetings. Then use tools such as Campfire from 37signals or IRC to allow real-time communication among people. Campfire or IRC beat email, wikis, and the phone, as it is searchable and a central place for communication to happen.

The harder you make it for your team to communicate, the less they will. This is bad as you want to put an end to poor ideas or weak implementations as soon as you can. Communication between individuals frequently happens outside the four- or five-person scheduled meetings. Progress often happens in the five-minute conversations held in a corridor instead.

Clarifying what you are making away from the big planning sessions means analyzing the high-level concepts that set out the main functionality of your site. Then you need to determine how to organize appropriate activities to create an application that offers personal utility, but then through repeated use generates something that offers social value, too. Understand that you are not just making a website for desktop use. Widgets, iPhone applications, desktop clients, and APIs all have their part to play.

This chapter will get developers thinking about developing small and adding features later, and will encourage designers to design so that new user interface elements can be added easily to the initial visual look. For the project manager, the aim is to understand the stages the application might go through and to adjust to the idea that code will be dropped and that redesigning is part of having a successful application. Failing fast and trying stuff out is the underlying idea.

Managing the Development Cycle

Building community software is a long-haul project, and getting to launch is less than half the journey: you will make the wrong decisions, particularly regarding database structure; you will change the design; that choice feature will be ignored, and your community will demand new and different features. Managing the competing desires of what you want to do and what your audience thinks you should do is hard. Two things constrain you: money and employee time. If you have plenty of money and time, you can figure out how to make the service work and continue to refine things. If you are constrained in terms of available people or money to hire them, you need to pick what to build or change. Virtually everyone is in the latter group. If you are in the former, good luck, and pay attention to your burn rate.

Managing the development cycle becomes the most important job for the product team. There are three main cycles in terms of running the show: the inevitable bug-fixing stage, the new-feature testing stage, and the main release stage. These cycles operate on conflicting time scales. You want bug fixes out the door as quickly as you can make them happen. During feature testing, you again want rapid deployment, but not to your entire audience. With a major release, you will want a bit of fanfare about the features, so these releases take longer to plan. The first bug-fixing cycle might take a day or days, new-feature testing will take days or a few weeks, and the main release stage is likely to take weeks or months.

Feature Prioritization and the Release Cycle

In the last three chapters of this book, we will look at how version control tools can help you manage the development cycle, but here we will look briefly at the feature prioritization and release cycle. Most of the companies I have spoken with use something similar to a monthly cycle for the release of major updates, but in between this they have interim bug-fix releases and test releases. The bug-fix releases are pretty self-explanatory. The test releases are a great way to find out whether new functionality is *worth its salt*.

Traditional approaches to release management have used a separately installed version of the software, which outside people can use to see new functionality. Newer thinking on this issue from Twitter, Dopplr, and Flickr is that instead of making a separate place for people to go, you add the functionality onto the live site. However, you make the visibility of this new functionality conditional based on the person viewing the site. So, you have a set of alpha testers who use the existing site and gain additional functionality. This takes the "click here for the beta version" approach used by Yahoo!, the BBC, and many others to another level. It changes how you develop software, but it can be hard to implement once you have a live site, as every feature then needs conditionality logic wrapped around it to figure out which version to show someone.

 Salt is important for maintaining health and was paid to Roman legionaries as part of their salary. The word *salary* derives from the word *salt*.

Choosing a Development Methodology

There are several good books on agile approaches to software development, so I will not reiterate their thinking in this book. I'm a fan of the Scrum methodology (a lean software development approach focusing on delivering software as shippable increments, rather than leaving months between updates; see *http://www.scrumalliance.org/pages/what_is_scrum*), as it seems to work well in mixed technical and non-technical environments. However, a critical point for any agile approach is that you must have buy-in across the company, as well as the time allocated at the middle management layer to apply it. Senior staff members and developers like agile approaches, but the internal middle manager for whom your project is just another in the heap can be the most resistant. You should check out Michael Lopp's book *Managing Humans* (Apress) for lots of great advice on software development management.

Collecting Audience Feedback

Collecting feedback from your audience is vital, but paying too much attention to it can lead you down the wrong path. Your earliest adopters will be a keen group of people doing advanced things, and what they require in terms of functionality will be different from the general person using your site. If you build for early adopters, you might make the site too complex for new people, or you might build something that seems like a really great idea but never gets used.

Early in the development of Nature Network (an online meeting place for scientists), we got a strong impression from focus groups that subscribers would host events, so we designed the event-creation system around this fact. It turns out that entering events into another event-management system was too time-consuming for many scientists. They already enter the event onto their own sites, which lack any sort of exportable feed, so they tend not to enter the events and associate them with groups as we thought they would. We should have waited to implement the functionality until we had enough people demanding it. Creating functionality that drives changes in behavior is very difficult to do successfully. It is often better to support existing behaviors and extend these, rather than offering a whole new workflow. Chapter 6 looks at workflow and change resistance.

Why Would People Continue to Visit Your Site?

Understanding why people would continue to use your social application is possibly the product team's most important task. There are some simple things you can do to ensure that they will feel comfortable getting started on your site, but one of the most important is to give them social context. If they arrive on their own, they might fiddle with a feature or two, but there is little to bind them to the site. They have little opportunity to interact with others. Compare this to arriving with a friend; they immediately have content or activity from someone they already know to interact with. An often-repeated myth is that social networking sites are for making friends. They are actually for continuing existing social relationships or supporting new ones made face to face.

Depending on the nature of your site, there are different ways to attract people to it and get them to use it and continue to use it. The *first use* experience is important. It needs to be positive. Critical mass and continued engagement can be achieved in several ways. It can come from a few vocal people, or many quieter people, or a bit of both. You need to determine how to get there; some of this will come from the role you see for your site. Are you encouraging new social relationships or supporting existing ones? What is the social context for the people coming to your site: a work or business relationship, a shared interest, or geographic proximity? All of this, as well as what activities you offer them, will impact how you attract people to your site and retain them.

Having social context gives a sensible reason for the site being on the Web. If your users are listing their intended trips and no one is looking at them, they may as well list their trips on a desktop calendar. For the first six months or so after Dopplr launched, people had to be invited by friends to use the site; this ensured that there was someone you already knew on the site.

Warmth and *a sense of belonging* might seem like odd terms to use when describing the Web, but they are key constituents in terms of how social interactions form and develop. Peter Kollack's 1999 paper, "The Economies of Online Cooperation: Gifts and Public Goods in Cyberspace" (*http://www.sscnet.ucla.edu/soc/faculty/kollock/papers/economies.htm*), lists four aspects of personal motivation for social engagement online.

Anticipated reciprocity means people are more likely to contribute on the basis of some future return. (Cory Doctorow calls this a *Whuffie*, which is the subject of Tara Hunt's book, *The Whuffie Factor* [*http://www.horsepigcow.com/book-the-whuffie-factor/*] [Crown Business].) Closely tied to reciprocity is the *sense of reputation* that people gain from repeated interactions with one another which can lead to recognition. A *sense of efficacy* comes from the interactions that people have with a community and observing the positive outcomes to which these interactions lead.

Finally, there is the *attachment* that comes from belonging to a community. People often describe themselves as a *Flickr-ino* or *Dopplr-ista* to show that they have a high degree of self-identification with these communities. They also often place links to their profile pages for these services on their own websites.

It is difficult to articulate these as goal-based or task-driven activities. Many people argue that there is no point to Twitter, but those who try it gain a lot from the interactions that occur there. The experience is the defining characteristic of most social software, not the feature list.

Thinking of the entire lifespan of user experience is helpful. The term *experience arc* comes from Adam Greenfield's book *Everyware* (New Riders Publishing). It describes a view of user interaction that starts from before people's awareness of your product and extends to after they have finished with your service. Product owners often focus on the stages directly involving their site and fail to understand the reasons people visit their site for the first time or what they might really be wanting. Also, they tend to miss the reasons for why they leave. The Apple iPod is a good example of a service that considers many aspects of the user interaction with music. Purchase, playback, hardware, and accessories are all part of the iPod and iTunes world. Adam Greenfield has an essay examining these mixes of products and services, which, while primarily focused on physical products, is thought-provoking in terms of the service design aspects of creating a web application; see *http://speedbird.wordpress.com/2007/06/22/on-the-ground-running-lessons-from-experience-design/*.

There are many ways to model an experience arc. A version I have used has the following stages:

1. Pre-awareness: Before the individual is aware of need
2. Awareness: Recognition of need
3. Search: Looking for a solution
4. Analysis: Choosing the right "product"
5. Acquisition: Making the purchase or commitment
6. Membership: Deeper involvement, self-describing; I am a...
7. Integration: Part of regular life; peer recognition in community
8. Expertise: Extending their knowledge, more depth
9. Withdrawal: Leaving the community with interest or need satisfied

It is worth exploring the individual needs and the product offering against each of these stages separately. This allows for needs and features to be more clearly matched up. Note that the first four stages occur prior to a user actually using your site.

Social objects provide only the basic mechanisms for these interactions to take place. The behaviors and language you attach to the objects will create the atmosphere in which the community will evolve. Your members will evolve independently, too, hopefully following the arc you defined earlier. Community memory is important in social applications. eBay and Amazon seller ratings are a simple example of this, but community memory exists outside of trading relationships. Allowing people to comment on or tag the content from other people is the essence of much social media activity. It is cyclic: I share some content and get feedback from my community, which will likely encourage me to continue my participation. If some of this content is entirely private, the sense of community breaks down. An example might be comments on content being visible only to the creator rather than to the public. By making the comments private, some of the warmth of the community is hidden. Allowing a variety of levels of disclosure will mean people can comment as they see fit: to a few friends, to a group, or publicly.

Summary

Building community web applications requires a lot of the same processes as building regular applications, but the influence of your audience will uniquely shape your application. A process of small, regular steps alongside some major launches will serve you well. Internally, you need to be able to agree on what your application is about and who it is for. Regular face-to-face meetings along with some detailed fleshing out will help a lot with defining your application. In terms of functionality, one or two main features is often enough, certainly at the start. Your community will expect your application to evolve and will be quite demanding about which direction they want it to go in. The trick is to be communicative and responsive to their needs, but focused on the few things that you want to do well.

CHAPTER 4

Creating a Visual Impact

Your audience will not see the code behind your website. They will see the user interface to your application through the web pages on your site. The goal of this chapter is to help you understand the difference between the visual approach to creating a web page and the visual approach to building a web application.

Before we explore how application design is changing, let me make an admission first: I'm not a visual designer. I can pick colors for the interior design of my house, but I know the final visual look of a website is best left to others. I know typography, copy, whitespace, and layout are critical to the understanding and emotional appeal of a website, but this book won't tell you how to create fantastic visual designs for the Web. For that, see *Transcending CSS* by Andy Clarke (New Riders Press) or *CSS Mastery* by Andy Budd (Friends of Ed).

 Jesse James Garrett distinguishes the code and the visual elements as the *skeleton* and *surface* planes in his book, *The Elements of User Experience* (Peachpit Press).

Instead, I will examine the uppermost layers of a web application and how they interact with the underlying code. So, I'll be talking about the HTML, JavaScript, and CSS that get delivered to the browser your reader is using, as opposed to the code that gets executed on your web server. This chapter serves as the introduction to Chapter 7, where we'll look more closely at what is actually going to happen in your application. This chapter is more about why visual design is important than how to implement good visual design.

Dynamic Interactions

The user interface for a community website is not the same as the user interface for a desktop application, and it performs more complex tasks than simple web pages. Nevertheless, web design lacks the tools that are required to create the sophisticated and consistent user interfaces we see in desktop applications. There are no NetBeans, Microsoft Visual Studio, or Apple Interface Builder-like tools that provide a simple graphical user interface builder for web applications. Dreamweaver filled this role for creating websites built from static pages, but web applications are more complicated than that.

The Power of Partial Page Reloads

This in-between application space has evolved from the ability to reload only part of a web page. Reloading only part of a page speeds up website interaction; there is less to (re)download, and usually it means fewer pages to navigate to achieve the same result. In-place editing has become a popular approach for maintaining content, such as profile pages, as opposed to going to a separate edit page. Google's Gmail popularized the use of the `XMLHttpRequest` JavaScript object, which lets you update only the parts of a web page that change instead of reloading the entire page. `XMLHttpRequest` was originally built into Microsoft Internet Explorer to support Outlook Web Access 2000, but then it was implemented in Mozilla 1.0 in 2002; today, it is available in Safari, Firefox, and other browsers.

 In his essay, "Ajax: A New Approach to Web Applications" (*http://www.adaptivepath.com/ideas/essays/archives/000385.php*), Jesse James Garrett introduced the term *Ajax* to describe the combined use of `XMLHttpRequest` with other technologies to create a better web experience.

Partial page reloads mean your interactions move from being based on pages to being based on the main element the page is about: for instance, the photograph, scientific paper, or song. This shift moves the design relationship away from pages and toward data, elements, and templates. This means that rethinking how design is practiced and identifying elements that can be recombined, as opposed to whole pages, is a better approach.

Designing Around Community-Generated Internal Pages

Traditionally, web design looked at entire pages and focused heavily on the content and visual look of the site's home page. Thanks to Google and other search engines, visitors to your site are much more likely to arrive on an internal page. People are also much more likely to link to an internal page. Again, the focus moves to the elements that become recombined with other content—in this case, the content provided by your community. It is arguably a harder design challenge to generate elements that can be recombined than to generate whole pages at a time.

The visual look of a site changes when it is built from templates with community-generated content and a more flowing style of interaction. Small numbers of pages designed with a more illustrated or handcrafted look give way to a lighter, less graphical layout that relies much more on CSS and icons than on single page designs with large graphical elements. The choice between a fluid or stretchy page layout versus a fixed-width design remains. A fixed layout with flexible internal sections is a popular choice for web application development, while setting a maximum width means that special coherency between elements can be maintained.

The unpredictability of the actual content to be displayed within templates means that these page layouts need to be more accommodating than typical static pages. Each page in a web application tends to be the result of someone's interaction with the site or be filled with content that your community creates. The majority of pages on a site will be for public display, but a site can also include a range of private pages for content upload and account management. Anything that is generated uniquely for a person is usually a private page. Such pages can have a different design treatment. A good example is the Flickr Organizr (*http://www.flickr.com/tools/organizr.gne*), which feels more like an application than a set of publicly viewable web pages.

These newer types of websites offer visitors the chance to do something. Often, a person can do several things on a page, and can get to a page from several different paths. To make sense of this, what becomes relevant are the people, the objects in the content, the actions, and the connections between them. On a page about a music track, for example, the tags might relate to the actual track, whereas on a page about the artist, they will relate to the artist and her entire body of work. The ability to comment means nothing unless it is clear what is being commented on. Identifying who owns or created something gives a lot of clarity to a page. The music track on an album page means one thing; the same track appearing on my own listening page means something different.

Finally, the idea of a page having a fixed position in a hierarchy also becomes less relevant. There is no longer a single contents page and a set order for exploring the site. Any route through the site can make sense, and most journeys will not start at the site's home page. In Chapter 13, we'll examine the kinds of navigation that are required to support browsing and discovery in social web applications.

Visual Design and Navigation

The reams of heavy graphical designs from previous years, which looked more like illustrations from a book than web pages, are largely in the past, though some of these applications, such as Fire Eagle, do have beautiful artwork. Today, social web applications tend to have minimal designs that let the content contributed by the community shine through. Figures 4-1 through 4-4 show some well-thought-out, well-designed social sites.

Figure 4-1. *The visual design of the now-closed Pownce*

Figure 4-2. *Fire Eagle showing my current location*

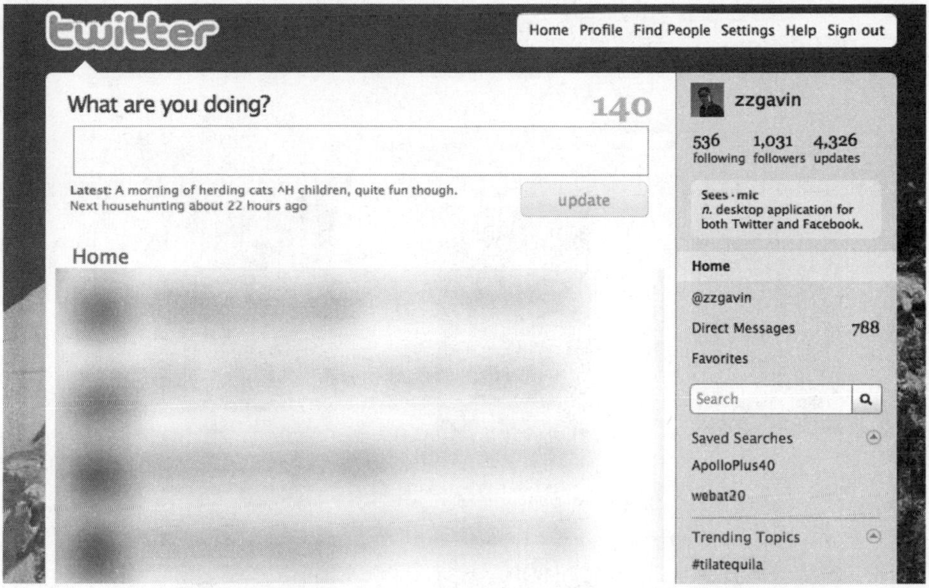

Figure 4-3. Twitter showing its pared-down visual look; messages from other people have been made anonymous (I provided the snowy mountain image in the background)

The shift from static to dynamic pages has impacted the work of the visual designer. Figure 4-5 shows this shift.

Depending on the type of application you are making, the amount of dynamic behavior that your site can express will vary. The more people that use your site in a social manner, the more likely it is to behave more like an application and less like a document-based website.

A social network is the most *application-like* of these examples. In these social communities, the entry points are generally internal pages—often a person's profile page—and the navigation flows from the content on the page rather than from any sort of hierarchy. However, such pages often include directions to the main centers of activity, as shown in Figures 4-6 and 4-7.

The main navigation of a site should include four to five key elements at most. These should focus on the site's primary objects: people, groups of people, and the content, usually emphasizing recent and relevant activity. The Flickr example shown in Figure 4-7 actually shows two levels of navigation: the main navigation elements, as well as the navigation for my photostream. The navigation elements on a site will change as the site grows and new functionality is added. For instance, the Map link on the Flickr site is a recent addition.

The Nature Network website, shown in Figure 4-8, has three levels of navigation. Nature Network is the social application that supports Nature.com, a science

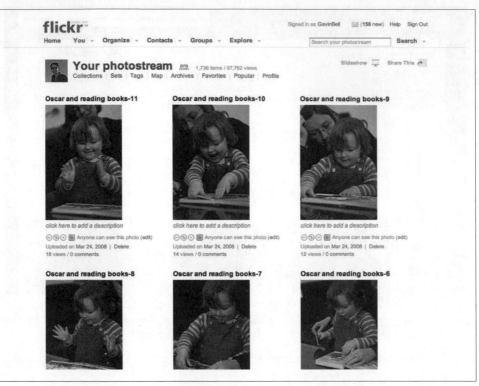

Figure 4-4. Flickr, which lets the photographs shine, keeping the page furniture minimal and out of the way

journal.* The left side of the page has two main links: one to the Nature.com home page and the other to the Nature Network home page via the logo.

On the right side of the figure, there are three levels of navigation. The topmost level is a common form of navigation that appears on other sites across Nature.com, and it provides a common reference for the social activities on Nature.com. For instance, Profile shows you your own profile page, Network shows you your list of friends, Snapshot gives you updates from everyone in your network, and Account takes you to your Nature.com account admin page.

The next level down is the Nature Network sitewide navigation showing each main content area, as well as a page to get to the private activity pages, labeled "You." Each of these sections has a submenu with specific options for that area. We decided not to use drop-down menus, so all navigation options are always visible.

---

* Nature Network is the social community brand from *Nature*, the science journal. I created some of the interaction design for social software for *Nature*, in particular the navigational elements in Figure 4-8.

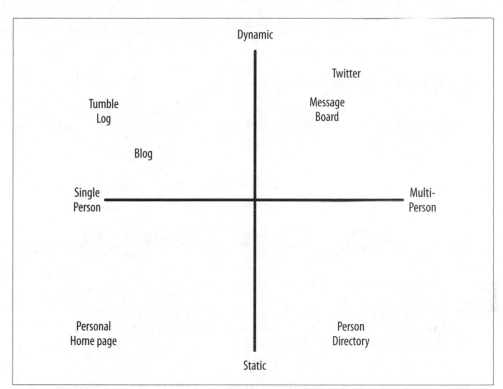

Figure 4-5. Shift from static to dynamic visual design

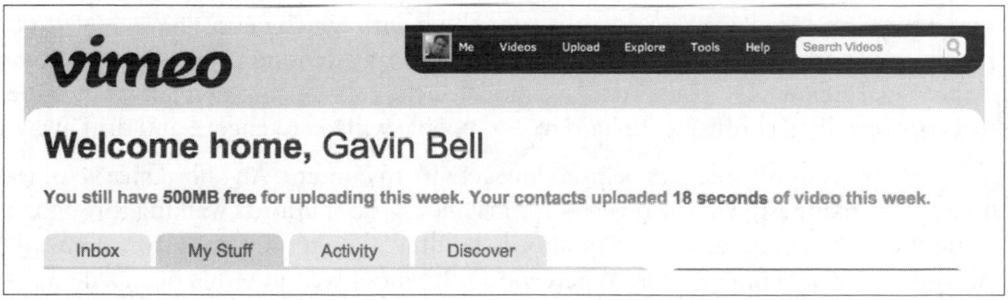

Figure 4-6. Vimeo, the video-sharing site, showing the main navigation options

This type of navigation represents a common compromise: how to provide navigation that shows off the functionality of a site for newcomers, how to show the relevant view of a site for a specific person, and how to represent the parent company, in this case Nature.com. The topmost menu allows Nature Network to act as a coordinating influence across other sites and brings all the social activity together.

Figure 4-7. The main navigation elements from Flickr; these are enough for you to start exploring the site

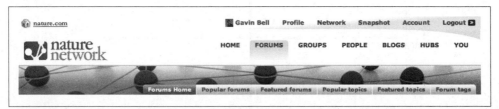

Figure 4-8. Navigation options for Nature Network

 The *Smashing Magazine* website provides many more examples of navigation menus: *http://www.smashingmagazine.com/2008/02/26/naviga tion-menus-trends-and-examples/*.

The focus is not on the pages per se, but on the people and the content on those pages. The navigation is spurred by the relationships between the content and the people who created it. This is a different way of thinking about site design. Jyri Engeström of Jaiku coined the term *social object* to describe something with which people have a relationship, be it a football team, a photograph on Flickr, or a scientific paper. You can have all the social elements in place and have modeled the relationship perfectly, but if the site is unappealing, confusing, or hard to use, people will fail to engage and drift away.

Creating and using affordances helps to link activity to content. An *affordance* is something that is manifested in the object—for instance, a door affords walking through, a window affords opening, and a cup affords holding. The term comes from James J. Gibson[†] and his theories on visual perception. It works well in terms of social application design. Creating simple, obvious prompts for action gives people clear cues regarding what it is possible to do on a page. The ability to add a comment and to clearly show what is being commented on is one example. In terms of navigation, placing elements so that they can be used as navigational tools works well, particularly for tags.

The core object page should have a clear purpose: to link to the creator and his content, and to provide a means for social interaction around that content.

† *http://en.wikipedia.org/wiki/Affordance*

Design First

A usability study found that people make up their minds about a site in seconds.‡ They don't take time to read the detailed copy before judging your site. They look for the next actions they can take, based on a quick, visual survey of the page. Good visual design is essential for making sites that people want to use.

The warmth and emotional context of a site come from the visual design. How you choose to portray your content, your use of whitespace and color, and your choice of typography all communicate what your site is about. Changing the color palette and typography can radically change the mood of your site. Visual designers are the people who will create this at-a-glance communication.

Page Types

There are several different types of pages to design for in a web application. The most obvious is the home page. On the home page, you want to summarize the purpose and attraction of your site. There are commonly two versions of a home page: one for people who have logged in and one for people who are just visiting (see Chapter 13). A lot of undue attention gets focused on the home page—it is an important page, just not the *most* important page. A home page for people who are not logged in acts as an advertisement, showing off the functionality and content of your site. An important aim is to get people to sign up for your site. In Chapter 18, I'll show several examples of home pages to help you decide which one might be right for your product.

The most important types of pages are those that represent a person to the rest of the site and those that host the her content. There will be tens of thousands of each of these pages on your site, and they will make up the bulk of your traffic. Spend time on these pages and iterate them gradually. These are the pages your members will regard as their own.

There are also two additional groups of pages. The *static pages* contain your help text, guidelines, API notes, and terms of service; the actual *application pages* are the forms-based pages that drive your site. The static pages are easy to deal with. Many resources are available to help you design flat pages of content. From a design point of view, the application pages are the most difficult to get right. These pages are tied to the code base once you have launched, and they have multiple paths and error states. A thumbnail flowchart is very helpful in documenting the flow of application pages (see Figure 4-9). Quick pencil sketches of each page can indicate which pages will need a full design and which can be created from a combination of elements. Chapter 7 explores the benefits of lightweight prototypes versus full graphical mockups.

---

‡ *http://websiteoptimization.com/speed/tweak/blink/*

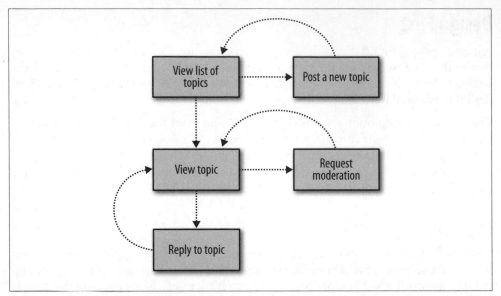

Figure 4-9. Message board software as a thumbnail wireframe representing page state and return paths in an application; the curved lines show the page returned to after performing the action

Forms in HTML can be difficult to do well, particularly when adding elements or explanatory text between form elements. It is worth having face-to-face discussions with the frontend developer, visual designer, and product owner before settling on a layout. In particular, be sure to explore the cost of changing or adding elements to a design.

The Amazon payment process is a good example of a complex forms-based application. It has changed quite a lot over the past five years, and it alters its behavior depending on whether you have ordered something from the site in the past. Several years ago, the Amazon site would always take you through all five stages of the order process. Now it will note your preferences from previous purchases and will give you the option to alter any detail from an order confirmation page. This reduces the number of pages you need to navigate from five to two or three, in most cases.

Search is also an area that can become complex very quickly. Many people adhere to the idea that a good search interface is one with many fields and buttons. Clever choice of default fields to search can simplify this radically. Chapters 7 and 16 explore search in more depth.

Designer Roles and Team Approaches

Designers who can write valid HTML and CSS are preferable, but first and foremost they need to be good visual designers. Designers inhabit a complex world. They need to wrangle with color, space, and typography, but they also need to design for applications. Ideally, your designer will be able to produce HTML and CSS pages rather than Photoshop JPEGs, but if not, he must at least understand how his design can be implemented in CSS across the main browsers. If he produces visual designs that require your frontend developer to spend days writing CSS, the product lead needs to assess the resulting complexity, which can be difficult or impossible to implement in CSS across all browsers. The frontend developer will have enough work ensuring browser compatibility across CSS and JavaScript. Note that some frontend people do just want the Photoshop file, but that does not obviate your designer from thinking about the CSS implementation as well.

Visual design approach

Different teams work in different ways. The web application company 37signals focuses on team collaboration tools and espouses a strong stance of getting the visual design done first and the code done second. Apple uses a similar approach (see the sidebar "Apple's Design Approach"). However, these approaches can often be the wrong place to start. We all have preconceived ideas of what makes something work visually, so we can get stuck debating color and font choice before we have worked out what the site should be doing. If your team has not agreed on the basic functionality of your site, you may end up debating surface issues and not understanding the underlying problem you are attempting to solve for your readers.

The 37signals and Apple approaches work for different reasons. In the 37signals case, with its "No Functional Spec" (*http://www.37signals.com/svn/archives/001050.php*) and "Interface First" (*http://gettingreal.37signals.com/ch09_Interface_First.php*) articles, it is easy to miss that the site is about the user experience, not the visual design. A preferable approach is one that avoids documenting human behavior, and instead focuses on creating experiences for humans to assess. Make something that is functional, not a (non)functional spec, to paraphrase the Apple and 37signals philosophies. This is a good idea, but first you need to get to the place where you know what you are attempting to build. In Chapter 7, I will introduce you to the service functionality diagram, which is a one-page document that you can use to get a basic understanding of what the new feature or service should be doing.

Apple's Design Approach

As we discussed briefly in Chapter 3, Apple has a seemingly novel way of working. It uses its 10-3-1 model to develop desktop software and interface elements for its operating systems. The basic model is a three-phase approach. During the first phase, it creates 10 fully worked-out interfaces for the new product or feature. These are entirely separate interfaces, not just color variations. Then, following a review, it creates 3 new interfaces using the best of the previous 10. Finally, it creates the final interface using the best elements of the three designs from the second phase. This approach allows Apple to find many different solutions to the same problem.

Alongside this, Apple runs a pair of important meetings that drive the project process. On a weekly basis, it has an open ideas meeting where people can suggest new ideas

---

for the current project. Later in the same week, the team gathers for a business meeting to assess current timelines and integrate new ideas.

This combination of exploratory design and rapid integration of new ideas produces products that feel cohesive and appealing.

At Apple, these are mainly internal discussions. The company rarely uses focus groups or consultants, so the process it uses is exploratory, looking at different ways to implement high-level functionality. The Photoshop files resulting from Apple's 10-3-1 model are both the functional spec and the interface.

Design-led approaches might well work for your company. They can certainly give you a quicker sense of what the application might feel like compared to the more traditional approaches.

Software design approach

If an interface reveals that the backend solution is lacking after the specification has been written and developed against and the interface has been polished, it can be expensive to fix. Developing the backend solution first often leads to a very data-centric view of the world, in which the user interface is there to provide the controls to the database. The person using the site is not the primary focus of the site. The users should be driving the application, not making decisions based on the need to fulfill parameters for a database function call.

Wireframes approach

A halfway house in design terms is often the *wireframe*. Wireframes present a complex mix of the content, layout, and functionality of a page. They give a sense of what will be on the page, but fall short of specifying an actual design. Capturing the content and functionality is important. Capturing the positional layout can constrain the visual designer in terms of how he might choose to position the elements.

Wireframes can also be as detailed as a full design, and as a result they can be time-consuming to produce. The page description diagram discussed in Chapter 7 allows non-design staff members to communicate what the page needs to do and say without resorting to wireframes. Lastly, wireframes are often produced by non-designers, so they tend to replicate existing designs or cram extra functionality onto the same page.

Wireframes fall between two positions: they are not as detailed as a visual design, nor are they functionally useful. If you feel you must use them, treat them as low-fidelity designs to be disposed of before launch. A mocked-up prototype is often a better choice.

Sketching approach

Sketching on paper or whiteboard is a final way of working to figure out the high-level structure of your site's design. This approach holds to the same principle as the design first approaches. You want to understand the problem quickly and not build something ill-founded and expensive. Writing code is costly, inflexible, and time-consuming. Sketching out the basic interface on paper, then sharing it and amending it face to face with designers, developers, and product management is a rapid way to explore prototypes. I have used this approach a lot, and it acts as a good replacement for informal wireframing, but you can miss important details with this approach, as it is rarely based on real examples. I would recommend it as a first approach to determining the flow of interaction in your application.

When doing design work, it is important to use real example copy. If you encourage the use of "Lorem ipsum" as a stand-in for real copy, you can miss details regarding how real people will interact with your site. This is also true if you repeat the same piece of real copy throughout the site. Make sure the product or editorial people on your team supply the designers with plenty of well-thought-out sample copy. This process will also help the product people solve potentially hidden problems. Generating this sample copy prompts the answering of many issues related to sourcing the content or understanding the roles involved in managing an item of content. An example might be a designer being supplied with dates for events—one case might have a range spanning many months, whereas another might have only a few weeks. The different time ranges will suggest different product and design solutions. Only when you get real sample data will you know which date range is going to be the common case. This upfront preparatory work will create a better product. The same is true in software testing, as we will see in Chapter 16.

Copywriting

As first mentioned in Chapter 3, the copy (descriptive and functional text) on your site matters, too. Getting the language right is critical, but too often it is left to the designer or the developer to sort out the details. What you label things matters to the *user*, which, by the way, is a dreadful word, but (so runs the joke) is commonplace in software and drug dealing. I have tried to avoid the word *user* in this book as much as possible. It is easy to make similar mistakes in the copy for your site. For some good examples, look at the language used on the sites referenced in this chapter.

Copywriting, interface design, and software development run hand in hand, but come from different people. Agreeing on the right language is important, and deciding on the copy often helps you understand the problem at a more fundamental level. It can make sense to agree on the copy before or in parallel with the detailed design work. Depending on the size of the site you are working on, you might have a single person whose role is to write the copy, or you might have a team working on it. Finally, all the copy on your site needs to be written from the point of view of a person using it. Therefore, explain and explain again. Make the language simple and clear, not gimmick-laden or too cute. From the main pages to all the help and recovery pages, it is important to get the copy right.

37signals has an excellent book, *Defensive Design for the Web* (Peachpit Press), that you might find useful when writing copy.

Summary

A good visual design for your website will help you to clearly communicate what your site is about. Web application design shifts the task to making templates that respond dynamically to what people on your site are doing. Hiring good visual designers who understand how their designs will be implemented makes the design work easier.

Understanding what you are going to build and then starting with a full visual user interface or a solid prototype is generally the fastest way to deploy a site. Save writing the code until you understand what you are making and how it will be used. Lastly, make sure you have your site's audience firmly in mind; think about the site from their perspective and use language and examples from their lives.

CHAPTER 5

Working with and Consuming Media

The world is already full of ways to produce content and form relationships. From the means of communication to the tasks people perform, contexts are created that people are familiar with. Each new website sets out to change, replace, or add to these means. If we fail to recognize these existing ways of doing things, we will set ourselves up for failure.

In this chapter, we'll explore how to positively engage with the status quo. We'll start by looking at media generation and consumption, and then at some examples of how people have developed sites to tap into the underlying human motivations that are present in all of these interactions.

Media Types Affect Consumption Styles

People consume content very differently depending on the media and the context. If you look at books, music, magazines, and films, you'll see that there are many different formats and types of publication. For example, music can be a public activity (played as background entertainment at a party or in a crowded setting at a concert), or a personal experience (heard through headphones in an office setting). Movies are historically a social experience, watched with other people and discussed later; but today, while most people don't go to the cinema by themselves, some might watch a film at home on their own. Reading materials tend to offer a more personal experience; people may sometimes share and/or lend newspapers and magazines to others, but reading books tends to be a personal activity.

From this quick analysis, you might draw some broad conclusions regarding media consumption styles. People engage with longer forms of media in a different social manner than they do with shorter forms: news, music, and magazines are shared at or near the time of consumption, whereas books and films are shared after consumption. Table 5-1 summarizes these ideas and introduces a breakdown of the *shared object*. Most types of media are shared socially and consumed personally, but usually one style is dominant.

Table 5-1. Media consumption patterns

	Access pattern	Consumption	Modality	Dominant pattern
Web	Non-linear	By page	Digital	Personal
Music	Non-linear	By track[a]	Digital	Personal
Movies/films	Linear	Entire work	Digital and analog	Social
Books	Linear	Entire work[b]	Analog	Personal
News	Non-linear	By story	Digital and analog	Personal
Magazines	Non-linear	By article	Analog	Personal

[a] Many people listen to albums in their entirety.

[b] Factual books are slightly different, as there is no plot per se, but consuming them as a whole is still relevant.

A significant element in terms of consumption style is whether the object is digital in nature. Of course, an online story is easier to share with a wide group of friends than a printed story, as you can share the online version with people not in your physical proximity. Digital objects are also much easier to gather data for. For instance, Apple's iTunes music software tracks which songs you have listened to from your collection. It is hard to imagine an easy service for paperback books that does the same thing. Although you can obtain reviews on a book you're interested in purchasing from Amazon, you'll have no idea whether the reviewers actually read the book or are decorating their bookcases with it. Stepping away from media, many hobbies are inherently non-digital, such as climbing and gardening. However, some of them you can track; for example, you can carry an altimeter and GPS unit to track your weekend hikes.

Returning to the length issue, smaller discrete elements, such as a story or a music track, work better online than something with a stronger narrative, such as a complete novel or a film. What we can summarize from all this is that consumption patterns differ radically: a single song by a music artist works well on the Web, but a book is harder to work with, and it takes much more time to consume an entire book than it takes to listen to a track on a CD.

Plots for books, films, and television programs present another issue. Spoilers can ruin a community experience if, for instance, someone reveals without warning important plot details to a person who has not yet seen the episode. Discovering "whodunit" separates the audience into two groups: those who know and those who don't. This is not an issue for music and is not relevant for most other printed and online media. Breaking news is also different, because a constant stream of new information is what is being delivered.

Analyzing Consumption Patterns

The differences in consumption patterns radically affect the kinds of online experiences you create for the people you want to attract to your site. A site for people who read books that mimics the behavior of a music site such as Last.fm would not work that well. Similarly, a site based on the Flickr photo-sharing website would not work for music sharing, as most people do not create music for public consumption in the same way they take photos. Two key criteria for social media products are that the content has to be digital in nature and the consuming or creating device can easily be connected to the Internet. A CD player is digital, but an iPod or a digital camera is digital *and* connected.

You need to assess what people are actually doing in the space in which you want to build a product. They may be using a competing online product, but if possible, look past this and examine what they are doing in terms of social relationships and current activities.

As I mentioned in Chapter 4, the term *social object*, coined by Jyri Engeström (who founded Jaiku and now designs social infrastructure at Google), has recently gained prominence. A social object moves the emphasis in social applications away from the action or the person and toward the combination of the object and its owner. To illustrate, the file *23489356408.jpg* is a specific picture, Gavin Bell is a specific person, but Gavin's picture of Oscar's birthday party is something much more meaningful. If we add a date and more contextual information, it moves from being only a picture to something that is rich in meaning. Figures 5-1 through 5-3 show this migration as a single element becomes a social object.

Figure 5-1. Oscar's birthday party—an isolated picture, 23489356408.jpg

Figure 5-2. Oscar's birthday party; this now becomes part of a bigger "picture"—a page

Figure 5-3. Oscar's birthday party with more context—now a social object, including responses from friends

Engeström describes conversations in the same light. The interesting aspect of the interactions that occur on Dopplr, Flickr, Jaiku, and Twitter is that the conversation happens around an identifiable object. For Dopplr it is a journey, for Flickr it is a picture, and for Jaiku and Twitter it is short messages. The conversation does not focus on the people first, or on the photo or the message; it focuses on both.

On Last.fm, the social objects are the music tracks that people have been listening to. Here the social object is not even annotatable. What is relevant is the aggregation of songs that a person has listened to. These individual songs combine with the person's identity to generate a view of her music tastes. For example, *http://www.last.fm/user/gavinb* gives a pretty good portrait of my music preferences. In fact, it's better than the portrait Amazon provides regarding my purchases.

If you publish your own content and host a community on the same website, there is an additional set of relationships to consider: those between the members of your community. Most people will simply participate passively in the community by buying the publication or the media. These people form the main part of the non-online publication world; we normally refer to them as readers of newspapers or books and so on. You'll also have to consider the relationship between your staff and the active community members, something we'll look at in the next chapter.

These more passive people form the majority of any audience or media-based engagement. The figures vary, but between 80% and 90% of the visitors to your site will come in, look, and leave. A small minority will contribute content. This is often referred to as the *Pareto principle* or the 80:20 rule. Derek Powazek notes the importance of this in community endeavors:

> That's not to say that the 80% aren't important—they are. Without them, there'd never be those 20% of writers. It's the balance that's important. Everyone gets to be treated like kings.*

On social community sites such as Flickr, participation levels are higher than typical message boards, though this tends to mean more active visitors rather than a higher rate of activity per visitor. The people who are simply reading the content are vital; without them, content creators would go elsewhere. They are the audience; they provide the traffic that observes the content that the 20% are making.

Collecting Consumption Data

Social objects require a unique identity, which is usually a single URL for a single object. I'll discuss URLs in much greater depth later in the book, but for now, it is important to understand the one-to-one principle regarding URLs. Having a URL for an object means you can refer to it and track it. You can use the object's behavior to aggregate it with other objects. Every object will, by definition, have an owner, so we can show all objects from a person or all new objects from your friends. Facebook's Mini-Feed does exactly this.

---

* *http://8020media.com/blog/2006/07/why_8020.html*

Collecting data on all of this activity is vital. Amazon is probably the most famous company in this regard. It collects data on every page you visit and then bases recommendations on the aggregated data it has collected. This is like the salespeople in a bookstore who note every book you glance at, which might get annoying quite quickly but is transparent and painless online. The seemingly passive readers on your site can give you all of this data for free. They can tell you what your most popular stories, people, or tags are. In Chapter 16, we'll explore how to capture and process this information.

Bradley Horowitz wrote about Yahoo! and its Yahoo! Groups product and came up with slightly different numbers to the 80:20 ratio, breaking community interaction into three categories:[†] 1% initiate, 10% respond, and 100% benefit from these activities. Depending on which system you look at, the figures will vary a bit, but the approximate ratios will not change that much. This is also true in the offline world; think of how many people read a magazine or newspaper and don't recommend any of the articles to anyone, let alone write about them to the editorial staff.

Media Evolves and Consumption Styles Change

This is a good juncture at which to look back at the media world. Newspapers have changed the most rapidly among the main publishing endeavors. The similarities between the creation of a web page and the writing of a news story have helped. Some newspapers, such as the *Lawrence Journal-World* in Kansas andthe *Guardian* in the United Kingdom, have taken community to heart and have reached out to bring their readers onto the newspaper's website. The advent of online news websites has even driven newsroom consolidation in such mainstream broadcasters as the BBC.[‡]

"comment is free"

Meanwhile, newspapers and magazines such as *The Economist*, the *New York Times*, the *Guardian*, and a host of others are exploring podcasting. Commenting and blogs are now becoming part of the standard newspaper website, and this is where the public reader interaction occurs.

The *Guardian* was an early adopter of this online interaction and decided to place the majority of its comment and opinion pieces in a blog titled "comment is free." The title comes from a quote by CP Scott, founder of the trust that runs the paper: "Comment is free, but facts are sacred." In its initial form, "comment is free" showed some weaknesses that can occur when strongly worded opinion pieces are left open for comment.

---

† *http://blog.elatable.com/2006/02/creators-synthesizers-and-consumers.html*

‡ *http://www.bbc.co.uk/pressoffice/pressreleases/stories/2007/10_october/18/reform.shtml*

Shortly after the "comment is free" blog was launched, Nico MacDonald discussed the weaknesses identified its initial form in an *Online Journalism Review* article titled "'Comment Is Free,' but designing communities is hard." The paper has since addressed many of these weaknesses (*http://www.ojr.org/ojr/stories/060817macdonald/*).

These weaknesses are common to many social software applications. The most fundamental weakness was the fact that a person's comment was not linked to his past comments because of the lack of a common profile page. This is a core tenet of social software: there must be an easy means of being able to establish a person's context by looking at his past output. The absence of a profile page allows mischievous people to agitate in one direction one day and in another direction the next day. Profile pages give stability to a community by providing identity. Bulletin board software offers profile pages, but they fall short in that they do not list a person's recent comments.

"comment is free" had one other significant issue: the people who authored the articles were not obligated to respond to any of the comments they received regarding their articles. However, some authors chose to respond to comments by writing another article.

Timothy Garton Ash analyzed this issue in "Mugged by the blogosphere – or how to find nuggets in a cyberswamp," at *http://www.guardian.co.uk/commentisfree/story/0, ,1819020,00.html*. He read all of the comments left on one of his posts and was confused by the experience. He called for a profile page so that he could figure out who some of the people were. While Garton Ash's desire for a profile page for each comment author is justified and an important feature for a cohesive community, there is another issue underlying the "comment is free" community: the authors of the original comment article rarely respond to the comments left on their articles. When launching a community site, it is vital to engage with the people coming to your site; if you or your authors keep themselves apart from your community, you can generate ill feelings.

The *Guardian* deserves praise for launching "comment is free" as a *post-moderated* forum in which comments are published first and then flagged for review if they are deemed inappropriate by readers, as opposed to a premoderated forum where every comment is read by staff members before publication. After all, opinion articles are usually written to evoke a reaction. By launching "comment is free," the *Guardian* was able to tap into this energy and attract a regular, if opinionated, group of people from across the globe. This endeavor has strengthened the *Guardian* brand and encouraged similar community projects at other media publishers.

The basic response to reading an opinion piece is to agree or disagree. By providing a forum for this to happen, the *Guardian* is addressing a need that exists outside the online world. It is allowing its readers to connect with other like-minded people who read the paper, as well as attracting people who disagree with the paper's general stance. This was not easily possible before the Internet. Local papers in the United States have already provided a forum for discussion, but the *Guardian* was one of the first national papers to do this widely and without requiring a *Guardian* journalist to read every comment prior to its publication.

Amazon: Reader Reviews Encourage Purchases

Amazon is a good example of how to build social software, particularly around books. (It now sells many other products, but its core offering is still arguably books.) Amazon has progressively added features that allow its book buyers to comment, rate, review, and list the books they like and dislike. The main social element on an Amazon page is the rating system, which is used across the site as an indication of the relative merit of an item. The rating comes from the people who have written a review of the book or DVD. People can add a 1–5 rating for a book or DVD and write a longer review if they desire. Figure 5-4 shows the rating system, Figure 5-5 shows other titles based on previous visitors' viewing habits, and Figure 5-6 shows the reviews of a DVD.

Figure 5-4. A product page on the Amazon UK website, showing the community-generated five-star rating for the Firefly DVD release

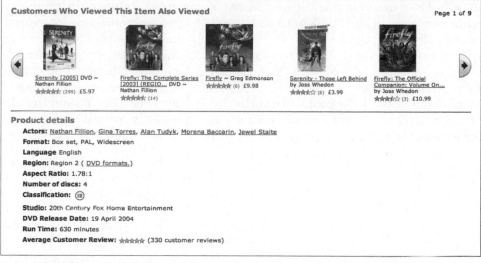

Serenity [2005] DVD ~ Nathan Fillion ★★★★☆ (299) £5.97

Firefly: The Complete Series [2003] (REGIO... DVD ~ Nathan Fillion ★★★★☆ (14)

Firefly ~ Greg Edmonson ★★★★★ (6) £9.98

Serenity - Those Left Behind by Joss Whedon ★★★★☆ (6) £3.99

Firefly: The Official Companion: Volume On... by Joss Whedon ★★★☆☆ (3) £10.99

Product details

 Actors: <u>Nathan Fillion</u>, <u>Gina Torres</u>, <u>Alan Tudyk</u>, <u>Morena Baccarin</u>, <u>Jewel Staite</u>

 Format: Box set, PAL, Widescreen

 Language English

 Region: Region 2 (<u>DVD formats.</u>)

 Aspect Ratio: 1.78:1

 Number of discs: 4

 Classification: ⑫

 Studio: 20th Century Fox Home Entertainment

 DVD Release Date: 19 April 2004

 Run Time: 630 minutes

 Average Customer Review: ★★★★★ (330 customer reviews)

Figure 5-5. Related titles based on customer viewing habits

Serenity [2005] DVD ~ Nathan Fillion ★★★★☆ (299) £5.97

Serenity - Those Left Behind by Joss Whedon ★★★★☆ (6) £3.99

Firefly ~ Greg Edmonson ★★★★★ (6) £9.98

Serenity (Newman) ~ Original Soundtrack ★★★★☆ (3) £9.98

Finding Serenity: Anti-heroes, Lost Shephe... by Jane Espenson ★★★★☆ (5) £8.99

Rate This Item to Improve Your Recommendations

☑ I own it x|★★★★★ Rate it

Customer Reviews

330 Reviews

5 star:	(304)
4 star:	(10)
3 star:	(6)
2 star:	(2)
1 star:	(8)

Average Customer Review
★★★★★ (330 customer reviews)

Share your thoughts with other customers:
Write your own review

Most Helpful Customer Reviews

56 of 57 people found the following review helpful:
★★★★★ **Amazingly good**, 3 May 2004
By **A Customer**
Why on earth did they cancel this? It's terrific!

Most Recent Customer Reviews

★★★★★ **just fab**
i am about half way through the series and it is just bloody brilliant. i got into Firefly after watching Serenity on dvd, which is also an excellent purchase. **Read more**

Figure 5-6. Customer purchasing habits based on aggregated data and some of the reviews for the Firefly DVD

Amazon then layers additional functionality on top of the rating framework. For instance, all the reviews can be rated on how helpful they were, and this information can then be aggregated onto the page for the reviewer. The rating of the review may even impact a product's overall score. Reviews can be anonymous, or the reviewer can be identified by name from a validated credit card. Anonymous reviews can obviously be written by anyone, and in 2004 the real names of some anonymous reviewers were accidentally displayed on Amazon's Canadian site, revealing that a raft of authors had written glowing reviews of their own books and sometimes less glowing reviews of competitors' books.§ (Of course, I'd never dream of doing that!) The provision of a real name builds a sense of reviewer trust. It is possible to see that the reviews that are rated more highly come from people who have left a real name. The majority of the Amazon.co.uk top 50 reviewers, for instance, are identified by a "Real Name" badge (*http://www.amazon.co.uk/gp/customer-reviews/top-reviewers.html*).

So, how does this relate to the basic process of reading books? It taps into two fundamental desires: people want to help others, and they want to feel knowledgeable. A review of a book saying that it is good for novices but runs out of steam if you are experienced is very helpful if you are starting a hobby. A detailed review of a book showing the book's flaws or correcting its mistakes allows the writer of the review to feel on par with the author, or at least to show his expertise.

From Amazon's point of view, reviews allow Amazon to determine which books are likely to sell well. The company can use the aggregated reviews and sales figures to determine which books are best for a particular genre. Amazon took a long-term approach to developing the site and did not look for an early profit. This meant it had time to build up the reviews and ratings for the books in its catalog. Amazon has almost every book in print, including new releases. It has gained something else as well: it is the de facto place to look for a book review. Amazon may not always be the cheapest place to buy books, but it has arguably become the library for the Internet. It allows other merchants to compete on price (via Amazon Marketplace), which adds credence to this argument. A recent Forrester report mentioned in the *New York Times*‖ showed that 52% of people who shop online do their product research at Amazon. So, that means more than half of online shoppers use Amazon to figure out what to purchase. Amazon also launched one of the first affiliate stores on the Internet. In later chapters, we'll explore how Amazon has become a part of the Internet, not something that is merely hosted on it.

New Services Respond to Evolving Needs

Music

In the 1980s, music came from LPs or tapes, and there was no way to automatically track via a computer which song you were listening to. So, a list of the songs a person

---

§ The article "Amazon Glitch Unmasks War Of Reviewers," at *http://query.nytimes.com/gst/fullpage.html?res =9C07E0DC1F3AF937A25751C0A9629C8B63*, covers the details of the accidental display of anonymous reviewer names on Amazon.

‖ *http://www.nytimes.com/2008/01/05/technology/05nocera.html*

had listened to over the course of a week would have had to be produced laboriously by hand. Today, the Compact Disk Database (CDDB), now known as the Gracenote database (*http://en.wikipedia.org/wiki/Gracenote*), holds track listings for virtually every CD produced, and provides the lookup service behind most online music services. Gracenote was generated by volunteers who entered into the database the track listings for CDs they were listening to, and it is now one of the unsung early Internet-driven collaborations. The magic glue that Gracenote provides allows any computer in the world with an Internet connection to give the CD or MP3 file playing on it a much richer meaning. Gracenote gives every track published a unique identifier, which means new services can be built on music that people are playing. This was simply not possible before the Internet existed. These catalogs of data are a key foundation, allowing social interaction around objects that are not native to the Internet, such as films, television programs, books, and, indeed, music.

These new services exist in different forms, from music sales to playlist management. The Apple service iTunes, along with the Apple iPod, is the leader in the sales field. The iPod is deservedly ahead in this market, and I'll discuss its merits in a subsequent chapter. iTunes is a very successful store (see Figure 5-7), but it also enables other behaviors. For instance, it offers recommendations if you shop from the store, and it shows you the relative popularity of songs. This helps to drive Apple's sales.

Figure 5-7. Radiohead in Apple's iTunes desktop software, showing the iTunes store

Last.fm takes a different approach to monitoring what music people are listening to. The data tracked from songs listened to on iTunes is aggregated onto a profile page, which other people can see. The critical difference between iTunes and Last.fm is the public data aspect of Last.fm. With Last.fm, you can add friends to a social network and discover other music via recommendations based on what people are actually listening to. There is a similar function in iTunes, called the Genius Sidebar, but it is based on private data.

Both services rely on data from Gracenote. They add commercial or social services on top of the basic behavior of people listening to music. Last.fm collates millions of actual tracks that real people have listened to, all of whom have profile pages. So, it gives a unique view of the musical tastes of many people. Last.fm has also created a global version of the conversations that people have about music, and has enabled interesting new behaviors, for example, Last.fm archives your listening habits so that you can see which bands you are into at the moment and how your tastes are changing. Last.fm is satisfying the desire to share tastes and explore new artists, if not the actual music for download.

Photos

Flickr originated as a side project from a gaming company called Ludicorp. The inventory management tool for the game was repurposed to become a photo-sharing application. However, what Ludicorp initially launched in 2004 is radically different from the service you'll see on Flickr today. The idea of a persistent photostream with unique URLs for photos and comments was not in the initial launch, nor were other key features such as tags and groups. The fact that Flickr launched without these seemingly key features is not the important point. What is key is that the company behind Flickr worked hard with its new community and generally delivered new features as people demanded them (as long as they related to Flickr's core business).

The advent of inexpensive digital photography equipment is one of the drivers behind Flickr's success. Photo-sharing websites have been around since the Web started (e.g., Photo.net), but they tended to be aimed at professional photographers. Flickr is aimed at everyone, and it attracts lots of professionals. Gone are the dusty slides and projector; today, photo viewing is a communal experience that you can enjoy wherever you have an Internet connection.

People have an innate desire to explore pictures from around the world, whether they are of places, people, or events. The structure within Flickr allows for easy navigation and discovery. Along these lines, the last Flickr feature I want to mention is the *interestingness* rating for pictures. Flickr uses many statistics to determine how interesting a picture is, from how many times it has been viewed to how many comments it has and who commented. Upward of 30 different factors are taken into account to determine the interestingness of an image. This allows Flickr to show the pictures that have facilitated a high degree of social interaction.

The photographs are the social objects, and these photographs, along with their accompanying comments, become a conversation. The pictures I place on Flickr document the events in my life and capture my friends' reactions to these events. I can also see my friends' lives depicted on Flickr. For the people I hang out with, Flickr provides a catalog of the events we have attended. However, you get these benefits only if you sign up (for non-members, Flickr is just a lot of pictures). Tags help to organize the content so that you can easily find amazing pictures of, for instance, the Grand Canyon, but Flickr only comes to life when your friends are there as well. This is a common issue with social networking sites.

One popular view is to look at images by tag, which gives you a selection of the best images identified by a particular term. However, tags can be problematic. For instance, searching for photos with the tag "digger" will produce pictures of an Australian cat called Digger and pictures of construction equipment, and searching for photos with the tag "otters" will produce pictures of otters and a few planes (I'll continue the discussion on this inconsistency in the use of tags in Chapter 13). Nonetheless, tags are a great way to show off the best images, and they encourage people to continue to use the site, even if they have no images to upload or comments to leave.

Video

Many video services—ranging from the popular YouTube to services such as Vimeo, Viddler, and Seesmic—allow people to shoot and then upload video clips. These sites are filled with lots of clips from TV shows, but among those are lots of homemade videos. For many people, available bandwidth at home is now at a level where video is a reasonable means of expression. These social services differ from music services in that a lot more video content is being generated by individuals, whereas music tends to come from record companies. Indeed, there is a seemingly vast appetite for video clips.

This harks back to the sense that viewing a video clip, like a movie, is a social experience. People more frequently call someone over to watch a video clip than to listen to an audio clip. Even more than with pictures, there is a sense of communal entertainment with video. Social tools around sharing video will behave differently from those around music, due to these differing consumption profiles. Music bears repeat listening, for example, whereas a film tends to be watched once. A Yahoo! research project designed to explore real-time video sharing is Zync (*http://sandbox.yahoo.net/Zync*).

New systems for tracking data are coming on the market. I've discussed some of the main ones associated with media, but in your industry, there will be others that are more relevant. For instance, it is now possible to track energy usage within the home, using a Wattson (*http://www.diykyoto.com/wattson.html*), and many more of these new tracking tools will be developed. Some of them may give you a basis for hosting a community. A good example is the Discovery Channel's funding of the Sharkrunners game developed by area/code (*http://www.playareacode.com/work/sharkrunners/*). This game uses real-time data from great white sharks. Players control their own virtual ships and receive an email when their virtual ship encounters a real shark. It is an example of the kind of community product that is already possible to create.

A burgeoning area for growth is systems that provide further complete data sets. A complete data set makes recommendation systems easier to create and content easier to map to identifiers. There is certainly money to be made in this space. In terms of geographic data sets, the UK Post Office sells the postal codes database and NavTeq or TeleAtlas sells satellite imagery of the Earth. There are many other new data sensors coming on to the market that will enable the creation and extension of new data sets.

If you are making a site that references external media or even something that you generate yourself, the easier it will be to track, and the simpler it will be to generate situations for comment regarding the media. The difference between music download and a paperback could not be starker. With both, it is possible to determine purchase data; however, without a deliberate effort on the reader's part, tracking data regarding the use of the book stops. A song has much more richness in terms of capturing and aggregating data than making it easily accessible simply by playing a version of it on a computer. Tom Coates discussed the issues of trackability and identification of digital objects, describing them as the "Web of data" (*http://www.plasticbag.org/archives/2006/02/my_future_of_web_apps_slides/*).

Summary

In this chapter, I showed how you should situate your application in the context of how people will use it. If the object of attention is clearly owned by someone, it can become a social object and not just an artifact. You need to understand the position your site fulfills with respect to the content or industry it is in. If your site is about books, you need to respect how people interact with and understand books. Many sites take a personal experience, such as reading books or listening to music, and record the act of consumption and make that social (or at least available for social interaction and comment). So, people are still listening to music on their own, but they are sharing the fact of their listening with others. The aggregate views on these personal data collections—for example, a person's favorite artists—provide useful stimulus for social comment.

Most of the examples I provided in this chapter have the following commonalities:

- A profile page, which represents the person and aggregates his content from the site into one place. These can be different pages, but the concept is the same.
- A means for the people on the site to find out who everyone is and what they have created.
- A means of finding the content on the site and a unique reference for that content.
- A means of commenting on or reviewing the unique items of content.
- A means of rating or marking as favorites the items of content.
- A means of finding the content on the site and a unique reference for that content via a search system and stable consistent URLs.

Look at the social product you are planning and see which features would fit in your project. How does the project fit the underlying needs of your audience? What basic, underlying need to socialize are you meeting? What is your social object? How do the social objects behave off the Internet? What common interactions happen around them? Answering these questions before you plan any features or decide on any technology will strengthen your project.

CHAPTER 6

Managing Change

'Cause people often talk about being scared of change

But for me I'm more afraid of things staying the same

'Cause the game is never won by standing in any one

Place for too long.

—"Jesus of the Moon" by Nick Cave
and the Bad Seeds

People get comfortable in their routines. When launching or changing a website, you are asking them to adjust to new contexts and unfamiliar ways of doing things. Even if a new product clearly offers a better way to do something, people—even those inside your organization—still may be unwilling to move to that new product quickly. Technology adoption rates are usually best measured in years, not months or weeks. Because modifying your website will affect your visitors, your workflow, and your site management processes, you need to look ahead cautiously as you plan for changes.

Resistance

People frequently reject change, preferring to stick with what they know. Generally, we like the world to stay the same, and at most we create change at our own pace. Think of how often you change the shop where you pick up your daily newspaper, your route to work, or even your parking space or seat on the train. There are many reasons for this, but the main reason is that some stability in life helps us deal with the rest of the unpredictability that life throws at us. Imagine being forced to take a new route to work every day due to unpredictable road or train and problems. The unexpected changes from one route to the next would disrupt your life and would likely make you resent the company that was responsible for them.

We all have to manage change on a daily basis. A common way to measure these events is to use *life change units*. Described in the 1970s by Thomas Holmes and Richard Rahe,[*] this approach lists events according to a 100-point scale, with death of a spouse at the top of the list. However, in relation to developing websites, the following are more relevant: change in living conditions is rated at 25 points, change in working conditions at 20 points, and change in work responsibilities at 29 points. Varying how people do their jobs has an impact on their lives. If you are extending your website into one that incorporates community, you should bear this in mind for your staff. It also has an effect on your members; you need to preserve some level of consistency between versions 1 and 2 of your site.

Different people react to change in different ways. Some groups on your website will accept changes, while others will oppose them. Most site redesigns or feature launches will engender some form of negative reaction, so you need to plan for this in the launch process. People grow accustomed to the way a particular tool or site fits into their lives and can get upset if it changes suddenly.

 The Myths of Innovation (http://oreilly.com/catalog/9780596527051/), by Scott Berkun (O'Reilly), explains how—through mismanagement or a failure to recognize the potential of the product—and why innovation frequently fails.

Schema Theory

Psychology offers some theories that describe more formally how we understand processes and situations. F.C. Bartlett developed *schema theory* in the 1930s (see *Remembering: An Experimental and Social Study* [Cambridge University Press]). Bartlett explored how people recall facts from stories over a period of a year since first hearing them. He deduced from this experiment that we create fairly fixed ideas for how things work. For instance, we have schema for how we expect a restaurant to operate: restaurants have tables and chairs, there is a menu to choose from, and food is brought out by waiters.

Congruence

The degree of fit between a situation and our schema is termed *congruence*, so using the restaurant analogy, a traditional Italian eatery is highly congruent with our ideas of a restaurant, whereas a Chinese takeout is not, despite the fact that both serve food. This congruence is important in websites, as it reassures the person using the site that a familiar situation is unfolding. If you change direction on your users by way of a poorly crafted addition or by trying to gain an entirely new audience whose needs are different from those of the existing audience, many people will be upset by the change.

[*] *http://en.wikipedia.org/wiki/Holmes_and_Rahe_stress_scale*

Adaptation

A second aspect of schema theory is *change*. The schemas that people have can change, but they do not change quickly; this process is called *adaptation*. The technology we use to access the Internet has changed gradually over the past 10 years, from analog modems to broadband and then to wireless broadband. Similar changes have occurred with cell phones; five years ago the idea that you'd be able to access the Internet on a phone-like device was laughable to most people, yet today the iPhone and similar devices now provide a good handheld web experience. Shifts in human behavior have occurred, too. The commenting that blogging allows on web content has led people to expect to be able to comment on more traditionally published material from established newspapers, broadcast, and magazines.

Schema theory gives us a good grasp of how people relate to the world, and it will help you understand your audience's expectations of your website. Realizing that people do not think of the world in purely task-based, goal-driven outcomes is helpful. Much user testing focuses on these details, and while the results of these tests are important, they do not tell the whole story. Understanding how your new web application will fit into the broader sweep of people's lives is vital. In Chapter 7, we will look at designing user experiences.

Rate of change

Understanding the processes people use to accomplish daily tasks will ensure a better chance of a good fit for your project. For example, Mint (*http://www.mint.com*) and Wesabe (*https://www.wesabe.com*) offer personal financial management services online, but both depend on three recently developed key factors: online access to statements; widespread, persistent Internet access; and probably most important, a high level of trust in third-party online services from companies such as PayPal. Because PayPal, eBay, and Amazon have made online financial transactions seem more ordinary, it is possible for Mint and Wesabe to move into their application area. However, until recently, the very idea that you would send your bank statements to a third party was unthinkable, and for many people, it will continue to seem odd for several years to come, as people don't change their habits and comfort levels at the same rate. This may seem obvious, but when the world is boiled down to "users" and "non-users," a lot of these subtleties can be forgotten.

Web Communities and Change

Web communities' vocal reactions to change are well documented. Here are a few examples that come from social software development specifically, as opposed to simply running a website.

Facebook is now a well-known and very popular social networking website. When launched, it was initially restricted to colleges in the United States, but in September 2006, it opened up to everyone. However, in the run-up to launch, Facebook added a new feature: the Mini-Feed (see *http://blog.facebook.com/blog.php?post=2207967130*). The Mini-Feed took information that was available elsewhere on the site and aggregated it into one place. So, for example, instead of having to visit the profile page of every one of your friends, you could see what was happening in your friends' lives on one page. The immediate reaction was overwhelmingly negative, as people felt like Facebook had turned into a stalker's paradise, even though no new information was being released.[†]

The strong reaction that this seemingly innocuous change generated came from two main misunderstandings (see *http://www.uie.com/articles/facebook_mini_feed/* for a more detailed analysis). First, the Facebook team, who had smaller networks of *friends*, used the product in a different manner from their keener users. Hence, everyone in their network was someone they had a connection to in the wider world. However, for many Facebook members, friends were a cost-free means of having a large social network, so people would add anyone to their Facebook. By showing activity from all of these people, many of whom had been forgotten, Facebook suddenly became a noisy place full of strangers.

This led to a second misunderstanding: people thought the people in the Mini-Feed were random strangers, and they worried that their activity was being broadcast to the wider world. Announcing this change before it happened, and trying it out on a smaller group of people first, would have revealed these problems earlier. Interestingly, within a few months, once people had adjusted to what a "friend" now meant on Facebook, the Mini-Feed became a valued part of the site and of many other social software products.

Flickr also offers a few examples of resistance to change. A few years after Flickr launched, Yahoo! bought the company. Unfortunately, Flickr took about 18 months to transfer old accounts over to Yahoo!, though all new accounts had to be Yahoo! ID accounts. This long migration from old to new accounts allowed time for dissent to ferment inside Flickr, so when the final forced migration date of March 20 was announced, a lot of people were unhappy about the change (see the now locked discussion forum post for a sense of the dissent, at *http://www.flickr.com/help/forum/32687/*). Many people wanted to keep their existing email- and password-based access to their accounts and did not want to have to use a Yahoo! account. An "old skool" movement started in reaction to the label Flickr gave to the existing account access mechanism.

The two systems ran in parallel for more than a year, offering the Yahoo! ID access mechanism as the default, but showing the old mechanism with a link to the older login screen, branding this as "psst, you must be old skool?" Even now, a year or two later, people still have "old skool" badges for their avatar images. Dan Rubin built some

---

[†] See the story at *http://media.www.easttennessean.com/media/storage/paper203/news/2006/09/11/Viewpoint/ New-Facebook.MiniFeed.Deemed.Creepy.Invasion.Of.Privacy.By.Some.Users-2264243.shtml* for more details and personal reactions.

templates for creating them at *http://superfluousbanter.org/archives/2007/02/flickr-old -skool-badges/*. Figure 6-1 shows an example.

Figure 6-1. Flickr "old skool" badges (from http://www.flickr.com/photos/danrubin/391594808/; used with permission)

In this case, the problem was not lack of communication, but rather leaving the issue hanging for too long so that the "old skool" login process became a badge of honor for early users of the site. Subsequently, when Yahoo! changed the login process for Up-coming, an event management website, the changeover had a fixed time frame of six weeks. (Mashable, a web application service provider, noted the change in approach (see *http://mashable.com/2007/04/19/upcoming/*). Yahoo! eased the process with a do-main name change, new functionality, and free T-shirts, giving the community some-thing else to talk about besides the change in login credentials. This time a lot of the fuss was from international users complaining that the T-shirts would be shipped only to addresses in the United States. People will always find something to complain about!

In April 2008, Flickr added video capability to its site. The majority of the community liked the change, but it was largely silent. The vociferous minority that disliked the change ran sitewide campaigns and protests, despite the fact that the videos were only 90 seconds in length and were not set to play automatically. Although some people reacted strongly, the integration of the video feature and the various ways to opt out of seeing video made the transition much smoother.

The Flickr team extended the functionality in ways that closely match how Flickr works, treating video as long photos and not video clips. The company maintained the schema that Flickr is a photo service and the album-flicking behaviors that the site evokes. All the existing functionality remained the same, but some of the pictures in the photo-stream have a small Play icon on them. Subsequently, in response to user requests, Flickr has added tools to restrict the use and display of video in groups, along with search functionality.

In addition, the Flickr team conducted a private feature release to gather feedback prior to the public launch. They then used the best of the content created in this beta phase to show off the video feature and to encourage the kinds of video that Flickr hoped to get.

Internal Workflow

External visitors are not the only people you need to worry about as you make changes to your application. Internal difficulties can also arise from changes to your workflow.

The term *workflow* is often used to describe a sequential process, but in a larger sense it can include a wide range of things. Every hobby or interest area includes some kind of workflow for participation, with vocabularies describing the expectations. For instance, *foreshadowing* (or spoilers) in a fiction book, revealing parts of the plot before the narrative does, is part of the workflow for reading. Prior knowledge of the route during rock climbing will lower the achievement level of climbing from an *onsight ascent* to a *flash*. Understanding the activities in your area becomes important when you are creating a community around something that is collaborative or has a complex workflow. Therefore, you should allow multiple entry and recovery points on your website for varying workflow needs, but have a strong narrative to guide people through.

Workflow changes when you gain a two-way community, but workflow questions often go unnoticed in the drive for the site or feature launch. In larger organizations, the people most affected by changes are often not consulted in the process of development. They are seen as internal staff members and not the ever-important external *user*. Even in quite sophisticated user-centered development approaches, the internal users of the system are often not represented.

This is puzzling, as these people are not hard to get in touch with; they are in your office. Sometimes this is exactly the problem: they are invisible, yet in plain sight. When looking at the scenarios around community software, the internal project team can often be quite small and closely involved in the development process, focusing on delivering the project for external consumption. There can be a larger team sitting alongside the internal project team, but it can be difficult to get their understanding and acceptance of the changes coming from the new system, they have already made an investment in adapting themselves to the old system. Surmounting this resistance is important so that their needs are accurately represented for the system they will end up running.

Commenting systems are a key example of where this can be problematic. Typically, one existing team generates content for a publication using a content management system (CMS). Then a social software project comes along and adds commenting to the CMS directly, or attaches comments to the existing articles. It sounds simple, but all the previous editorial jobs have now changed. Writers suddenly have a responsive and diverse audience to attend to, not just editors. These changes need to be factored into the working environment, and time needs to be allocated for the job. The next step, comment moderation, will raise additional issues, such as who does the work on holidays, how should escalation of moderation requests through editorial be handled, and how to avoid libel cases.

These issues *should* be addressed before functionality is launched, but there are a surprising number of examples where the workflow clearly did not account for how the Internet operates. For instance, the *Los Angeles Times'* wikitorial experiment was a brave idea. (See *http://www.guardian.co.uk/technology/2005/jun/22/media.pressandpublishing* for an analysis of the story.) The paper took a provocative editorial on the Iraq war and allowed anyone on the Internet to edit it. However, it did this on a Friday, and when the external editing shifted the document to pornographic content late on Saturday night, it decided to remove the feature entirely. The Internet runs 24 hours a day and is accessible from countries outside your own; the staff seemed not to realize that starting with a contentious topic right before the weekend was poor planning. This is an extreme example, but there are many others where the change in role, particularly for the editorial staff, is not clearly defined and communicated.

In the "comment is free" example discussed in Chapter 5, the challenge of keeping up with anonymous comments created a major disconnect between the experience of the reader commenting on the opinion piece and the author of the piece: the conversation separated, and with a few exceptions, the readers discussed articles among themselves. Several years later, the *Guardian* has addressed many of these early criticisms, but it remains a challenge to integrate broadcast-style opinion writing, as it has been done for years, with personal commentary.

Twitter is bringing these issues to the forefront more frequently, given the ease with which content can be reused via its API. The technical hurdle is now quite low for including third-party content from the Internet, but a proper editorial process is still needed to ensure that you are including content that is appropriate. *The Telegraph* used a search feed from Twitter on the 2009 budget day in the United Kingdom, taking every post that mentioned the hashtag #budget and displaying it on its home page in real time and unfiltered. The resulting comedy as Twitter users abused the service was short-lived, but it was a quick lesson in how the Internet can respond to poorly thought-out attempts at engagement (see *http://www.guardian.co.uk/media/2009/apr/21/telegraph -twitter-budget-twitterfall-embarrassment* for further details).

Community Managers

Unless you are already doing community-related work on your website, you are unlikely to have the manpower to handle such work if you decide to add this feature. Even an editorially led company does not have the right people on staff for such a task. The community manager role is not marketing, editorial, or technical in nature. You may have to fill it from outside the company, although internal staff members can sometimes do the work. It requires a level head for making judgments and a willingness to talk to people online.

The community manager is the public presence on the site. This person talks to the members, reads contributions, and helps set community standards. The community manager is usually the main moderator on the site, though this person may receive help from other nominated users (non-staff members) on a volunteer basis. If you have other editorial teams, you need to ensure that everyone is clear regarding what he is entitled and expected to do. Traditionally, editorial teams have been the first port of call for conversations with the community—receiving emails or letters—but the conversations have largely been one to one and private. Now this responsibility will shift to the community managers and this community interaction will often be done in public. The community manager needs to learn from the editorial team and then feed back the day-to-day knowledge he is gathering about how your community thinks and behaves. If this task is ill-managed, it can become a real problem—the company can become two-headed in the way it deals with the community.

Summary

Change is complex to manage and is inherent to launching a new website or launching new functionality on a website. Humans dislike not being able to control change at their own pace, so encourage people to adopt your new tools by understanding what your community is trying to accomplish. Add new functionality so that it extends (rather than conflicts with) their existing ways of thinking. Internally, change will create challenges, too, primarily manifested in terms of workflow management, but also in the relationships your staff will strike up with their new community. Pay attention to how you manage this, especially if you have both editorial and community management teams so that your company can speak with a common voice.

CHAPTER 7

Designing for People

Building a website that people use socially is quite different from building desktop software or service-based websites. Desktop software has a model that traditionally serves a single person to complete a set task. Service-based websites follow a similar model.

Interaction design provides an underlying methodology that helps to shape social software applications with contributions from many other areas. This type of design work is the main differentiator between applications in a similar area, as there can be many ways to approach the same task. This chapter will look at how creating social applications differs from creating other software, and will explain how to run these kinds of projects. The chapter also explores some new methodologies for creating applications based on Activity Theory and the social object. The chapter ends with some guidelines for and examples of designing social applications. It is often said that the quality of an application is in the details; this is the chapter for those details. Dive in!

 A site design is the combination of the site's content and activity, so simply copying the design of another site for use in your site will not work. A real estate site modeled after Flickr, for example, will not work, even though both would be using photography. Modeling your site after a "popular site" is not a good starting position: you can borrow subelements from that site, but not the entire site. Being influenced is different from copying. You need to create the design to understand how to evolve it.

The article at *http://www..37signals.com/svn/posts/1561 why you -shouldnt-copy-us-or-anyone-else* from 37signals puts it perfectly: "Copying skips understanding." Sadly, this is a common bad practice. See *http://www.flickr.com/groups/web_design_ripoffs/pool/* for many more examples of misguided copying. This is different, however, from building on a social network tool designed to provide a base. For more on these, see "Social Platforms As a Foundation" on page 151.

Making Software for People

Traditionally, developing software was a very computer-centric process: programmers had to turn information and the environment into something the computer could understand. We have moved a long way from this, thankfully, and punch cards and paper tape are museum pieces now. However, developing social web applications still presents a challenge, in that supporting the needs and activities of the individual while fostering community and social interactions means technical solutions are no longer sufficient. For clarity, social interaction runs a wide gamut, from commenting to annotation, chat, uploading pictures, cooperating on tasks, and discussion.

The same problem can be solved in many different ways. A common expression describing successful sites is "it is all about the execution." Unpacking this phrase reveals that it is not computer cycles that are important; it is the social and cognitive aspects of the relationship between the person, the site, and the community that make an application "feel right."

Waterfalls Are Pretty to Look At

A classic model for software development is the waterfall model. The idea of completing one phase, then the next, and the next one after that until the project is done has an innate appeal, but it is a poor approach toward solving complex problems. Dr. Winston W. Royce described the waterfall model in 1970, in "Managing the Development of Large Software Systems" (*http://www.cs.umd.edu/class/spring2003/cmsc838p/Process/waterfall.pdf*). In fact, he raised it as an example of a *flawed* model.

One limitation of waterfall approaches to software development is that they expect a division of labor. For instance, Adam Smith (*http://www.econlib.org/library/Enc/bios/Smith.html*) noticed that pin manufacturing could be increased if each person focused on only one aspect, rather than creating a whole pin himself; this was the start of the assembly line and the segregation of worker tasks. The waterfall approach works when there is a fixed plan that can be devolved into separate, non-overlapping tasks, but good software development has to be more interactive than that.

Fixed schedules are another limitation of waterfall approaches to software development. For example, waterfall approaches make sense when you are building a house. The foundation comes first, then bricks, then windows, the roof, and so on. These activities have a fixed order that is known in advance. Since most software projects are entirely about making something unlike what came before, you can't expect them to follow a fixed schedule.

A simple "build the backend and then stick a user interface in front of it" approach is doomed to failure these days. Why do I say "doomed"? Just as a builder wouldn't turn what should be a kitchen into a living room without drawing up new plans to reflect the newly intended usage, implementing the backend of an interface without thinking about how it will be used will lead to similar clashes of functionality versus intended usage.

What approaches can you use to determine what to build? The field of interaction design can help you determine the appropriate things to build and how to present them. The full scope of interaction design reaches from the visual design back to the models for information storage.

Interaction Design

Interaction design[*] can help you design software that groups of individuals can use to describe, discuss, and build on their world. It draws on psychology, groupware design, collaborative systems design, user-centered design, as well as some of the newer models coming from human–computer interaction.

Earlier chapters of this book examined the software side and the visual design aspects of building a site. What is left is the glue that brings those two aspects together. You can represent visual design in code, just like you can a database schema. The interaction design is how the problem is represented and the solution is developed. It is closer to psychology than software development. You need to understand both the motivations of the people in your subject area and the activities they are trying to perform.

The interaction designer is often viewed as either the person who creates the wireframes, or, in some places, the person who builds the Flash applications. Neither of these descriptions captures what an interaction designer can bring to a project. Many teams do not have a full-time interaction designer on staff; instead, the role falls into a number of other disciplines. On smaller teams, for instance, it is frequently part of the visual designer or client-side developer's role.

Some teams make the project manager do the interactive design work, though in that case it tends to be more akin to information architecture wireframing work. The product manager might be the closest fit if there is not space for a separate role. Much of the work of a product manager involves defining the behavior of the application, which is close to the interaction designer's role. Having a separate person manage the interaction design process while working alongside the people who implement the design work forces the entire team to reflect on and discuss each feature prior to its implementation. This can help the team focus on solving the interface problem rather than simply implementing it, resulting in a better user experience. The polar opposite approach reduces tasks to line items on a spreadsheet, which keeps the team from contributing to or understanding the project, often leading to problems.

---

[*] There are many books on interaction design and many more on usability. Dan Saffer's book, *Designing for Interaction* (Peachpit Press), is an excellent introduction to the area.

Individuals choose to use social web applications. Remember, the elusive quality of the user experience, and not the feature spec list, will win people over to your social web application.

There is generally no company mandate that says this is the web application you need to use to do your job. There is a high degree of personal choice and variety on the Internet in virtually every application area.

Identify Needs with Personas and User-Centered Design

User-centered design (UCD) is a persona-led approach that focuses on a known set of users who can be interviewed and have their needs assessed. Many other definitions and approaches reflect the breadth of what is called UCD. (The approach I describe in this chapter is not the only version of UCD that is valid; it is just a common one.)

UCD is a great improvement over the waterfall approach. Understanding and keeping the needs of your users at the heart of your software project is always a good idea. However, UCD tends to be used primarily in larger companies, as it can be an expensive approach if executed to its fullest extent. UCD was developed in the late 1970s; Jared Spool gives a short history of the origins of the approach on the IXDA mailing list at *http://www.ixda.org/discuss.php?post=33885#comment33966*. An early term in UCD development was *usability engineering*. There is much disagreement over what constitutes UCD, but a focus on the needs of the user, rather than the needs of the software system or a specific set of tools, is a good starting point.

UCD separates the product from the preferences of the designer. We are prone to make things that we would like to use ourselves. UCD introduces the persona to handle this; each persona represents a core use case for the area you are working in. Behind UCD is a model that emphasizes the person as an information processor. The model attempts to determine the needs of the individual and map this onto a set of goals that can then be implemented as a set of tasks.

A *use case* is a combination of a thumbnail sketch of an individual who might use your services tied to a set of tasks he can perform on your site. An example use case might be *Simon*, a 27-year-old project manager who is fed up with Microsoft Project. He is looking for a shared project management tool that his team can use on the Internet. A persona like *Simon* might, for example, look at tools such as Basecamp from 37signals. Generally, personas have a lot more depth to them than just age and role. Developing personas is a good, fun activity that your team can take part in. The difficult part of using a persona is ensuring that creating and using it is not just a fun way to spend the afternoon. *Simon* and friends need to become an active element in product planning, and as your product matures or evolves prior to launch, you need to update your personas. Other common approaches include storyboarding and scenario planning.

Designers and marketing people tend to like personas. Developers often struggle to see the value in them, but they can be a useful tool in understanding who your intended users are. If personas are overplayed, they can also take on an unassailable role on some projects, negating common sense. A persona that is frequently missed is the internal user, often on your own staff; she is as much a customer of this process as the people who come to the site. She is also a simple persona to sense-check, as you can actually talk to her. Personas for social software also need to take into account the social interactions *between* the people using the site, something that they traditionally have not included.

Along with the persona, UCD practitioners use a variety of other techniques to elicit information, including structured interviewing, card sorting, and contextual inquiry. Their focus is on helping the system designers become closer to the domain experts who will be using the system. Mike Kuniavsky's *Observing the User Experience* (Morgan Kaufmann) offers a thorough overview and tutorial on many aspects of UCD.

You have many advantages over the people who developed UCD tools back in the 1980s. Before UCD, designers and developers of, for instance, healthcare insurance packages or hotel management software were generally not well versed in these particular business areas. Today, in many cases the tools in UCD help software teams understand the working practices they are automating.

Talking with Potential Users

Most people have no idea what software is capable of doing, so they cannot raise genuinely useful ideas. As a result, you need to approach these people indirectly, and instead ask what they do and why they do those things. From these interview notes, you can build a composite picture of what your potential audience will want. Henry Ford is often quoted as saying that people would have wanted a "faster horse" before he popularized the motor car, suggesting that people find it hard to imagine the real solution to their problems. This process of researching and understanding allows you to determine how your product will impact how people are currently behaving. Techniques such as prototyping and sketching allow quick exploration of these ideas.

If the product you are building is something that *you* are likely to want to use, as is common with startups, characterizing its features and interaction becomes an easier problem to solve. In larger companies, or for those who are targeting a diverse audience, this separation makes product creation more difficult. UCD can help you connect with people who are different from you. In an agency environment, where there might be a new client every few months coming from a completely different business area, UCD is essential. A lot of UCD is about getting inside the user's head, so if your team comprises active users, you can shortcut this process. Often what is happening on the personal scale is a rapid evaluation and iteration with periods for reflection and understanding, but these are internal processes. When we move to the wider scale of building for others, we need to make these processes more orchestrated and systematic.

Naming Influences Perspectives

You need to be careful to use labels that other people will understand. Many sites make too many implicit assumptions about people's levels of understanding. Correctly capturing and critically assessing these assumptions in the initial planning phase of a project is key so that prior to launch, you can reevaluate this list of assumptions as a point of reference before presenting the site externally. The language you use in your project will become an internal form of shorthand that visitors to your site will need to learn. What to call things when represented on your site can become a long-running debate internally, and can influence your users' perspective. Calling the initial post on a message board a *question* as opposed to a *topic* will encourage a certain style of posting from the community. Calling the post a *question* is likely to promote short, direct posts, whereas calling it a *topic* would instead encourage more open-ended contributions.

Picking the correct language for your site is a difficult task, as the language on your site needs to meet many requirements. Short is good, but so is applicability; context is important, too. Drawing on your community to help you define these requirements is an essential part of product design (particularly in terms of later refactoring). As a result, customers are moving into a more active role in terms of product formation.

Common Techniques for UCD

UCD has numerous techniques and approaches. Rather than review every technique, here are some of the most common:

Contextual inquiry
> This is an on-site observational and semistructured interviewing technique aimed at users to get them up to speed with how your community operates currently. It is composed of the techniques that follow:

Task analysis
> Task analysis is the process of decomposing a high-level task into fine-grained, single steps to better understand implicit thinking and assumptions. An outside expert in the area for which you are developing needs to review the analysis data for consistency. This reviewer should not have been involved in the task analysis. Effectively, task analysis involves two reviews: one to assess the task, and one to check that the assessment makes sense.

Card sort test
> This is a process that is intended to discover content and group activities. Identify content or activities (but not both in the same test) and put them on small cards. Ask people individually to sort them into as many categories as they see fit. This test is useful for determining how people see a content area. This test can also be used to determine activity paths (determining the logical temporal ordering of a task).

Focus groups

These small-group focused discussions are helpful for obtaining buy-in with senior stakeholders and gleaning opinions on product direction. If they are not well planned, they can result in data that is difficult to analyze or that simply confirms prejudices. A good moderator will help during these sessions so that you can concentrate on what is being said.

Usability testing

Usability tests can be run in several ways from formal, one-way or video-based tests of implemented systems to simple paper prototypes. It is amazing how people will misinterpret your well-intended designs. These tests are easier and cheaper to arrange than most people think, particularly with paper prototyping.

Design consequences

This is a good technique to get beyond the idea that only one person can draw up the interface. Take a multidisciplinary group, and give everyone the same design problem and seven to eight minutes to sketch out an interface for it. Then have each participant pass it to the person on her right, and ask that person to draw the results of clicking on what she sees as the appropriate link. (See Leisa Reichelt's post at *http://www.disambiguity.com/design-consequences -a-fun-workshop-technique-for-brainstorming-consensus-building/* for more details on her technique.)

These techniques are really important, and you can use them anytime and as often as you like throughout the project, or anytime you are developing new functionality. Some companies see this as a task to be done only once during the life of a project. That is not true—you can come back to it again and again.

Running Interaction Design Projects

UCD will help you develop a model of the requirements of the different people coming to your site. The process develops a lot of internal documentation from personas and the various task-based approaches. You can run UCD projects in different ways; some of them take a "design upfront" approach, and others are more iterative in their style. The more iterative approach fits better with agile methods, but it depends on the scale of the project. Agile is a software development practice that emphasizes working code rather than copious documentation. The focus is on iterating in short cycles with working models—"design upfront" is better than "code upfront" in most cases. Building a suite of code without an idea of the final user interface (or needs) is a recipe for disaster with a social web application.

A larger UCD project can take on a life of its own, almost becoming a full project prior to your building the actual application. UCD projects frequently deliver fully fledged wireframes, which can seem like mockups for the actual application. There is much discussion on UCD mailing lists regarding whether showing this output to clients is a good idea because the output can look like unfinished site designs, even though it is valuable work. If you are an agency building sites for other companies, you will have an in-house approach to this problem. If you are an internal team, these documents can be important tools to get better engagement with other people in the company. Later in this chapter, we'll look at other document types like interactive mockups.

 A key difference between wireframes for websites and wireframes for web applications is that the application can have multiple implementations and actually has functionality, whereas a website tends to be simply read.

Reaching the point where you have a good model of the people, objects, and activities that your site will represent means you can settle on a user interface. Determining what people can do and designing how it looks on-screen can occur simultaneously and is best mocked up as an interface to allow those actions to occur together.

Using Agile and UCD Methods

UCD and agile development methods can seem to operate in opposition if you allow them to run their natural course. Agile likes rapid iteration; UCD generally likes long time periods for research and then a firm plan. However, some practitioners are more flexible in their approaches. Today, a guerrilla UCD movement is in full swing, with practitioners viewing UCD as a tactical tool and a long-term analysis tool.

UCD and agile development methods are not impossible bedfellows, but both require careful management and introduction. Leisa Reichelt, among others, has talked about the washing machine model for doing interaction design in short bursts alongside and slightly ahead of agile sprints (*http://www.disambiguity.com/waterfall-bad-washing-ma chine-good-ia-summit-07-slides/*). The work is led by the interaction design, and the user interface design work informs the software development work. This approach feels like a natural extension of how small teams work and draws on the open source idea of "ship early and often."

As noted earlier, one of the main drawbacks to the waterfall approach is the inflexibility and the single big launch. Developing an application a month at a time with a release each month means you can try things and course-correct if you make a bad move. Combining this with interaction design work means you can intelligently react to your community. Grand plans over multiple quarters look great on a Gantt chart, but they mean you are often building the product you think your audience should have, rather than the one they really want.

Typically, these Gantt charts are tied to staff availability and a firm product launch date, so there is very limited or no flexibility. The common approach is to aim for 100% and then cut features if it looks like you'll miss your deadline. Also, product planning done in August, resulting in a launch in April, means you are building the product that was appropriate eight months prior to launch. Big features do take time to create, but linking several big features together into a monster release is rarely a good idea. This approach also tends to stifle any experimentation and testing along the way.

Aim for small, regular releases. Work up to 100% with a functioning product; don't leave yourself with half a product and gaping holes because you started something too big that then had to have major pieces cut from it.

Getting agile and UCD to work well together requires some flexibility from both the designer and developer teams in terms of language and sharing common documents, which might have previously been private. Having both teams working in the same building—ideally in the same room—helps. It makes conversations easier and allows the background social interaction to develop. A lot happens in a company that does not take place in a meeting room or through email. When your teams are physically separated, this type of communication can't happen easily.

If this is not possible, at least have your teams meet regularly so that these personal relationships can develop. Rather than working in isolation and handing finished work to one another, designers and developers should work hand in hand and make live prototypes that can be used with test subjects. This process tends to bring developers on board with the product at an early stage, and avoids designing features that are impossible to implement.

The popular JavaScript library JQuery includes an excellent plug-in called PolyPage (*http://24ways.org/2008/easier-page-states-for-wireframes*), which is a great tool for creating interactive wireframes that handle state well. All social applications have a logged-in state, a logged-out state, and many others. This plug-in helps you to automate state changes while allowing you to keep a single mockup page for each actual page in the application (rather than having four files corresponding to four different states in the application). Using this tool is a great way to bridge the gap between design and development.

You do not have to start out with a grand plan; instead, you can build the system in an iterative manner, which seems like common sense. It is easy to lose sight of this in a larger company, when work goes to "design," and then to "development," and before you know it you have a waterfall. Hard discipline boundaries are unhelpful, and they are one of the advantages that small startups have over larger companies, as there is not another project to get assigned to or to compete for staff within a startup company. Also, in a startup company, there is likely to be more overlap between roles, as there is no budget for an interaction designer, an illustrator, a usability consultant, and six different types of software developer.

Planning a site does take time. Rushing the planning phase so that you can start writing code means you will most likely have a poor understanding of what you are making. If you take the line item approach, you are likely to have as many views of each item as there are people on the project. Ten features and 10 people likely means perhaps 100 different viewpoints on how the application will operate. English is an imprecise language, compared to software code, in which every word has a single meaning. A brisk planning phase is also likely to lead to a feature-led, rather than a person-led, design approach. The features rack up without a thought as to how they will integrate, each one lost in a set of written requirements documents, a situation that is sometimes known as *creeping featurism* or *carbuncle design*.

Taking the time to create visual mockups of each feature means there will be less ambiguity in terms of what is being built and how it will operate. The balance between static mockups in Photoshop and functional prototypes made from HTML and CSS will depend on your team and the project, but try to avoid the "home page as Holy Grail" school of design. There is one home page, but there are thousands (or millions) of content pages, so spend your time making the content pages shine—the home page will evolve. The search engines of the world will know the content pages just as well as they know the home page; many more people come in via a content page than via the front door.

Even a quick hand-drawn sketch communicates a lot and can be quickly iterated. Many social applications start out on a sheet of paper or a whiteboard, as shown in Figure 7-1.

Combining agile and UCD methods requires some flexibility and a clear understanding of expected or assumed roles and responsibilities, plus an acceptance that some work will be thrown away. Iteration will mean some dead ends and the need to reassess some decisions. In fact, it can be more strongly stated that unless you have found some dead ends and thrown away some prototypes, you probably have not found the best design for your application. The psychology term *confirmation bias* is used to describe people's tendency to notice evidence that supports their initial point of view. Exploring several prototypes helps you move past your bias.

A good ground rule is that code should not be developed unless the design has been prototyped. The behavior-driven design approach also supports this model of working, as you determine what should be happening in response to user interaction rather than building features.

Beyond UCD

UCD is far from the only approach to help you decide what to build, but it is one of the most dominant. As noted earlier, UCD came from the computer-driven cognitive psychology models of the 1980s. Understanding how we process information in specific situations was helpful; it lifted our interactions with computers from text-based interfaces to graphical ones. Focusing on the goal and decision-making aspects, however, kept the focus task-based. Today, there are much richer interaction models that we can support, and tools to derive them.

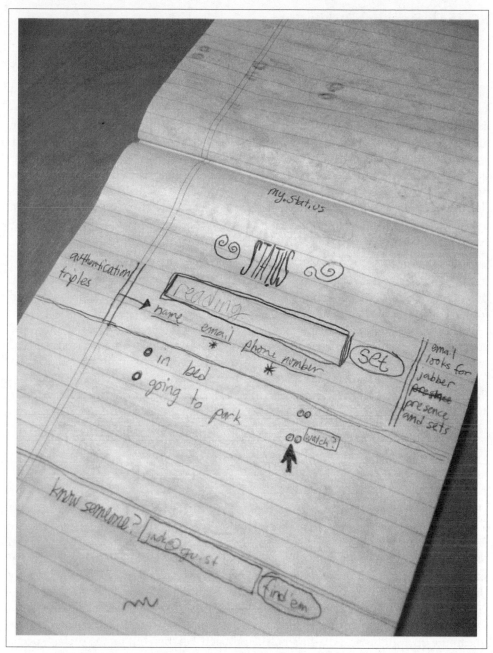

Figure 7-1. Stat.us, the original concept sketch for what became Twitter (http://www.flickr.com/photos/jackdorsey/182613360/; used with permission)

HCI and Information Architecture

Cognitive psychology overlaps with the wider discipline of human–computer interaction (HCI), which sits between computer science and psychology. Cognitive psychology is not the only area of psychology that offers a means to develop applications, however. There is much to be explored in the areas of social psychology and other social sciences. One of HCI's early influences came not from psychology, but from architecture and design. *Information architecture* took thinking from urban planning and the work of Kevin Lynch (*The Image of the City*, The MIT Press) to help understand hypertext information systems. *Hypertext* is the now-seldom-mentioned term used to describe some of what the Web represents. The idea of links within text taking you to other pages is much older than the Web, which dates from about 1990. Hypertext ideas date back to Vannevar Bush and the memex in 1945, through Ted Nelson in the 1960s, and to academic work in the 1980s and 1990s. (For more information, see the ongoing ACM Hypertext conference series at *http://www.acm.org*.)

Information architecture describes how information is organized so that it is relevant to different user populations. Formal organization of information is the main tool set, but library science has contributed a lot. Controlled vocabularies, taxonomies, and formal descriptions of content as objects give a solid handle on large amounts of content. These tools are really useful if you are publishing the content yourself, but if the content largely comes from your community, it is hard to get people to effectively use taxonomy (Chapter 13 explores this in more depth). The navigation aspects of information architecture are very useful for getting a sense of which pages act as thoroughfares.

 Information Architecture for the World Wide Web (*http://oreilly.com/cat alog/9780596527341/*), by Peter Morville and Louis Rosenfeld (O'Reilly), is a great book on the topic of information architecture.

UCD works with information architecture to produce a site. *User experience design* is a good term covering both areas. Jesse James Garrett's book *The Elements of User Experience* (Peachpit Press) gives a useful frame of reference for the overlap of visual design, interaction design, information architecture, and product strategy. His initial work is eight years old now, but the idea of separate layers has stayed with the industry (*http://www.jjg.net/elements/pdf/elements.pdf*). One point to note is that a pure UCD and information architecture approach to building web applications can miss out on the social interactions between individuals. The intraperson interactions are impossible to capture on a sitemap, and a goal-based approach can miss out on the social aspects. On the next few pages, we'll look at some other models of design.

The Craftsman Approach

Dan Saffer coined the term *craftsman* to describe the experienced designer who works with little traditional UCD research to back herself up. Compared to many other companies, Apple does little external research, and it doesn't use focus groups. It does have a very coherent model of what each product should do, which often includes a clear picture of what is extraneous. This means that Apple is not actively engaging the prospective purchasers of its products, instead it's designing for them. Apple is very concerned with proprietary boundaries, and as such, it rarely makes its design processes and iterations public. Instead, hard work behind closed doors produces the iPod or the iPhone. Developing products without reference to the customer is hard to pull off consistently. It requires tremendous talent and discipline, and very few companies can do it time and again.

However, due to budget constraints, many of us work in a similar manner. Making something that you would use is the goal. In open source software development, this is known as "scratching your own itch." A craftsman will use his skills to create things, and hopefully he makes things that are useful to himself or his friends. Customer requirements are immediately obvious, and people tend to make things within their knowledge and ability. For instance, Basecamp from 37signals came from a project management tool for managing client work; Last.fm came from a passion for music and a desire to find new things to listen to.

With this approach, you're designing for a core problem or experience, so you need to be clear in communicating this. You need to be aware that additions will muddy your message and potentially obscure the value of your product, which in turn will mean people will be unsure of what you are offering.

The farther away you move from your core interests, the more likely you are to go astray with this approach. Designers can be led into a case of "designer knows best" if there is not genuine knowledge of the subject. Their prior design experience can lead them to falsely make assumptions about how another community behaves.

Another argument for the craftsman approach is speed, as conducting a series of UCD studies means you are spending time understanding and not building. For some teams, this seeming lack of activity is too much, and they will push on to the build phase as soon as possible. The risk in pushing on is that you may end up building the wrong thing through lack of understanding. Rapid iteration of code and swift progress from prototype to application are possible with frameworks such as Ruby on Rails. This rapid iteration and visible prototypes can give a sense of real progress, but unless you have a good idea of where you are heading in terms of the overall user experience, this development can be a direction-less wiring up of blocks of code, leaving the interaction style and experience ragged.

Small iterative prototypes allow you to make progress while not committing to a long-term plan. You can run tactical UCD projects in the month before development and then use them to adjust what you are making each month. In large companies, this style of working becomes more difficult, as staff members are allocated to other projects, and getting the right people at the right time becomes increasingly complicated. This leaky information management as staff members move in and out leads to a weakened product vision and can result in poorer products.

Software development is sometimes thought of as a production line, though it doesn't happen in a factory. It is best seen as a series of bespoke work, each piece unique and tailored, perhaps made from some common patterns, but each cut to fit.

 A common approach to software development and interaction design is the use of patterns. This is not a formal patterns book. However, *Designing Social Interfaces* (*http://oreilly.com/catalog/9780596154929*), by Christian Crumlish and Erin Malone (O'Reilly), and its companion site at *http://www.designingsocialinterfaces.com*, offers a patterns-based approach to social interaction.

Learning to Love Constraints

Your product should not attempt to be all things to all people. Bespoke products fit well or suit their surroundings perfectly, but they tend to be designed exactly for that purpose. The potential that a complex interface such as a desktop application might have is limited on the Web. Many popular web applications do one thing well and stick to one approach to addressing a complex area. Constraints are beneficial; although they can seem to limit your market, they help you communicate what your product is about and give it coherence. Certainly for version 1, you should pick one approach or technique for doing things, as opposed to offering a choice. Every time you offer a choice, you increase the amount of code you need to support and you introduce complexity into the user experience.

The impact of product design changes can be widespread, and supporting mixed modes of usage adds more complexity than you might expect. This process has what is commonly known as a *ripple effect*. Explore what happens when you change something, prior to implementing it. For example, adding private groups to an application complicates every page that has to list activities in groups. At first, this might seem like a simple change, as the group pages are the only pages to which you must add new functionality. However, you also must consider the personal activity pages, any summary home pages, pages that list tagging behaviors, and search pages. I'll talk about documentation styles that can help to track this later in the chapter.

Do not ignore constraints or, worse, attempt to build elaborate workarounds for them. These constraints are likely to be known about already by people in the area. Bandwidth, privacy, and rights management all impose constraints on how you might decide to run your project. Establish your constraints and avoid the temptation to work around them using reams of fragile code or overly elaborate interfaces. It is best to keep your project simple so that you can quickly communicate it to others, and it is easy for them to understand.

You can put arbitrary constraints on your project. For example, Twitter, Jaiku, and Pownce all took different approaches to near-time communication. Twitter does not support groups or file upload. Twitter is the simplest of the three and at the time of this writing is the most actively used product. It is simple in many respects: in terms of the functionality offered, the modes of social contact, and the media types it supports. Clearly, simplicity is not a negative attribute; in fact, it is far from it.

Twitter has even dropped features. For example, it is no longer possible to see the "with others" view of a person's profile, which gave you the view of *twitter.com* that other users saw individually, but without the private subscriptions that you did not have access to. It was like dropping in on a conversation: great for providing context, but expensive to generate a unique view of every person's timeline based on the viewer. Simple products are attractive. Jaiku and Pownce are great products, but the group aspect of them complicates the interface. Twitter remains the same product from your iPhone, to your IM, and on the Web. This high degree of consistency across the three platforms makes it much easier for people to develop a relationship with the medium they prefer. Consistent interfaces are easier to learn. It takes a long time for Twitter to make changes to the interface, because it is pays attention to the interface and doesn't just add features.

Some of the more challenging constraints tend not to be design constraints; they come from power hierarchies present in larger companies—the middle managers for whom your bright ideas are just another project and intransigent IT departments resenting your step outside the neat world of vendor-supported software. Focusing on the design problems and using them as a means of persuading senior staff members to add their influence to your project is a good way to get around these difficulties.

Working on separate hosting facilities and using an external contract staff will allow you to work around constraints in the short term, but over time, you will need to integrate with their world, just not for the initial phase. See Chapter 17 for a discussion of integration issues in larger companies.

Connecting passion to the design and development cycle will ensure that good and true things get made, as the team needs to make fewer assumptions regarding how other people think and behave. If you are not in this position—say, you are an agency or you are working in a large, multiproduct company—find appropriate constraints to hold on to. Make what you think is the best choice for your members.

Keeping Experiments Quick

Time is the primary constraint most of us grapple with. BarCamp (*http://barcamp .org*) and Hack Day (*http://hackday.org*) have shown that short sprints can produce great results in a couple of days, rather than weeks. But what you'll get from this short development cycle are quick applications, not finished products.

The early phases of a project should be the time for experimentation and rapidly trying out ideas, not for ensuring that your initial prototype works on Internet Explorer 6. There is a persuasive argument toward hacking the first iteration out as quickly as you can, but you should expect to throw a lot of it away. You can create something you can really test quickly and determine whether you are going down the right path. These hacks are not the product—they are not even the foundation for the product—but they can point you toward something of value and indicate that you need to keep looking.

If you have a live application already, creating lightweight user interface prototypes on top of the live data can be a very useful approach. Chapter 16 discusses how to deploy these prototypes and the current version of the data at the same time.

Larger companies often get this initial phase wrong: the pace slows, the planning documents pile up, and no one knows whether the application concept will work, but already it is becoming fixed in stone. The untested idea is now too expensive to kill. A quick prototype can provide a course correction early on and save money in the long term.

"Failing faster" is a good way to describe this process. No one has consistently good ideas, so you need to try lots of ideas and see what works. It is not easy to maintain flexibility in large companies so that rapid prototyping or proof-of-concept work is possible. Getting allocated designers and developers to build something experimental is often difficult, but rapidly iterating on your initial ideas will pay back many times over in the mid-term, even if it means not going forward with that particular idea. Schemes that allow designers to use 20% of their time at work to explore personal projects can be very helpful for exploring tentative ideas.

Figuring Out the Social Aspect

Choosing and understanding the right social object early in product design is critical. Starting with the wrong entity or providing insufficient support for interaction around the object can make your site feel empty or purposeless.

Social objects need to act as hooks for conversations. An early version of Flickr was based on real-time sharing of pictures. When stable URLs for images and the ability to comment were added, people were given a means for commenting on what was happening in their friends' lives, not just reacting to pictures. The picture was always the social object, but the support for interaction in the web-based version became much stronger and longer-term.

The trip on Dopplr, the track on Last.fm, and the bookmark on Delicious all provide a means for a conversation to continue or to be initiated. Only some of these objects will bear the fruit of social interaction, but the potential is there for interaction to occur. However, determining the right conditions for these personal exchanges to occur can be tricky.

Volume of content, privacy, and detail are three important aspects to pay attention to. Each aspect impinges on the other. High volume needs a low level of detail. Twitter at 140 words would be much slower-paced than the 140-character limit that Twitter currently uses. A high degree of privacy means low public volume and the sense of a dormant site. Creating a sense of vitality on your site is important. You want to show the active accounts, not the dormant ones. Content size (or ease of generation) will influence the rate of content production, so the appropriate interfaces will change between a blog and a microblog. Twitter and Flickr have more in common in terms of interface than WordPress.com and Twitter do.

Subjects, Verbs, and Objects

Social software should feel like a conversation. *The Cluetrain Manifesto* by Chris Locke et al. encouraged companies to think about their relationship with the consumer and engage with them. In a similar manner, sites that hosted content used to put their brand above that of the person using the site, and some still do. On a social website, the important person in the relationship is the individual and her relationship with her content and her friends. Some good advice: get out of the way of your users as quickly as possible.

Many sites languish in the area portrayed on the left side of Figure 7-2 because they fail to adequately create opportunities for community interaction that are not directly brokered by the creators of the site. Or the site is too hands-on in terms of community management. The reach or surface area your organization can present is tiny in comparison to the surface area that a community can generate through its own content. Strongly directed communities that have a high degree of editorial involvement can be a success, but success depends on how much of an investment you want to make in terms of time. A high degree of involvement will create something closer to your brand; less control leads to activity that you are supporting rather than initiating.

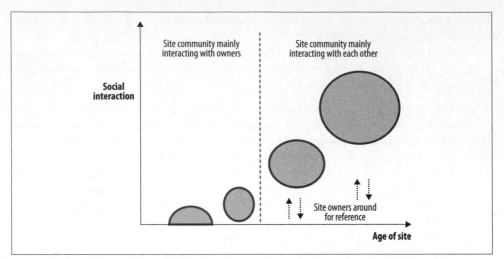

Figure 7-2. Models of community interaction showing (from left to right) decreasing levels of direct support from founders and increasing community interaction

Theories for the Future

While researching this book, I came across several approaches that have inspired my thinking on the design of social applications. Given the shift to a social web and away from a traditional desktop model, new approaches for thinking about interaction are essential.

Activity Theory is an alternative model for the way human beings use everyday tools and process information. The theory starts with the idea that the focus of human existence is our social interaction; in fact, that consciousness derives from social interaction. Activity Theory was originated by Lem Vogoysky and Aleksei Leontiev, and essentially it focuses on the idea that all human activity is social in nature and by engaging in this activity we are changed by it. An activity is composed of a subject and an object, mediated by a tool (counting, writing, signage, etc.).

I think Activity Theory is a great new direction in terms of understanding the social web. The basic model explains humans as social entities that perform tasks, of which the important tasks are social in nature. Each task has a context and its completion is not in isolation; the tasks change us (albeit fractionally sometimes) upon their completion. Every task has a social understanding.

For instance, which aspects of the Flickr site are social and which are individual in nature? We find that even the task of uploading a photograph, itself done by one person from a single machine, is essentially a social task; that is, the reason one uploads a picture is to share it with others.

The concept of the social object is roughly derived from Activity Theory with contributions from Actor Network Theory:

- *Find your object.* There should be a primary social object for relationships to focus on.
- *Work out the verbs.* What is the activity that the social interaction is hung upon?
- *Make it easy to discover new objects and activities.* Make it simple to find new objects and obvious how to interact with these objects. Support a social context.

Activity Theory is more of an orientation for understanding social interaction than a clear framework for analysis. If this intrigues you, read *Acting with Technology: Activity Theory and Interaction Design* by Victor Kaptelinen and Bonnie A. Nardi (The MIT Press).

Activity Theory has inspired other ideas. Don Norman's article, "Human-Centered Design Considered Harmful" (*http://www.jnd.org/dn.mss/human-centered.html*), suggests that the need for detailed personas has passed and that we should focus on more generic designs based on the activities being carried out by individuals.

This approach marries up well with an agile "fast and lean" approach to software development. Quickly analyze the things your intended users are actually doing and then make clear design documentation regarding how to match this to an actual implementation, and don't worry too much about the individual differences.

The book *Thinking in Systems* by Donella Meadows (Chelsea Green Publishing) describes a model of how complex non-linear systems work in the world. It looks at big issues such as poverty and environment degradation, so you might wonder why it is relevant to social software design. Much of the behavior in social applications is non-linear, but is gradually becoming linked via federation and aggregation. The approaches in this book let you step back from the detail of the specific task and think about the wider context of the person's social interactions.

Internet applications are increasingly central to our lives, so we need to design tools that pay attention to what is important rather than what is plentiful. The Web needs more intelligent tools to help us filter and understand our environment. Systems Theory is one approach that can help.

Including You, Me, and Her Over There, Plus Him, Too

Social applications should be filled with people. This means there are at least five viewpoints to keep in mind when designing pages:

- The user who is not logged in
- The logged-in user looking at her pages
- The logged-in user looking at other people's pages
- Potential group memberships
- Admin views

Historically, UCD has focused on the individual user. Much of the interesting activity in social web applications comes from the interactions between lots of people. UCD will help us understand the use for an individual, but we need to look at other techniques to understand the impact of social networks. The primary activity most people are engaged in on social applications is the sharing of information. Sometimes this information is entirely public, but often it is restricted to a particular group of individuals. The views in the preceding list show the differences between the owner viewing her page, a friend viewing that page, and a non-member viewing that page. These are important to capture early in the design process.

Moving Quickly from Idea to Implementation

The sooner you can create a version of your product that people can give feedback on the more likely you are to build something small and useful or to decide that the idea was a bad one and stop work on it.

Larger companies tend to spend a lot of time planning the work, compared to small startups, which tend to spend more time doing the work. This is an unfortunate artifact of having shared teams. It is sensible to share a personnel department, but sharing a development team can be frustrating. Time spent planning is not a bad idea per se, but if the planning entails busy senior managers discussing detailed written feature lists, it is likely to be expensive and slow. Most companies do not have enough development staff, so projects tend to spend a lot of time in the planning phase so that the scarce developers have had all the "complex" decisions made for them. I'd argue that this is a false economy.

Earlier I wrote about the line item approach and its negative impact on building great software. It takes a good imagination to read half a dozen line items and see the same thing as the person who wrote them—let alone be able to visualize the social interactions between the people on the future site that these features will allow. Much has been said about the importance of user testing; this first stage is just as important. Time spent prototyping several possible implementations will generally lead to a stronger solution than more time spent honing the description of something on a spreadsheet.

By prototyping possible implementations, I do not mean trying out color or layout variations, or trying different behavior patterns to solve the problem. There are different ways to get a working design model—from simple paper-based prototypes to interactive mockups to fully fledged products. Each model is more expensive, less flexible in representation, and more time-consuming to create than the previous one. The right one for you will depend on the type of problem you are solving and the amount of time you have. A reasonable guide is the more novel your product, the more detailed your prototype should be.

The common approach of arguing about a final feature specification in a management meeting that is then handed over to a design team is weak in comparison. Good applications come from trying out many approaches to the same problem, and these approaches need to be visual and interactive in nature. Allowing design to be explored is important; however, too much focus on data-driven design can result in visual design decisions being made purely by *A/B testing*. This process will create two live versions of your product and automate the alternation between them so that it is possible to measure any differences between each approach.

A long planning phase can leave the product manager or interaction designer waiting for the development team to start work. This pause can lead the product manager or interaction designer to spend his time generating more ideas. The small, simple idea at the beginning grows into a richer, more exciting concept, which often gets management support. Thus, instead of launching a cheap and simple version 1, the team starts building version 2 before they have even launched the first one. The project then becomes too expensive to stop because so much time has been invested in it, but the basic ideas have not even been road-tested in a simple version 1 launch. Startups rarely get to this point, as they usually lack sufficient funding to get to the baroque stage without a launch, though this hasn't stopped a few from trying.

 "Shipping a 1.0 product isn't going to kill you, but it will try" (*http:// www.randsinrepose.com/archives/2006/04/20/10.html*).

Early user interface work combined with rapid development, prototyping, and user testing will quickly hone the application to a smaller size. The best iPhone applications are a great place to learn about efficient use of interface design. Doing a few things really well is much better than offering everything poorly.

For instance, imagine that you want to sell a book about wine tasting: you could build a recommendation service application to sell other books, or you could get a review of the book and post it on a site.

However, both of these are single, closed tasks; there is no need for a return visit. Think in terms of a service that will create something of longer-term interest. An example in this case could be a wine reviewing service. People who buy the book must like and drink wine, so dip into their ongoing lives. Encourage them to share with other readers their experiences with the wines they have enjoyed or hated.

Assuming a country-specific service, partnering with a retail chain to run a monthly tasting, with people coming back to the site to share experiences and opinions, would be one approach.

Allowing people to create a diary would be another option. Let them rate wines they have tasted, and use this as the means of generating a recommendation service for other wines to try. Perhaps you could make the data anonymous so that people can have private diaries if they wish, but use all the data for recommendation purposes.

Local wine tasting clubs could be created from regional readers who are willing to participate; this way you could generate face-to-face social interactions that will help facilitate interaction on the site.

The key is to provide something that is not time-consuming for the readers to do, but that gives more value in return for them. Linking this to the book content and providing source content for the next edition from the community interaction should also be effective.

Explaining to Others What You Are Doing

As briefly mentioned in Chapter 3, at some point, you will probably need to document what you are doing for new staff members or for review. One document that is helpful is the page description diagram (PDD). This has the benefits of the wireframe in that it is quick to create and modify, but it avoids the positional bias that the wireframe brings along with it. A wireframe is meant to be a sketch of how the site might operate, but too often it becomes how the site is laid out; the position is fixed in the wireframe. The PDD is an ordered list of the elements that need to appear on the page. It is a three-column, landscape page with the top left as the most important (or distinctive) element and the bottom right as the least important element. A final column for notes is recommended; this is particularly helpful for describing the behavior of the page elements. A clickable prototype imparts a lot more information, but it is also more work to create and uses different skill sets. Figure 7-3 shows a sample PDD.

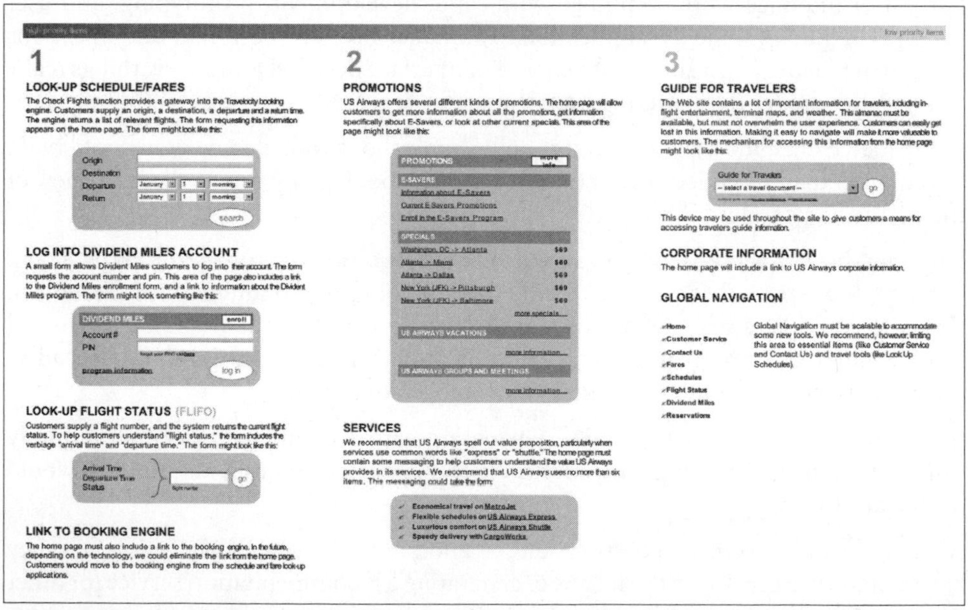

Figure 7-3. Sample page description diagram (http://www.7nights.com/asterisk/archive/2005/04/page-description-diagrams)

Creating Service Functionality Documents

Capturing the overall behavior of a new feature and how it affects the existing functionality is an important task. You can do it by writing and updating detailed documents of site behavior, but a more straightforward approach is the Service Functionality Document (SFD) shown in Figure 7-4. This is ideally a single-page document that summarizes what the new feature will do and who it is aimed at. It should include the following:

Title
> A short descriptive title that emphasizes functionality.

Aim
> Describes why the application is being created and includes the justification for it. Only one aim is allowed.

Goal
> Explains what needs are being addressed. It is more task-based than the aim is.

Assumptions
> Lists all the assumptions being made for the product.

Out of scope
> Lists what the functionality will not do, and is as important as what it will do.

Who will use this
> Identifies the main groups of people who will use the functionality.

Tasks
> Lists the actual tasks being implemented and a description of the functionality.

Context
> Any supporting information that is required.

Navigation
> Thumbnail of any logic flow in the application. This is useful for error states and completion screens.

Connections to other SFDs
> Lists any other SFDs that are affected by changes in this functionality.

Short, one- or two-page documents are more likely to be read and revised than anything that is four to five pages in length. The example in Figure 7-4 is a version I have used; the information it captures is the important thing, not the specific layout. Feel free to take these and modify them as you see fit.

Calculating Content Size

Determining the right amount of content to request for an object on your site and the granularity at which to model it is classical information architecture work. You want an amount of detail that is meaningful, but that also carries value. Twitter has shown

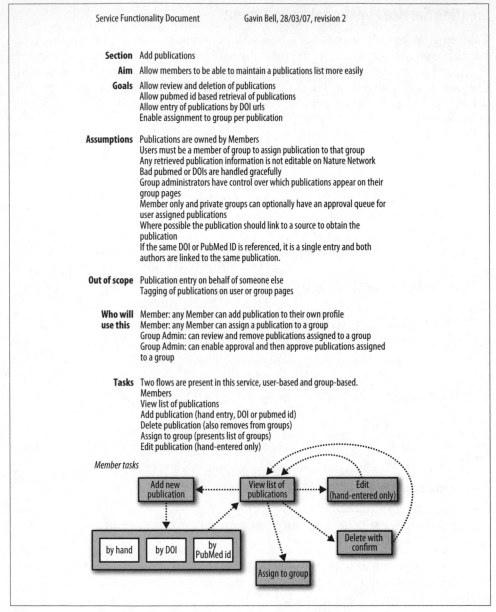

Section Add publications

Aim Allow members to be able to maintain a publications list more easily

Goals Allow review and deletion of publications
Allow pubmed id based retrieval of publications
Allow entry of publications by DOI urls
Enable assignment to group per publication

Assumptions Publications are owned by Members
Users must be a member of group to assign publication to that group
Any retrieved publication information is not editable on Nature Network
Bad pubmed or DOIs are handled gracefully
Group administrators have control over which publications appear on their group pages
Member only and private groups can optionally have an approval queue for user assigned publications
Where possible the publication should link to a source to obtain the publication
If the same DOI or PubMed ID is referenced, it is a single entry and both authors are linked to the same publication.

Out of scope Publication entry on behalf of someone else
Tagging of publications on user or group pages

Who will use this Member: any Member can add publication to their own profile
Member: any Member can assign a publication to a group
Group Admin: can review and remove publications assigned to a group
Group Admin: can enable approval and then approve publications assigned to a group

Tasks Two flows are present in this service, user-based and group-based.
Members
View list of publications
Add publication (hand entry, DOI or pubmed id)
Delete publication (also removes from groups)
Assign to group (presents list of groups)
Edit publication (hand-entered only)

Member tasks

Figure 7-4. Sample Service Functionality Document; this document attempts to capture what is happening in a new piece of functionality and the impact on the rest of the site

value in 140 characters, and people become quite chatty on Twitter. It encourages a somewhat terse style of language. The blog post, now more than 10 years old, has for many people become a less common way of expressing themselves. There is a definite attraction to the microblog style of writing. Blog posts take time to write, and the constant interruptions from attractions on the Internet, work, and family life mean there is seemingly less time to actually write. Anecdotal evidence on Twitter indicates that microcontent has led to a drop in blogging and an increase in continual partial attention (CPA). Linda Stone described the CPA affliction in 2005 (*http://radar.oreilly .com/archives/2005/06/supernova-2005-2.html*). We are bombarded with information and the continual drip, drip of content only makes us hungry for more.

In the 1950s, B.F. Skinner ran some experiments on pigeons, giving them a pellet of food in response to pressing a bar. He altered the rate of delivery so that some pigeons consistently got one pellet for every press, some got one for every 5 presses, and some got one after a random interval of between 3 and 10 presses. The pigeons in the last group took the longest time to stop pressing the bar after they stopped receiving pellets.

The social application update cycle (and email) is very similar to the Skinner experiment. It is impossible to know whether there will be some content for you when you check your favorite application. If you make the content size small and deliver it often, you will mimic the behavior of the B.F. Skinner pigeons, which can be good for your application, but you may also irritate people by encouraging them to check constantly. A natural part of human nature is to monitor and check. There is a trade-off, however, as people have a limited capacity for this monitoring. Failure of some social applications can be partly due to frequent checks that return valueless information.

Yet, there is still a need for a format to encapsulate significant thoughts and experiences. Filtering tools are becoming vital as we are all generating items of content from our interactions with the world.

Don't Let Your Users Drown in Activity

Imagine you follow 150 people, each tweeting two or three times per day on average, creating about 400 updates per day. You don't need to read all of these updates, but reading none of them misses the point of being part of Twitter. Scale this up to using half a dozen social software applications and you have a lot of data being pushed to you on a daily basis. Add email and meetings, and you end up with a lot of items to attend to. A whole field of study is devoted to the so-called *economies of attention*.

Social applications generate a lot of information. In early 2009, Facebook and Friend-Feed both began offering a real-time river of activity of your friends on their sites. The Activity Streams initiative (*http://activitystrea.ms/*) is attempting to allow this kind of activity streaming as a more commonplace service in the future. Behind all of this content lie the activities on your site. What verb describes the actions that your application allows? *Posted/listened/commented* are all represented now. In Chapter 16, we'll look at collective intelligence approaches to filtering and making sense of this volume of data. A more commonplace means of doing that is a simple search.

Implementing Search

Search often comes last on the list of things to design and build; it's almost an after-thought. Two factors contribute to this: it is hard to build a decent search interface when you have a sprinkling of test content, and the common, visually led design approaches focus on pages you can navigate easily. Search is likely to be an area of the site you revise often, sometimes completely replacing the functionality.

Search is one of the common first places for new visitors to a site to explore. This is particularly true if these new people arrive without a defined social context and some people to interact with (see Chapter 18 for ways to counteract the blank-page feeling that some sites create). Search is actually highly context-based, too. The search you offer people who've not yet signed up on your site will be different from the search you offer site members. A search for people is very different from a search for events; in particular, how the results are displayed will vary a lot. People who are members will see their social network represented in the results, and the results for each person can be a compound result showing a summary of their content contributed or their recent activity. Table 7-1 shows the variety of search types across four different social applications.

Google is not the perfect example of how to do search. Google is trying to solve a really tough problem: how to provide a generic interface to thousands of different types of people. Hence the minimal interface and plain results listings. You don't have Google's problem; you generally have a good idea of the types of people using your site, plus you have another advantage: you can tell the difference between an event and a person on your site. Internet-wide search engine providers have very little information regarding the types of content they are indexing.

Table 7-1. Search in social applications showing the variety of content types and potential results

Site	Default content	Results type
Dopplr	Single search interface for places, people, trips, tips, and questions	Specific results for each type of content
Twitter	Two separate search systems for people and content	People and Twitter messages on different pages
Flickr	Photos and video	List of content as thumbnails, with many options to reorder listing and advanced search
LinkedIn	Separate searches for people, jobs, answers, inbox, and groups	Specific listings for each content type; advanced search available

Using the different content types that inhabit your site is a great way to improve your search tools. In the Nature Network site I discussed in earlier chapters, my colleagues and I created separate indexes for our content types: people, publications, forum topics, events, and blog posts. By using separate indexes, we could represent each search result, correctly showing the time and date for an event and the thumbnail for a person.

Initially, we kept the searches local to each content area: if you searched from a forum page, you got results corresponding to forums and navigation supporting your starting context of the forums. However, this meant we missed out on a sitewide search. Later we added an *elsewhere* feature that showed the search results matching each of the other content types (see Figure 7-5). This meant we could add a sitewide search.

A subsequent revision will likely replace the Ruby on Rails custom search tools that were created with a specific search product such as Solr. This evolution of search products is quite common. If the design decision to support context-relevant search early had gone the other way and produced a Google-like plain search list, it would be hard to retrofit. Plain lists tend to homogenize content and behavior.

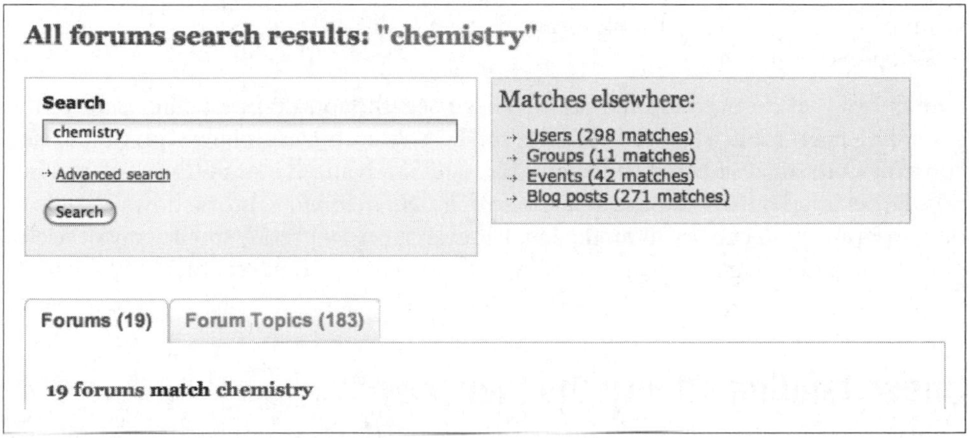

All forums search results: "chemistry"

Search
chemistry
→ Advanced search
Search

Matches elsewhere:
→ Users (298 matches)
→ Groups (11 matches)
→ Events (42 matches)
→ Blog posts (271 matches)

Forums (19) | Forum Topics (183)

19 forums match chemistry

Figure 7-5. Nature Network search for "chemistry" showing the main results for the forums, but also the matches across the site in the "Matches elsewhere" section

Member-Specific Search

Member-specific search is important on any site with private information. There will be a pool of information that is available only to the person conducting the search. You can add this information into normal search results or create natural interfaces for browsing this content. The activity stream is simply a search for the recent activity relevant to one person, when looked at from a search point of view.

On top of this, and based on that person's previous interactions with the site, the search results can be ranked by relevance specifically for the person. Not every site needs to support person relevance searching—for instance, it doesn't make a lot of sense on an A–Z listing—but in most places considering the individual in the search will be helpful. Basing this on previously viewed content would be one approach: personalized search is a mix of recommendation algorithm and search; run the search and then weigh each returned element against known liked content or types of content. If you have a model for the interests for a person, using this to filter the content makes sense. Make sure the reasons for filtering are evident. You do not want to create an unmanageable black box.

Advanced Search

The perils of advanced search are many. Every project seems to immediately throw up a need for an advanced search capability. There is a seemingly special content type or requirement that means a simple search box cannot reflect the true complexity of your glorious content. I'd argue that this is usually the wrong starting point, with the exception of time-based searching. The more you can make the simple search useful and meaningful in terms of results, the better your application will be. Make an excellent basic search, and then let people modify the search results. Prompting them to use an advanced search as a near default means that generally you have not done an adequate interaction design job.

Sometimes you do need to offer an advanced search, and despite what I said in the preceding paragraph, advanced searches can be very useful, especially with time-based content. Offering text-based shorthand for regular advanced search users is a real bonus. For example, the web page at *http://search.twitter.com/operators* shows a range of operators that you can use to modify a basic search on Twitter. A small array of useful options is better than many edge cases. As always, when it comes to interaction, simple is better.

Understanding Activity and Viewpoints

I believe *activity* is a great point of view from which to look at how social software can develop. However, determining the appropriate frame of reference from which to work can be difficult. Recently, I used non-fiction books as an example in a talk I gave at the O'Reilly Tools of Change 2009 conference. I wanted to explore how to extend the relationship beyond the simple book sale. An obvious idea is to get readers to review the books they have purchased, but this suffers in two respects: people do not buy books directly from publishers, and a review is another closed activity, like purchasing. Reviewing makes a lot of sense as an activity on a site such as Amazon; it continues the relationship post purchase and can lead to further purchases. The situation is different with a publisher, however, as the publisher has a more limited repertoire from which the person can select.

Furthermore, there is a difference between those who buy books and those who have read the books they bought. If you have read a particular book, you have something in common with the other people who have read that book, and perhaps you have a desire to meet and share ideas or experiences with them. The publisher can work with this difference, as it is a subject specialist in this area. Having read the book, the reader will be able to perform different activities. So, by building a product to support these new activities and the potential social relationships that spring from them, the publisher will be able to create a longer-term service, one that supports an open-ended relationship rather than one ending in a purchase receipt.

This open-ended aspect is vital. Focusing on making money too early can result in a closed relationship that simply ends at the sale. Making money is important, but building a longer-term relationship that can result in multiple sales is a better position to be in. People in their teens and 20s also expect an immediate two-way relationship. Providing a service that supports this kind of two-way interaction means people have a reason to come to you to extend their enjoyment of the subject.

Make sure you focus on the viewpoint of your actual audience or user population, not on the one you think you have or wish for. Then build out an activity that is a good match for this group of people.

Recipe Books: An Example

Over the past few years, if you had been developing a website aimed at people who cook, you would have built different products as the swing from retail to community took place. Here is a thumbnail sketch of how these sites might differ from one another:

Version 1
> Encourage further book purchases based on books other people bought that were similar to the ones you bought (the Amazon model). This is a good approach, but it's impersonal.

Version 2
> On the site, offer the ability to list the books the current user owns, to discover people with similar likes and dislikes. This adds a personal layer on top of book sales. It implies that people have a profile page on your site.

Version 3
> Extend the profile page and allow people to list the recipes they have cooked. Let them list and rate specific recipes and modifications they made to the recipes. This shifts the model from being purely about books to being about cooking and people.

The shift from the book as an indivisible entity to the content within the book is important. The content size becomes more granular thanks to better URL mapping and more content coming online in the examples.

The second shift is the move from aggregating everyone to personal curation of content. This seems like a small shift, but it is the start of a social rather than a retail product. The image site FFFFOUND! allows users to put any image from across the Web into a collection. You can then get pictures recommended to you based on the pictures from other individuals which you have liked. An interim model for book lists might use ownership as a proxy for recommendations in a community. A current model for cookbooks might use the actual recipe cooked, referenced from the page number in the book. Each version gets closer to the real activity the person is performing. Most cookbooks sit on shelves; only a few recipes are used from each one. Finding the actual recipes cooked and making recommendations on them could be more interesting.

The cooking sketch is probably enough to start making a prototype using a couple of authors and some friends. Nothing further should be done until the workflow around the recipe to web transfer is understood. How would you best get the event of cooking a recipe out of the kitchen? It might be best handled as an application on an iPhone or similar handheld device. Other questions then flow: what about recipes from the Internet? How might duplicates be handled? Taking this idea to a prototype stage will help you to understand whether there is a real product here or whether this is just a flash-in-the-pan idea.

Remembering the Fun

Social applications are not work; they are often useful, but this is not the same thing, so you need to make the experience of using them enjoyable. A term from the hotel industry gives the right context: *delighter*. These are pleasant surprises that appear in your room on your second or third night, or perhaps on a repeat visit. In web applications, they make the sustained interaction with a site more satisfying, as it retains the air of discovery. The logo on the Dopplr site changes depending on where you are traveling to; the scrunch noise and tiny explosion when you delete some items in Apple applications and the scroll wheel zoom on Google maps are additional examples of delighters.

Remembering that your community is there out of choice and not out of obligation will help you create the right tone. Building something that is enjoyable and satisfying to use makes people more likely to stay. Kathy Sierra (*http://headrush.typepad.com/*) describes it as the "I rock" experience. Applications should make the person using them feel good first, not think that the product is good first.

Twelve Ideas to Take Away

Here are some product creation guidelines that I covered in this chapter. Think of them as a framework for planning the interaction within your application; a quick takeaway to keep your application on track:

Understand the activities people are doing
> Do enough research so that you understand the area for which you are creating a product. Use limited documentation to ensure a shared overall understanding of what is being built at a high level. Make sure you capture the activities people want to do as well as what they are doing.

Use personas to shape product creation
> Use personas to ensure that you address your users' needs and not what you think those needs are. Also consider storyboarding as an approach.

Create prototypes as part of product planning

Do not just write documents when planning your product; make prototypes and test them with people who might use your product. Documentation is rarely up-to-date, whereas a prototype is actually used.

Create a visual design before implementing any code

Agree on the look and feel of a product before the bulk of the backend code is written. In particular, agree on the actual language to be used on the site pages. This means you agree on what is being created. Ensure that the backend code is realistic and possible.

Plan your URLs as part of the product design process

Every page should have an agreed URL or URL template before code implementation work commences. Every URL for an item of content or a person should be a pretty URL, one that is short and meaningful. No URL should change once it has been published.

Build the smallest thing you can

Focus on doing a few things well, rather than many things poorly. Solve 80% of a problem, rather than dealing with every possibility. Simple, clear applications are much easier for people to explain. This means the number of users of your application increases through word of mouth. Small applications are also easier to maintain, and cheaper as well.

Launch with an API and RSS feeds

A social web application should have an API so that people can build other products that work with your application. Let them provide alternative interfaces or additional functionality; focus on doing a few things well. RSS feeds let people easily move their content onto other places and platforms. People, tags, and content, as well as the site, can all generate RSS.

Link people to content and to one another

Ensure that the content is clearly linked to the person who contributed it. Provide contextual prompts to encourage response to this content. Support weak and strong ties between people on your site: weak could be comments or Twitter @replies, and strong could be a subscription-based following of others.

Build on top of other people's components and services

Use components such as OpenID and OAuth to simplify the experience for others, but also use other services such as Get Satisfaction for support or Fire Eagle for location management. There is no need to implement all of these services yourself, though make sure you can handle downtime on these services.

Release regularly and make iterative changes

Once you have a live product, pay attention to feedback and make gradual changes in the direction you want to take the product. Flickr added permalinks and Twitter added @replies due to feedback Can you imagine either site without those features now? Regularly updated products are responsive to community needs, even if they are not delivering what the community is asking for most loudly. Flickr took a long time to deliver printing; Twitter took a long time to deliver stability.

Scale when you need to

Technically, scaling is difficult, expensive, and time-consuming. If you do it too early, you will have hardware sitting idle or you will launch late. If you do it too late, you will have downtime and angry users. Build as much of your site to work in an asynchronous manner as possible. Return the results to the actual person viewing the site and make the rest of the updates later. Alongside the need for asynchronous design in terms of interface, there is the size of your audience to consider. If you build to support stadium-size audiences, your site will feel empty at launch. On the other hand, if you build tools to support interactions with a handful of people and you try to support thousands, your site will feel unmanageable with this volume of content. You will need to revise your site design and interfaces as your community grows. The carefully crafted interface you launch with will not be the one you have a year later.

The Web is not the only interface

Do not design your site exclusively for the Web. Mobile devices such as the iPhone and application interfaces such as Instant Messaging and email are perfectly appropriate mechanisms for interacting with your product. Too much focus on the Web can shut out these audiences from using your product. Dopplr shows that iCal can be a great interface for showing who is visiting your home city. SMS, IM, and email can work perfectly as a command interface to your content once the identity of the user has been confirmed.

A baker's dozen gets you one extra, and we can't leave out search:

Support search as a primary task

Search interfaces are tricky, despite the seeming simplicity of Google's interface. Everyone has a different set of advanced search needs, and determining which content should be searchable in different contexts also draws out differing opinions. Determining a good default set of information to search will help, as the earlier section on search showed this is very site-specific. Providing search results in context so that the information is presented meaningfully, rather than a simple plain list, makes your site a lot more usable.

Summary

Building social web applications requires that you try to understand your community's needs and desires, and what might make your new product central to their lives. It should operate in a social manner, creating objects for social attention and interaction. Building a small and focused product with clear mechanisms for social interaction is a good starting place. Assess your potential application. Does it have a core social object and a means of interaction around it? If not, go back and think again.

CHAPTER 8

Relationships, Responsibilities, and Privacy

People inhabit social web applications, and as a host, you become responsible for their interactions. Chapters 7 and 15 explore how to build for the individual and manage the unruly whole. This chapter pauses to look at the role *you* will be taking on as site owner or manager, and some of the situations you will need to consider for features and API design.

We Are in a Relationship?

Looking back to 2000, there were few sites in which the site owner had more than a transitory and often commercial relationship with the people visiting the site, let alone the ability to establish a persistent relationship with them. There were plenty of examples of web communities then, as Derek Powazek's 2001 book, *Design for Community* (Waite Group Press), demonstrates, but they were not the dominant form on the Web. Sites such as Photo.net and MetaFilter.com were starting to show how interpersonal relationships on a website might be realized.

Until recently, the idea that you might integrate your audience and your content was strange, regardless of whether you were a company, a newspaper, or even a celebrity (e.g., Stephenfry.com). Many companies do not want this relationship made obvious, or are reticent about including their community directly alongside their content.

Sometimes it might seem inappropriate. Direct customer comments on a product page from a manufacturer have been a step too far for many companies. That's changing, however, as the Kodak page on the 2008 Zi6 pocket video camera shows (*http://www .kodak.com/eknec/PageQuerier.jhtml?pq-path=13063*). It contains dozens of reviews of the Zi6 camera, many with responses from Kodak employees. Reviews range from one to five stars, and even the one-star reviews are still on the site. Kodak's willingness to leave the negative reviews is a strength. Common sense would say that even good products get negative reviews, so by including them on the site, Kodak provides a more realistic picture of its product. Your products will get both good and bad reviews on other sites, so presenting a falsely rosy version on your site is of dubious worth.

Adding readers, customers, or any other people to your site changes the relationships that are possible. They become the audience or user population; they have a relationship with you as the host, and also among themselves. In this case, *themselves* does not mean *homogeneous mass*. There are multiple groupings of people who know one another. Some are new to the site or visit infrequently. They talk to one another; they "favorite" one another's content; they argue; and they make friends, just like people in the real world.

Personal Identity and Reputation

By having people place their content on your site, you are giving them a persistent identity, not just a flimsy screen name. Calling myself *oreillybookauthor2009* makes me anonymous and unique. At the time of this writing, that string yields no search results on Google.com. Tying together content and identity is important; it gives weight and solidity to a person's online form. (For more on linking when identities change, see "Changing Identities and Linking Content" on page 188.) It encourages people to behave well, too, as they are defined by their actions within a site.

However, if I create a new identity and use it on only one site, I can say whatever I like, as it has little connection to me. This can be dangerous for the owner of the site, as I can act with impunity and provoke or cause mischief. If that account gets banned, I can come back as *amusedhecklerwaitingforsnow* and continue to provoke. Without any content or interactions for people to discover who I am, people will be less likely to trust me, as we explored in Chapter 6.

Creating profile pages that aggregate activity and encourage people to provide identities gives potentially transient identities some weight and meaning. These profiles might be the formal ones relating to trading ability, as on eBay and Amazon. Or they can be an integral part of using the service, such as the profile (about) page on Blogger or the profile page on Twitter. The responsible approach is to link the activity to the identity of its creator so that it is clear who made or said what. This linking strengthens the community and gives a stronger scope for introductions and interactions.

Handling Public, Private, and Gray Information

Potential privacy issues arise when summary information is shared on users' profile pages, but it is undeniably useful to show some information about a person. You should take care that you are not disclosing more than your community might expect you to. The limits to appropriate sharing vary with each site. For example, showing who someone regularly interacts with is probably inappropriate, whereas showing a person's favorite bands aggregated from listening habits is usually acceptable. And, of course, people are often sensitive about displaying their real-time location and information about their children, for obvious reasons. A basic rule: if you feel uncomfortable knowing a particular fact about another person, tying that data to that person's identity for public consumption is probably not a good idea.

There are two different contexts for considering privacy. The first is aggregated or summary information. Most listened to, most visited, and most popular are all examples of this kind of aggregation. Commonly, this happens anonymously for central pages, but as noted earlier, it is also displayed on individuals' profile pages.

The second context is the actual content the people share. Both fall under your control in terms of designing the product. Both require that you have a strong sense of what you are trying to build, and how people will interact with the service.

A piece of information can be public or it can be private. The first case is simple and tends to be what most people design for. Twitter started as a fully public service;* privacy was added a few months into the initial development phase. (*Private* in this case means people with a private account have control over who sees their messages.) Privacy is a popular feature request. Supporting privacy is important, but it is easiest to add it early in the development process so that you do not need to revise large amounts of code to support excluding private items from aggregation pages, search capability, and plenty of other places you'll discover in testing. Implementing privacy after initial development requires a lot more work than planning for privacy at the outset; I can speak from experience with Nature Network.

Groups and other ad hoc collections of people fall into the gray area. Is an item of content public or private? It depends on who is looking at the page. This is also true for private accounts. The followers of a person become another implicit group of people. There are other groups depending on the structure of your application.

You want to make sure that you have no gray pools of information whose privacy state is unclear. These gray pools sometimes appear because a privacy layer was applied late or because of changes in privacy levels. Different applications take different approaches to privacy. On Twitter, an account is binary: it is private or it is not, but it is possible to change the privacy state. However, if you make an account private, your previously published content will still appear in searches (as of the time of this writing). This is arguably a minor case, but it stems from the original structure of Twitter where everything was public by default, and search was added later after Twitter purchased another company.

On Flickr, privacy comes in several flavors, but it is more closely linked to the content than to the person who posted or created it. Privacy is set per item, not per account. Individuals are granted access to specific photos in an account, not an entire collection. This model is more complicated to understand, but it is substantially more flexible. It

---

* *http://www.140characters.com/2009/01/30/how-twitter-was-born/*

is also more appropriate for photography; you might not want to share pictures of your family with everyone, but you are happy to share pictures of a conference publicly.

Ensuring that you put the right information in front of the right person means always knowing and checking who is looking at a page, an RSS feed, or an API call. Failing to check identity in any of these methods for any feature will result in an automatic privacy breach and lots of irritated people. Building identity management into the core of your application makes this a lot easier to do. Chapter 16 looks at implementation of privacy in more depth.

Privacy and Aggregate Views

What about summary data tools that create aggregated views? These can range from tag pages of images or messages to activity summary pages. Twitter again gives some interesting examples of this via its API. Twitter makes it possible to find the words used most frequently by a person. You can also see the people she sends @replies to most often via third-party tools such as *http://tweetstats.com*. Other tools such as Mr. Tweet (*http://mrtweet.net/*) recommend people to follow. The interaction between these tools is private to the person requesting it. Imagine how different a place Twitter would be if these summaries and recommendations were listed publicly on your profile for all to see. Some information is definitely for private consumption only.

You can create many types of summary tools, but in general, detailed statistics or personal data should be shown to the account owner only. Simple counts are enough to show the level of activity that a person has generated. Be careful about what you list as public information; some people would argue that displaying the number of followers on Twitter has turned chasing higher follower counts into a competition to the site's detriment.

Statistics, such as the Flickr stats shown in Figure 8-1, are interesting to, but they are too detailed to show on the Flickr image page itself.

Personal information regarding the specific actions of an individual is best kept private. This includes summaries of interactions with a specific person. Sharing that I have 800 favorites is fine as a summary item, but showing by default the top five people whose pictures I mark as favorites might be giving away too much information. Context is very helpful. Figure 8-2 summarizes my listening habits for 2008. This is useful information and does not personally disclose someone else's activity, so I'd be quite happy to share this information, though other people might disagree and wish to keep their summaries private. Giving control over the publication of information such as this is the right thing to do. In "Setting Exposure Levels" on page 115, we will discuss providing such controls.

Tagging is slightly different in terms of how it operates. You might think a simple summary of all the uses of a tag on a site would be straightforward to create. However, such a summary would include all the private tagging from everyone in a basic

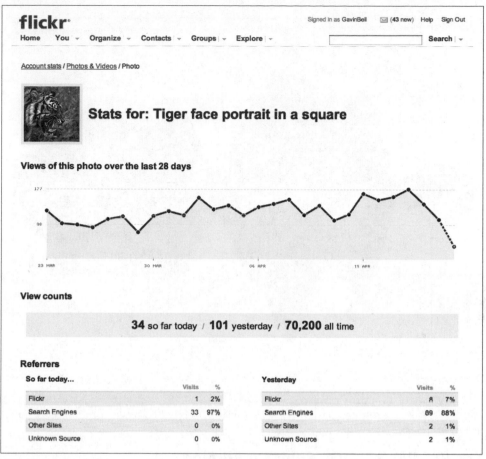

Figure 8-1. *Statistics for a tiger picture on Flickr*

implementation of the feature. In this case, you are not disclosing which person is actually doing the tagging. However, you need to ensure that tag aggregation refers only to public tagging activities so that you create a model of the site that everyone shares, not one that includes private data. Depending on your site URLs and data structures, it might be possible to reverse-engineer which tags are being used by which groups so that filter data sets include only public data before displaying it. It is important to exclude any private access that your own administrative account has in these situations, or ideally to create new accounts without privileged access for this kind of public summary work.

Generating partial views that include the private content the viewing person has access to, as well as the public content, is a big undertaking. It needs to be of significant value to you to provide, because it greatly complicates the search system design as very little information becomes cacheable. Chapter 16 expands on this topic.

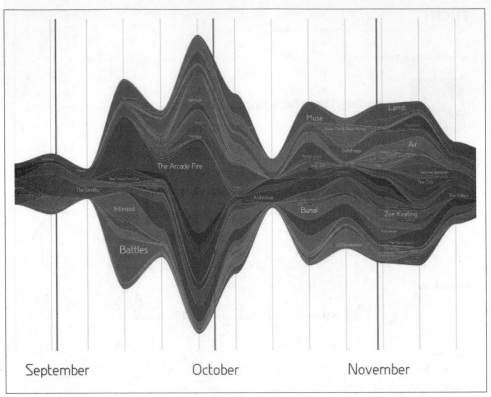

Figure 8-2. Part of my listening habits from 2008 generated by http://aeracode.org/projects/lastgraph/ using Last.fm data

See But Don't Touch: Rules for Admins

A similar situation exists for site admins. Normally, admins can access all the data on the site, even data that is *private*. The Twitter history article noted earlier (*http://www .140characters.com/2009/01/30/how-twitter-was-born/*) mentions the need for private admin accounts to help identify and test personal spaces:

> We had an admin page where you could see every user. As Head of Quality for the company, it seemed like my duty to watch for opinions or issues from our users. This caused confusion, though, when family members of our team were suddenly being followed by a seemingly random person. Thus, Private Accounts were born.

Once a site is live, the need for a private account for admins still exists to ensure that everyone is behaving. Many sites offer admins a web-based means of assuming someone else's identity by altering their URLs slightly. Inserting a parameter before the path or appending a parameter will let the logged-in admin become the viewing person. It is an extremely useful technique, but it is a powerful tool and therefore it is important not to abuse or reveal it. Seeing a problem from the point of view of the actual user can make the problem much easier to debug.

Ensuring that your users are aware that a private account is private—*unless* they request help or break the terms and conditions for use—is important in developing your community's trust. Internally, it is important to have good practices; for instance, only approved staff members should have access to admin accounts, and all accesses should be logged and subject to a regular audit. Social applications are now in the mainstream, so the temptation to dip into a famous person's account becomes more likely.

Private by Default?

A different viewpoint on privacy is the private-by-default stance of Dopplr and the now defunct Pownce. Both of these sites encourage the model that *my data is private unless I decide to share it with others.* The data flow is based on the person specifying who sees her information. It is strongly permission-based. Adding a person in Dopplr gives that person access to your information; it does not give you access to that person's information, though reciprocation is encouraged.

Starting with the premise that information is private, and you are explicitly sharing information with others, changes the basis for aggregation. Locations in the world, known as *Places* in Dopplr, are the main focus for public aggregation, rather than people or trips. Even this is anonymous in Dopplr if you are not logged in. Once you are logged in, you see the activity of your friends for that city alongside any planned trip you have to the it (see Figure 8-3).

This private-by-default model works well for sites with relatively low volumes of data exchange. People tend to travel only a few times per month at most, and people used Pownce daily rather than multiple times per hour. Sites with a higher volume of content, such as Flickr, Twitter, and Last.fm, however, do not fit as well with the private-by-default approach. Defaults are important; they set an expectation for use of the service. Many people do not change the defaults, so if you make the site private, most people will operate it as a private service. Another difference is that private sites tend to operate in a push mode. Dopplr makes content available to the subscribing user, so it works better with a lower-volume content stream. Being able to share your content with someone and have that be a high-volume feed would not work as well.

Setting Exposure Levels

Sites usually have two levels of disclosure for your users: one level that you set in the design of the environment to specify content as public or private by default, and a second level that users create. The second level is called a *digital publics* by danah boyd. This term is deliberately plural as each person has a separate one. All users have a different set of people who follow them and who they follow on a social network (see

Figure 8-3. *The New York page from Dopplr showing some data relevant to the author, along with more general information*

Kevin Marks's comments on danah's longer article at *http://epeus.blogspot.com/2008/04/digital-publics-conversations-and.html*). Essentially, this mimics our normal life. People don't have a homogeneous set of friends and relationships, so why should they have one on the Web?

Complications can arise when you allow designation of multiple levels of friendship on a social network. Flickr, for example, offers four levels of relationship: contact, friend, family, and friend plus family. When Flickr launched, offering multiple levels was the recommended best practice. Most sites now offer a simple follow or no contact level of relationship. Photography is slightly different. The most common use of the friend or family setting on Flickr is to control access to photos of children. LiveJournal.com lets you create multiple lists of people from your complete contact list and set the functionality for each list, eliminating the need to set the access per person.

Content can require specific privacy protection, too. On the Flickr service, the original uploaded image is given a secret URL so that only the person who owns the photograph can determine who gets access to the original. This version does not have a guessable URL, and it is not accessible via the API without the appropriate permission.

Determining the right balance between public and private data will depend on the content turnover rate on your site and your preference as the site designer. If content changes rapidly, public will be a good default. If there is a lot of sensitive information in the content, a multiple-list approach to sharing information will be appropriate. Fully public sites do exist. Last.fm is a good example of a site without a private account; though you can hide some activities (see Figure 8-4).

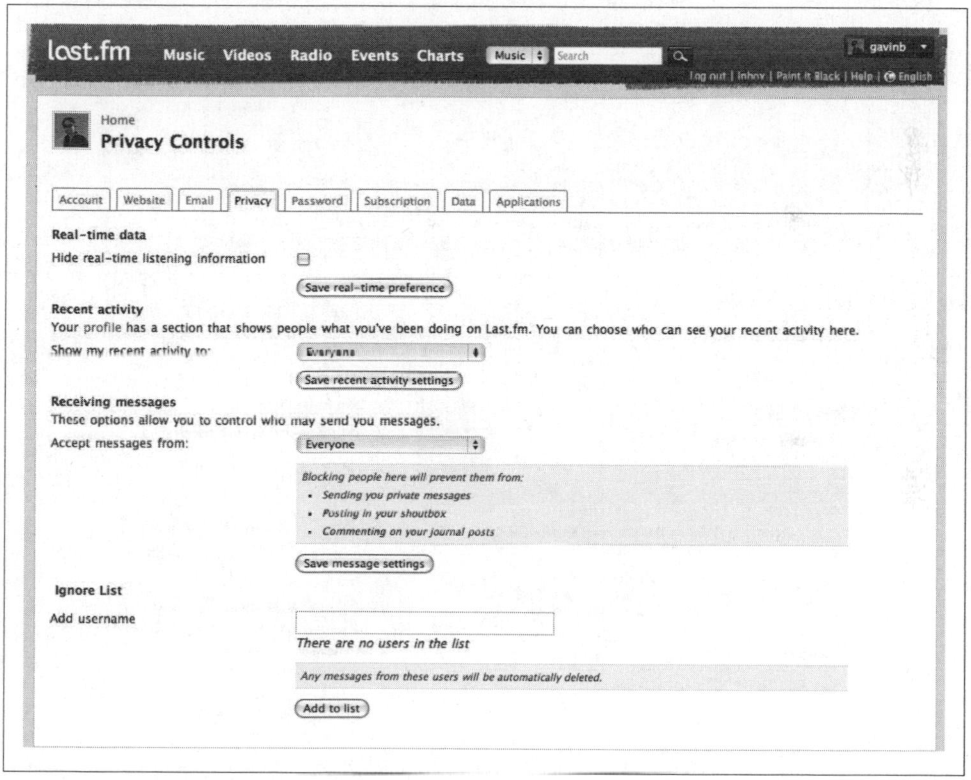

Figure 8-4. Last.fm privacy control settings

If you offer a private type of account (see Figure 8-5), you will need to create a public face (see Figure 8-6) for these profiles. Typically, this will have a small amount of summary information about the person, but usually it will not have any of the site-specific content from the person. The site still hosts a profile space for the person, but the person is opting not to share her content with others in a public manner. This seems to go against the idea of having a profile page; in fact, the only people who will be able to see the content from this person and thus wish for additional context are people who the contributor has already approved to see her content. The public face allows her to be seen on the site but avoid having to share more than she wishes to. It also provides a discovery mechanism so that new people to the site can find these users, with whom they might already have a firm relationship.

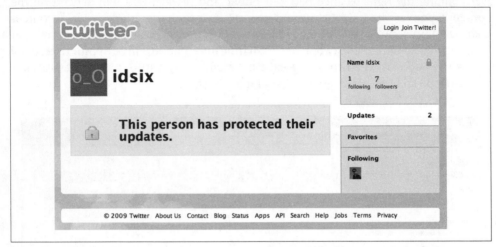

Figure 8-5. Private profile on Twitter

Figure 8-6. Logged-out view of a profile on LinkedIn

Once you have created these public views, a mechanism for editing them is required. Figure 8-7 shows the editing interface for Dopplr. All sites require the means to edit a profile page, and this page is always displayed differently for people other than the owner. At a minimum, it will not have an edit profile link. On sites such as Dopplr, this public profile is an additional step out of the ordinary, as it is a public face for non-users of the site. A similar situation exists with the LinkedIn profile. These pages are visible only if you are completely logged out of the sites.

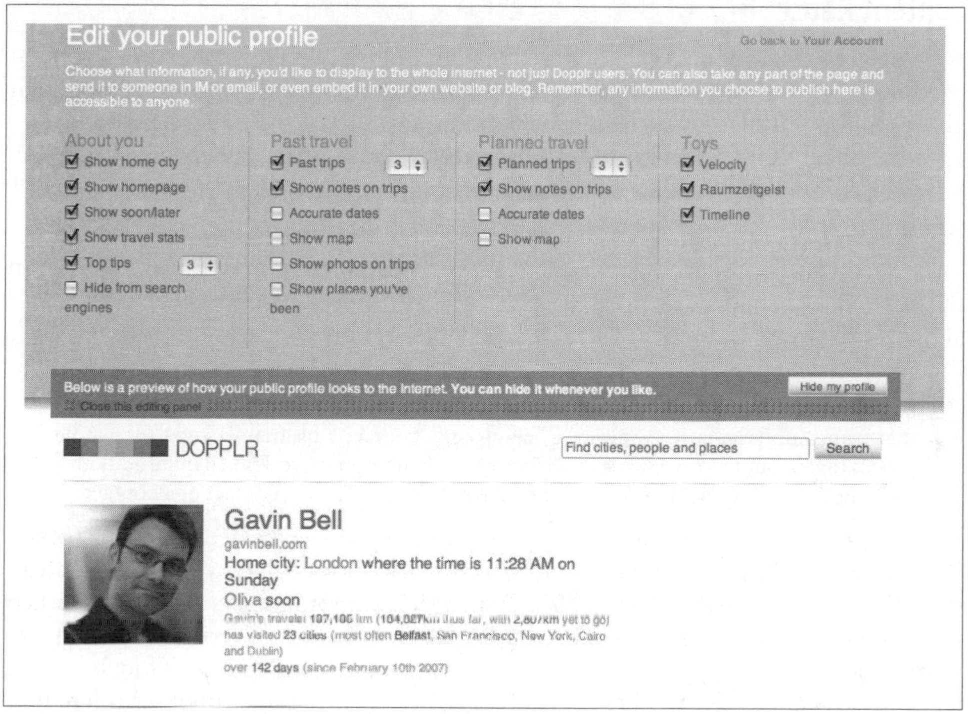

Figure 8-7. Public profile in editing mode on Dopplr

The Dopplr example is interesting because it is customizable in terms of how much personal information a person shares. Chapter 12 discusses how to create these different views of a profile page.

Managing Access for Content Reuse, Applications, and Other Developers

Looking beyond the immediate context of your website's interface, sharing your data through APIs raises additional privacy concerns. Unintended outcomes from APIs are more common than you might expect. Misunderstanding how the API works and inadvertent outcomes from using personal credentials for the API client can lead to private information being shared with the wrong people.

The specifics of identity management and the password antipattern are covered in Chapters 12 and 16, along with discussions of OpenID and OAuth.

Content Reuse

APIs are about sharing content, for the most part. Many APIs allow for external content generation, giving users another way to get their content into the system. APIs that allow for content reuse, which let information flow out, are the more dangerous ones in terms of privacy. APIs need to be as watertight about privacy as the main website, but your community's understanding of how APIs operate is likely minimal.

For example, Jeremy Keith, a web developer and author, developed a Flickr API application on his site, Adactio.com, which allowed redisplay of photos from Flickr within the context of his site, called Adactio Elsewhere (*http://adactio.com/journal/988/*). It allowed arbitrary display of any image, and you could browse contacts, too:

> The Flickr section pulls in my contacts, my newest pictures and the newest pictures from my contacts. Clicking on a thumbnail brings up a larger view of that image. Clicking on that brings up a larger view again. Clicking on a contact's username starts the whole process again but this time you see their contacts, their photos, etc. I find it quite addictive clicking through to pictures from someone who is a contact of a contact of a contact.

Shortly after he launched this functionality, a question was posted on Flickr (*http://www.flickr.com/help/forum/20686/*), followed many months later by an irate thread (*http://www.flickr.com/help/forum/50508*) in which a photographer who had marked his images as "All Rights Reserved" complained that the larger version of his images were appearing on Jeremy's site. What was happening was that the Google search engine was simply following links that eventually took the search robot from Jeremy's page to the pages for this photographer. However, many of the users of Flickr felt that it was Jeremy's fault that he was displaying the images, even though he was not storing them. The issue is difficult to judge clearly: the main photographer opinion is that the bigger image use did not count as fair use. The situation resolved itself with the initial complainant's username becoming a special-case exemption and no photos being served from Jeremy's script for that photographer.

Google's robot blindly following links led to the images being indexed. The fact that in 2007, Jeremy's site was already highly linked to meant that the versions of this photographer's images became highly ranked on Google. People cannot easily understand whether the images are real copies or are included via an API call. The Flickr API was designed so that "All Rights Reserved" images can be displayed if requested by username, which meant lots of other tools could use the API to make tools based on access to photos from a specific user. Clean URLs and simple interaction design meant that Jeremy's site was easy to index. It is a complex situation to get right and one that some people had a strong reaction to, so it became heated quickly (it's also a good example of community, host, and developer, all pulling in slightly different directions). The entire thread is worth reading to see what sorts of issues can be thrown up unexpectedly by API usage and the kinds of fixes that get demanded.

Even simple, non-API-based aggregation can be hard to get right. For instance, I set up a private blog (a non-public URL) for my first son and wanted to aggregate the public photos from Flickr into one place for my parents. A simple and quick means of doing this was to use a Tumblr microblog, but I failed to notice that Tumblr inserts a link back to the source for content. I had inadvertently leaked my private blog in an attempt to simplify access to the photos for my parents. Google came, crawled the links on the Tumblr blog, and followed the links back to the non-password-protected private blog and indexed the content. If I had thought this through more carefully and not rushed, I would have removed the link on Tumblr pointing back to the source links on my blog. I would have also added *no-index no-follow* metadata in the HTML for the pages on my private blog in case Google inadvertently found it. This stops a search engine from indexing the content and stops it from following any of the links on the page.

Many sites now have a mobile version of their content specifically designed for a device such as an iPhone. The security on these versions needs to be as tight as that on the main site, even when they are launched in beta. Launching without the same security measures in place just encourages opportunistic hacking of your content.

Don't Give Away Too Much Power

Structuring your API so that there is a read-only version with no authentication and a separate authenticated version that gains access to private accounts is quite common. The authenticated version is also used to access the write capabilities of the API. The majority of access to your API will be read-based, but managing control over whom you allow to create content on behalf of your users is important. Giving write access via an API empowers the application to act as that person to create or delete content. Chapter 16 discusses the security aspects of this, and Chapter 17 explores how to structure an API so that you manage the capabilities of the API appropriately.

On Twitter, there is a rash of applications that want you to authenticate so that they can send a message as you. Typically, this is described as *tweet the results or tweet this*. Often, this is a one-time usage, but some applications, such as Loopt and My name is E, among many others, keep the password and send messages without the explicit permission of the Twitter user.

Impressing upon your API developers the need to respect the people whom they are getting to use their applications is important. No application should send what is essentially an advertising message without the explicit permission of the person using the application. Another common transgression is spamming the email address books obtained from Yahoo! and Gmail. Both of these activities seem like a great marketing ploy, but both will quickly generate a negative reaction from your community. It is your responsibility as the API creator to set and enforce the guidelines regarding use of your own API.

Licensing Content

Earlier I touched on the issue of rights management in the Flickr example. Let's return to this now and look at the potential for giving your community control over their content. The common default on social applications is to take a non-exclusive, world-wide, and perpetual license on any content that is submitted. This means you can display the content someone puts on your site and retain the content even if the person leaves. This is the norm for text-based content. With photographs, it is common to remove the image content when the person deletes his account, but to retain the right to display any previous conversations.

The norm is to assign "All Rights Reserved" to your users to indicate that they own the content and wish to protect it beyond letting you host it. The Creative Commons (CC) license gives another option. It provides a staged option between content that is *copyrighted* and content that is *in the public domain* (see *http://creativecommons.org/about/licenses/*). It breaks the rights down into different elements: requiring attribution, commercial usage, whether the image can be modified, and the ability to redistribute the content. All of these elements are supported within the CC license. My own pictures on Flickr are licensed as *Attribution Non-Commercial No Derivatives*—otherwise known as BY NC ND (this is quite popular on Flickr)—which means that I require attribution, someone reusing my images must credit me as the photographer, I permit non-commercial usage without explicit permission, and I wish the image to be used unedited. Furthermore, I do not allow derivatives of my images without asking me first; and I am at liberty to grant more flexible licenses if people ask me.

In fact, a whole interface is dedicated to searching for CC-licensed photographs. The CC licenses are free to assign to your content and can be used for many types of creative work, from blog posts to songs and videos. They allow reuse of the licensed content and incorporation into other sites in a clear and managed way. Chapter 17 will explore the potential for integration into other sites in more depth.

Summary

This chapter highlighted the issues regarding privacy and rights management for your community. Recognizing that you have a new set of relationships to manage is the essential starting point. Flickr is not terabytes of JPEGs; it is a community of photographers who care about the pictures they have taken. You need to think about how you construct the dynamics of sharing and privacy in terms of the relationships and activities you are enabling. Simply copying the behaviors of one site and applying them elsewhere will not work. The Dopplr example highlighted the care you need to take with private information. Finally, it is vital to ensure that your API respects the rights your community has assigned to their content.

CHAPTER 9

Community Structures, Software, and Behavior

There are thousands of communities on the Internet. Some are vast, some are tiny. Each is unique, but some common behaviors emerge in similar contexts, depending on how the community is hosted, on the participants' relationships to one another, or on the subject matter. In this chapter, we will look at several general types of communities and then review some common types of social software infrastructure.

Community Structures

Communities are not a new concept. People have existed in communities since before we started to farm the land. What is recent is the ability to form communities that are geographically distant and entirely interest-led. For instance, prior to the Internet, if you wanted to find local hi-fi buffs, you needed to hang out at your local hi-fi or record shop. Now you can find dozens of hi-fi communities on the Internet, and the only barriers are language and the times people are awake.

All communities are a form of group, and so they follow the behavioral patterns that groups exhibit. People in groups tend to identify with the group as a whole; they will sometimes be unwelcoming to strangers and will form norms for group behaviors. They also have a common history which will be referenced from within the group. Finally, you cannot make a group. You can create the conditions for a group to form and encourage the formation, but you cannot force people to interact socially online.

Publisher-Led

Publisher-led communities are quite common on the Internet, as publishers engage with their readerships on their own websites. Traditionally, a newspaper publisher might have invited letters to the editor; now the conversation can occur alongside the editorial on the newspaper's website. These concurrent conversations are becoming common on news websites, and they are the norm for electronic publications. Even in book publication, community efforts are widespread in the travel sector.

The tension between the publisher-derived content and the community-generated content needs to be managed carefully. It is important to distinguish between the two, but not to discriminate against the community content. It is easy for a publisher to regard its own content as "better" and to hold the community-generated content in a lower esteem. This can manifest itself in many ways, from isolating it in a separate place to placing it beneath the publisher content in each context. Community-generated content differs from the content that publishers create. One difference is that publishers pay for their content, whereas community content comes from an interest or passion about the subject being covered; love, not money, is the driving force behind its creation (see *http://rooreynolds.com/2009/05/07/alternatives-to-ucg/* for a discussion of terms the BBC could use for the content that comes from its communities).

The increasing use of blog software to power online publication of single-interest news sites brings with it the built-in ability to comment on the content. In turn, this is raising the expectations people have for more traditional printed publications. This pressure is felt in many other areas of publishing—in particular, in sports, hobbies, and academia.

Interest-Led

The interest-led community is a very common model. The intention behind many message board installations is to support a common interest. Frequently, someone in a group will say, "I'll set up an *X* for that and email you all." The *X* is typically a message board. Message boards can be run by enthusiasts or supported by various companies and organizations. Typically, they are not for-profit or subscription-based. It is entirely possible to support a reasonably large community message board for less than $20 per month. It is also possible to make these costs back in affiliate income or text-based advertisements. Hence, there are thousands of small community endeavors out there.

However, the complexity of software integration means these tend to be based on the customization of single products. Often, a message board hosts the comments on the articles posted on the site's front page as well as other forums for discussion. This simplifies or even removes the software development work, because there is one user registration database to manage, and therefore one set of profiles and a single audience. However, this can limit the potential for future development, because you are dependent on the product development of an external piece of software.

Product-Led

Product-led sites have a particular product at their core, where there is a commercial relationship. There are two real groupings here depending on whether the host creates the product (e.g., Apple) or is a retailer of the product (e.g., an Apple retailer). The

---

focus tends to be on customer support, which is different from publisher- and interest-led sites. The company or retailer has a much more overt role to play, mitigating the complaints of its customers.

These discussion boards can be a tremendous company resource to learn from. For instance, the Apple customer support boards are full of non-Apple and Apple members helping one another. Widespread issues with new hardware surface here, and Apple sometimes intervenes to get more details directly from customers. Apple is not unique in running boards such as this, but many companies avoid this kind of direct customer involvement online, certainly on their own sites.

Another approach is to use an external company for customer support. Timbuk2 uses Get Satisfaction (*http://getsatisfaction.com/*) to host its customer support (see Figure 9-1), and links to Get Satisfaction from its customer service pages. In 2008, the integration was a more explicit embedding of the Get Satisfaction content; today, thanks to the addition of Timbuk2's own blog, there are now two community aspects to Timbuk2: a blog and a discussion forum.

One advantage of this approach is that you can host potentially negative conversations at a distance from your own company site. This separation of service and product news works well for product-led company sites, but it probably wouldn't work as well for more editorially focused sites. For a product company, the object that is being discussed is usually a physical, software, or service object. Because the product and the discussion are tightly intertwined, separating the discussion is harder to do on, for example, a newspaper.

Supporting Social Interactions

In social applications, there may not be a traditional message board or discussion space. Instead, the interaction is likely one-to-one around the community-generated content. Applications such as Facebook and MySpace are obviously social software, too. They are not sites that you can copy directly. They evolved from something much smaller and simpler. They are places with which you can integrate. Upcoming and Delicious are good examples of this type of community, and many of the newer Web 2.0 companies fit into this space as well.

There is a definite community interaction between individuals in social applications, but the start of this interaction is based on the user's own content. The initial social interactions will be between people the user knows, rather than the community at large. The community grows when people find that the product and the social interactions they engage in are useful. Compared to a discussion board, the focus in social applications is on the objects, which can range from photos to events, rather than a discussion about the subject. That being said, many social applications also host a discussion board, too.

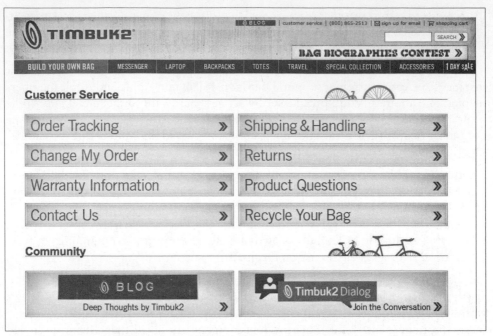

Figure 9-1. Timbuk2 support pages showing the Timbuk2 Dialog branding of the link to Get Satisfaction

The actions that bind the community in this case are usually based on sharing, commenting on, or rating content coming from others. On sites such as Delicious, Upcoming, and FFFFOUND!, the content is added to the collections of each person using the site. On Flickr, the photos are owned by each person; they can be commented on, but they can also be marked as favorites, which is a simple form of rating system. On Digg and other news aggregators, the flagging of stories allows the relative popularity of each event to be shown.

Social Applications for Teenagers

Facebook and, especially, MySpace are different from other applications we've discussed thus far in this book, because they have a large number of teenage members.

Teenagers rely on these social applications for communication. Twitter is a post-teen product; it has little bearing on teenage life. Research from danah boyd in 2009 reaffirms the idea that this age group sees email as not being relevant to them. They live their lives in one social application until their interest wanes and the next one becomes popular. danah solicited questions on Twitter from adults prior to some research with teenagers in Atlanta. The following excerpt gives a sense of their attitudes:

Question:

> @shcdean: What future do they see for FB or Twitter.

Response from danah (*http://www.zephoria.org/thoughts/archives/2009/05/16/answers_to_ques.html*):

> They don't use Twitter. When asked, teens always say that they'll use their preferred social network site (or social media service) FOREVER as a sign of their passion for it now. If they expect that they'll "grow out of it," it's a sign that the service is waning among that group at this very moment. So they're not a good predictor of their own future usage.

This book is aimed primarily at people developing software for adults. Teenagers and younger children often behave quite differently from adults. Features such as personal messaging are much more important to teenagers than to people of college age or older. Other issues such as the lack of a credit card (and legal issues) mean you need to approach design for these age groups in quite a different manner.

Non-Text-Based Social Interaction

These application examples show that the medium of exchange does not have to be simply words. These applications generate a community because they are designed for sharing information. This "architecture of participation,"* as it is frequently known, can be hard to get right. Balancing the needs of the application so that it works well for the individual and is used repeatedly is one set of problems. Making the application successfully social involves finding the right mechanism to turn that individual activity into an ongoing conversation or something that can prompt further social interaction between regular groups of people.

On Delicious, the simple aggregation of the bookmarks from an individual's social network offers a useful feature, but it is not conversational. The Add to Network feature lets people connect to one another but doesn't establish a conversation; as a comparison, on ma.gnolia there is a Give Thanks feature (see Figure 9-2) that allows anonymous appreciation to be shown among community members. In Flickr, the conversation is more obvious in that it is a response to a photograph; however, the lower-level interaction of "mark as favorite" is still there.

There are two levels of social interaction here that allow for lightweight community engagement between the members based on the sharing and appreciation of content objects. On Delicious and FFFFOUND!, they are anonymous in nature. On Flickr, the *favoriting* action is named to an individual; people are more likely to follow closer friends on Flickr, so there is the opportunity for more personal social interaction. Table 9-1 shows some other non-text-based means of social interaction.

---

* Tim O'Reilly coined the phrase in 2004 (see *http://www.oreillynet.com/pub/a/oreilly/tim/articles/architecture_of_participation.html*).

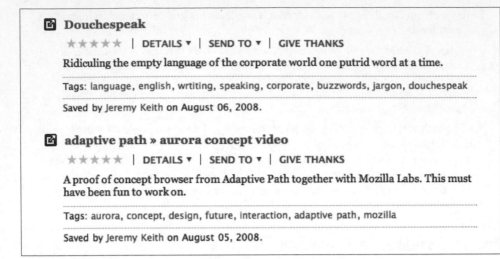

Figure 9-2. An element from ma.gnolia showing the Give Thanks feature; this shows up as an anonymous "thanks" on your private activity view

Table 9-1. Types of non-textual social interaction

Type	Action	Example sites
Anonymous	Add to library	FFFFOUND!
	Add to library	Delicious
	Give thanks	ma.gnolia
	Mark as helpful on reviews	Amazon
Named individual	Favorite	Flickr
	Loved	Last.fm
	Visited/Liked	Dopplr
	Share	Google Reader

A primary difference between the anonymous and named means of social interaction is the depth of personal ownership or relationship that exists. In the anonymous case, the interaction happens on content that is generally not created by a person; the act of mark as favorite is largely curatorial in nature. Amazon is the exception, but the rating on a personal review is not a hugely personal interaction. This model suits communities in which the content is more important than the person associated with it. It is possible to form a stronger bond with any of these people, but it's also possible to interact only once.

Where there is a named interaction, it is happening between a group of people who know one another or who are acting on content that is owned by someone. A photo taken by a person is quite different from an image a person found and liked on the Internet. This model suits interaction between small groups of people where the person is as important as the content. Note that there can be different directionality in these actions. In Flickr, a favorite is directed at the photographer, but for Dopplr and Last.fm the action will inform the friends of the person performing the action. Figure 9-3 illustrates the interaction pattern for Dopplr with its visited and liked service. The model operates purely on mouse clicks, making it quick to use.

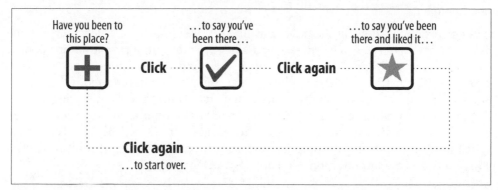

Figure 9-3. The user interaction flow for visited/liked on the travel site Dopplr (used with permission, Matt Jones); the model consists of simply clicking, once to mark it as visited, a second time to say you liked it, and a third time to reset

Non-text-based social interaction is not the only way to generate this conversation; the examples are to illustrate that you do not need to focus on the exchange of words as the sole driver of community. Lightweight social interaction that is often purely driven by mouse clicks can be a very positive reinforcement for community cohesion. Generally, the more personal actions are only positive in nature: "add to favorites," "like," "this is good." Due to their low cognitive overhead, it is common for people to mark many items in this manner. Each time they do this, the recipient gains positive reinforcement. If there was a requirement to tag the content at the same time, the rates of activity would drop, because it stops being a semiautomatic gesture and becomes a conscious act.

Assess how you can add these kinds of lightweight social interactions into your own application: the large community-content-focused activities, which will generally be curatorial in nature, and the more personal praise-bearing activities. The flow of social interaction around a site is important. An individual returning to a site and finding that someone liked her contributions is likely to be more positively disposed to the site.

For this to happen on a frequent basis, the interaction needs to be click-based. As noted earlier, with a click it is possible to mark several items as good in the time it takes to tag only one item. Make sure this click action is available via your API and encourage developers to add this to their applications. Finally, these lightweight operations can form the beginnings of social relationships between individuals on a social application. An indication of interest can lead to later addition to their social circle.

One side effect of the "mark as favorite" action is the creation of long lists of favorites that won't provide further value if left as a list. "Mark as favorite" should act as a within-application bookmarking service; the lists of favorites should then offer actions that are relevant to the content. The ability to act as a curator of the content that you find interesting appeals to a large number of people. Better tools should be offered to help people manage these interesting items of content—offering permission to republish is one example.

A simple example showing the desire for this sort of support is on Delicious (*http://delicious.com/tag/toread*). The `toread` tag frequently comes from people adding bookmarks to their collections from the content they find on Delicious. They use the `toread` tag as a marker for later reading on the content they have found. On Google Reader (see Figure 9-4), the ability to share an item of content is an interesting implementation of the favorite model. The items can then be republished elsewhere—for example, on FriendFeed or other activity stream aggregation services. This is a social activity based on private consumption of content from RSS feeds, in contrast to the addition to a personal collection that happens on Delicious.

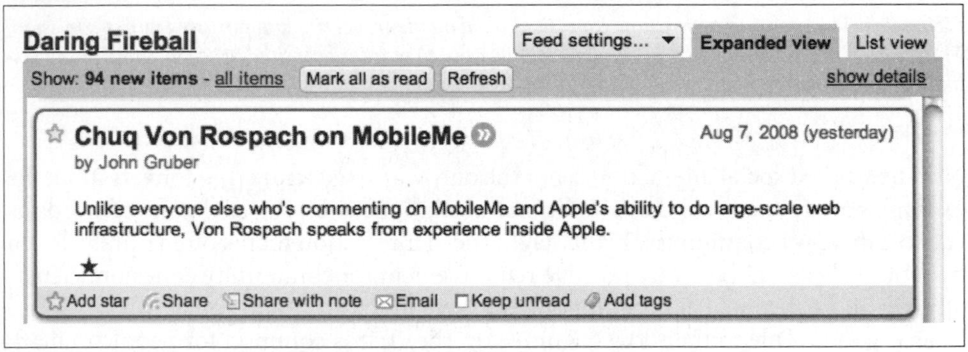

Figure 9-4. An element from Google Reader, showing the Share feature

Competition: Making Games Social

Another good means of developing community can be competition. Many games, among them *World of Warcraft*, engender community. People form clans, and there are strong in-game social dynamics. These sites tend to follow similar paths as the interest-led communities, but people arrive with a solid persona from the game. A new form is the alternative reality game (ARG) where people play games based on real-world physical locations or real-world data, using the Internet to coordinate activity.

Plundr (*http://plundr.playareacode.com/*), for instance, turns public Wi-Fi access points around the world into virtual treasure islands, and players pose as pirates. Sharkrunners (*http://dsc.discovery.com/convergence/sharkweek/shark-runners/shark-runners-hq.html*) takes real-time shark location data and allows you to pilot virtual research boats to track real sharks. There is even a Firefox-based ARG called The

Nethernet (*http://thenethernet.com/*) that attempts to make a game from your browsing behavior. With The Nethernet, you visit sites and gain points, or fall into a trap that friends set on the site; you can even take on challenges, such as "use the Web for a week without visiting Google." I raise these examples to show that the kind of community you are creating need not be tied only to your own site. The potential to have real-time location as a factor in your websites is shown by these more experimental uses of the Internet. The launch of the Apple iTunes App Store for the iPhone in July 2008 will encourage many more location-aware applications, because the iPhone offers an effective mechanism to determine the current location of the device.

Gaming communities can be short-lived because they are often event-based, but a wider community can persist. A good example of this comes from Penguin and Six to Start and their "We Tell Stories" project (see Figure 9-5). Six authors each wrote a story and six questions stemmed from each story; if you could answer the questions, you'd win a prize (*http://www.sixtostart.com/blog/2008/03/27/we-tell-stories-whats-yours/*). This ARG placed Penguin as a brand at the center of a gaming experience, but one that was still connected to fiction and storytelling.

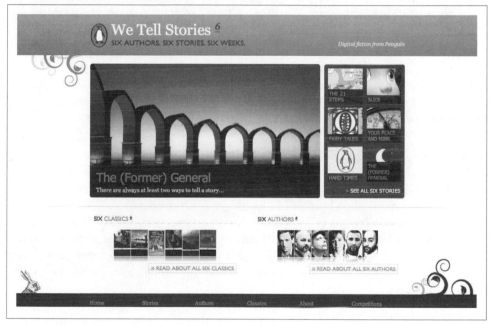

Figure 9-5. We Tell Stories, a storytelling game from Penguin that uses the Internet as a place to tell stories and play games

Content Creation and Collectives

Many sites on the Internet set out to allow people to create and share content. Blogger, which launched in 1999, popularized the idea of regularly maintained personal websites, as opposed to farms of cookie-cutter home pages, which had been the norm on Geocities and others. The idea that an individual should regularly update a website on his own seems obvious now, but was less obvious then. This shift from maintaining a static page of content to becoming a publisher marked a significant change in individual activity on the Internet; anyone could become a publisher.

Fast-forward to 2009 and there are dozens of content creation sites. Often, content appears in reverse chronological order, with the most recent content at the top of the page. There is frequently a profile page that represents you and a page that represents the content you have created, with each item of content getting a permalink. The permalink is important as it allows for reference outside the context of the hosting site. It allows the individually owned item of content to exist on the Web in its own right.

Aggregation of this content often happens within a *river of news* view. Dave Winer coined this expression in 2005. He means a page that contains a timestamped list of the last 50 or 100 items. Older items drop off the bottom; if you come back in an hour, there will be some new content at the top:

> There's another kind of reader, an aggregator, that works differently, and I think more efficiently for the human reader. Instead of having to hunt for new stories by clicking on the titles of feeds, you just view the page of new stuff and scroll through it. It's like sitting on the bank of a river, watching the boats go by.†

—Dave Winer

Personal aggregation and republishing experiments also started around 2005. Jeremy Keith's *Adactio Elsewhere* (*http://elsewhere.adactio.com/*) is an early example of such an experiment. He wrote notes on the implementation of an aggregator on his blog (*http://adactio.com/journal/988/*).

Many of these services are microblogging tools that allow the person to curate short pieces of text and pictures. The sense of community is less explicit than in a service such as Flickr that does not allow republishing. These tools started as personal content republishing systems and short-form blogging tools. For instance, Tumblr (see Figure 9-6) has specific interfaces for adding different types of content. This recognizes people's desire to republish or share content with others. The social network around Tumblr came later. The ability to follow other people using Tumblr was added after the initial launch. The community is formed from individuals using the same tool to create content for themselves.

Social Microblogging

Lastly, there are the social microblogs, the most popular of which is Twitter. These are text-only and tend to be limited to 140 characters for ease of transmission via SMS, the cell phone Short Message Service that delivers text messages. For these purely

---

† *http://www.reallysimplesyndication.com/riverOfNews*

Figure 9-6. Tumblr, a popular microblogging service that allows republishing of content and content creation

text-based social services, the core driver was social from day one. One of Twitter's early names was Stat.us (*http://www.flickr.com/photos/jackdorsey/182613360/*). The idea came from sharing your IM status messages on a more persistent and immediate basis. These services incorporate a social network into their operation, so instead of the impersonal river of news from everyone or the river of news from one person, they can offer a river of news from the social network of everyone.

The popularity of these services is intriguing. Why would sharing 140 characters (frequently fewer than that) with some people become a popular and much-copied activity? The answer comes in two parts: a technical explanation and the more interesting social answer. Technically, because Twitter limits the number of characters in a message to allow it to be sent and received over SMS, IM, and the Web, as well as on desktop applications, everyone can find a medium for participation that suits their lifestyle. The social reasoning is more complex. Twitter provokes strong reactions. People love it or they declare it pointless. It operates as a way for you to dip into what your friends are doing or thinking in close to real time.

People use Twitter for many purposes: to ask questions, get opinions, arrange to meet one another, make social commentary, exclaim at the world, and simply to say what they are up to. It fills the space between a blog post and a phone call or IM. It has become a supportive framework for asking questions and getting advice. Twitter seems particularly popular with freelancers and others who work on their own. It provides a channel for day-to-day chatter for them and for people who have a wide social group. These services are arguably supplanting blogging for a lot of people; they let the simple thoughts head into the light of day. Twitter and tumblelogs work equally well in this case. However, blogging and longer forms of writing are still important for communicating complex or longer ideas.

Pownce (*http://pownce.com*) also fell into this category, but instead of a steady stream of short text-based updates, people shared video and audio files or invites to events, or asked questions. This model is also much closer to email in nature. While you can send the update to everyone on your list of friends, you also can pick and choose who receives each update each time. This fine-grained privacy model does mean that a lot of the activity on Pownce was hidden from public view, but there are many cases where you might want to selectively invite people to meet, and Twitter or a blog post would be an inappropriate means to do this. Six Apart bought Pownce in late 2008, and expects to implement the Pownce functionality in future products.

Who Is Sharing, and Why?

Activity-centered design is a good approach to application design, helping you figure out who your audience is and how your application fits into their lives. Understanding the kind of relationships you can facilitate on your site is important. Different communities operate in very different ways; some are share openly, while others are tightly closed.

Competition Between Peers Skews Interaction

Scientists can work in any field they want, if their credentials can secure funding for them. So, there is essentially perfect competition in the field of science: people are free to move into any area of study at will. Compare this to the web developer; although the companies that two developers work for might be in competition for customers, the developers themselves can help one another without being in direct competition. There is no restraint (of trade) for scientists in terms of the areas they can work on, whereas web developers cannot start working on whichever site they decide looks interesting. (Of course, the scientist is bound by funding, plus access to reagents and equipment, so it is not an entirely level playing field.) A secondary factor that skews interaction is that the scientist is judged on his recent work, which must be novel to enter into a science journal. Little credit is given to activities outside publications based on original experiments.

Thus, ideas in some areas are very easy to take and use. The same is true in television; a new TV format is a heavily protected secret. The means of implementing the idea are well understood; it is the idea that is unique. So, elaborating on a new idea in public can be detrimental, as others may exploit it. This is one of the reasons that some areas are less social than others. There is a potential for information sharing, but it will be in the areas of implementation and technique and not in the area of idea generation. The social interaction will be in the low investment activities, as these are less exploitable. Highly valued, unpublished content will not be shared so willingly and will at least require credit in terms of paper citations.

Talking About Things That Are Easy to Discuss

Photography hobbyists converse endlessly about which cameras and lenses to purchase and less frequently about the process of taking pictures, even though that is the focus of the hobby. This is not for competition reasons; the key aspect is one of performance. When on the Internet, the person is not taking pictures, so she turns to a metaconversation about the subject. Put another way, I can tell you how to take a good picture, but only you can take that picture. If there is merit to be gained in highly evolved written materials, it is unlikely that this will become the core social object for exchange on your site.

I realize you are not building software to support scientific communication, but looking at the degree of collaboration within your subject area is an essential aspect of good community design. There is always a trade-off between the amount of effort and the degree of collaboration required compared to the ease of capitalizing on that effort. Using this understanding can help you to determine which things people on your site will discuss openly. The next section looks at common types of open social exchange. As you read, think about the area you are creating a product for and determine the content to be exchanged and the motivations for the exchange of information.

How Are They Sharing?

The defaults that you set for your application will have a huge impact on how people will use your site. If you set them to be fully open and public, you might encourage a lot of chatty social exchange, whereas a fully private setting might lead to longer and deeper engagement among smaller groups. People rarely change the default settings on a web application, so picking the right settings to create the kind of environment you think will work is your job. Do not think that an option will be reversed by the majority.

Being Semiprivate

Pownce's semiprivate options, as opposed to making everything public, more realistically reflected the way people interact in the real world. Likewise, many people use Twitter, but they keep their updates private. We need both a public and a private means of social expression. The people involved in each private exchange are not the same every time. This is an area for experimentation and growth. LiveJournal has supported the notion of multiple friends lists for many years. These new social broadcast services generally start with a default of "everything public," which does make the user experience simple, but misses part of how we interact socially.

Lifestreaming and Social Aggregation

Applications such as Jaiku have been offering *lifestreaming* since 2006. This is an aggregation of a person's content from multiple web applications—for example, a blog,

Twitter, Flickr, and Upcoming. Jaiku itself also provides a microblogging service as part of the native offering. Lifestreaming applies the river of news view to multiple services, and then typically builds a social network around these streams. Tumblr and FriendFeed (see Figure 9-7) also offer this kind of service. FriendFeed makes it the core of its offering. Aggregation is based on consumption of RSS feeds from these external services, and sometimes the content exchange is authenticated by OAuth (which is discussed further in Chapters 12, 14, and 16).

Figure 9-7. FriendFeed showing people and the services they provide to FriendFeed; each icon represents a content source the person offers

The rise in popularity of these services is driven by a desire for a mechanism to follow the updates from friends, who might use many services. Essentially they are acting as RSS readers for people, as opposed to standard RSS readers that are more focused on sites. The context is the person and you are reading the content the person is generating. You could join every service your friends are members of and add them to your network, or you could add them one by one into folders in an RSS reader. These lifestream applications allow the individual to make available the content he wishes and then his friends can follow him. Centralization is a recurrent theme in the design of social networking sites; everyone wants to be a hub, not a spoke.

Given the number of services many people use and the volume of updates they can generate, lifestreaming services can aggregate a lot of information. Jaiku has an excellent feature that allows the reader to decide which of the offered streams of content she wishes to see (see Figure 9-8). The scaling issue here is a personal one; following 150 people on FriendFeed might easily deliver more than a 1,000 updates per day, with only 6 updates per person.

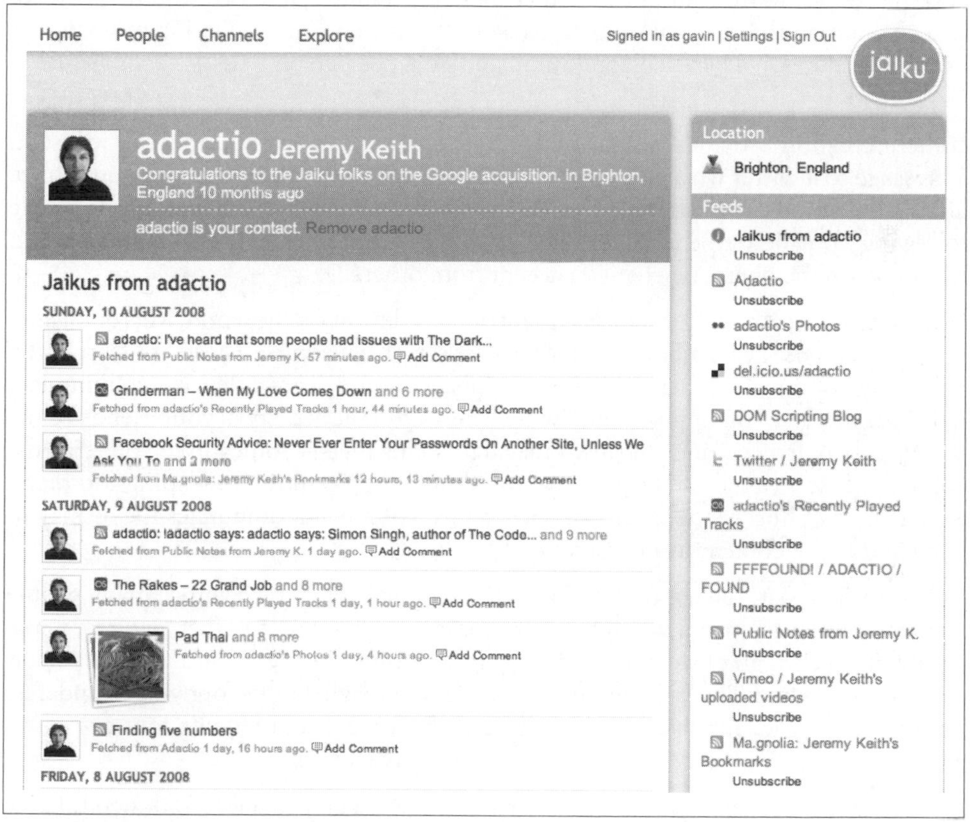

Figure 9-8. Jaiku showing, on the right side of the screen, the ability to unsubscribe from some of the feeds provided by a person

These kinds of aggregation services will only become more common as the number of social web applications increases and people start using a wider variety of them to express themselves. There is a finite limit on the amount of time that someone has to read updates from social software applications; better filtering and recommendation services will help determine what might be of interest to each reader.

Overfeeding on Lifestreams

Even if you have a moderate social network, reading all the updates from every social application your friends use can be overwhelming. In the future, tools will need to manage the flow of information more intelligently. Hints of these exist in the Jaiku unsubscribe approach, whereby you can selectively stop receiving some types of updates from friends. Another approach is to *sleep* an overly noisy person, thereby making his updates disappear from your stream for 24 hours. FriendFeed has a range of mechanisms to reduce the number of entries displayed. For instance, it uses "and 7 more" as a hint that someone is being prolific. The truncation of the updates from someone and the "and 7 more" hint indicate that there are additional items from this person, and clicking on this text will show the rest of the entries. These filtering mechanisms need to operate on a per-web application and on a per-person basis.

Many web applications use these lifestreaming services by offering more than simple content creation activities in their feeds for a person. Both Seesmic and Qik will send a message to Twitter when someone is using the service. Some services will announce all of your actions to Twitter by default, making for a very noisy experience for people following you. Better-behaved applications follow Postel's Law: "Be conservative in what you do; be liberal in what you accept from others."

What is relevant activity for your site might not be relevant for the world. Microblogging services such as Twitter have an understood set of behaviors. These are learned by observing community reactions and behaviors. To some degree, they are communicated in the design of the application. Twitter shows you the activity of your friends below the entry box for creating your own messages. This means you can see your friends' context when writing. So, be sensitive to dominating the flow by sending too many messages in a short space of time. If you do this, your avatar dominates the display of what should be content from everyone.

Other norms exist, such as not sending automated messages on Twitter; many people feel that is akin to spamming. If you are sending information to other services, make sure there is enough of a context for the information to be meaningful for the person reading the update. The FriendFeed experience is somewhat more forgiving of updates, but the updates ideally should comprise newly generated content, not context-bound actions such as "watched," "viewed," or "added to favorites."

Managing the amount of content that is shown in an aggregated feed is difficult. Facebook algorithmically chooses which items to show, so it is guaranteed to be incomplete. Flickr allows members to choose from one to five pictures and from friends or friends and contacts. Setting these options limits the number of photos the person can see, but will include at least one update from everyone. Twitter shows everything. FriendFeed shows some of everything, but will truncate the display for services that are being used heavily—for example, "and 25 more photos."

Good management tools that give your community control over what items of content they do and do not see are increasingly important. The ability to control rate and volume should be theirs to set. Allowing muting or selective unsubscribe capability is useful. Noting which people someone pays attention to and which people are less attended means you can offer everyone an overview they might recognize based on activity patterns they have set. Being respectful of the time your community spends with you is important if you want to keep them.

A Simple Core for Rapid Growth

LinkedIn, Friendster, Facebook, and MySpace all offer a complex variety of options for activity management. At their core, they all have a profile, a social network, and some form of group communication tool. Why were these applications successful and many others not? Because they had made a good assessment of their core audience and good organic growth plans, plus they offer features that match the needs of their communities. (At the time of this writing, Facebook is dominant, but it is not the last word in social networks.)

All of these applications are now large endeavors offering many different functions, but they all started with a relatively small, useful idea aimed at a specific group of people. This focus on supporting a group of people or activity is important, because it gives a sense of coherence and purpose to the site. MySpace honed in on the music scene in Los Angeles, Facebook started with college students, and LinkedIn focused on fostering external business contacts. danah boyd and Nicole Ellison provide a good analysis of the beginnings of social networks at *http://jcmc.indiana.edu/vol13/issue1/boyd.ellison .html*, where they also trace the origins of social networks, from SixDegrees.com in 1997 through mid-2007.

Federation Versus Centralization

All the services mentioned so far are centralized, in that one company runs the system and generally the software is not open source, but access to the content is open. These *software as a service* companies are the bread and butter of the Web 2.0 product space. Identi.ca, based on *http://laconi.ca/trac/*, and similar federated microblogging services, such as FETHR (Featherweight Entangled Timelines over HTTP Requests; *http://brdfdr .com/*), offer a new approach. They are Twitter-like applications, but they allow you to set up your own instance of the software on your own server. This federated approach allows individuals to customize and control the data and user experience of their microblogging platform.

This wave of federation activity follows the activity around identity resulting from the popularity of OpenID, and it is in part a reaction to the centralized nature of larger social networks. The ability to move your friends and your data from one service to another is laudable, as companies do go out of business, get bought, or change direction. However, you rarely get to influence the actual direction in which these products are headed. Running a federated social network means you have control over your own software. This is a recent area of development. Figure 9-9 shows the migration of isolated to centralized to federated applications.

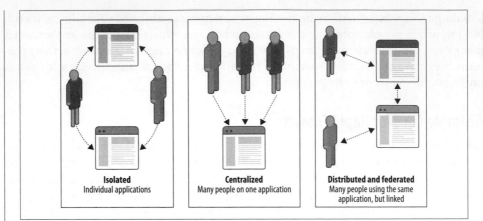

Figure 9-9. *Centralized versus federated versus distributed application models*

Social software development seems to be moving in cycles. First, experiments with new ways of building things result in a distributed model, with software available for download and installation on many personal servers. Individuals rely on desktop aggregation to manage the multiple servers. This corresponds to installed WordPress or Movable Type.

Next, some people decide there is money to be made, so larger centralized services come into existence. Individuals can follow multiple people from a single large service provider. Aggregation happens on the server, but it is possible to form stronger community bonds between people as the community begins to have an identity. Facebook, Flickr, and TypePad are good examples of centralized services.

Now, in 2009, with identity becoming a strong part of the equation, people are heading back into an experimental period. Do I need the centralized servers if I can host my own content? A federation of multiple servers and software installs, linked with a consistent identity, is one future that is being explored. Locally hosting personal content and licensing it to remote aggregation and federation services is being proposed by some people. A federated model suits the way the Internet operates, but it is harder to make money from, though they can avoid scaling issues.

The proliferation of services such as Google Connect, Facebook Connect, and TypePad Connect are indicative of this need to reconnect across the Web. A common identity being used across multiple services is advantageous. Whether these centralized approaches or the fully distributed model wins or, more likely, whether they coexist, remains to be seen.

Social Software Menagerie

The rest of this chapter will look at the staple components of social software. These generally correspond to the open source applications you can download and install.

They are the application areas that most people are familiar with, but they are typically used alone. They are social in that people can interact by using them, but they differ from the previous services because they normally do not have a social network swirling around them. You might use one of these as part of a larger site and integrate with it, which is a lot easier now than it was in 2005.

Blogging

A *blog* is a single- (or group-) authored listing of short to medium-length essays, opinions, or commentary. Blogs are almost always sorted in reverse chronological order, with the most recent posting at the top of the page. They generally allow (registered) comments on each posting. There are many variations on this general theme; many blogs include lists-of-links-type postings and photographs, too. The standard 400–500-word blog post is still the most common. Blogs tend to have a theme, but given that they usually have a single author, the theme can drift depending on the author's interests. Group blogs tend to stay more on topic, but they can run out of steam, as no one person owns them.

Blogging is, in general, a "me to you" conversation, though there are, as ever, variants such as asking people to be guests on your blog. The blogger is usually clearly identified with her content, and she is the person who responds to comments and emails about her site. The writing is personal in style and often opinionated; these are personal spaces for public consumption. Loose parallels can be drawn with interior decoration, fashion taste, or type of garden the person prefers. All of these are for public view, but the individual gets to determine how they look and behave within a few boundaries. Merlin Mann gives some good rules for what makes a good blog at *http://www.43folders.com/2008/08/19/good-blogs*. Good blogs have a personal voice with an area of focused interest. They are interesting and encouraging; they make you want to react to what the blogger has written. Good blogs require some effort.

A blog can be a strong community feature; simply offering a space for your employees/colleagues to talk to your community opens up the relationship. A company blog is almost an essential item today for most organizations. It provides a simple and cheap means to converse with people who are interested in your organization, and it is also a means by which you can start the conversation.

Authenticity is very important. If the CEO is blogging, it should be the CEO who replies and actually writes the text. The blog should come from identified people and not be written like a press release, though you can put press releases on your blog, too. The effect you are aiming for is semiformal at most, but ideally it is informal. You are starting a conversation, not broadcasting. Posting regularly does help, but you want the significant announcements to stand out. Thus, there is a balance between just making announcements and chatting; you want something in the middle for most company blogs. If you have no major announcements for a while, ask for feedback, but be explicit with your users about the guarantee or lack thereof that you will address all comments.

In the face of a crisis, a blog can be a real boon (or a complete millstone). Once you realize the situation is not going to resolve itself quickly, you need to communicate with your community. Apple and MobileMe, Joyent and Strongspace, Six Apart and Movabletype.org all exerpienced a type of systems failing and used their blogs to communicate with their users. Apple (*http://www.apple.com/mobileme/status/*) didn't provide a means for people to comment. However, in the cases of Joyent (*http://www.joyeur.com/2008/01/16/strongspace-and-bingodisk-update*) and Six Apart (*http://www.movabletype .org/2008/08/website_outage_update.html*), comments were allowed, and the company responded to the questions that were raised.

Community blogging

If you are a publisher, you can open your blog and let readers have blogs, too. *Le Monde*, the French newspaper, did this several years ago using WordPress (*http://www .lemonde.fr/web/blogs/0,39-0,48-0,0.html*), and many others have done this since. It is a big step and might not be the right one for every publisher or company, and probably is a bad fit for a product company. However, if you have a wide-ranging community and vocal individuals within the community, it might work for you. There are different ways to approach this. Many companies set up a separate domain to host their community blogs. Some companies set up a whole other brand to host a community blog, such as the publisher Seed Media and its brand, Scienceblogs.com.

Depending on your subject area, you may need to recruit bloggers to your new site, importing their old site as you do this. However, you also might get flooded with applications. If you are starting a blog for a community that was unaware of blogging, you can be in a good position, but you will need to be aware that bloggers do move on to other blogs, particularly successful ones. Establishing the relationship early on between you and your bloggers in terms of entry, exit, and benefits is important. If you have your own internal blogs and you also host external community blogs, you need to be clear about the position of each type of blog—in particular, the amount of support you give each in terms of promotion. If the blogging community thinks you are taking them for a free ride, they will be quick and vocal in their disapproval.

Another aspect of blogging policy is clarifying ownership of content and any possible clashes in editorial voice. If you publish your own content and publish content from bloggers, you need to be careful to communicate which is which. Readers are likely to want to know this, as they have a relationship with your brand. The blogger will want to see who created the content so that he has an identity that is separate from your brand. If this is not done, when bloggers disagree with the editorial line on a certain issue, it can have unexpected impacts on your company.

Creating a blogging system

A lot is involved in choosing a full-blown content management system (CMS). open sourceCMS gives a long list of advice, but blogging software is not really a CMS as the enterprise software defines a CMS (thankfully). An enterprise CMS is a hugely complex product capable of integrating with many subsystems, and offers a large amount of configurability. Enterprise CMSs tend to be publishing systems first and community tools second, if at all. A blog is a community tool first and a CMS second.

A simple install of WordPress or Movable Type suffices as a blog for many companies, and the fact that many of your readers will be familiar with these well-known products makes them attractive options. A reasonable approach might be to integrate these tools with your own software. The editing and management interfaces from both WordPress and Movable Type represent thousands of hours of work, which is hard to replicate in-house cost-effectively. That being said, creating a simple blogging product is a trivial undertaking. Ruby on Rails has a demo for creating a primitive blog application in 20 minutes. If your needs are more complex, there are maturing applications in the community platform space. If your needs are primarily for blogging, Six Apart offers Movable Type Pro and Automattic offers WordPress MU. Refer to Chapter 16 for further discussion.

Commenting Is Not the Same As Blogging

Commenting is often lumped in with blogging, as some people see them as essentially the same things. They have strong ties, but they are definitely not the same in terms of behavior. *Commenting* gives a user the ability to append a piece of text to content that you as the site owner have created or published. So, typically it is publishers that care about this distinction. Newspapers allow comments on their stories, science journals allow comments on their articles, and on many social sites, users can comment on user-generated content.

The key differences are in how the conversation is managed. Typically, a blog post will have the author managing the conversation. In commenting, however, the editorial team manages the conversation. Technically, a commenting system looks like a headless blogging system, as often the actual content that is being published flows through an older system. (Commenting systems tend to be bolted onto existing publishing systems; this is the quickest way to implement them.) Rebuilding your technical architecture to support community interaction online, as the *Guardian* has done, will give more flexibility than just connecting to existing systems would (for more information, see *http://blogs.guardian.co.uk/inside/2008/05/the_web_on_the_move_xtech_2008 .html*).

This subtle difference gets clouded in the wider Internet, because people refer to the comments on their blogs or on YouTube as comments. Most of these situations are essentially blogging, though. A counterexample is solicited book reviews; these *are* comments, because it is not the author who is soliciting, but rather, the publishing company is making the service available.

In terms of implementation, there are fewer and more expensive options available than in the case of blogging. Pluck offers commenting as a commercial service, as do many other companies. These tend to be quite complex products that can interface with your (likely bespoke) in-house content production system and also with your identity management tools, and then finally with your web publishing system.

Where is commenting appropriate? This is a tricky question to give a simple answer to. Many articles in the world that are open for comments don't have any. Always offering comments on everything you publish is likely to make your lack of community interaction more prominent. Striking a balance between making the stories that will get comments and the amount of editorial time required to support this new kind of interaction is key. Chapter 6 mentioned changes to staff responsibilities; this is a good example. To get effective commenting working on your content, you need an editorial team who is actively opening enough articles to satisfy a broad cross section of your audience—enough articles that they still have time to create the new ones, but not so many that most are not commented on. Meg Pickard at the *Guardian* suggests that the comments should be off by default on all content. Turning on commenting is as much an editorial decision as a publishing decision.

Commenting systems are often run in premoderation; all comments are viewed and vetted prior to publication. This allows the company to ensure that everything meets the appropriate guidelines, but also makes the company legally responsible for all comments on the site, as it becomes the publisher of the content. See Chapter 15 for more details on the legal issues involved in commenting.

In the science world, many journals have tried commenting with either one article per monthly issue opened for comments, or every article on the site open to commenting. In both cases, the level of community comments was low. One article once a month will interest only a subset of the readership, and leaving everything open to commenting can reinforce a sense that "no one is commenting, so why should I." Although these lessons are from science publishing, they apply to other publishers.

Groups

If you have a site that covers more than a single issue, people will want to create groups. There is an inherent desire for cohesion among humans beings, and creating a group represents people's desire to find others like themselves. These groups are a subset of the general population on the site, so they are always subgroups.

Group Formation

You can support group formation in a variety of ways. The primary choices center on the types of groups you allow and visibility. The standard group on the Internet is a public one. A person creates a group that is then available for other people to view and join. He runs the group and can be a member of the site staff, a member with special powers, or any member of the site. Membership can be open, application-based, or criteria-driven. Finally, visibility can be private or public.

A less common format is email-based group creation, which Pownce used. Any individual can create a group based on a selection from her personal network. Publisher/owner-derived groups are also common; staff members pick the areas they think will be appropriate, and the community is unable to create groups for themselves.

Groups should have listings of its members, which supports the cohesion that people seek. Many message boards fail in this regard, because it is hard to see who is a member, other than by looking at the content. Membership of a group generally confers the ability to participate in the group's activities. Some groups allow some level of interaction with the group without becoming a member, but this is generally limited to responding rather than initiating activities.

Management of groups needs to be simple and visible. The ability to see new content and see active and new users will help, and monitoring tools are key. Most groups can get away with a single person running the group, but many fare better if the owner has some support. Titles for these roles can be hard to define. The owner or administrator is the person who set up the group, and the people who help are often called moderators. Flickr (see Figure 9-10) played with this idea and let groups come up with their own names for these titles. Some clear community guidelines are vital to help members and group admins know what to expect from one another in all roles. If admins behave badly, people will leave the group.

If you allow community creation of groups, you can expect a high drop-off rate in terms of group creation. Most of the groups created on your site will fail to thrive. Hopefully, between 10% and 20% will gain enough interested people to become viable. Groups provide an important focus for your community to congregate around and help shape the experience from "who are all these people" to "these are people like me." They act well in combination with social networks that let people identify their friends.

Group Conversation

Group members need some means for interacting with one another. Message boards are one of the most common tools used to facilitate this interaction. There are three basic elements: the topic, which is the initial post; any replies to that topic; and the forum or board to which the topic has been posted. A *pool* is a new group activity space and it represents the collected media from participants in the group; a Flickr photo pool is a good example. There are many other types of group functionality, including collective editing tools and real-time conversation features. We will primarily look at the message board, because it is the dominant means of interaction.

Conversing on message boards

Message boards are very popular; thousands of sites exist purely as message boards. Message boards can be powerful tools to generate community. However, they can also be prey to opportunist behavior. Many message boards, particularly technical ones, are plagued by people who jump in, ask a question that has already been asked several

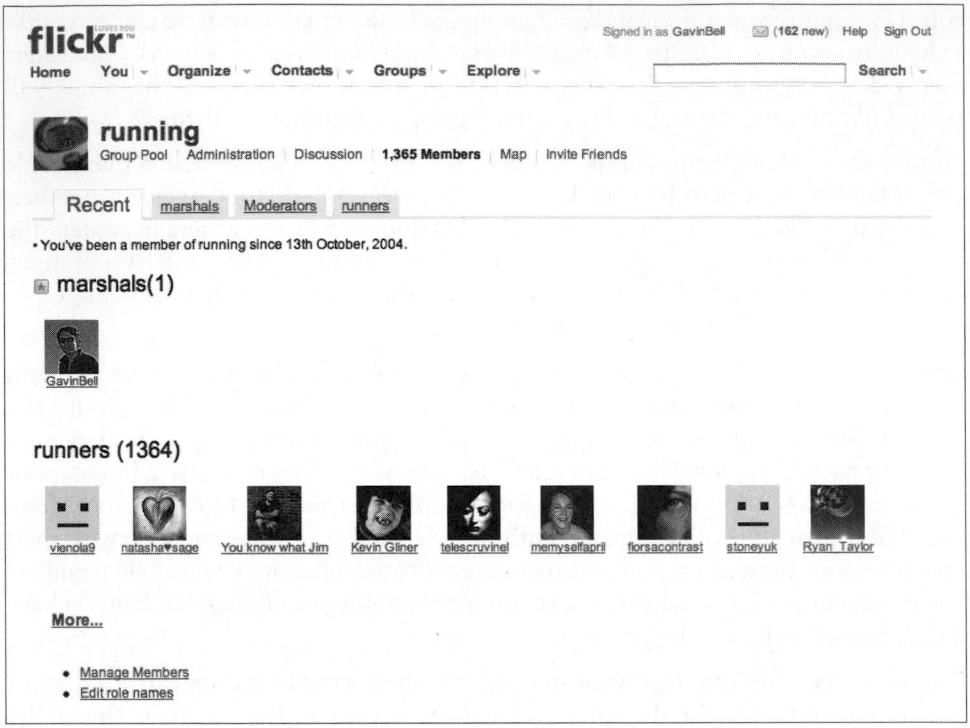

Figure 9-10. Names of roles in Flickr that allow group owners to customize their titles

times, get the answer, and then leave. This interaction adds nothing to the community; instead, it drains the energy from the existing members and in fact can drive people away if it occurs frequently enough. Many message boards operate on a question and answer basis. Some manage to get to the level of conversations about the issues, rather than just answers.

There are a few things you can do to counteract this leeching behavior. There is a balance between making it too hard to contribute and thereby putting off people who will stick around and get involved with the group, and making it too easy to ask a question so that you get inundated with people asking the same ones. To do this correctly relies on using the existing content in the message board to provide answers to the person asking a question. The person often wants an answer quickly, and rather than making it easy to ask a question, you should make it easy to find an answer.

Tagging is important for making this work; if you do not use tagging, text analysis of the question may be appropriate. You need to get to the essence of what the question is about and use this to suggest similar questions that have been asked before. Matching a new question to existing questions is much easier than matching questions to answers, though this is dependent on the subject area. Simple text matching of tags against the text in answers can work, though it tends to bring up longer threads, simply because they have more text content in them, and so more content against which to generate matches. However you implement it, you need to use the existing content as a filter to stop new questions from being asked.

Filtering questions is a polite mechanism to get people to read the existing content on the site first, including the FAQs page. People rarely do this, so by highlighting it for them, you make it so that they are much more likely to read some of it and hopefully find their answer.

Message board design is a combination of information architecture and interaction design, as every site is, but the linkage is very direct in message boards. The software provides a framework for a huge volume of community-generated content. By providing tools to aid in the curation of this content, you can help the community gain more value from their conversations. It becomes an archive of answers and content rather than a series of transcripts of conversations.

Tags Create Navigation

Nature Network uses tags extensively to allow discovery of conversations. Science is a multidisciplinary subject, so any single conversation might have a large number of communities that it could interest. Hence, Nature Network decided not to support subforums. Every topic can be tagged, and the tags act in two ways (see Figure 9-11):

- Within a forum, clicking on a tag will narrow the focus to topics tagged with the corresponding word. So, from *Physics* you can view only the optics topics in that forum. Here, the tag acts as a filter.
- You can also broaden out and see any conversation tagged with that word in any forum. This is using the tag as a search term.

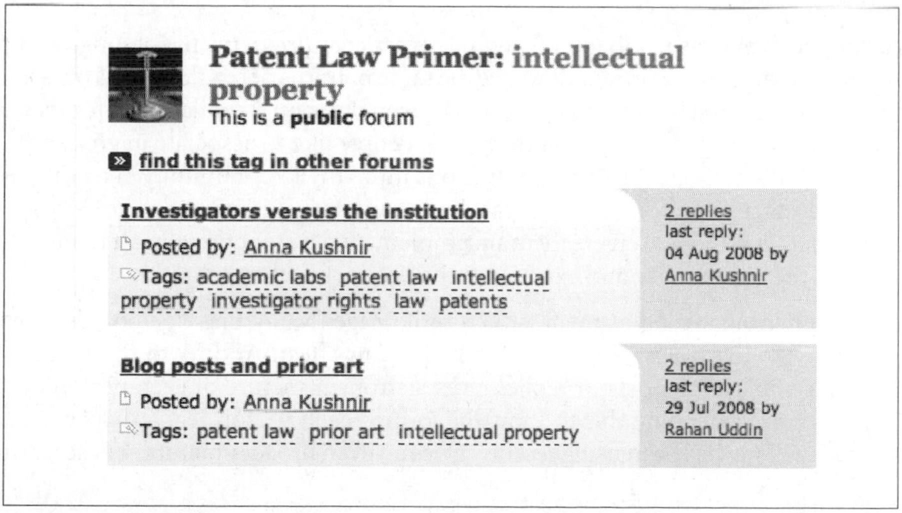
Patent Law Primer: intellectual property
This is a public forum
find this tag in other forums
Investigators versus the institution
Posted by: Anna Kushnir
Tags: academic labs patent law intellectual property investigator rights law patents
2 replies
last reply:
04 Aug 2008 by
Anna Kushnir
Blog posts and prior art
Posted by: Anna Kushnir
Tags: patent law prior art intellectual property
2 replies
last reply:
29 Jul 2008 by
Rahan Uddin

Figure 9-11. Nature Network content tagged with "intellectual property" on the Patent Law Primer forum

Finally, you can see the forums in which the tag occurs. The ability to move across the message boards/forums by using tags makes the topics or conversations the main object of interest, instead of the focus being the forum and subforum hierarchy. You need a large number of areas of interest to benefit from this approach, but it has application outside the realm of science; for instance, Get Satisfaction uses a similar approach on its site.

If you do not use tags on your message board, you can track which conversations your community values from search engine keyword analysis. This will give you a sense of the topics for which people are being referred to your site. Then you can editorially decide to embrace this or attempt to steer your community in a different direction. Monitoring the overall activity in terms of raw counts is important for scaling and determining ad revenues, but you need to understand what your community is actually discussing. Ideally, you will know this, because you and your colleagues will be involved in those conversations; however, if you have a busy site, you cannot track every conversation.

Communities develop their own personalities, and within them there are various roles the members can take on. I do not mean the more formal admin and moderator roles, but the types of community behavior that mature societies develop online. For example, Marc A. Smith at Microsoft Research looked at millions of Usenet‡ messages in the late 1990s. He determined that there are definite types of people in terms of community engagement. Roughly paraphrased, they are the ask-and-leave types, as already discussed; the person who acts as the backbone and answers the majority of questions; the infrequent regular who dips in and generally asks questions; and the announcer who brings news to the site.

Returning to the ideas in Chapter 3 and the *experience arc* (a profile of long-term potential interaction with a product), we see the same patterns of regular versus occasional usage happening on Usenet. No research has been done on a similar scale for message boards, but the same patterns exist there, too. People like to associate in groups. They enjoy social interactions, but resent intrusions into "their" community. Treating message boards as a place for social interaction is important; it is easy to get lost in the technical details of how to create them and implement new functionality. It is important to also see the community and experience the product as they see it.

One strongly humanizing element is the profile page. Many message boards provide very simple profile pages—almost name badges, in effect. Adding to these pages by aggregating the last 10 posts or replies gives a stronger picture of each person on the message board. Extending this to show the forums each person regularly participates in and the tags she has been using recently gives an even broader picture. These features

‡ Usenet is the Internet news service that was very popular in the 1990s. For more information, see Marc's paper, "Invisible Crowds in Cyberspace: Mapping the Social Structure of the Usenet," at *http://research .microsoft.com/research/pubs/view.aspx?pubid=798*.

are very helpful in determining the relative trustworthiness of someone posting on a forum. Metrics such as the number of posts she has made or the length of time a person has spent on the site are also helpful, but showing the actual content she has contributed is more valuable.

Making message boards

You can create a message board in many ways, while retaining the same forum, topic, and post arrangement. One of the primary tasks is to figure out the URL structure so that people can consistently reference a reply in a forum post; fixed-length pagination makes this a lot easier to achieve.

Other issues to consider include placing images in posts and making thumbnails of larger images. Decide whether you want to allow nested threads in your topics and how you will handle quoting or other internal references to replies. Nesting tends to encourage drifting within the topic. Being able to easily quote and reply directly to another reply is important because it lets people create more useful conversations.

People will often want to edit a reply immediately after posting it because they discovered a typo. Allowing this for, say, 15 minutes is quite common; auto-timestamping the edit helps in following conversation flow. Some forums do not allow edits if someone has replied.

Tagging content is a relatively new capability on message boards. It seems like a better way of implementing the kind of intent behind subforums, but without the restrictive hierarchy. Tags also help in terms of information retrieval. Sometimes all participants in a topic are allowed to add tags, so the person answering the question can assign more accurate tags than the naive inquirer might have. Auto-suggestion based on topic content will help to control the potential explosion in tags assigned to topics. Depending on how well structured the subject area is in which you are operating, you might be able to seed the tag word list with appropriate terms.

How you handle moderation is important, too; simply removing offending posts can disrupt the flow of conversation. Most communities operate in post moderation; that is, people complain about an item of content after publication. So, there are many ways to determine whether something merits attention (see Chapter 15 for more information on this important topic).

Message boards and the like are great if you want to host an open conversation on a topic, but sometimes simply drawing lots of content together is enough for people to feel part of something.

Group Aggregation Tools

Aggregation is an important part of establishing a sense of togetherness. People want to see what they have made, and through this are hopefully inspired to make more things. Certainly, this is one of the important aspects of the photo and video groups on Flickr, Vimeo, and YouTube. Sometimes the content they "make" is simply images, but video content comes closer to collective blogging. The aggregation allows people with a specific interest to share content with one another, which may spur further conversation, but the sharing is the primary activity. Tools such as this are relatively simple to create once you have a group structure in place. For each social object, an "add to group" function places the object in the appropriate group. This was abused in Flickr for a while, because people tried to game the "interestingness" function by placing their pictures in front of as many people as possible. That abuse aside, content aggregation for groups is a positive feature for most sites.

FriendFeed has added an interesting mode of group creation and sharing on its site. Its groups are called *rooms* and people selectively reshare items of their content in a room. This creates a river of news on a topic, much as a lightweight group blog might create. It is a surprisingly effective mechanism for following an area of interest and, when combined with the commenting facility, for understanding community viewpoints on a subject.

Collaboration Tools for Groups

If your group is looking for a more concrete outcome than simply ongoing conversations, there are other tools to look at. Table 9-2 lists some collaboration tools and the situations for which they are best suited. A full-blown wiki is sometimes the right solution for document editing, but they are often misused. Wikis need to have a definite purpose in mind. If used as a community note-taking tool, they can quickly get out of hand.

Another approach is to use the wiki page, which is a shared document much like Google Docs or WriteBoard from 37signals. Often, people want a means of writing and amending a document in a small group, and a shared document facility is perfect for this. Lastly is the community review of a document that often is written by one author. In this case, a document uploading and commenting service is very useful. The author uploads a document and then the rest of the group comments on the web page about the document. The author can then upload revised versions for further comment.

Table 9-2. Collaboration tools

Community	Purpose	Tool	Outcome/example
Anyone from the community	Directed information capture	Wiki	Set of coherent notes on a well-defined project, such as *http://microformats.org/wiki/*
Known individuals	Collaboratively edit a document for a known purpose	Shared document editing tool with revision tracking	Usually a single document; Google Docs is a good example
Single author and re-view panel	Gathering feedback on a draft	Upload and comment system, allowing multiple uploads and commenting	Revised document or images; Basecamp supports this well
Anyone from the community	Ongoing discussion	Web-based chat system	Searchable archive of conversations/great replacement for email; see FriendFeed or Campfire

A final example of a useful group tool is a web-based chat service. These sit between email, Twitter, and IM in terms of their functionality. They have the non-real-time benefits of email and Twitter, but the immediacy of IM when the participants are online together. Campfire from 37signals is a great example of this kind of functionality. This kind of web chat tool is a good replacement for multiple emails, particularly in a team setting. If the kind of communication you are trying to support is more akin to office chatter than to formal questions and responses, this might work for your community. The rooms in FriendFeed are an open-aggregation-based version of a similar concept.

Social Platforms As a Foundation

Instead of writing your application entirely from scratch, there are other ways to build it while avoiding the trap of copying another site, as noted in Chapter 7. Several of the larger Internet companies have released platforms upon which you can create applications of your own. There are four main development types:

- Facebook platform and the Google OpenSocial framework
- OpenSocial Container; Shindig (*http://incubator.apache.org/shindig/*) is a common reference implementation
- Google Friend Connect, Facebook Connect, and TypePad Connect
- Drupal (*http://drupal.org*) or BuddyPress (*http://buddypress.org*), an extension to WordPress, and many other open source products

The first option is to create an application that runs on top of the Facebook or Open-Social application platform. Your application becomes tied to these, but you gain the benefits of their huge existing audiences. The Facebook platform works only with Facebook, but you get access to its 200 million users. OpenSocial works with a wider variety of social applications, such as LinkedIn, MySpace, Ning, and several Google products such as Gmail.

Facebook and OpenSocial applications are a good way to connect your community with the large communities on these other platforms, but you need to have your own product to connect it with. Solely pursuing a social strategy based on Facebook or OpenSocial is limiting. Admittedly, few people are doing this alone, but think of these applications as a means of supporting your community and ensure that you develop an excellent experience for your own site, too.

An OpenSocial container is the opposite of creating an application. You implement a set of defined OpenSocial services and then other OpenSocial application developers can deploy their applications on your site. LinkedIn did this in late 2008, with Hud-dle (*http://www.huddle.net*), WordPress (*http://wordpress.com*), and SlideShare (*http://www.slideshare.net*) (*http://www.slideshare.net*), among others. There are real advantages in building a social application in this fashion. Essentially, you are connecting with another community in many cases and gaining additional functionality for your own site.

There are also many ways of allowing login with preexisting credentials, and these bring the existing community along, too. The Facebook Connect, TypePad Connect, and Google Friend Connect tools are designed to bring the social relationships that people already have on these services to other sites. Connecting these social products involves little actual development; cutting and pasting some code is the usual approach. These tools allow a simple login process, commenting tools, and persistent profiles for the people who are visiting your site. They represent a simple first step in adding community to your website.

Drupal and products such as Movable Type Motion and BuddyPress are community platforms. They offer a large amount of functionality upon which to base a new application. All three are extensible and well supported with active developer communities behind them. They are primary content management tools first and social networks second, so they have good tools for community management and content creation. If they contain the majority of the functionality you need, they can be a great place to start. They can also act as a useful adjunct to your core application by providing the generic discussion forums or blogs that you might need.

Ning and White Label Social Software

Rather than building your own social web app, you can use one of the many providers of white label social software. These companies provide a basic framework of discussion and blogging, as well as the ability to create a social network. Ning is probably the most famous of these, but there are others, including Pluck, Jive, and Mzinga.§ They can be a very cost-effective means of launching a product. These tools differ from those in the previous section as they focus on the community aspects first, not the content management aspects. They also tend to be hosted products and commercially licensed as opposed to open source and/or free.

Over the past few years, the minimal set of functionality for a social network application has consolidated into a firmer set of features. Several companies are now offering similar white label social applications. If you do choose to use these companies/products, you run the slight risk of having a site that looks like everyone else's. You may lack that unique proposition that keeps people on your site. However, if creating a social networking product is not the focus of your company's business, these products can be a good choice. The rest of the book will be helpful in terms of understanding what you might get from one of these providers.

Growing Social Networks

A social application has at its core a list of contacts. These lists are becoming the new address book. The ability to have an address book of contacts online is not that new, but over the past decade or so, these address books have taken a much more active role. The address book has become an activity tracker and aggregation tool. Each person on the list is someone who can potentially generate activity that we will then see. Adding someone to a contact list in a social application is an expression of interest.

Social networks are now the foundation of most community-focused online endeavors. To quickly dispel a myth about social networks, they are not for finding new friends, they are for staying in contact with existing friends. You may meet and add new people in real life, but the primary focus of a social network is maintenance, not acquisition. The creation of the application platforms and various Google Friend Connect or Facebook Connect products bears witness to the strength of preexisting social contacts.

A well-defined activity is at the core of many successful social networks. This means you can communicate the main intent of the site in a few words. For Flickr, it is "share photos"; for Dopplr, it is "shared traveling intentions"; for Last.fm, it is "music listened to"; for Twitter, it is "share context." In this way, it is possible to get a sense of what the site consists of quickly.

There are other ways to approach this. For instance, the profile-led approaches of LinkedIn and Facebook allow people to gain a first-time persistent online presence, one they can update as they move from job to job. However, without some means of communication, they would be dry places. The communication tools on these profile-based sites allow people to feel and act as humans and ensure that the provider has

§ See *http://www.web-strategist.com/blog/2007/02/12/list-of-white-label-social-networking-platforms/* for a pretty comprehensive list which has been updated through 2008.

more up-to-date profiles. Turn the clock back 10 years and these sites would have been static page templates and not rich with social ties and communication.

The social contact formation tools you offer make a big difference in terms of the rate of growth of your site and the types of social engagements that will occur. By this I mean the type of "friending" you offer. The default pattern has become "asymmetric follow," which means "I can follow you, but that does not mean you have to follow mean, nor do I need to approve your request to follow me." There are several other variations—among them automated follow and follow-back or request-based approaches—but there is a real benefit to the asymmetric model. It requires no additional work on the part of the followed person; she simply gains more followers. It might not be the right model for your application, but it should be the starting point.

Creating a successful social network involves tapping into a genuine need; you need to get people to sign up and return to your site to create and share in something of value. Depending on the area you are working in, the kind of approach you take will be different. The websites for Barack Obama (*http://www.my.barackobama.com*),‖ Facebook, and Dopplr offer something very different from one another, but all have a social network at their core. Social networks are about two aspects in tandem: a group of friends and colleagues, and a shared set of interests or an activity or item of content. The former is almost a given; it is trivial to set up a networked address book. The hard work is determining the right approach to supporting the activity the community wants to participate in.

Summary

Communities have many different reasons for being, and there are many different ways to support them. You need to explore why you are hosting a community, then decide which tools you need to support it. Your own community will probably not be a perfect match for any of these examples, so you need to understand your motivation for creating a social application and how you will enable the members of that community to interact with one another. The next few chapters explore issues regarding creating social networks and the mechanics of how to create successful ones.

‖ See *http://www.technologyreview.com/Infotech/21222/?a=f* for an analysis.

CHAPTER 10

Social Network Patterns

People want to interact with one another. We are a social species. Solitary confinement is, after all, a punishment. Doug Ruscoff put it beautifully at the O'Reilly Tools of Change for Publishing conference in 2008: "Contact is king." Content and context are important, but social contact drives our society. So, if we are inviting people to our websites, we should give them something to do that encourages social contact. Simply installing a message board is not enough. Talk is fine, but its transitory nature can make it a weak glue to bind a community together.

Sharing Social Objects

As we have discussed throughout this book, social objects provide a focus around which people can interact. Even sites that cover the same general subject will have a very different feel depending on which objects receive focus. Flickr, for example, started out as a place to discuss photographs, not a place to discuss photography. Unlike its predecessors, it wasn't a photo gallery, either.

The photography site Photo.net is a great place to discuss photography and a good example of early content-driven social software. The site was founded in the late 1990s. On the site, the links between the photographer, his discussions on the forums, and his photographs are present, but the photographs tend to be shown in galleries rather than as a regularly updated stream of photos. The same can be said of PhotoBase and other gallery-led sites: they offer photographers the ability to show off their pictures, but this capability is not connected to the lives of the photographers. These older sites were also designed for smaller volumes of photography, coming from an age when you scanned in your best pictures.

Making photography a narrative experience—a set of individual photos with their own information as opposed to a set of galleries—created a different type of interaction. It let Flickr keep up with the vastly greater flow of pictures from digital cameras, but also moved the type of interaction away from critique of photography and toward commentary on the lives of the people who you knew on the site. This was a small but significant change.

Relationships and Social Objects

Social applications are about who you know in a much more immediate way than any other kind of website (by this I do not mean who you want others to *think* you know, though that does happen). Social networks are about friendship and regular contact. The kinds of interaction that you create on your website should support the real-world social interactions that occur around your own content. I think it is really helpful if the social interaction is connected to some content that is owned by your members. If they have something they feel they own, they are more likely to come back to care for and tend to their content. To put it another way, if you have spent time creating and annotating some content, you are more likely to respond if someone else comments on your stuff, compared to a message board that you contribute to from time to time, where the sense of involvement is less immediate and less personal.

A broader set of examples of social objects will help you understand:

- Jim and Chris are chatting about last night's game, discussing the poor offence of the home team. The game is the social object.
- Sarah and Jessica are having lunch and they discuss what to eat, and then move on to their friend Claire's love life. Their friend's relationships are the social objects.
- Yvonne and Tim meet to review the work for the week in their one-to-one relationship. The projects are the social objects.
- Simon and Oscar are fighting over a toy tiger. The tiger is the social object.
- Hettie and Jacob are lunching in their retirement home. A letter has arrived for Hettie with news of her granddaughter Monica. The letter about Monica is the social object.

There are many other examples, but I think these give you an idea of the shared social object between the actors in the situations. There is a lot of variety in what a social object can be, but it is always something directly connected to the person or his interests. This gives a strong reason for people to care about the interactions around the object. The interactions on a social network site come from the person's friends in general, but also from his wider circle of fans and acquaintances. This gives him a directness and intimacy that is hard to fake. Note that the object is not passive. The people around the object are always doing something with the content, even if it is by reference.

For more on social objects, see Jyri Engeström's "The Case for Object-Centered Sociality" (*http://www.zengestrom.com/blog/2005/04/why _some_social.html*), Tom Coates's "The Future of Web Apps" (*http:// www.plasticbag.org/archives/2006/09/my_slides_from_the_fu/*), and Hugh MacLeod's "More Thoughts on Social Objects" (*http://www.ga pingvoid.com/Moveable_Type/archives/004265.html*).

Determining the Right Social Object

I've referenced the subject of modeling objects several times already in this book, but at the level of the social object. A good social object is one that can be regularly created by everyone on the site and has the potential for spurring open discussion about the object or other person-to-person social interaction. Flickr and Twitter follow exactly this pattern. Dopplr and Last.fm rely more on other forms of person-to-person interaction. A Dopplr trip might prompt two people to arrange to have lunch, for example.

Once you have a primary social object, a range of activities and secondary objects can fit around it. The ability to comment is core to most social applications; similarly, marking something as a favorite is a popular feature. Secondary objects usually stem from aggregations of the primary object.

The primary and secondary objects might not be tangible, but they are still the focus of your site. One of them should be the dominant object. Many of the sites in Table 10-1 allow some form of discussion or other information generation, but there is a primary object that stands out. The table also includes some secondary objects. Often the activities lead to the generation of the secondary objects.

Table 10-1. Primary and secondary objects for common sites

Website	Primary object	Activities	Secondary objects
Last.fm	Music track	Listening, commenting	Artist, album, faves, recommendations
Flickr	Picture or video	Viewing, commenting	Faves, places, groups
Dopplr	Trip	Coincidences	Places, tips
Twitter	140 characters of wit, cynicism, or fact	Posting	Faves and hashtags; for example, #hifi

If you cannot determine what the object is or you have more than one, you are in a bit of a quandary. It is probably time to reanalyze the activities of your community to determine why you are asking the community to come to your site. Confusing conversation about a social object is often the common problem here. The social object will be the generator of conversation. Simply having the means for conversation without a social object can lead to a lack of focus. In Flickr and Dopplr, it is clear that the primary objects are the picture and trip, respectively. Once you have discovered your primary object, then you can give it a home on the Internet.

As Tom Coates wrote in "The Age of Point-at-Things" (*http://www.plasticbag.org/ar chives/2005/04/the_age_of_pointatthings/*):

> It's like there are two views of the world—the solid one around us and the Matrix-style flowing green lines one. In this second world, until you give a thing a name—until you can point at it in greenspace—it simply doesn't exist.

The concept of a fixed URL, which acts as an anchor for the social object, is important. These are commonly called permalinks and are discussed in the next chapter.

Published Sites Expect Audiences

A photographer's space on a gallery website often does not provide enough room to involve the audience. The audience is likely unable to leave comments on each piece. There is no direct personal involvement. The site is designed so that you can look at the work, not leave behind your interpretation of it.

Likewise, a site for a band and their music is great for finding out about the artists and their work, but such a site is often broadcast-only; the information is there to be read. Any community endeavor is unlikely to involve the artists directly.

Newspapers are an interesting edge case, as they can turn the news into a social object, but they tend to attract a very hardcore news junkie audience. The social object isn't necessarily the article, but the emotive issue, which will often attract polarized viewpoints. A good magazine example is the *What Hi-fi* forums at *http://whathifi.com/Fo rums/*. The editorial staff is heavily involved in the conversations on the site, which makes the place feel very welcoming and open.

In all three of these cases, you can make the photographer or band or paper the social object. This will work for a smaller subset of the audience, generally the committed fan. Broader growth occurs when you give your audience some means of content ownership or creation. The broker of the connection can then move from being the host to being the connections between the people on the site. This gives people a substantially stronger reason to return to the site. The host's attention is finite, so the direct connection is weak. If the connection can be between the members of the audience, it can be much deeper, as there is more attention to go around. There is no functionality on these published websites for the intentionality of the audience; they cannot do anything on the site other than passively observe.

On the professional photographer's website, the task can be to commission the photographer, to allow people to admire his work, to allow people to purchase his work, or just to provide information. On a social-object-based site, the photographs become part of a conversation that involves the viewer, as the viewer has a direct connection with the photographer. Jimmy's photograph of Sarah on holiday with Kate is much more meaningful for a particular group of people who know Jimmy, Kate, Sarah, or one of their friends. The site moves from being about viewing and conversing about photographs to telling stories about friends.

The band Radiohead allowed listeners to remix the audio for two tracks from their 2007 album "In Rainbows." Radiohead offered "Nude" and, later, "Reckoner" as source files for people to experiment with. People bought the music and then got a GarageBand file (see Figure 10-1) containing the separate tracks, which they could then remix and upload to *http://www.radioheadremix.com/*. Nine Inch Nails (NIN), another band (see Figure 10-2), offered a similar process and a wider range of music from their catalog on *http://remix.nin.com/*. The NIN service is still active in 2009. Both bands have offered the means for fans to get deeply involved in their music and create sharable content that can be embedded and rated.

Figure 10-1. Radiohead remix site showing the most popular remixes of their track "Nude"

Deep and Broad Sharing

A quick personal aside: the attachment I have to Flickr is deep. Some of my most significant personal events are told on the site. The photograph of the arrival of my first son is one of my pictures on the site. I can take the picture and put it anywhere I want to on the Internet, but I cannot move my friends' reactions to his birth and put them on another site because the event has already occurred. I can't easily shift my friends to another site, and I can't make the people on my new favorite photography site relive the experience of my son's arrival. It is locked in time and space to Flickr.

Figure 10-2. Nine Inch Nails audio source tracks in GarageBand for remixing

Moments such as this are not something you as a site owner should actively chase people to share with you; that would be a bit odd. However, enabling people to live out part of their lives on your website will mean that this depth of involvement becomes part of their experience on the site. You cannot make people share these personal moments. They will do this only if they feel comfortable with the site and the social relationships they have there.

Imagine someone who turns wood for a hobby. He creates turnings and shows them to his friends as he creates them, building a relationship with each success or each split piece of wood. His activity forms a dialog with a potential community, but the activity comes first. These interactions will likely develop longer-term, deeper relationships. Alternatively, he could have a trophy-cabinet-like photo gallery of finished pieces. The reaction in this case would be less genuine and less frequent, as the readers have not experienced the pain and joy of the person making the pieces.

This is simple group psychology: people like to feel involved. The enormous (and personally worrying) rise of celebrity culture stems from the incessant detailing of Britney, Amy, or Jude's life. We are meant to feel some connection because we see them drunk in the street or we see what they wear every day. It works because people love to gossip. You can make use of this need, but be sure to turn the focus to your readers and the microcosm of their lives.

Sometimes the entity around which you would like to draw your community together is hard to access. Arguably, there is a need for privacy whenever the social object is an entity of value—in particular, when it is in written form. In science, a discovery is communicated in written form, so to publicly share it prior to publication is very risky, and although the discovery of new knowledge is the exciting part, it is also the most private (until it is published). Ideas remain valuable in science. On the Web, ideas are cheap, but implementation is key. Thus, scientists are unwilling to share ideas that are close to their experimental work. If ideas are valuable in your domain, such as new TV show formats, you need to think hard about what social objects you can create a community around.

It is worth understanding why people share content online and how you can harness their motivations for continuing to do this. Amazon's Listmania service (see Figure 10-3) is a perfect example of harnessing people's innate desire for social contact. There is no financial reward for creating a list: the sole satisfaction comes from curating a list of things you care about, which is visible only on the Amazon website, yet there are thousands of these lists. People gain value from collating a list of books around a subject area or tools for a hobby, and they perceive value from appointing themselves experts in the area. These lists then become something they can maintain as their area evolves, adding new books or tools, or removing ones they deem no longer appropriate. Amazon also counts the number of times a list has been read, and each list can be marked as helpful by people who have read it. This counting gives each person maintaining a list a game in which to participate: who can have the best list.

Figure 10-3. An Amazon Listmania list for software development books

People share for many reasons: they like to feel like an authority on a subject, they share for altruistic reasons, they want to give away information, or they simply like to make lists. Websites help us organize information, which helps us understand the world a bit better. However, no one site can meet all of our needs for sharing and categorizing information. There are hundreds of specialist sites—for instance, Cork'd for people who like wine.

Tools such as LiveJournal, Vox, Tumblr, Dopplr, Delicious, Upcoming, Flickr, and Last.fm all convey some aspect of my life to my friends. I noted in Chapter 5 that conveying these aspects is easier if the social object is digital in nature. The data capture is more straightforward than with analog media. A CD player is dumb compared to the same track in iTunes, so connectivity is important, too. If we use the Internet a lot, we end up with our lives spread across many sites, each with a different community, something I'll return to later in this chapter.

Capturing Intentionality

As I just mentioned, LiveJournal, Vox, Tumblr, Dopplr, Delicious, Upcoming, Flickr, and Last.fm are useful in helping me to organize aspects of my life; these sites were created so that people could participate on them. This architecture of participation means I can, at a minimum, interact with others simply by putting content online. This content is usually tagged, so it becomes part of a rich corpus that other people can explore. This can generate network effects, as the many contributions create a greater whole.

Successful sites are ones that people can use on a regular basis, without having to spend a lot of time doing so. Add the means to find and follow friends plus search the content, and you have the basis for interesting network effects to occur. These activities need to be intrinsically useful and allow for easy discovery of other people's content; otherwise, you may as well perform the activity privately on your local machine. The driver for getting people to place their content and activities with you is not that they can share the content. Rather, it is the useful service, and the sharing is often a side effect. The degree of attraction for sharing varies among domains. For Delicious, the bookmarking tool, sharing is a side effect; for Flickr, the sharing fits with how we culturally use photographs; for Upcoming, sharing and discovery is the main draw.

Each social application is capturing an intention to organize and communicate information and is redirecting this from a solo activity into something that creates a greater whole. The music I have listened to is recorded by Last.fm. I can see which bands I like and which have fallen out of favor. On its own, this is useful, but when all my listening habits are combined, I can gain much more. I can listen to the music my friends like or get recommendations for new artists. The collective nature of the site encourages my attention. I give the site something small and it returns that information as something that is much richer.

Often we share our content with other members of the site and, by implication, with the rest of the world via search engines. However, we feel we are sharing our content with a group of known individuals. Flickr is not a photography site, though it looks like one at first glance. A critical aspect of why people keep returning to Flickr is that the pictures are their friends' pictures. Flickr tells stories about their friends. Flickr has made it easy to add images to the site and easy to discover photos and friends. Strip away the friends and what does Flickr offer? It still has a good set of photo management tools and arguably acts as a backup service for your pictures, but the value at the heart of the service is gone

Successful sites capture small, discrete activities for their community to take part in and enable the social interaction in a manner that does not overwhelm the user.

A different example is Dopplr, a site for regular travelers (see Figure 10-4). The trip is the key activity on Dopplr, but another activity is possible for the less well traveled. They can subscribe to a calendar showing which of their friends are visiting their home city. So, sites with a stronger focus on two-way interaction, such as Twitter, do not work as well for passive members.

Figure 10-4. Dopplr London page showing upcoming trips from my friends

There is a strong curatorial aspect to a lot of social software applications: you're either creating your own collection of content or you're managing a collection of content from other people. Both Delicious and FFFFOUND! (see Figure 10-5) encourage a model of adding content to a library. This requires less work than generating new content, so the threshold for activity is very low, and thus it becomes easy to participate. Compare this to the amount of work involved in writing blog posts or taking pictures. Both Twitter and Last.fm also have a low thresholdfor participation.

Cohesion

One important factor in creating social web applications is the degree of togetherness or cohesion that your community feels. This can be evaluated at several levels, including the individual, the group, and the site:

- For the *individual* level, cohesion comes from the personal connections to the people the individual has chosen to connect with on the site. These people are her friends and colleagues.

- At a *group* level, the sense becomes one of membership or belonging: "I take landscape photographs." Natural subgroups can also come into play. A counterpoint might be "I'm a fashion photographer, I'd never shoot landscapes."

- At the *site* level, the cohesion is again about belonging and identity. Individuals perform actions on the site that enable them to identify with the site hobby or interest, and through these actions they discover others with like minds. They can take on a collective identity, a concept called *scibling* for ScienceBlogs and *Flickerenes/ites* for Flickr.

Making a noun and verb from the name of your site is surprisingly useful. If people can identify with your site, you are in a good place. Avoid faking or *astroturfing* this; it should be a genuine community activity.

Figure 10-5. An image stored on FFFFOUND!, which allows people to easily add images they find on the Web to a personal collection

Filtering Lists by Popularity

Social software creates lists, lots of them. You are going to want to display these lists for the people using your site. However, some of the more obvious ways of doing this are not ideal for a variety of reasons. Ideally, you want lists that change over time. Simple lists of the most popular tags on a site tend to become quite static once you have a decent level of traffic.

Another aspect to consider is lists with a scale, whereby being high on the list is seen as being good, people will try their utmost to be first on the list. This instinctive urge to compete can lead to people changing their interactions with the site to get themselves on the list, as opposed to how they'd normally use the site.

Say you had a recently updated profile page, with each profile ranked based on the frequency of edits and then the top three of these were featured on your home page. A person can manipulate this profile page editing system with just a minor edit. Adding or removing a single space will appear to be a legitimate edit, but he is really just faking activity. This person will often be on your home page as his page appears to have frequent edits, albeit he is just manipulating spaces. He is not really contributing something to the site, but rather is doing something for self-promotion. If you have lists, you want people to appear on them because they are actually contributing to the community.

The algorithms for tracking these lists and filtering out the manipulations can get quite complicated, as they tend to track multiple factors (single factors are much easier to manipulate directly). *Programming Collective Intelligence* (*http://oreilly.com/catalog/9780596529321/*) by Toby Segaran (O'Reilly) has great examples of how to run complex analyses of these kinds of lists. It also discusses some algorithms that you should find useful in managing lists. In the following subsections, we'll analyze some typical kinds of lists and some useful factors you might want to track on your site. (The Flickr interestingness algorithm is another excellent example of this in action; we'll explore it in more detail in "Calculating Popularity Across a Site" on page 168.)

Filtering Lists to Show Recent Content

There are many reasons to have a list of recent actions on your site. A list is one of the easiest ways to show fresh content on the site. Recent lists are also the most vulnerable to abuse if implemented in a simple manner. Sadly, you need to think about every list on your site in terms of how it might be misused, inadvertently or not.

Let's start with the most basic and simplest implementation and show the work required to create something better. We will look at a profile update tracker. The phrase "last five updates" can have a lot of different meanings, depending on how your system is implemented. For instance, the five updates could be five changed pieces of information all from the same person. A basic implementation would treat these changes as different updates and then the person would be listed five times. So, we need to aggregate information together to represent a person.

In another scenario, the person updates her publication list with three new publications. Is that three publication entries or one composite entry? The answer depends on the context of the page. If it is her page, all three publication entries would be listed. If the publications are for a group she belongs to, perhaps all three entries should be listed. If the publication entries are being put on a main section page, probably just one of them from that person should be listed. As you can see, there is a need for balance in terms of the amount of information displayed on public and personal sections of a site; on the public section of the site, content from other people needs to share the page. On the site and section home pages, which are commonly the most highly trafficked individual pages on a site, you will want to show off the best content for the site, not just any old updates. These pages act as a means to convince new people to come and join the site.

Personal aggregated streams of content also need careful thought. These rivers of news views that show the updates from the people you follow on a social network can easily flood the reader with content. The name varies from site to site: Dopplr calls them a *journal*, and Nature Network calls them a *snapshot*; the name varies. Most sites will show you everything your community generates. In this regard, it is worth discussing further how Facebook and Flickr handle content. For instance, Facebook operates a black box model to news feed stories. You can alter various parameters, but it is impossible to guarantee that any one of your friends will see a particular update (see Figure 10-6). This has an advantage in that it allows for deniability, but the lack of control frustrates many people. Facebook changed to a real-time 100% delivery model in early 2009.

Flickr, on the other hand, takes a different approach to feed management, one based on volume of pictures (see Figure 10-7). It is possible to turn off photos from contacts and reduce the number of photos from five per person (the default) to one per person. However, it is not possible to get every photo from everyone you follow; you can get as many as the most recent five from everyone. Given that people often upload large batches of photos to Flickr, this is a fair and content-sensitive approach. How far back you allow people to go in an activity page is something else you need to determine. You can find more on this in Chapter 13.

Nature Network, meanwhile, offers a river of news aggregation service that spans multiple content types. Launched in June 2006, the service offers a simple view of everything that has happened from your network on the site. Over successive launches, we added new content types, forum topics, and replies. We also removed group join notices and aggregated replies to the same topic. These changes came from growth in community size, experience using the site, and feedback from the community. The growth-driven changes are noteworthy: the tools that work well when there are hundreds or a few thousand people become cluttered when there are tens of thousands of

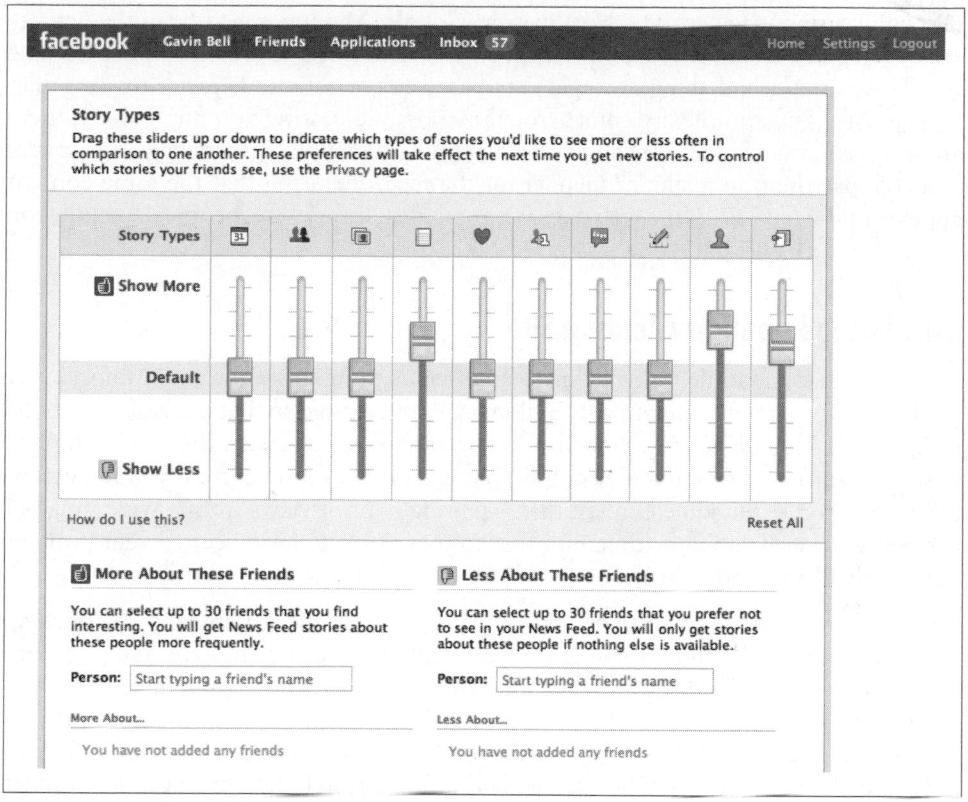

Figure 10-6. *Facebook news feed preferences*

Figure 10-7. *Flickr from your contacts settings showing the ability to alter the volume of photos seen*

people or more. However, building community features that are scaled to support thousands of interactions can feel too big in scale if the actual community size is small.

Understanding the need to view updates will guide you in putting the right number of updates with the right level of detail on the right page. On personal pages, you can use more detail and more updates; on public spaces, you will want less detail. Offering a minimal view and linking to a more detailed view can work well in many cases. Ideally, you are supporting "at-a-glance" viewing of content, with the option to delve deeper.

One last point of complexity: many people will want to follow along with the site via a feed, either in an RSS reader such as Google Reader or NetNewsWire, or increasingly in a widget start page such as NetVibes or iGoogle. Making a feed from the activity page seems like a simple idea, but it means your activity page must comprise a single list. This is not a bad thing; a single date-based list of activity is easier to scan than several lists. The complexity comes from any possible nesting you might do. If there are seven comments on a post and you collapse them on your activity page, make sure you collapse them in a similar manner for the feed. Ensuring that the same content appears in the feed as on the web page is a good idea. Otherwise, people depending on the feed will miss updates.

Calculating Popularity Across a Site

Tracking what is popular on your site is an obvious thing to want to do. Almost every site has some form of Popular page. Building a Popular page so that it is resistant to the influence of individuals determined to be on this page can make the page complex. Basically, you want to show the content that lots of people are currently looking at or rating. So, you want some content that is getting a lot of views from a wide range of people. You need to factor time into this so that the list can reflect current popular items, not all-time-popular items.

A robust popularity system can be a major feature for a site. The Popular pages of Digg, Delicious, and Flickr show some of the best content on those sites and the pages are justly very popular. For Digg and Delicious, these pages are the site's main features and showcase some of their most interesting content. Since these sites are large and successful, they have a lot of content to draw on. Making a popularity list soon after you have launched can be much harder, as there is not enough data to calculate a robust measure of popularity.

There are many downsides to popularity lists. Popular pages can create self-perpetuating lists, as people see the popular items and then alter their own lists to either maintain or achieve a position on the Popular page. People will also try to figure out your algorithm so that they can stay on the list, which can create unwelcome behaviors.

A good starting point for a Popular service is that the originator of the content cannot influence the popularity of the item he created. A simple Popular service would count every view of the item of content; however, this would allow an individual to repeatedly view her content to bump up her rankings. Discounting the views of the creator means that only other people's views count. There are other, subtler things the creator can do; however, posting content to many groups is a common behavior to encourage views.

Flickr has a technique called *interestingness* that powers its Explore section. This is a good example of the kind of complexity that a popularity system can require. Flickr initially did not have a Popular Pictures section; it launched the interestingness feature in August 2005 (*http://blog.flickr.net/en/2005/08/01/the-new-new-things/*), more than a year after Flickr launched. Waiting allowed Flickr time to collate a lot of data and test ideas regarding how the system should work. What it eventually released was the result of much internal experimentation. The feature recalculates the interestingness of the daily uploads to Flickr everyday, so the relative position of photos changes over time.

 This discussion draws on conversations with Cal Henderson and Kellan Elliot-McCrea from Flickr, as well as various presentations from other Flickr staff members. I've not seen any code or implementation details.

One mistake the Flickr team admittedly made when they first launched the interestingness feature was to allow visitors to rank the pictures. This was the only public ranked listing on the entire site. Some people did not like the introduction of such explicit competition, while other people immediately started to hack the feature to get as many of their pictures on the interestingness pages as possible. Posting to many groups was one of the undesirable behaviors that resulted from this. People started joining groups just to put pictures in front of other people, not to participate. A later iteration of interestingness dropped the overt ranking.

Stamen Design, a San Francisco-based agency, has done some visualization work on Digg's Popular pages (*http://stamen.com/clients/digg*). Visit labs.digg.com to see some of the work Stamen has been doing regarding real-time visualization of the activity on Digg. This is different from a text list of popular content; rather, it is an attempt to show how the community is actually behaving. This real-time interface works well for news stories, but probably wouldn't work as well for other content. Watching the stack visualization (*http://labs.digg.com/stack/*), as shown in Figure 10-8, for a few minutes gives a good sense of what the community thinks is important right now, something that is impossible to see on the main site.

Commenting, Faving, and Rating

Determining popularity and real-time interest is great for showing aggregate popularity on a site, but personal interests and interactions are also important. Several tools that allow for one-to-one social interactions are described in the next section.

Commenting

The most obvious tool is commenting, which is the ability to leave text comments on items of content created by others. This is probably the dominant means of social interaction on many sites. It is also one that you should probably custom-build for your site because this will give the closest fit to your own content.

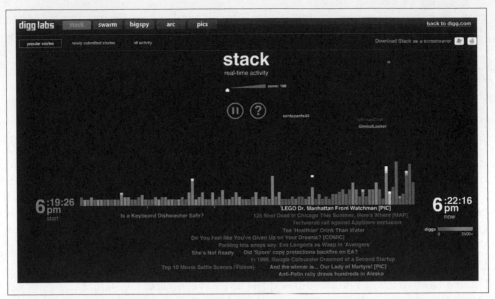

Figure 10-8. Digg Labs' stack visualization, which shows real-time "diggs" on stories (created by Stamen.com)

The blog evolved from a regularly updated home page, gaining archives along the way; comments were a later addition. Indeed, many famous blogs, such as Kotkke.org and Daringfireball.net, rarely or never have comments. Some people turn them on only selectively.[*]

As a primary means of commenting, the provision of a simple email address suffices. The TrackBack system (*http://www.sixapart.com/pronet/docs/trackback_spec*) originated from this way of thinking. Essentially, TrackBack supports the idea that "I'll write a blog post in response to your blog post." TrackBack is an automated mechanism that notifies a blog when a new article on another blog references it. Commenting does not define blogging, any more than permalinks do; it is the combination and selection of these elements that make the medium effective. The other primary source of commenting behavior comes from message boards; some blogs behave much more like a message board with hundreds of comments per new post. The *Guardian*'s "comment is free" system behaves like this (see Chapter 5).

There are three key characteristics of a good commenting system, beyond the mere ability to leave a comment:

---

[*] At *http://a.wholelottanothing.org/2008/08/27/becoming-an-old-blogging-man/*, Matt Haughey explains why it is not a good idea to allow comments. John Gruber described why he doesn't have comments in a podcast; the relevant transcript is on *http://shawnblanc.net/2007/why-daring-fireball-is-comment-free/*. Essentially, both Matt and John feel that comments should be made via email or on your own blog.

- There must be a clear link between text identifying the person leaving the comment and the person's profile on the site. Unlike blogging, generally everyone on a commenting system has a profile on the same site.

- There must be an ability to easily follow up on further comments made, which helps to maintain conversation. This pertains to both the person whose content is being commented on and the people leaving the comments. It is just as important to notify the people who have left comments that they have received comments themselves.

- The person who owns the item of content needs to have tools that allow him to control which comments appear on his content. He should be able to delete any comment left by another person on his content.

It is icing on the cake if you can allow a person who left a comment to edit it. Note that it is important to mark such edited comments, typically with a system-generated time-stamp and the word *Edited*. Showing which comments have been changed is important because it makes it clear when someone has altered what he previously wrote. If someone writes something heated and then retracts it later, the responses that immediately follow the heated comment will not make as much sense if there is no signal that the heated post was changed.

A preview mode for the comment creation can also be very helpful, particularly if you decide to allow links or other pieces of HTML on your site. Many systems use a simple text markup language such as Markdown or Textile for this.

Faving or Marking As Favorite

Commenting can be a very effective way of facilitating interaction among members of your community; however, there are great benefits to be seen from non-text-based interactions as well. Marking something as a favorite is probably the most common of these. There are several others: "add to library" on Delicious, "liking" or "marked a place as has been" on Dopplr, "sharing" on Google Reader, and One-Click Purchase on Amazon. These are low-cognitive-overhead activities, meaning there is no need for a long interaction; instead, you just click and move on. There is no text to be entered, as there is with tagging or commenting. On Twitter, the act of faving posts from other people is quick and simple, and works well within the list view or over the API.

The star has become a common icon for marking something as a favorite, closely followed by the heart. Typically, the icon is an outline and the act of clicking changes the color and fills in the icon. The icons then appears in the activity list for the person who owns the content. Essentially, it sends an "I liked this" message to the creator. For the person who marked it as a favorite, the item gets added to a list of other favorites, acting as a service-centric bookmarking tool. Some services—such as Delicious, FFFFOUND!, and Flickr—make this list of favorites public (see Figure 10-9), and if you decide to do so on your site, it is essential that you explicitly communicate to your users that their favorites will be public; it is not always immediately clear to people that others can see their favorites.

Figure 10-9. Notification in a Flickr activity stream that people like this picture of spices

I mentioned earlier in the book that we can make more of these collated lists of content, as they capture the best content from the site for that person. There are two ways to use these lists: as the basis for further recommendations and as a list of content with which users can be invited to do more things. If you view the act of marking as favorite as a save-for-later activity, you can offer a range of contextual actions for your users to perform. Republishing is one possibility, but so is resharing the content with other groups or individuals. This latter activity works well with events, as there is no contention over ownership of the content.

Better management tools are required for favorites. The default listing is a list of content in reverse chronological order. Some sites allow searching within your favorites. Displaying associated tags or showing people whose content you have marked as a favorite would be helpful in gleaning more value from favorites.

Looking briefly at desktop applications, there are many related actions that can be done on RSS feeds. NetNewsWire, as shown in Figure 10-10, shows half a dozen specific activities for a single feed. Desktop applications have a rich interface potential. Web applications have less opportunity to offer this richness, but they seem to rarely offer even a few of these. Consider what activities people might want to perform with the items they have marked as a favorite, and then add these as options to the View Favorites section of your application.

Rating

Rating content also falls into the category of activities requiring tools with low cognitive overhead. Rating on a five-point scale (known as the *Likert* scale, *http://en.wikipedia .org/wiki/Likert_scale*) is fairly common, alongside a simple yes/no rating. When used as a voting mechanism, it can be effective. For instance, Digg uses the rating system to show the popularity of its news items. Amazon uses the scale for rating products. You need to carefully think about whether you want to include a rating system on your site

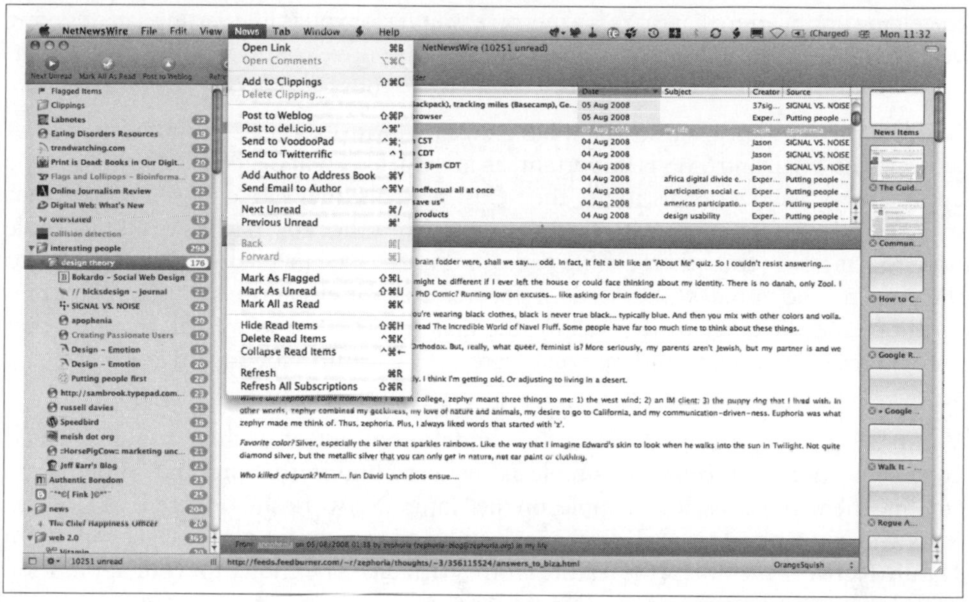

Figure 10-10. NetNewsWire news contextual menu showing possible actions for a news item from an RSS feed

so that you don't change the dynamics of your community. Imagine Flickr with a rating on each picture; it would be quite a different place. This is why I view rating as a separate social activity from favorites. Giving people the ability to express dislikes as well as likes means people can overreact to the negative and attempt to game the positive. Rating means competition among your community, which you might want, but can be unhealthy. Think carefully before you add a negative rating system. Even a ranked positive system such as gold, silver, and bronze can leave the bronze rating looking like a negative comment.

Rating content that is not community-generated, as Digg does in general and Amazon allows, can work well, but remember that many people will see your site as a competitive environment.

Internal Messaging Systems

When you're developing a website, at some point someone will suggest a personal messaging service so that your participants can talk to one another privately. And although there are advantages to having such a service, you must consider the disadvantages as well. Private messaging is basically like creating an internal email system, and everyone on your site has email already. Sometimes people want to create personal messaging services as a means of driving return traffic to their site. Thankfully, this is on the wane. For instance, when you receive a message on Facebook, you no longer get just an envelope; instead, you now receive the content of the message as well.

Receiving notification that there is a message waiting for you is like getting a card saying you missed a package delivery; it's annoying. It may drive traffic to your site and generate ad impressions, but it is just as likely to drive your users away.

Building private messaging so that it integrates well with existing communication services such as email and SMS is important, as more people will be likely to adopt it. One approach is to allow people to use their existing tools: they can choose any recipient in their network, similar to what Twitter offers. The other approach is to allow people to send a message from their profile page. In this case, the mechanism is connected to the person. The former works well for Twitter, as Twitter is primarily about communication, and the latter works well for the majority of sites, so we will focus on that mode. Preserving privacy and ease of use are critical features for any private messaging service.

You must give people on your site the ability to opt out of or limit any unsolicited communication. This can be as simple as clicking a button that prohibits others from sending them messages; for example, on the Nature Network site (Figure 10-11), clicking a checkbox turns off outside messaging and allows receipt of messages only from Nature Network members (the feature is off by default). The choice for your application may differ, but allowing opt-out is important.

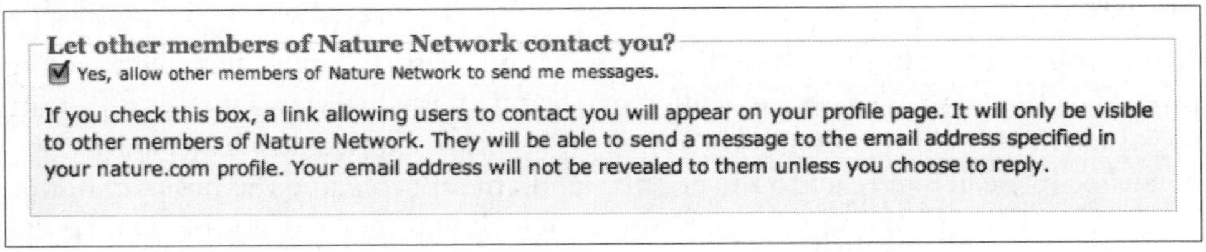

Let other members of Nature Network contact you?
☑ Yes, allow other members of Nature Network to send me messages.

If you check this box, a link allowing users to contact you will appear on your profile page. It will only be visible to other members of Nature Network. They will be able to send a message to the email address specified in your nature.com profile. Your email address will not be revealed to them unless you choose to reply.

Figure 10-11. Nature Network personal messaging opt-in preference setting

It is important to notify people when a message is waiting for them. By far, the most common means for this is to send an email, though sending an SMS or text message to a phone is becoming more common, but has associated costs. The email should contain the content of the message and a link to respond to it. Giving away someone's email address is not desirable (for the recipient or the sender). So, you need to be careful who you set as the From: and Reply-to: addresses in any emails you send; these should not be the personal email address of the member who is sending the message. Your application is generating and sending the message, so this gives you a great opportunity to get this right.

One approach that 37signals (and others) have used to create a useful messaging system is to allow for replies from a web-based exchange via email. Every message comes from a unique address that corresponds to a conversation, and the entire conversation is archived on the Web. So, it is possible to use email to simply respond to the message. 37signals uses this approach in its Basecamp project management application (see *http: //37signals.blogs.com/products/2008/04/new-basecamp-fe.html*). No one needs to see any actual email addresses, and there is an archive of all messages for that conversation in one place on the Web, instead of being lost in an email inbox. This is a good design pattern to copy. Extending this a little, it is worth allowing multiple email addresses for individual people so that your members can have these notifications sent to a separate email account if they wish. Supporting multiple email addresses per account is generally a good practice anyway, as people change jobs, and they are known by different email addresses—for example, their home and work email addresses.

One unfortunate use of personal messaging is as a spamming mechanism. If you allow personal messages to be sent on your site, some people will abuse this capability. One way to curtail the abuse is to make the ability to send a message dependent on another factor. The simplest system is one in which any signed-in member can send a message to another signed-in member. The next level allows people to opt out of this feature, making this more palatable for many. The level after that is requiring that an established relationship exist before messages can be sent. A two-way relationship is an obvious choice. Twitter allows for an interesting variation—if I am following you, you can send me a direct message, but if you are not following me, I cannot send you a direct message. This asymmetric system works well, as it allows personal replies to a broad audience, without the load of following everyone back. Further curtailment can come by making the ability to send messages based on length of service, meaning it is not something you get immediately on sign-up (note that this can be off-putting to new members).

Some communities will want personal messaging available earlier and require it to be private, whereas for other communities private messaging will be covered by email or Instant Messenger. Personal messaging places another level of responsibility on your site: if you can encourage people to use email, you can keep your application focused on doing useful things. Dopplr, for example, could have built an internal personal messaging system for contacting people about trips, but instead it uses email (see Figures 10-12 and 10-13). Once this email is sent, all the replies will occur via email, as opposed to being hosted on Dopplr. Hence the emails come from the sign-up address.

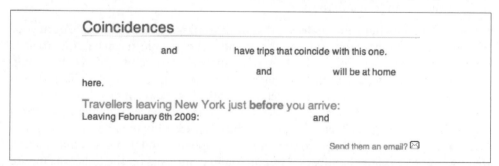

Figure 10-12. Dopplr trip page offering an opportunity to send an email to specific people in New York, with names removed for privacy

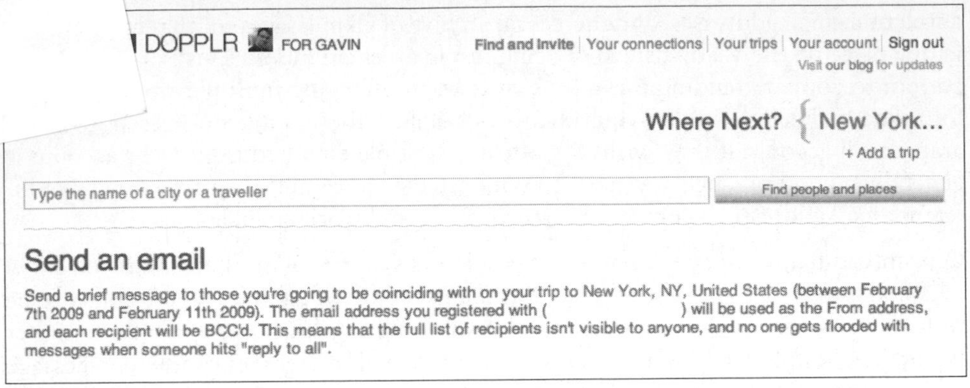

Figure 10-13. Dopplr trip email introductory text, explaining that the email will come from the sign-up address

Friending Considered Harmful

Dopplr's design director, Matt Jones, coined the expression "friending considered harmful," and it neatly sums up a problem with current social web applications. The intent of most sites should be to share experiences and information, but the focus is often on growing your social network. "Friend" is an unhelpful term. If a certain person is your friend, other people must be something else. The concept of "friend" can be useful in terms of privacy, but there is already a level of privacy between members and non-members of a site.

Shared activity can be much more useful than determining the difference between friend and not-friend. It does require a change in language on the site. *Sharing* is a useful word to describe what is happening. It might seem like just playing with words, but it shifts the emphasis to the activity on the site. A flat privacy model makes for an application that is easier to understand, too.

Privacy is an issue, but you can deal with it by creating subgroups of people from your list. If you want to share something with a specific set of people, it can be easier to have a named list of known people with whom you want to share. Reciprocation of friending, a common social cue, will blur the boundary of friends versus contacts. This is due to the impoliteness of responding to a "friending" with a "mark as contact." Your network now has people who think you are a "friend" and you might have originally added them as a "contact." FriendFeed has even created the odd capability to allow "fake friends." You can add someone, but not receive any of their updates, and they get a confirmation that you are "friending them back." Merlin Mann comments on the ludicrous nature of this idea, saying, "this is a major breakthrough in the make-believe friendship space."[†]

† *http://www.43folders.com/2008/08/26/pause-button*

Named lists make this a lot easier socially. You control who is on your list, and they get to see some specific material. Ideally, though, you should keep to one level of relationships. It makes development a lot easier, as maintaining even a two-level system of friend and contact requires a lot of special case code.

Sharing Events

Many other kinds of sharing are possible on the Internet. One other area I want to touch on is event and conference management. The very nature of these time-based objects means they have a different consumption profile than something such as a photograph. We cannot be aware of a photo before it is created. It is taken, uploaded to a site, and then we can experience it. However, an event has a phase during which people can decide whether to attend or not. Also, once an event is over, it is no longer possible to attend it, so the chance to participate with the object is different for an event compared to a photo, a song, or even a TV program (a TV program or film can be repeated).

The consumption profile for an event is from the future to the end of the scheduled time for the event. For virtually everything else, it is the other way around. It moves from "it will happen" to "it has happened." There is then the possibility to react to the event, just like we can react to seeing a photo. In Chapter 5, we looked at different types of media and how we handle them in the world. Events can be seen as a different type of media. There are a range of verbs we can use to describe our interactions with them: *attending, sponsoring, speaking, organizing,* and *missing* are some of them.

There are many ways to approach social interaction around events. Upcoming allows anyone to list an event, and people can then mark the event as "interesting" or "attending." Other software treats the community around the event as a collective whole. For instance, CrowdVine allows attendees of an event to import external data such as Twitter streams or Flickr photos onto a profile that is populated by answering a few relevant questions. CrowdVine sites generally are ephemeral in nature, in that they last for the duration of the event, and then people export data from them back into their core network. See *http://blog.crowdvine.com/2008/08/29/crowdvine-vs-ning/* for a discussion of how CrowdVine differs from generic social software.

Summary

Finding the right activity and social object around which to build your site is much more important than the tools to grow your community. From the immediacy of Twitter to the slower but valuable exchanges of Dopplr, finding the right balance is difficult. Social objects and verbs are the important takeaways from this chapter: find the thing that people are willing to share and give it a handle. Enable the right verbs for these objects to become something that can be the focus of interactions among individuals. Along the way, build something that is of initial use to a single person. Do not start with a "social network;" instead, enable one to evolve.

CHAPTER 11

Modeling Data and Relationships

Turning things, people, and relationships from ideas and sketches into social objects on the Web means creating URLs that people can use to access them. You need to represent these social objects in a data model, mapping the people, for example, to a series of user ID fields, and then linking these user IDs to the videos they have uploaded and the comments they have made. Behind the URLs is a database that holds the relationships between all of these items.

People, location, and group membership can seem simple to model at first glance. A person has a name and a login ID, probably a profile, and an avatar image. However, locations can change when you factor in time as a variable. Do you keep the current location only? The answer will depend on the type of application you are developing.

Anyone coming to your application will need to use a URL to access the social interactions and content on your site. If you create these URLs without any thought, you can end up with a site structure that is hard to understand. Good URL design is a key starting point for good data modeling.

Designing URLs

In the late 1990s, the rush of people and companies to get online meant that well-meaning guidelines were largely ignored and people created URLs any which way they wanted. Tim Berners-Lee wrote some good guidelines early on for how to manage URLs (see *http://www.w3.org/DesignIssues/Axioms.html* and *http://www.w3.org/Provider/Style/URI*), but it wasn't until the dot-com crash in 2000 that there was time for reflection and a new focus on making the Web a high-quality place, rather than a shanty town.

A URL can be seen as a name for a thing; if you change the name, you lose the thing. This does not generally happen with books or places, so it should not happen online either. With that in mind, three particular problems are common when people create URLs without regard to any design guidelines:

Reference

You will change your technology at some point; the script names and languages will not be the same, and this means URLs will no longer work. So, using a current function name and the templates to include, or referencing the current software implementation such as */cgi-bin/script.pl*, is not a good idea. A change in technology will result in lots of broken URLs.

Transience

Too many URLs change after they are published. This is particularly true of news sites, but also true of advertising microsites, which disappear. Poor maintenance practices also lead to changing URLs. There should be no reason to change a URL, so pick a good one when you first create it. At a minimum, provide a redirect to the new location, if you must change it. Your site will hopefully be full of interesting, exciting content that other people will link to; if your URLs change, these links break. Also, search engines index content at a specific URL. Carelessly change the URL, and your content will drop out of the search engines.

Uniqueness

An object should have one and only one unique or canonical URL that represents it. Presenting multiple URLs that claim to be the same object can mean different people will use a different URL to link to your object. Keeping to one URL means everyone links to the same one, and algorithms such as Google's page rank will score all the links against that one place.

In Chapter 16, I talk about URLs in more detail, but for now it's important to know that you need to think about the design of your URLs. Weird characters such as parentheses (which are common on Wikipedia) and commas (Vignette StoryServer is guilty of this) make for odd URLs. They can break in email clients that are not expecting commas or parentheses as part of a URL.

 Dan Connolly's 2005 article, "Untangle URIs, URLs, and URNs," at *http://www.ibm.com/developerworks/xml/library/x-urlni.html*, gives a recent overview of what's happening with URLs and related technologies.

Getting to the Right URL

In February 2009, Google announced a new `link` element for defining a relationship between entities on the Web. The canonical element is meant to help with the problem of multiple URLs pointing at the same object (*http://www.google.com/support/webmasters/bin/answer.py?hl=en&answer=139394*). This is particularly an issue with query string parameters:

```
<link rel="canonical" href=
    "http://www.example.com/product.php?item=swedish-fish"/>
```

Another issue with URLs is the widespread use of link-shortening services. TinyURL (*http://tinyurl.com*) is one of the more famous of the early entrants into this area. Link shortening came about because the long URLs that were being created in the 1990s wouldn't work in many email clients without wrapping. Twitter, with its 140-character-per-message limit, drove a rapid increase in the number of link generation services.

This has led to a new problem: a proliferation of shortened URLs that point at the same things on the Internet. Sometimes the same URL will have half a dozen shortened URLs pointing to it. A solution is to create a means to point at the main link, much in the same way that the earlier `rel="canonical"` defines the primary URL.

The initial proposal was to use the previously obscure `rev` element from HTML that declares a reverse link relationship. Unpacking the `rev` link element states that the canonical version of the URL this HTML document points at is the one in the link `rev` header. So, *http://bit.ly/ILMg*, which links to *http://oreilly.com/catalog/9780596518752/*, could contain:

```
<link rev="canonical" href=" http://oreilly.com/catalog/9780596518752/">
```

The rev canonical proposal came from Flickr's Kellan Elliot-McCrea (*http://laughing meme.org/2009/04/03/url-shortening-hinting/*), based on conversations with Google's Kevin Marks. Conversation continued in early 2009 with concerns about links breaking on the Internet as a result of link shortening companies going out of business (see *http://joshua.schachter.org/2009/04/on-url-shorteners.html*). RevCanonical (*http://revcanonical.appspot.com*) is an application that can test whether a page has a canonically shortened URL defined for it. For instance, it can tell you that *http://www.flickr.com/photos/gavinbell/35378445/* has a shortened URL of *http://flic.kr/p/48jMc* already defined for it.

Permalinks

People need to be able to address social objects, to find them again and share them, in order to build conversations around them. The shift from galleries to individual photos took advantage of a key idea emerging on the Web: the permalink. Jason Kottke (*http://www.kottke.org/00/03/finally-did-you-notice-the*) and Matt Haughey (*http://a.whole lottanothing.org/2000/03/caroline_wishes.html*) were instrumental in popularizing the idea that a blog post should have a permanent URL. The idea stems back to Tim Berners-Lee's writings at the W3C; his essay at *http://www.w3.org/Provider/Style/URI* is still very relevant now. Here is a short excerpt from the essay:

> Cool URIs don't change.
>
> What makes a cool URI?
>
> A cool URI is one which does not change.
>
> What sorts of URI change?
>
> *URIs don't change: people change them.*
>
> There are no reasons at all in theory for people to change URIs.

The permalink gives the piece of content a handle, a means of allowing interaction with the world. You can attach comments to it, you can reference it from other websites, you can put it into other social systems, and you can query it. In the case of Flickr, the connection between the pictures and the person is direct and immediate. The display of pictures as a reverse chronological list is heavily influenced by the permalink and blogging.

Putting Objects on the Internet

Many of the things we turn into social objects are already native to the Web or are digital in form. Most people's pictures and music are digital. However, the more obvious media consumption-led services such as Flickr are not the only kinds of social software services it is possible to create.

It is also possible to take data from sensors and put it on the Internet. For example, information regarding the electricity consumed in my house is available online at *http://pachube.com*, via a current cost meter (*http://currentcost.com*), a device that tracks energy meter usage. Pachube is a data aggregation service for sensor and machine-generated data. It makes pretty graphs such as the one shown in Figure 11-1. Using this combination of data, the energy consumption for my house can be aggregated into other services such as AMEE (*http://amee.com*), another data service. AMEE is aimed at tracking energy usage worldwide. My electricity consumption becomes part of the Internet through these two services.

The more obvious media consumption-led services such as Flickr are not the only kinds of social software services it is possible to create.

Determining what gets a good URL and how the actions around that are expressed can be a bit of a black art. The primary object needs to get a unique identifier, and it needs to be associated with the person who created it. When you take into account the actions that are possible around that content, you need to map those to the software that runs your site. All of this must be done while generating a URL that meets the qualities I described.

A typical solution has been the Apache mod-rewrite module that can take otherwise awkward URLs and create *clean URLs* from them. In addition, routes in Ruby on Rails (*http://guides.rubyonrails.org/routing.html*) have helped the cause of clean URLs a lot by integrating the URL design into the application layer. Designing decent URLs requires a different skill set from designing interfaces and page layouts. Generally, the task falls to some combination of information architect, lead developer, and product manager. Attaching accurate URLs to wireframes whenever they are being discussed will help to bring other people on board. URLs are invisible to most people, so you need to make people see them, before they will engage with the design of them.

Not every URL on the site needs to be perfect and clean, but URLs for your important objects, such as people, places, and social objects, should be clear, short, and if possible,

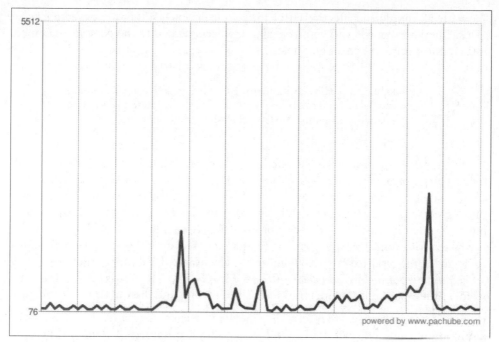

Figure 11-1. Pachube.com visualization of current cost meter data from my house; the big spikes represent the kettle boiling

meaningful. Any URL that corresponds to an action that might be sent via email or be bookmarked should be properly designed.

> Append the URL of the page at the top of every wireframe or mock that you work with. People will see the URL and start to think about its design as part of the design process.

Short URLs are better. URLs with more than about 60 characters will break in an email. With the caveats noted about URL shorteners, you should consider creating one for your application. Dopplr with *dplr.it* and Flickr with *flic.kr* have already done this. Analyzing your web server logs for 404 errors (File Not Found errors) can tell you whether you have broken URLs already.

The following are good URL patterns:

http://www.dopplr.com/trip/person/trip_id
http://www.flickr.com/photos/person/photo_id/
http://www.last.fm/music/artist/album_id

These are all simple and effective URLs for people or objects; they are called *hackable URLs*. Chop off the "id" and you have all the objects related to the person for Dopplr or the photos for that person on Flickr.

 Hackable is a positive attribute for a URL. It means that it is human-understandable and can be easily modified. Usually, these URLs have a clear pattern and a structure that allows for guessable combinations.

Another interesting example of URL design is Oakland Crimespotting, (*http://oakland.crimespotting.org*), which scraped the Oakland (California) Police Department's website to visualize crime in that particular neighborhood. (Subsequently, they got an implicit agreement to use the data; this is a good example of forgiveness, not permission, in terms of building services.) By creating *geo-URLs* (URLs that link an event or object to a place for crimes), Stamen, a San Francisco-based design agency (*http://stamen.com*), made the reported crime data more socially usable. URLs are of the form *http://oakland.crimespotting.org/crime/2009-02-18/Type/id*. The URL breaks down into a label for crime, then a date, then a type (such as an assault), and then an ID for the offense.

Many of these identifiers are internally generated by each company, due to a lack of commonly agreed upon external identifiers or multiple providers of identity. There are some commonly agreed upon standards for books (e.g., ISBNs) and airport codes, but most *things* do not have a tidy preexisting list of identifiers.

Issuing Identifiers

The world would be an easier place to navigate if everything came with an RFID tag (a common type of radio frequency tag often used in shops) or a bar code. Unfortunately, often by the time something is popular, the possibility of a simple worldwide identifier is no longer feasible. Even with books, there are often multiple ISBNs for the same one (the ISBN represents the edition, not the actual work), but services have been created to give items unique identifiers. For example, the motive behind CDDB, a music lookup service now known as Gracenote, was to calculate a unique code for every music CD, creating a single identifier instead of the thousands of CD stock codes generated by hundreds of recording labels. Another example is Equity, the UK union for people working in entertainment. Their membership policy enforces a unique professional name,* one of the few places where people have unique identifiers out of choice.

If you can find something that already exists on which to base your identifier, use that. Many travel sites use the International Air Transport Association (IATA) and International Civil Aviation Organization (ICAO) airport codes. Book sites commonly start with the ISBN and manually handle the mapping of editions. Ensuring that your

---

* *http://www.equity.org.uk/HowToJoin/ProfessionalName.aspx*

identifiers are simple and that your API and website call the same object by using something such as "w38y2wy" may seem obvious, but it is necessary advice. The right approach to issuing identifiers will probably evolve, rather than spring fully formed in version 1 of your site.

Auto-generated database keys, which tend to be simple number sequences, are fine for some things, but these are generally equivalent to your actual user count or post count, and you might not want to divulge your counts to just anyone. Lastly, not every database or language generates sequences in the same manner, so if you generate your own number sequence, you will control this and not leave it to the whims of another system designer when you or someone else ports your code. Like URLs, not every identifier needs to be hand-crafted, but issues of security will encourage generated keys for many areas. Privacy is a key driver of this need.

Identifying People

Representing people on your site is important. There are usually three notions of a person in a system. The internal database representation is usually a numeric key and is used internally. The other two are used by the person on your site: the private name by which the user logs in (typically this is the email address the person signed up with), and the public screen name by which other people know this person. Randy Farmer provides a good overview of these concepts at *http://thefarmers.org/Habitat/2008/10/the_tripartite_identity_patter_1.html*.

There is some variation; some sites let you use the public identifier as the login username and some sites allow use of OpenID. Most sites put the public identifier (screen name or username) in the URL for the person's profile page, too. Table 11-1 shows what some popular sites use to identify people.

 Do not use a person's email address as a public identifier, as it is too easily harvested by spammers.

Table 11-1. Identifying people on sites

Site	Private login key	Public identifier	Public ID in URL
Flickr	Yahoo! username	GavinBell	Yes, though can be different from public ID
Twitter	Username or email	zzgavin	Yes
Dopplr	Email or OpenID	zzgavin	Yes

For more information on how to build admin systems and separate user and administration identities, refer to Chapter 16.

Using Data-Driven Site Design

While I was with the BBC, I worked on a project called Program Information Pages (PIPs). The aim was to create web pages for every TV and radio program broadcast by the company. The format */programme-name/yyyy/mm/dd* seemed like an obvious choice for the URL, but the problem is that programs repeat.[†] The key insight was to model the episode, not the broadcast. Creating a single page for an episode means there is a focal point for all conversation about that program.

Exploring the information we had available from internal database systems and the current broadcast behavior became the basis for the URL design. Repeats were one of the main issues. These may seem like a curious television problem, but many events occur more than once. For example, Jane Austen's *Pride and Prejudice* has been made into several films, a few television series, and a radio play, so a simple *pride-and-prejudice/* URL would not work; the version would not be clear. A monthly meeting is another good example.

To focus on data first might seem at odds with the approach on activity as the core that I outlined in Chapter 7, but unless you can effectively give a handle to the objects in your community, it will be difficult for people to interact around them. This is particularly true if the content (object) is preexisting, such as music, video, crimes, or books. The next level of focus should be on behavior. What verbs characterize the interactions that you want your community to engage in around this content? Page layout comes after you have determined the *what* and *how* of your site. High-level sketching on a whiteboard can be a very effective way for a small team to understand the objects and actions. But be cautious about jumping to detailed wireframes before you understand the data. Those initial sketches should not be transformed into elaborate wireframes; try several different approaches to the problem, then review. Iteration at this sketching stage is cheap and easy, so take time to explore your ideas.

Handling Containment

The problem of containment can creep up on you. We encountered it at the BBC. Sometimes an entire program is broadcast within another program. Saturday morning cartoons are a good example of this. Another example is a side trip. If I fly to San Francisco and stay a night, then I go to Sebastopol and stay there for a few nights, and then return for another night to San Francisco, the trip to Sebastopol is inside a primary trip to San Francisco. The early trip modeling for Dopplr thought of all trips as return trips from home. So, this became a "London to San Francisco and back to London," then "London to Sebastopol," and finally another "London to San Francisco" trip. Including the notion of a side trip solved this problem. The default remains an "out

---

[†] Tom Coates wrote an excellent review of the work we did together to answer the question about programs that repeat and their URL structures. You can find it at *http://www.plasticbag.org/archives/2004/06/developing_a_url_structure_for_broadcast_radio_sites/*.

---

and back" from your home city, but now the web interface supports multiple legs on a trip; see Figure 11-2.

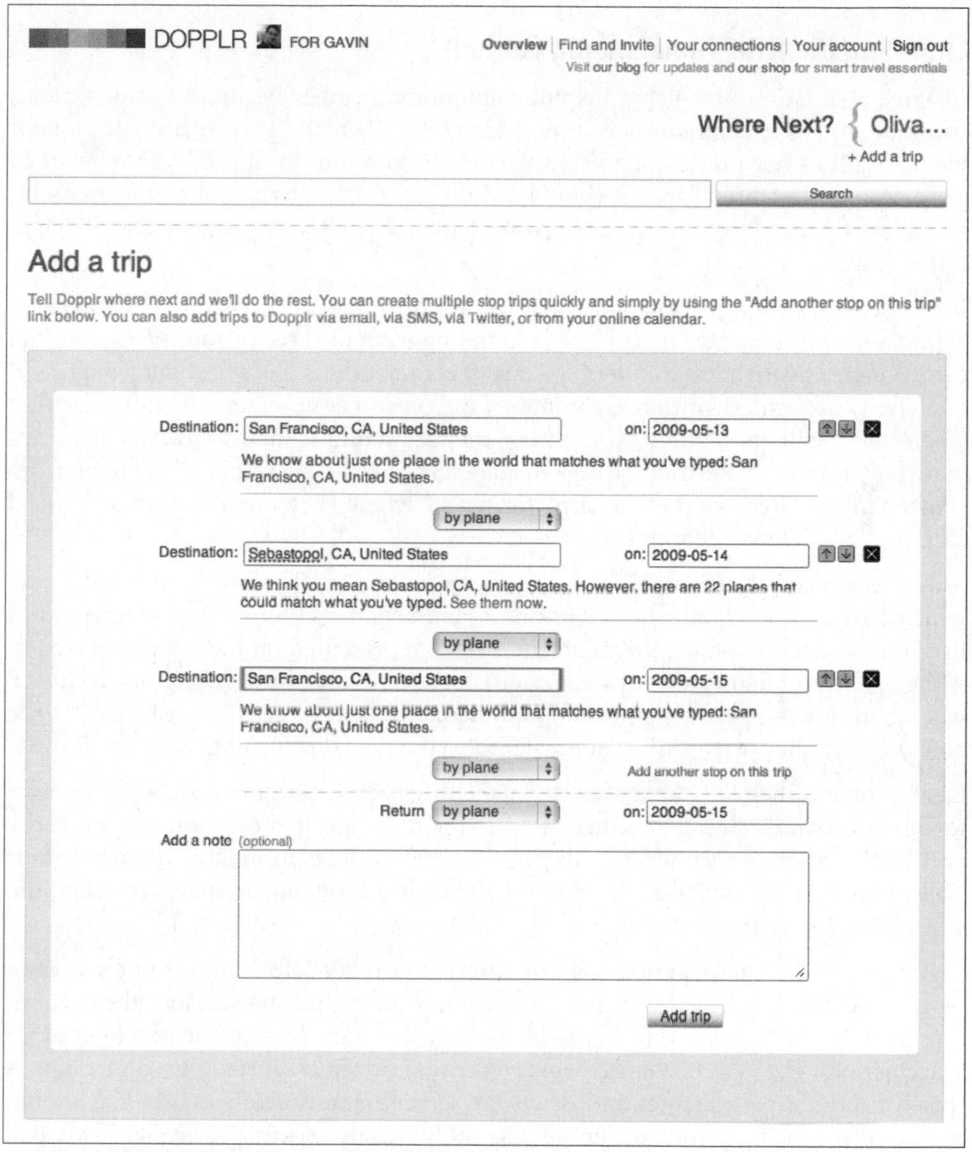

Figure 11-2. Dopplr supporting trips inside other trips

They are not always obvious, but anywhere time-based activity occurs, there are likely to be containment issues. Podcasts have segments and a DVD video has chapter points. Travel with side trips and also most games (e.g., a match in a set for tennis) have these kinds of containment issues, too. If they exist in your domain, you can decide whether they are important enough to represent. Time management can be tricky in other ways, as the next section shows.

Changing Identities and Linking Content

Imagine a situation in which a helpful community member becomes a support staff member (this is a common occurrence, in fact). When the person becomes a staff member, all of her previous contributions to the community should remain as they were posted; the staffing change should not affect the previous content. One useful bit of advice for marking the ownership of content is to always ensure that it has a timestamp.

It is worth examining where and when you need to make it known that someone is acting as a staff member. If you have a founding team of three or four people and an early community of a few hundred, your staff contributions will stand out from everyone else's, particularly if they are commenting on someone's content. Consider that when staff members comment on content, they are acting as themselves, not as a company representative. Restrict the urge to mark "STAFF" on everything that comes from staff members. Reserve that "stamp" for places where they are acting in an official capacity; it will have more impact.

A different example of identity and content comes from the Theyworkforyou.com site, which creates a much improved version of Hansard, the UK government's record of Parliament. Each Member of Parliament (MP) is represented on the site and linked to what he has said. However, MPs do resign or lose elections; for example, my local MP will stand down at the next election and there will be a new MP. Ensuring that the content from the current MP is not assigned to the new representative is important.

Lastly, there is the tricky area of personal identifier reuse, and many different options for how to handle this. The simplest option is to assign identities once, even if the account lies dormant. However, this generates bad feelings from later arrivals to your site, as the "good" names get used up by the early adopters who may stop using the site, but still have the identifier.

Many sites allow a grace period of six months of inactivity before an account name can be claimed. An email to the current owner confirming that she will lose the account due to inactivity is polite. Automatically reaping dormant accounts irritates people; a grace period offers some balance between the two extremes. A point worth making is that if your company creates and issues the screen names members use, you should reserve the right to terminate service and prohibit sale of these identities. This will discourage squatters and fake accounts.

Identity and Context-Dependent Views

Profile pages are a good example to show some of the issues that come up when modeling the activities around a page. Imagine a social web application. Every person gets his own page. How many different instances of that profile page with the same URL will you need to create? Let's take a look.

My view of my profile page includes private information, such as a count of visitors and a link to edit the page, and uses the URL format */people/screenname*. Figure 11-3 shows such a profile page.

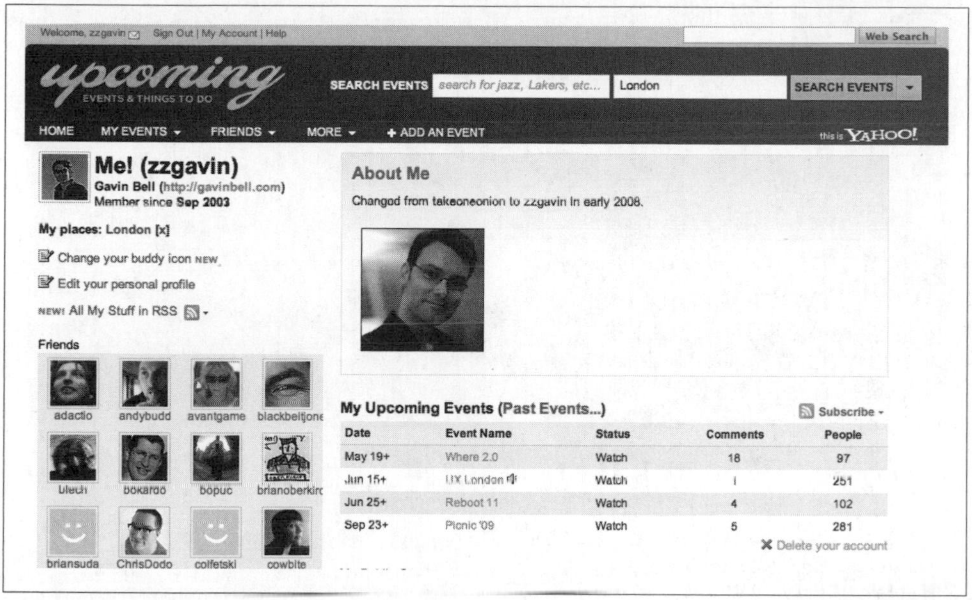

Figure 11-3. Profile page from Upcoming, showing the private links for account deletion and profile editing

Your view of my profile page will have a different behavior if you are already connected to my profile on this site. If not, there will be an "Add As Contact" link (the exact wording varies). Both views will have the same */people/screenname* URL as the profile page.

The logged-out or search engine view of a profile page has the same URL as well. However, the viewing person or search bot is not a member of the site, so no special activity is possible, unless the site is semiprivate. LinkedIn offers a different page to non-logged-in members, as docs Dopplr (see Figure 11-4), but still using the same */people/screenname* URL.

Editing profile pages requires a different URL, and it doesn't need to be a clean URL. You can do this via Ajax and in-place editing, but moving to a different page will give the user a place to update all of her details at once, rather than section by section.

Feeds and syndication give alternative representations of the same content and different URLs. A feed version can actually mean an Atom and an RSS version of the page. Usually, this is a stream of updates to the page content. In terms of modeling, this brings

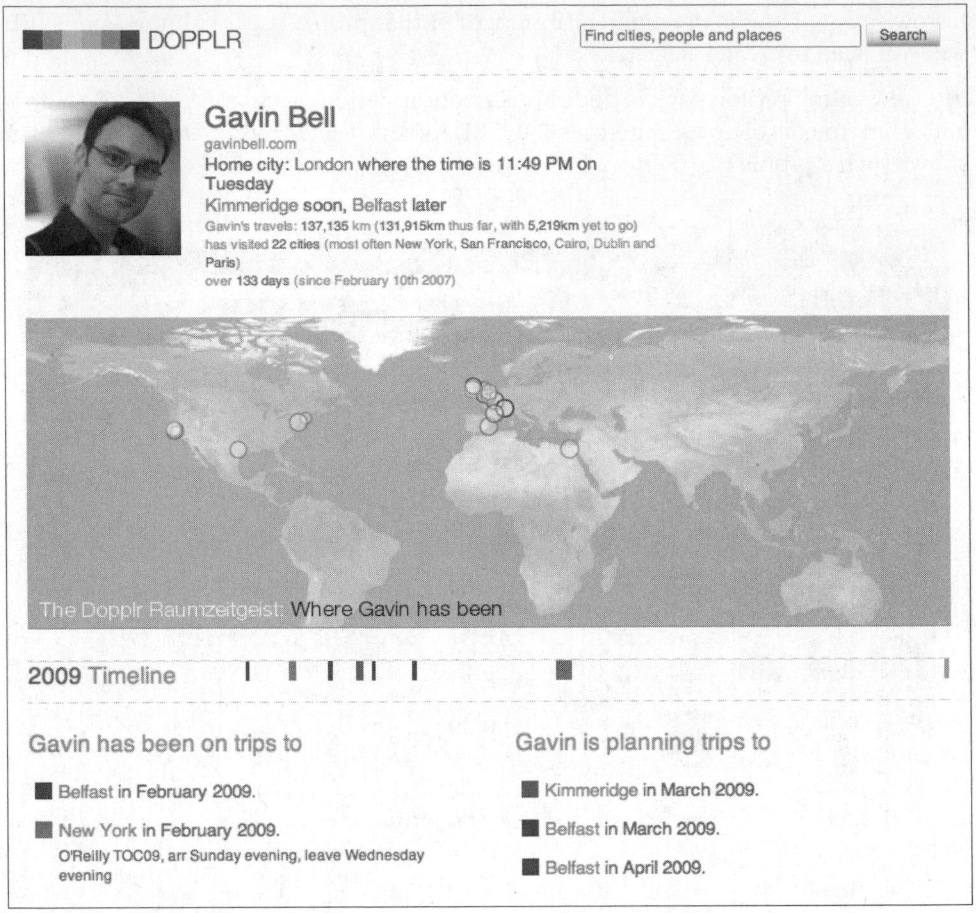

Figure 11-4. Dopplr public profile page

a time perspective into the representation (see "Considering Time Implications" on page 206 for more information). Syndicating content on one web page to place it on another page on the Internet is a common technique. This will give the page a different URL, that of the hosting page, but it is still another representation of the same content from the social application (see Figure 11-5).

Aggregation takes updates to the page content and merges them with other updates to the site. The video example in Figure 11-6 covers this with more appropriate content. Profile pages tend to have slower updates and there is less scope for aggregation.

The mobile version of the profile page can use the same URL, but the page content will be laid out differently on some devices. Deliberately designing for mobile devices might seem less of an issue now that phones such as the iPhone and the Google Android are available, but it is worth examining what information you think will be important in a mobile context. Typically, less information is displayed. Some sites are now producing

Figure 11-5. Syndicated content from Flickr to another website, clearly showing the source and ownership of the images

Figure 11-6. Video clip of my son on Vimeo

a specific mobile version of their sites. For instance, *m.flickr.com*, shown in Figure 11-7, is a great example of what can be done. It shows the version of Flickr as seen on the iPhone. It is a complete reworking of the interface for the site, as suited to a mobile context.

So, after all this discussion on versions of profile pages, it turns out that there are eight versions of this page. However, four of them use the same URL with different behavior that is based on who is viewing the page. The editing version plus the reuse versions in feeds, syndication, and aggregation will have different URLs.

Finally, some of the content on a profile page might be represented as an hCard microformat (*http://microformats.org/wiki/hcard*). An hCard holds business-card-like details about a person. These microformats allow for simple content reuse. They are a simple HTML markup pattern that makes publicly visible content machine-readable. Formatting your content as microformats creates a read-only API on top of your normal page content, for relatively little additional effort (see *http://allinthehead.com/retro/301/ can-your-website-be-your-api*). In the case of a profile page, supporting hCards allows anyone viewing the page to more easily add the person whose profile it is to an address book.

Figure 11-7. m.flickr.com

Exploring a Video Example

A piece of content might be reused and may appear in different contexts. A video is a reasonable example to consider, so let's look at some ways to link to, include, or reference video on a site.

The video itself is accessible through a URL pointing at the file, but the video lacks context on this URL. The URL points at the server farm for media, not the page representing the picture.

The default home for this video is a part of a person's account on the service; in this case, Vimeo. All the metadata about the video is available from this page, which will have a unique URL known as a permalink. The URL should show the connection between the person and the video using a format of *eg/videos/person/video_ID*. Figure 11-7 shows such a video clip.

When a video appears on a tag page, it is the tag that is being represented and the video that is being included. The */videos/tags/tag_word* URL structure by nature does not allow for specific videos to be referenced. Nor is this desirable: a video should have a single URL that points at the original object. Every other instance of the object is by reference to this page.

Many sites have a Featured section. Persistence is hard to maintain in these kinds of URLs. Using */featured* and pagination is a common practice. Adding an additional date-based URL structure alongside the default allows exploration of the featured content by time. For instance, */featured/yyyy/mm/dd* is a reasonable approach.

Videos can be represented within a group page. Usually they will appear on a group page when a user manually adds them, as a paginated listing, as in */group/groupname/videos/*, with subsequent pagination. Note that there will never be a */group/groupname/videos/video_id* URL, as the video belongs to an individual, not the group.

Videos can appear in site search results on the basis of any of the video's metadata. For instance, a video can appear in web search results on the basis of the text associated with the page on which the video is displayed. This matching is based on a more limited set of metadata than the site search offers, but it is useful for bringing additional traffic to your site.

Also, the owner of a video can incorporate the video onto another site, either as a Recent Updates badge or by some form of HTML or JavaScript. In some cases, it may be the plain URL that points at the media file. Alternatively, another person may want to include the video on his site. Often, this is via an HTML and JavaScript code fragment that allows for easy placement on another site.

Incorporation into someone else's site or application via an API is another possibility, but this can lead to complex issues. Ensuring that your API follows the same permissions and rights management that you expect of people using your site is a good idea. Content included by an API call is likely to be arbitrarily based on some search terms. For instance, all pictures of cats should return only images that allow reuse if the call is not originated on your site. Educating your users about the API and what it might mean for content is also important. Allowing the people using your site to set Creative Commons licensing for their content so that media-sharing permissions are clearer is highly recommended. This makes the available options much clearer, from All Rights Reserved to public domain and Creative Commons options (for more information, see *http://creativecommons.org/*).

Searches based on location proximity are quite common now for images and increasingly so for video. GPS-derived latitude and longitude values are often embedded in metadata content coming from phones and cameras. Location metadata deserves a section of its own, so see "Entering the Geoworld" on page 201 for more details.

Lastly, content can appear in response to command-line or IM application commands. This is largely experimental at the moment, but there is a large scope for command-based requests for information. Video is not a good use case for command-based requests, but text-based content is very suitable. While it is possible to return metadata about photos and videos in a text-based interface, we often need to see the actual images to determine whether they are the right ones.

Twitter had an experimental AOL Instant Messenger (AIM) and Google Talk–based interface for its application, which is offline as of this writing. It was a great way of interacting with the site when it was running. Command-line interfaces can run over SMS, email, and IM. Figure 11-8 shows the initiation step for a text interface. Ping.fm generated a unique code for me to send from my AIM account so that it could associate the AIM account with my Ping.fm account. For the right kind of content, it provides a very immediate and responsive interface to your application. Aardvark (*http://vark .com*) is a new entrant into this area, using IM and email as a means of asking questions of your social network. The interaction style feels very natural and conversational. The questions are then sent to people who Aardvark thinks might be able to answer them based on analysis of the words in the questions and tags that people on the service have applied.

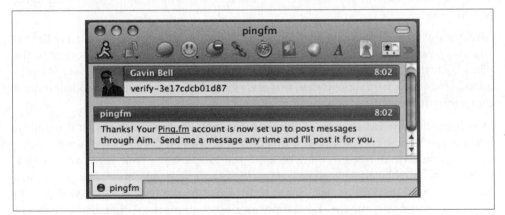

Figure 11-8. Setting up Ping.fm to allow posting from AOL Instant Messaging

Content can appear in a wide variety of contexts, but the overriding need is to ensure that raw files are not separated from their context and metadata. You want people to come back to your site to find more excellent content. Another way to put this: the content and the person should travel together. With social applications, everything is owned by someone.

Thinking that you are making an application only for the Web is a mistake, despite the title of this book. Your content will appear in many different contexts beyond the site you create to host it. The API in particular can be responsible for a huge percentage of the accesses to your content. Flickr is the largest user of its own API. A significant factor in the growth of Twitter was the use of Twitter's API by dozens of clients. Twitter would be a different (smaller) product if all access had to be purely via the website.

Aggregating Data to Create New Content

Chapter 17 goes into more detail on API design, but while we are looking at data modeling, one aspect to keep in mind is the benefits of having people make things with the content on your site. Uncomplicated URIs and well-documented data structures simplify integration with external tools. The graph shown in Figure 11-9 was easy for me to produce from Last.fm. All I needed to supply was my username and a date range, and then the LastGraph application (*http://lastgraph3.aeracode.org/*) produced a chart of the music I listened to while writing the bulk of this book.

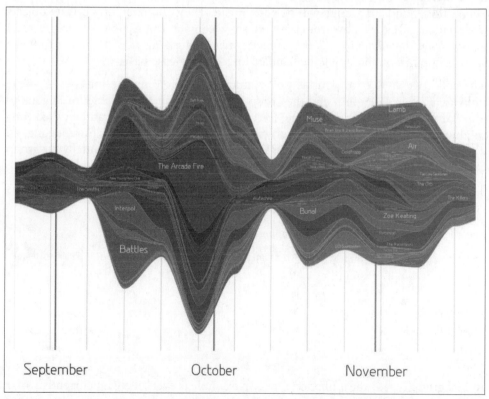

Figure 11-9. LastGraph image showing my listening habits, generated from data stored on Last.fm

This ease of embedding and integration means people are more likely to discover your service and then make it part of their lives. I'll pick up on this topic in Chapter 17, but I wanted to raise it here so that you realize that the data modeling is not just for your own site; you want to make it possible for people to integrate their data on your site with data from other sites to make clever, interesting things.

Exploring Groups

Now that we have looked at the individual and the object, let's look at modeling a larger social entity, the group, discussed earlier in Chapter 9. What is a group? A simple definition is that a group is a collection of individuals on a site who share a common interest.

Personal groups, similar to email or buddy lists in IM clients, are much less common than public groups. Essentially, these are subgroups of a person's contacts from his social network. The user may select the people in his subgroup, or it could be compiled from metadata—for example, all contacts in London. These kinds of groups offer a good mechanism for managing volume on social networks, but more work remains before these kinds of groups will be widespread. They are inherently private objects and so their URLs will flow from how you show contact listings: for instance, */profile/zzgavin/contacts/londonfriends* or */profile/zzgavin/contacts/foodies/*. Deciding to make these groupings public should be handled on a case-by-case basis.

The collective view of a group is pretty much everywhere on the Internet. A single individual creates a group, and the group is usually publicly available for anyone to join. Group names must be unique; for example, only one group can be called *Austin*, but there could be another group called *SXSW-Austin*. In terms of modeling, an obvious approach is to associate the user_id with a group object. Essentially the group becomes a container for the people and conversations associated with it.

There are many ways in which people can join groups and determine who can see its content. Table 11-2 shows some of the possible combinations.

Table 11-2. Group types for social applications

	Permission to join?	Public content?	Participation for non-members?	Public existence?
Private	Yes	No	No	No
Semiprivate	Yes	No	No	Yes
Public (by invitation)	Yes	Yes	No	Yes
Public	No	Yes	Yes	Yes

A final group type is the affiliation type. An example is everyone who currently works for Google on a career-oriented site such as LinkedIn. In this case, the origination of the group comes from automatic processes at LinkedIn, not from an individual creating the group. Membership is based on metadata from the profile of the people who use the site.

With Nature Network, we had two different entities that performed the function of a group: a people-led construct called a *group*, which was primarily for people to show non-employer affiliations, and the more common group with a discussion board, called a *forum*. We were trying to shortcut affiliations, as this is what groups on Nature Network were, in effect, but the structure was not satisfactory. In hindsight, it would have been better to let a critical mass of people arrive before attempting to create organizational or affiliation-based networks. This also shows the importance of language. We were trying to express the concept of a formally organized group of people, such as a company, professional association, or university department, and chose the more general term *group* so as not to dissuade a company or association from joining.

There remains a difference between wanting to be an active member of a community and simply belonging to a group. One of the issues we were trying to resolve was slow versus fast community interaction. The affiliation type of community is generally slower in activity rate than the chattier forum type. An example activity for an affiliation would be publications from the group, which would come from members in the group publishing newspapers, which is a slow activity. A subject-based forum might encourage group members to recommend publications, which is a quicker-paced activity.

Handling Groups and Privacy

Adding groups to your site will complicate every aggregation page on it. Tag pages for a person or sitewide need to be filtered for private group content. Every group page needs to filter for access before showing the content. Despite all of these complications and a dramatic increase in testing requirements, groups are a valuable addition to your site. However, bear in mind the extra code complexity and pages you will be creating by implementing groups.

A group starts with an invitation, which is a complex object. An invitation from one member to another is a relatively straightforward situation. Sending an invite involves the requesting member picking a person from her contacts list and sending him a (potentially personal) invite. To join, the invitee must check his email, click the invitation link, and accept. The invitation link must be keyed to the invited member; it is directed at him, not toward anyone who finds the link or guesses an invite URL. Using a non-sequenced number for the invites helps keep them secure. This process implies a check that the person is logged in. If you are already checking that the invite is addressed to the person, adding private groups involves no additional work, as the invite is correctly being opened by the right person.

If you allow arbitrary invites to be sent to email addresses rather than existing contacts, the flow becomes more complex. In this case, you need to place the invite on hold until the person has completed the sign-up process, and then the invite can be processed. A final complication is if the invite has been sent to someone who is already a member;

he is likely to be logged in and an invite should begin the process to create a new account. It should also offer him a chance to add this new email address to his existing account. Catching this situation would involve noting that the person was already logged in, but was trying to process an invite for another email address. An option to verify the invited email address would work. Then, after verification, he could automatically be taken through the invite process. Allowing multiple email addresses to be associated with a single identity is important, because it allows people to be properly represented on your site.

Adding privacy to your site creates complexity. Every page needs to check who is viewing the page and act appropriately. Privacy has additional issues for scaling, plus your API will now require authentication to access the private content on the site, as well as a range of new methods to deal with checking for privacy. The Guest Pass functionality on Flickr resolves privacy for people who are non-members (see *http://www.flickr.com/ help/guestpass*). It is a special key that unlocks a specific set of photos on an individual's account. For example, a Guest Pass can be sent to grandparents so that they can see pictures of their new grandchild.

Handling Privacy and Scaling Issues

Early in Twitter's history , it offered an interesting feature called "with_others," which allowed people to see the posts from people that someone else followed. For instance, you could drop in on their conversation and see the context of the @replies for those people who you were not following. If everyone has a public account, this is a great feature. Once people start to have private accounts, which they could on Twitter, scaling becomes a serious issue. The impact for Twitter was that every tweet needed to be checked against the person who was viewing, and at 20 tweets per page, that was 20 additional requests. The likelihood that two members will follow the same people is near zero, so every "with_others" page view had to be requested from scratch. Sadly, this feature is no longer part of Twitter. It was reasonable to remove it, however, given the scaling problems that it was having.

This is not the only example of privacy causing scaling issues. Every site that has the potential for private and non-private data to be mixed on the same page suffers from this. This is particularly true with social applications, where the question of privacy changes with every individual. When you add privacy to your application, examine the areas of your site where you aggregate information and assess the impact.

Some readers might expect the bulk of this chapter to be about SQL and data normalization. This is an important area in designing efficient systems that will scale well, but to get the most out of your system, database storage, indexing, and relationships must be quite fluid. Technologies such as *memcached* make a huge difference in how your system can be set up. Chapter 16 will look at some approaches that are appropriate for social software applications. A clean, perfectly normalized database schema is unlikely to occur with social software. Many polymorphic relationships are present, such as the one between a tag, an object, and a person. Multiserver setups are very common, so there is the complexity in maintaining coherency among the write servers, the read servers, and their cache. Issues exist immediately post-write when the read servers and their cache have become invalid. Add in network latency, potentially cross-continent if you are big enough, and this is a real problem. Let's focus on modeling the problem you are building an application for and leave implementation until later.

Making the Most of Metadata

Metadata creates connections between content on your site; it is in your interest to support it. For photography, there is the data held in EXIF (EXchangeable Image File) format, which is embedded inside the data of each digital photo describing the parameters of the photo as taken in the camera. Similarly, for video there is clip length and camera type. Books have publication information such as page count, edition, publisher, and ISBN.

If you treat metadata as a means of enabling organization for your site, it can give additional structure for a little extra work. Every item of metadata you add to the site is a possible link to something else on your site and additional discoverable information for people searching the Web. Place, time, and intrinsic file format information are the most obvious types of information to gather. In addition, there is a wealth of sensor data to come from new devices connecting to the Internet, from Arduino and ZigBee electronics to embedded GPS and even e-book readers. In time there will be a lot more data to associate with individuals.

However, one of the best types of metadata comes from your users, who will add tags to their content, and in some cases will tag other people's content, too. These tags provide a good means of organizing your site. Machine tags are a special type of tag that uses a key/value paring such as name:gavin to make data values explicit. They are useful for getting better value from simple tagging (for more information, see *http://www.flickr.com/groups/api/discuss/72157594497877875/*). Machine tags allow for a key/value pair as a single tag; this means you can store *lat:51.0234* as a single tag and not have to guess which of the numeric values in the four tags "lat, long, 51.0234, 0.003" is the latitude and which is the longitude.

Some of the data you capture will be really messy. Place of work and address information is notorious for being noisy data, as there is a lot of variance in how people relate address information. Getting the place of work and street address for a university department from 10 people at the same department can result in 10 variations on the address, depending on how complete or abbreviation-laden each one is.

Normalization is hard, because you will usually not have a fixed list of places to work with. Auto-complete and auto-suggestion can be effective here. Depending on your country, you might be able to get a postcode or zip code database. Then you can start determining location based on postcode first. If that is not possible, a *type and suggest* interface can work well, where the input from the user is automatically used as search input while she types.

Connecting the Relationship to the Content

Due to the complexity that adding privacy introduces, there are other approaches to the design of social web applications. You can make the default such that all content is private. This might seem like an odd decision for a social application, but several successful applications already do this: for instance, Wesabe in the financial sector, Dopplr for trips, and Fire Eagle for location data.

With this default of everything being hidden comes a rejection of the levels of social relationships in terms of contacts. With Dopplr, there is one level of relationship: either you are sharing trips or you are not. Interestingly, with Dopplr, the direction is outward: you choose to make your trips available to a person; there is no reciprocation by default. It can be summed up as "I want you to know where I am, not express a level of friendship rating between us." This push model is the inverse of the standard "watcher" model that is common in many other social software applications. In this case, privacy is handled outside the application. If you do not want people to know you are taking a quick trip to Paris, don't enter the trip. There is no subdivision in the application. Not every content area can follow this model; it works well for content where there are a small number of significant events (e.g., on Dopplr). For a higher-volume social object such as photography, the push model would be akin to spamming.

Modeling Relationships

A common practice is to import contacts from a variety of sources to seed a new membership on a new application. Importing from the webmail services of Yahoo!, Google, and Microsoft is very popular. Alongside simple importing of an address book file is vCard data. A vCard is very similar to the previously mentioned hCard microformat; email programs can export vCards. Subscribing to another social network is also possible. Within Dopplr, it is possible to subscribe to another social network for weekly updates. These are useful services, as they avoid the pain of identifying the same friendships again and again.

The focus of each social application differs: a social application for wine tasting will have a different audience from one for photography. You might not want a bulk import of contacts, but want to merely offer the ability to add or invite these people to your new service. A related point is that few services support the idea of gradually losing touch with someone. A fair portrayal of normal social existence is that we make friends and over time we make new friends and lose contact with former friends.

You might have added someone on Flickr two to three years ago, but if you have not looked at her photos or interacted with her for some time, should Flickr suggest you are no longer really friends? Flickr could do this subtly, by not showing her updates as often, but this feels disingenuous to your relationship. Tools to reduce connections become more important as the audience on your site grows. *Pruning one's social network* is becoming a popular phrase in some circles, but there is very little software support for this kind of activity. It is possible to "unfollow" people one by one on many services, but there are few bulk pruning tools.

Underlying these social relationships is the idea that a single social network is evolving: the Internet. Each of these social networks connects people who already inhabit this world. Many people have a single profile URL, which they give to new applications. I usually use the same profile URL, *gavinbell.com*; other people might use their blog URL or one from another social network service. Commonly, these sites allow for listing of other services, so I can list Flickr, Dopplr, Upcoming, and Twitter. Each of these will have a link to my profile on those sites. If the XFN (XHTML Friends Network) microformat `rel="me"` attribute is placed in the HTML for these links, this explicitly says that you are the same person at each end.

On *gavinbell.com*, I have the following line of code:

```
<a href="http://flickr.com/" rel="me">flickr</a>
```

The corresponding Flickr profile page has the following code, which I've simplified slightly:

```
<a href="http://gavinbell.com/" rel="me">gavinbell.com</a>
```

Both sites point at one another and both have `rel="me"` on the links. They form part of a composite *me* on the Internet. We need better tools to manage these longer-term relationships, particularly as the time during which we have these kinds of relationships grows into years and we move around the world. The Google Social Graph API (*http://code.google.com/apis/socialgraph/*) is one tool that lets you explore the growing concepts of distributed identity, in particular the use of XFN microformatted links.

Entering the Geoworld

In 2008, location started to become a significant aspect of social networks. There are now commonly available data sets that connect coordinates to place names and postcodes (e.g., *http://geonames.org*) and offer an excellent resource as a free starting point. Geonames.org is a community-generated database of location data and place names. Determining location is now relatively easy in areas of the world where there are Wi-Fi and 3G phone networks.

Skyhook Wireless (*http://skyhookwireless.com*) offers a product called Loki that connects your web browser to its data set offering location. This is the same data set behind the location services for the iPhone. Yahoo! has its WOE data set (*http://developer.yahoo.com/geo/*) upon which two interesting products are based: Fire Eagle and the Places section of Flickr. The World Wide Web Consortium (W3C) is running a new working group to define a secure and privacy-sensitive interface for using client-side location information in location-aware web applications. The current draft is available from *http://www.w3.org/TR/geolocation-API/*, and the main working group page is available at *http://www.w3.org/2008/geolocation/*. Finally, there is an increasing availability of GPS services in everything from phones to cameras.

One of the core services these companies offer is the mapping between the three types of location identifiers. A coordinate system such as latitude and longitude or the GPS WGS84 divides the world into a common grid reference. People generally know a place's name, but few can readily give you its grid reference. Unfortunately, the name of a place has a lot of ambiguity in terms of where the area begins and ends. A *gazetteer*, which is a word list of place names that map to locations, can help determine the exact location of a place.

The third type of location identifier is postcodes (or zip codes), which refer to a precise area of land and, if complete, can be quite accurate. Linking postcodes to one another is a complex process and both the place names and postcodes change over time. Postcodes generally exist to support mail delivery, so if the volume of mail to a certain area increases, the number of postcodes will increase, too. This is the model for the United Kingdom; other countries vary.

Modeling where someone is located generally comprises two values: where they declare as home and where they are now or when the activity associated with the object took place. Frequently, with media such as photographs or video, the person is no longer at that location, but the metadata describes when and where he was when it was captured. Using the Geonames.org library, it is possible to get someone to enter a place name and then produce a list of places for him to choose from. Nature Network uses this approach, as do many other location-based applications. This will give you a home location, which for many simple applications, is enough to allow proximity-based matching.

More complex applications where you care about the movement of the person require a near-real-time location-tracking system, or one that can dynamically report location quickly. In this case, I suggest that rather than trying to create these types of systems from scratch, you should look at Fire Eagle (discussed in the next section), which offers a person-based location management application with excellent privacy controls. The iPhone, Android phone, Nokia phones, and others offer real-time location tracking and proximity matching for mobile use.

Once you have obtained a location, you will at some point want to publish the data and give it a sensible URL. This is a tricky endeavor. A URL such as */country/county* or *state/town* seems entirely reasonable, but when you try to project a country's structure into the application, it becomes immensely complex. Making location URLs consistent, hackable, and meaningful is tricky.‡ Capital cities are often exceptions to the state or county requirement. In the United Kingdom, for instance, there is a "Greater London" construct that deals with the complexity of county and metropolitan area boundaries.

Organizing content by place is an excellent idea, but it is also quite difficult. Simply put, determining whether two things are near each other is pretty straightforward, and determining whether something is within 20 miles of a place is slightly harder. However, determining whether a place is in Texas is really hard. Texas is not a simple shape, and determining whether a place is located there on the basis of the actual state boundary means you need a special type of database that can handle shape files. Flickr released the shape file data set under a public domain license (see *http://code.flickr.com/blog/2009/05/21/flickr-shapefiles-public-dataset-10/*).

Simple approaches to geolocation, such as point and radius, will, however, get you a long way with less effort than using shape files. This approach is good for quick experiments. These are based on latitude and longitude and a fixed distance from a point, giving you 5, 10, or 20 miles from the point defined. If you are dealing with postcodes, you will get the center, known as the *centroid*, of the area the postcode covers.

Flickr generates pretty accurate shape files from the geotagged photos it has had uploaded (*http://code.flickr.com/blog/2008/10/30/the-shape-of-alpha/*). Lots of other companies have done great work in the geocoding area, but Flickr has been making it into a good story, and that is why I used them in Figure 11-10. Using photos does lead to interesting artifacts. Note that the shape file boundary expands out into the bay in front of Houston, but on Flickr, it is still seen as being Texas from the point of view of the photographers.

‡ This pair of blog posts describes the URL design approach for Flickr Places: *http://laughingmeme.org/2007/12/10/flickr-a-place-of-our-own/* and *http://geobloggers.com/2007/11/28/the-overdue-flickr-places-blog-post-part-i-urls/*. They give a great overview of the thinking behind linking people, places, and social objects.

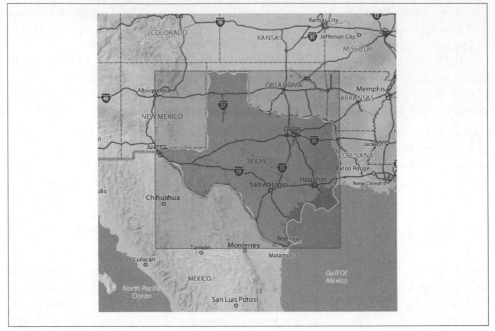

Figure 11-10. The shape file for Texas, as defined by photos contributed to Flickr (http://flickr.com/photos/straup/2971287541/; used with permission)

One caution about geodata is in order: posting a picture of something and associating its location with it makes it easier to find that object in the real world. Earlier in this chapter, I didn't provide the URL for the Pachube images in Figure 11-1, because if you know which URL on Pachube is mine, you can note when we are not using power and therefore are likely to be away from home. I'm not expecting any reader of this book to come to my house and rob me; the point is that geodata connects the real and virtual worlds very concretely. Make sure the geodata you include in your applications explains this connection and has adequate privacy protections around it. The default setting in the Dopplr badge is to show the month of travel only, not the dates, so that unfamiliar visitors to your blog don't know exactly when you will be away, as Figure 11-11 shows. It is possible to show these as exact dates, too, as Figure 11-12 shows.

Figure 11-11. Dopplr badge without dates

Figure 11-12. Dopplr badge with dates

Changing location can still be a hard problem to solve. The notion of home and where you are now is challenging enough to implement. Allowing people to change their home location is essential, but effects of this can be complex. If you are delivering location-based content, do you reset all the previous location information, essentially starting afresh with the new location? The people from the old location will still be friends, but their most local content may no longer be of interest. Assuming that location will change is a good way to plan your product.

Becoming "Brokers of the World"

Fire Eagle, a service from Yahoo!, is what is known as a *location broker*. Fire Eagle knows where its members are in the world at any point. You can tell other applications to ask Fire Eagle where you are and allow these applications to update Fire Eagle. Importantly, Fire Eagle handles the privacy around this information for you. You tell Fire Eagle what each application is allowed to do and to what degree to share information, from the exact location to country level. For more information about Fire Eagle, see the interview with Tom Coates, the product manager for Fire Eagle, at *http://www .ygeoblog.com/blog/2009/02/06/irregular-interviews-1-tom-coates-yahoo-geo-technolo gies-and-fire-eagle/*, where he discusses the creation of the service and some future ideas.

An important distinction with Fire Eagle is how it handles application-level permissions versus user-level permissions within each application. Fire Eagle handles only high-level application permissions. For example, a Facebook application has access to my data. It is then up to the social network to handle who can see this data. This clean separation between data access and data viewability means Fire Eagle never needs to know who your friends are, just where you would like to share your information.

Essentially, Fire Eagle offers a complete location management service. However, you can imagine a similar service for social network invite delegation that accepts invites from previously accepted people. Other examples of brokers exist as well. For instance, Last.fm is almost a music broker tool; it knows lots of detail about its users' tastes, and uses those details to pick music for them. A broker for money management is also possible. In addition, Twitter is becoming an availability or communication broker. Broker services are about automating and managing data on your behalf; they will become increasingly common as more of the material world comes online (see "Information Brokers" on page 253).

Considering Time Implications

Not considering when something was published can have a significant impact on your site. If you doubt this, the story from *Wired* at *http://blog.wired.com/27bstroke6/2008/ 09/six-year-old-st.html* and *The Times* (UK) at *http://technology.timesonline.co.uk/tol/ news/tech_and_web/article4742147.ece* might convince you. It is about a huge United Airlines stock tumble. A Florida newspaper had an automated popular story section that placed a 2002 story about United's bankruptcy proceedings from that year on the home page. This was then picked up by Google's daily visit to the *South Florida Sun Sentinel*'s news home page. The story was undated; Google's news engine apparently automatically assumed a 2008 date. An analyst then picked up the story from Google News and pushed it to Bloomberg, and within minutes the United Airlines stock was tumbling. Its stock price dropped from $12 to $3, then recovered to $11 over the course of the day. See *http://24ways.org/2008/ghosts-on-the-internet* for more.

Errors like this do happen from time to time. The issue, however, is not one of accuracy. We can get very accurate timing, down to milliseconds. Ruby and other languages can even handle calendar reformation in England from the 1500s (see *http://www.ruby-doc .org/core/classes/DateTime.html*). Time is defined by *http://www.w3.org/TR/NOTE-da tetime*, which extends the ISO 8601 definition by mandating the use of a year value. Associating the right date with the right piece of content and action remains the issue.

But what happens when you have more than one possible date? Looking at Flickr, the picture at *http://www.flickr.com/photos/douglascountyhistory/2714248706/in/date taken/* has four date values that can be associated with it. The picture was taken around 1900, scanned in 1992, placed on Flickr on July 29, 2008, and replaced later that day. Which dates should be represented here? This is a difficult question to answer, but currently the date of upload to Flickr is the best date represented in terms of the date URL format, */photos/douglascountyhistory/archives/date-posted/2008/07/29/*, plus some Dublin Core§ RDF (Resource Description Framework). Flickr uses 2008 as the value for this image. It's not accurate, but it's a reasonable compromise for the millions of other images on its site.

In terms of newspapers, the BBC uses the following tag:

```
<meta name="OriginalPublicationDate" content="2008/12/18 18:52:05" />
```

along with somewhat unclear URL formats such as *http://news.bbc.co.uk/1/hi/technol ogy/7787335.stm*. The *Guardian* uses nice, clear URLs such as *http://www.guardian.co .uk/business/2008/dec/18/car-industry-recession*, but it has no marked-up date on the page. The *New York Times* is similar to the *Guardian* with nice URLs such as *http:// www.nytimes.com/2008/12/19/business/19markets.html*, but again no timestamps. All of these papers have all the data available, but it is not displayed in a useful manner.

---

§ Dublin Core is a standardized minimal set of metadata used to describe arbitrary resources (see *http:// dublincore.org/documents/dces/*).

Syndication formats are better at supporting dates. For example, RSS *cyber.law.harvard.edu/rss* uses RFC 822 *tools.ietf.org/html/rfc822* for dates just like email, so dates such as Wed, 17 Dec 2008 12:52:40 GMT are valid, with all the whitespace issues that entails. The Atom syndication format uses the much clearer *tools.ietf.org/html/rfc3339* with timestamps of the form 1996-12-19T16:39:57-08:00. Both syndication formats encourage the use of last-modified timestamps. This is understandable, but it's a pity because the published date is a very useful value. The Atom syndication format supports "published" and mandates "updated" as timestamps; see the spec for Atom at *http://tools.ietf.org/html/rfc4287* for more detail.

The hAtom microformat is a good catchall for much of this kind of work. The embedded nature of the microformat means the date will always be directly associated with the specific piece of content (see *http://microformats.org/wiki/hatom-examples*). A microformat works by nesting semantic information around the actual content to be displayed. The timestamp is included in the metadata for the link. For example:

```
<a href="http://www.ablog.org/2009/posttitle" rel=
    "bookmark" title="posttitle">
<abbr class="published" title=
    "2008-07-10T14:07:00-07:00">July 10th, 2008</abbr>
</a>
```

Making it easier for people searching for your content in the future should be a priority. We've discussed tagging content and geotagging content. Now it is time to get the timestamps right on our content. "How do you know when something happened?" and "how can you find other things that happened at the same time?" are fair questions. A range of tools are available in either hAtom or RDF to specify time accurately alongside content, and they are not hard to implement, particularly as Google now supports microformats and RDFa (*http://www.w3.org/TR/rdfa-syntax/*) from its search product.

Another way to handle date-based information is by generating and processing iCalendar or *.ics* files (see *http://tools.ietf.org/html/rfc2445*). These files are handled well by Apple's iCal, Mozilla's Thunderbird, and Microsoft's Outlook 2007 and onward. They allow event information to be efficiently represented in a calendar instead of as simple plain text. Some applications like elmcity.info, a generic local events application created by John Udell, use these calendars as the primary means of information exchange. Others like Dopplr and Upcoming primarily use them as a means of information output, though Dopplr will subscribe to an iCalendar file as a source.

Looking Beyond the Web

From the iPhone to Bluetooth and sensors making non-desktop information, the Web is changing. An undercurrent in this chapter has been the focus on data modeling over page presentation. Get the data modeling right and you can build the service to support any platform. When Twitter and Flickr were being designed, the iPhone didn't exist, yet via specific HTML templates and applications using their APIs, both services thrive on mobile platforms. Non-desktop platforms will offer new kinds of behaviors or affordances, which will allow your application to do new things with them, but the greatest benefit is being able to work equally well on many devices. The advent of the iPhone in particular is blunting the sharp web-only focus that was present until recently. Building a service with mobile web, SMS, IM, and email interfaces is entirely possible, but optimizing for one of them too early can make it very hard to get your service to work on another platform. FriendFeed allowing inline commenting on content streamed into it meant that it was harder to build an effective mobile version of Friend-Feed. The simple posting style of Twitter suits the multiplatform world better than a threaded commenting model.

A large part of the near future rests on feeds and lifestreaming. RSS is nearly 10 years old, but it took 6 to 7 years to become widely adopted. The lifestreaming meetings that are happening in San Francisco (*http://therealmccrea.com/2009/01/08/live-blogging -from-the-activity-streams-meetup/*) as I write this book illustrate one possible future. Activity streams are an attempt to allow actions that happen on one site to easily appear on another site (for more information, see *http://activitystrea.ms/*).

The Open Web, a combination of OpenID, OAuth, and similar protocols, talks of a related future of coherent identity linked to a single account. The RSS adoption story is relevant here; social applications with networks of relationships and streams of activity are barely five years old (three or less if you look at mainstream adoption). What this will turn into is hard to predict; I'll have had my own punt at it in this book. However, building your tools so that you are flexible in terms of aggregation and your API will mean you can adapt easily. Some form of lifestreaming will become a part of social applications.

Summary

Social software and communities are all about relationships between people, places, and things. To make these relationships work in a social software application, it is important that you understand the activities and implications of the behavior present in the world you are modeling. Privacy has an enormous impact on modeling any social application, and implementing it will change the kinds of decisions you can make.

Picking the right objects, giving them persistent identifiers, and then looking hard at the roles of the individuals using your application will give you a good place to start implementing it. Place, time, and context will add layers of complexity depending on the type of application. Lastly, realizing that the objects in your world will connect and become part of other applications is an important design criterion. Making a useful API and working with brokerage services will help your application in the long run.

CHAPTER 12

Managing Identities

Identity is an essential part of how people interact online. The faith you have in someone's identity will color your interactions with that person. The "Real Name" badge on Amazon, for example, clearly identifies who is writing reviews by using the reviewer's name from her credit card, giving the reviews more credibility. Profile pages for the people on your site are another key component of this. In this chapter, we'll look at the wider issue of identity on the Internet and how this affects your site.

Existing Identities

People will come to your site with an existing identity on the Internet, but all too often we ignore this potential context and set up new identities that they cannot reuse. A simple example is the square avatar, which is a visual representation of a person. Sites usually recommend that people choose an image to use for their avatar. Most people use a photo of themselves, but this is not obligatory; providing emotionless defaults tends to encourage people to add their own image and give a better representation of their identity. Many sites use a 48×48 pixel image, but some use an image that's 60×60, and others use one that's 128×128 pixels. Lately, the trend is for larger avatars. If you request one of the standard sizes, people are more likely to have an image of the right size on hand. Do not force people to find an image of themselves, open an editor, crop the image, and then export it because you think a 160×120 image suits your design. They may just think it is too much effort and not provide an image at all.

 When determining the size of an avatar to use, keep it to a multiple of four. This will make JPEG compression work better, as it is based on groups of 4×4 pixels. Allowing animated GIFs will make for distracting screen furniture and is best avoided.

Forms of Identification

Ideally, it is best to require users to log in with their email addresses, reserving the screen name for use as a public identifier within the application. Thus, there are four significant pieces of information that identify a person, and the recent OpenID system adds a fifth (I'll discuss OpenID later in this chapter). Table 12-1 describes the significant pieces of online identification.

Table 12-1. Online identification information

Data	Description
Email address	Used to identify the person outside your application and for account confirmation and password reset.
Password	The means of proving who someone is once he has confirmed his email access.
Name of person	The real name of the person; usually requested as first and last names. This can be optional; see "Real Names Versus Aliases and Screen Names" below.
Screen name	An internal name for your application, which has two benefits: it avoids using an email address as a public identifier and avoids duplication in terms of real names. Some systems allow this to be set only once, which is probably a good idea. People tend to reuse the same unique handle on multiple sites.
OpenID	A new system offering an identity that will work on multiple sites; URL-based.

Email

Identity online is still fundamentally based on email. Virtually every site will require you to use email to verify your identity. Email is used for password reset links and other forms of account administration. Sadly, it is often abused by spammers, so it is also fragile. The account administration emails that you will send from your site can look like spam in that they have small sections of text and URLs to click on. So, how do you manage to get your emails to your members? It helps if your communications come from clear email addresses that clearly identify your company's name. Encourage your members to add your email address to their address book, so your messages will stay out of their junk bin.

Real Names Versus Aliases and Screen Names

Depending on the type of community you are running, whether people use real names may become an issue for you. In general, I think people displaying their real names is important in many contexts. People should stand by what they believe in. The use of an anonymous screen name derives from message boards and Internet Relay Chat (IRC), a real-time text-based chat service. On social applications where people will have long-term personal relationships, real names are much more common. However, there are many contexts in which people might not want to use their real names. If someone were inquiring about a financial problem or psychological condition, he might want to do this under a pseudonym. Many hobby websites are frequented by people using a pseudonym so that they can chat during their work time, or at least make sure their hobby isn't associated with their professional persona.

Amazon implemented its "Real Name" system to improve the credibility of its reviewing system. Amazon uses the name from a validated credit card as the means of verifying the name of the reviewer. The Nature Network site also encourages the use of real names; if people want to associate published papers with their profile, it gives more validity if the name on the profile matches the name of one of the authors of the paper.

OpenID

The problem of creating a new account for every site and ending up with multiple accounts has been recognized for years. Microsoft's Passport system was an early attempt at solving this problem. OpenID is a new solution that makes the problem of identity management somewhat easier. It allows people to have a single account that they can use with multiple websites. It provides a means of authenticating that someone is who he claims to be, and it simply shows that the person has the right information to verify an account login. OpenID has no means of knowing whether he is actually the person he is claiming to be or he gained the account information illicitly. This makes it a lightweight system, but it offers a similar level of security to the common email account. It is possible to add additional layers of security on top of OpenID.

An OpenID differs from email in that it is URL-based. My OpenID is *http://gavinbell .com/*, the same as my personal domain. I delegated this from another provider, which is something that the OpenID specification supports. I added two lines of code to make this happen. Delegation means that I can pick a domain of my own choosing while using an OpenID service provider to manage the actual protocol exchange. It allows for vanity OpenIDs rather than ones explicitly tied to the service provider.

Developers are likely to use OpenIDs, but most other people will use services from larger providers. This leads to a hurdle for less technically aware audiences, as their understanding of URLs is that they are typically places to visit. This is likely to be a short-term issue, because owning a Facebook page or MySpace account is helping people to realize that URLs can represent people, just like an email address can. However, do assess the level of technical understanding of your members and present OpenID in ways that they will understand. Many services offer an OpenID, so name these services rather than expecting your members to know that they can use their AOL identity as an OpenID.

RSS, OpenID, and OAuth Adoption

The last major shift in how the Web works for the general public was RSS, which early adopters were defining around 2000. It took about five to six years for people to become comfortable with RSS as a technology, mostly because it is now hidden inside tools such as Netvibes, iGoogle, and the Yahoo! start page. This embedding hides the raw acronym-laden technology and packages it in a user-driven manner. You can download a *widget* (a mini application for use on a Mac), put it on your Mac OS X *dashboard* (a desktop application that Apple uses for hosting widgets), and it will show you the weather or stock prices or the latest blog feed for a site. People don't need to know (or care) about the technology.

Now along come two new technologies at once: OpenID and OAuth. These authorization tools will take time to become embedded and hidden away. The beginnings of this are apparent already in systems such as MovableType4. Instead of asking people to use their OpenIDs, MovableType4 asks people to use their AOL ID or their Live-Journal ID, both of which are OpenID providers. It doesn't matter that they are Open-IDs; it is an underlying technology, not the reason to use the ID.

A similar story can be told for OAuth. We do not need to blatantly show the technology to our audiences; we need to explain the purpose and the implications of what we are doing. An architect knows about the load-bearing properties of the glass she is using for a set of steps; the client cares that it is transparent, whereas the architect needs to know the supplier and the technical details. The same story is true for us: we don't need to show off the names of the technologies of everything we use to make our sites.

There are two sides to the OpenID story, and a lot of details, which I'll cover in Chapter 16. Essentially, there are OpenID providers that offer OpenIDs to the general public, much in the same way as there are webmail providers. In fact, there is an increasing overlap in webmail provision and OpenID provision.

Then there are sites on which you can use an OpenID. These used to be called *OpenID consumers*, but now they are known as *relying parties*, to avoid confusion with members of the public, who are also known as consumers. If you are building a new application, it is relatively easy to become a relying party.

OpenID has seen rapid deployment. Both Yahoo! and AOL allow everyone who has an account with them to use it as an OpenID. So, there are hundreds of millions of OpenIDs, but the actual number in use is lower, and the number of relying parties is lower than the number of deployed OpenID providers on the Internet, particularly from established websites. New startups and new projects probably should offer OpenID-based login, but refactoring existing identity systems is slow work. Accepting OpenIDs is a bit more involved if you have a bespoke login system already, as you will need to modify your existing sign-up code. While writing this book in 2008–2009, I saw a gradual increase in the number of companies accepting OpenIDs; uptake seems to be faster than with RSS.

OpenID works well as a replacement for simple email address and password-based login systems. To support systems such as banks or other similar sites, additional security tools such as a secure login token from RSA are needed. *

Tips for Account Registration and Verification

There are many elements to creating a secure account registration system, and it is easy to miss one of the important ones, such as never sending passwords by email. The following list gives a good set of guidelines for creating a secure system:

- Require email verification. Without email verification, you have no proof of identity. Ensuring that your members can give you an email address and then receive an email with a unique code at least proves they have access to that email account.

- Never send a username and password in the same email. This is a common mistake; actually, you should never send passwords via email period. By sending both in the same email, though, you are giving away all of the identity information for a person in one neat package. People really do scan networks for passwords, so avoid sending passwords by email.

- Do not provide a password reminder service; provide a password reset link instead. The person's email address is obviously included in the email, so by including the password in the reminder service, you have given the whole game away.

- Never use email as the public username on your site. This is an invitation to spammers. Email addresses are important and valuable, so respect them. Though they are readily available, unique names, let people pick their own usernames.

- Avoid weak passwords. Help your readers choose a good password. Give them real-time feedback as to how good their password is. You are protecting everyone on the site by ensuring good passwords. Mixed case, numbers and letters, punctuation, and length can all be used. Avoid using words in the dictionary.

- Do not use a maiden name or place of birth as a reminder question. Bank sites use these questions and it muddies the security.

- Allow people to pick their own screen name; there's a better chance they will remember it if they choose it.

- Use at least 256-bit SSL (Secure Sockets Layer) to protect password login to a site.

- Never store an unencrypted password on your site. Instead, store a hash of the password. There is no need for you to ever store an unencrypted password for your users.

- Never tell someone which of the username or password was incorrect when a login fails. If you give separate advice on password and username being incorrect, you

---

* RSA is a company specializing in security products; it helped to define the OpenID standard.

are starting to chip away at the security of the service. If both password and username remain private, a fraudulent person needs to guess both.

The Need for Profile Pages

Once you have a number of people on a site, it is helpful for them to be able to identify one another on a recurring basis. A common way to do this is to give them a profile page. Profile pages have been around for a while; message board software has had the notion of a *user's page* for a long time. However, look at the more distributed world of blogging: people can leave a URL that represents them, but it will not be able to hold a record of their contributions to that blog or to other blogs—it is simply a calling card.

Who Really Exists on the Internet?

There are several levels of identity on the Internet. The one that most technical people are familiar with is the highest level: owning your own domain name that you alone use. To have a domain such as this requires some technical sophistication and a level of investment. You need to purchase a domain name, obtain a hosting account, and often install software. Some systems, such as Tumblr and TypePad, obviate the need for the latter two requirements, but you still need to buy a domain name.

Below this level is sharing a domain, where a friend or relative offers some part of her hosting account. Most small companies fit into this category.

Then there are the various profile pages on the Internet that people also call *home*; for example, a profile page on Flickr.

The last level of identity on the Internet and the most common is the email address, but it is not a domain name. Virtually everyone who accesses the Internet will have an email address, so all identity needs to work at this level.

Occasional use of the Internet on a friend's computer would be an example of someone who was on the Internet but did not have an email address. There are also a surprising number of shared email addresses in use. Difficulty in setting up computers and email software with more than one account makes this issue persist. Family email addresses and spouses who share email addresses are the most common examples of this.

From people owning multiple domains to people sharing email addresses makes for quite a spread of identity types to manage. But focusing your efforts on the email-address-owning side of this balance will cater to more people. Do not expect everyone to have a domain of his own.

Profile Page Anatomy

A profile page on your website that represents a unique person is a real benefit. However, a lot of pressures and requirements dictate how this page should be constructed. The page needs to represent two aspects of the person: his activity on your site in terms of content or of the activity she generates, and her wider existence on the Internet. The profile page also needs to allow other people to add her to social networks that your site supports. Often, more than one type of page is needed to represent a person; essentially *public pages* represent the person on your site and *private pages* offer the person tools or unique views of the site. Many sites separate the activity page from the profile page; for example, Flickr has a profile page and a photos page. However, some sites, such as Facebook, Twitter, and Dopplr, keep the activity and the profile pages together. Chapter 13 explores these activity pages in greater depth.

Let's look at some typical profile pages and see what features are needed to update them. You can ask people to put many types of information on their profile page. Some of the information is simple in structure and some of it is more complex. The complexity of the information on a page is a good guide as to whether to use a new page for data entry. Geographic locations, publications, and affiliations are good examples of complex data which is best entered on a separate form. These types of content often require multiple stages of entry or a confirmation stage. Most other types of content work well on a single, editable form on a profile page. On these types of forms, all the displayed text fields can be made editable and there is a single save control at the base of the form. Table 12-2 shows some of the typical information to include on a profile page, and how you might want to gather or display the information.

Table 12-2. Profile page information

Property	Description
Real name	Allow first and last names to be entered separately so that you can use the first name as a greeting.
Screen name	Make this obvious and visible; it is also likely to be used in the URL for the page, so consider allowing it to be set only once (see Chapter 11 on URLs).
Gender	Consider whether you need this information at all; certainly make it optional to display.
Age	Determine whether you need to gather this information for legal reasons; make it optional to display.
Email	Gather this as part of the sign-up process. It should not be publicly visible, but optionally visible to contacts.
IM (Instant Messenger)	Make this optionally visible; consider making this an active link, AIM, or similar.
Web page	Create a link to the person's web page for her wider identity on the Internet (see Chapter 14 on the XFN microformat).
Bio	Provides a free-form description of what the person does.
Interests	Displays lists of films, music, and authors; very common on websites with a more social focus.
Location	Geographic location is an increasingly important area on the Web (see Chapter 11 on modeling data).
Current affiliation	Useful on job-related sites; displays job title and employer.

Property	Description
Previous affiliation	Allows maintenance of a record of previous affiliations. Can be simply a list of job titles and employers, or can be more complex and include dates of employment.
Recommendations	Provides the possibility for recommendations or endorsements. Control over display of recommendations should reside with the owner of the page.
Publications/examples of work	Offers links to external content that might be appropriate, depending on the site.
Avatar	Provides a visual identity for the person.
Add to network/friend or contact indicator	Allows you to add someone to a viewing network, or allows an indication of the current relationship status. This link should be displayed only in context. Logged-in people can add someone they do not know to their network. For people who are already connected, it should show state.
Link to person's network	Provides a link to the network for the person or a sample of the network; on some sites, such as LinkedIn, display of this is under the control of the profile owner.
Recent content/activity	Shows the recent updates from the person, or a link to the person's content on the site.

Real-World Profile Pages

How detailed you make profile pages for your audience will depend on the depth of engagement and type of relationship you have with them and they expect to have with one another. There is also the degree of familiarity that you expect within social networks. Despite claims to the contrary, the majority of social networks consist of pre-existing groupings of friends. People tend to add people they already know or have met. Among web conference attendees, there is usually a post-conference rush to add interesting people they met at the conference. For a few years, Flickr was the primary focus of this activity. Now it is Twitter and, to some degree, Dopplr.

Pownce

Pownce had a nice approach to profile creation: simple and basic, but also fun. Pownce chose to make gender choice entertaining; rather than the simple defaults of male and female, Pownce gave a wide range of words to choose from, such as *dude*, *gentleman*, and the more prosaic *male*. Pownce was about sharing content with your friends, and this approach to sign up gave character to the site and reflected the air of friendship underlying it. The help provided in the green box alongside the sign-up fields was useful and encouraging, as shown in Figure 12-1. Figure 12-2 shows the profile.

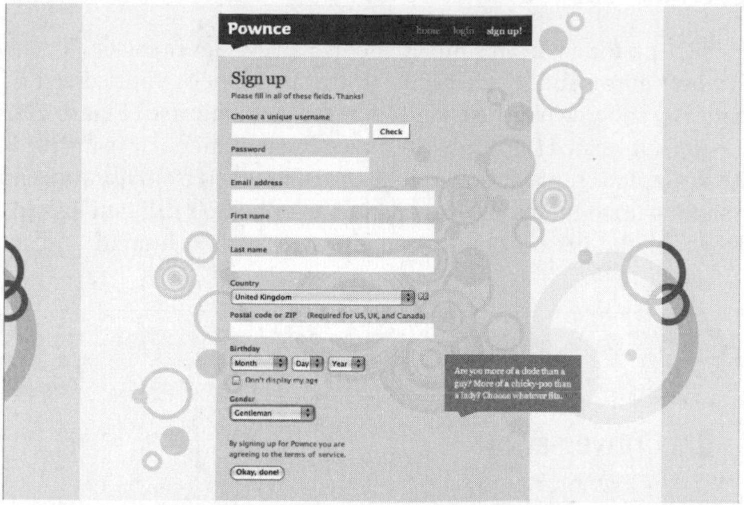

Figure 12-1. Pownce sign-up form: simple, straightforward, and friendly

Figure 12-2. Pownce profile showing updates from contacts

Twitter

The Twitter sign-up form is even simpler and uses a few clever tricks. When you create a profile, Twitter automatically checks for the availability of your screen name (username) and clearly shows what the URL will be for your page (see Figure 12-3). Twitter also tries to stop automated sign-ups, often used by spammers, by using the ReCaptcha service. The ReCaptcha service shows pictures of text taken from library scans and asks the person signing up to enter the words. This is an extremely difficult task to automate, so it ensures that the person completing the sign-up is a human and not another computer.

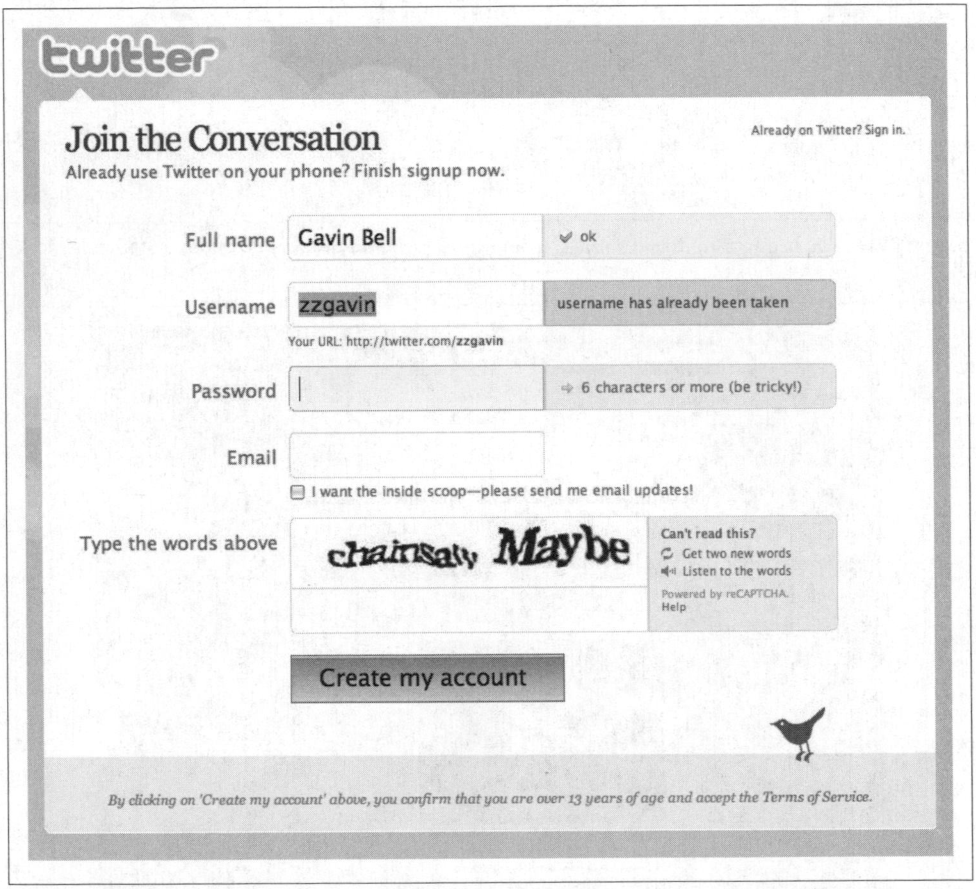

Figure 12-3. Twitter sign-up form, showing profile name checking and the ReCaptcha antispammer measure

The sign-up happens over HTTPS, which is respectful, given that you are supplying an email and your password. Lastly, Twitter gains opt-in mailing list preferences as part of the sign-up. This is a good, simple, minimal profile to capture (see Figure 12-4). It can be extended with a bio and an avatar later.

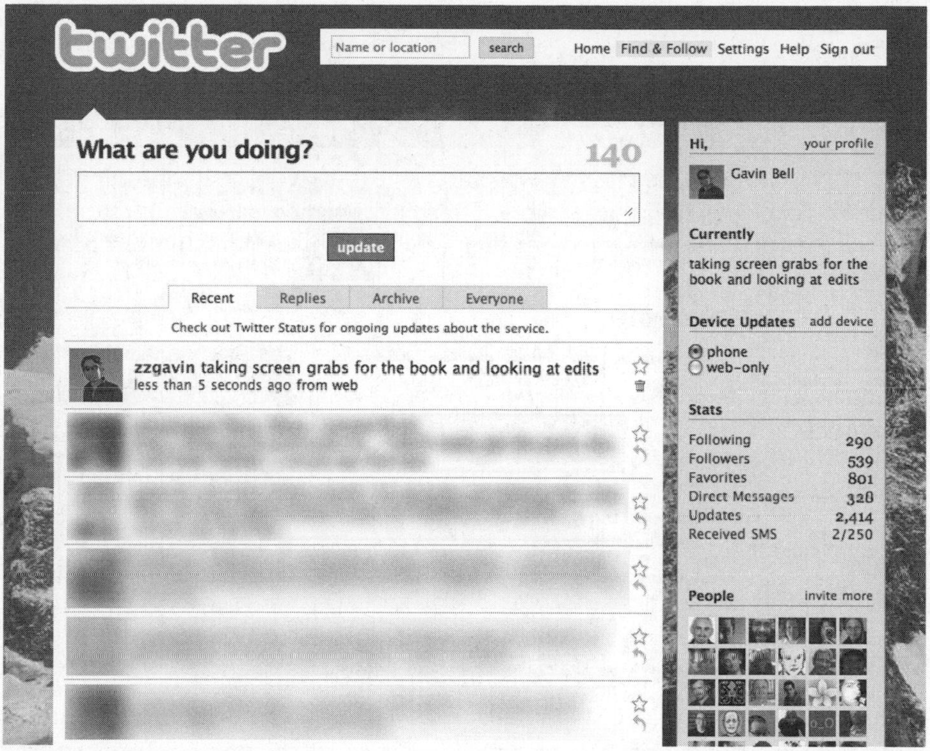

Figure 12-4. Twitter profile

LinkedIn and Nature Network

LinkedIn (Figure 12-5) and Nature Network (Figure 12-6) have formal profile pages. The relationships come from a work or professional context, rather than a purely social context. Completing the full profile on LinkedIn is a lot of work, but LinkedIn lets you fill in a little bit at a time, suggesting the next piece to add and showing the percentage you have completed. This is a clever feature, as full profiles help LinkedIn to connect people, but expecting people to spend an hour or so completing forms in one step is unreasonable. A few minutes here and there over months or years is not noticed.

Traditionally, marketing departments have wanted to get as much information about new sign-ups as possible. This has often resulted in long, detailed sign-up forms. The LinkedIn version is a good example of a gradual registration approach. Creating a system whereby people can sign up as quickly and easily as possible is the starting point. Then you need to create multiple opportunities for them to add information to their profile. The "percentage complete" prompt is a gentle encouragement. Map out all the information you would like to obtain and see where on your application you can capture this information with the least amount of effort on behalf of the new member.

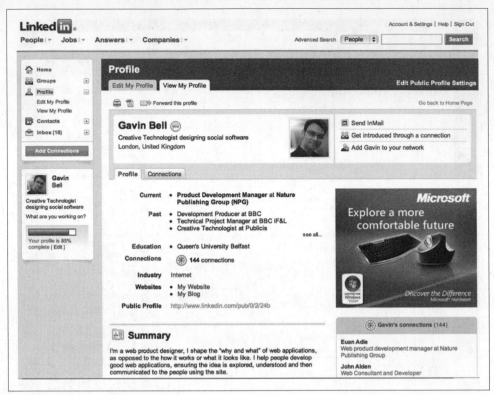

Figure 12-5. The LinkedIn profile, which can be filled in gradually, one element at a time, over months or years

All activity on a site can be valuable data in terms of building up a person's profile. A behavioral tracking system such as this will look at all aspects of a person's interactions across the site, including people, content, and activities.

Nature Network in particular wanted to create a means to find people who are practicing scientists in particular fields so that members could strike up a relationship for collaboration. Hence the decision to allow one-way relationships, adding someone to your network does not automatically add you to their network. This works well for famous scientists, who are not obligated to automatically add every junior researcher who follows them.

Nature Network was keen to allow people to add publications, as these are the lifeblood of practicing scientists. The product also had to take into account other people who may not have a science publication. So, contributing a publication is not a mandatory part of sign-up; limiting Nature Network to only published scientists would create an age restriction of mid-20s, as it takes time to be published in science. It is best to have as few mandatory aspects to your profile as possible.

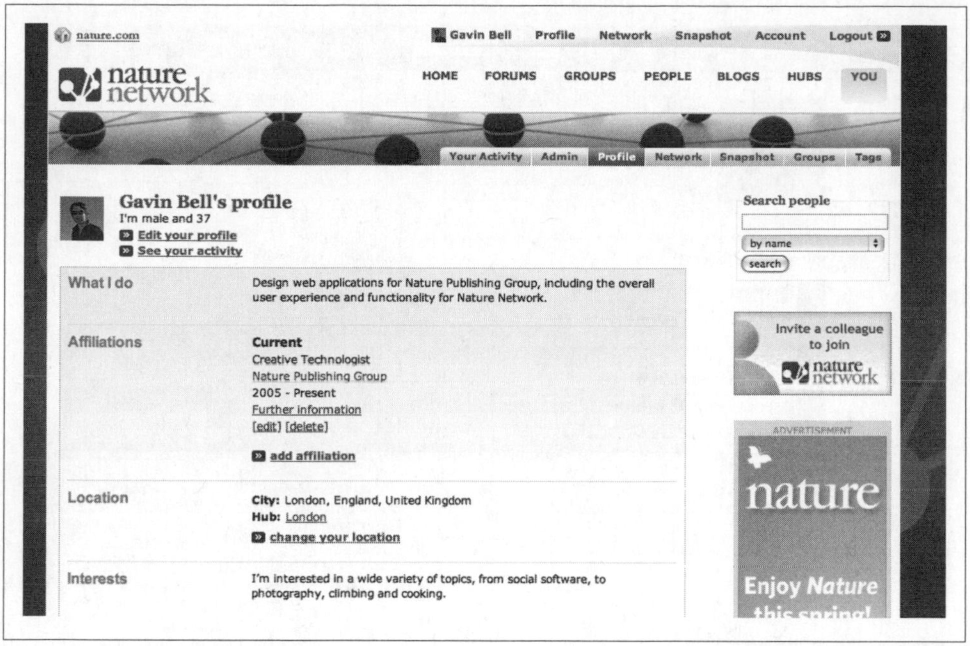

Figure 12-6. The Nature Network profile, which is aimed at scientists showing affiliations and publications

Personal network member maximums

One curious aspect of social networks is the desire of some users to add as many people as possible to their network. They essentially turn it into a game, trying to find the system maximum for the social network. Regardless of what content area you work in, there will be someone who will try to add everyone to his network. If you have a page that naively lists all updates from a person's network for the past 24 hours, this manic follower is going to create unexpected stresses on your infrastructure.

Activity Pages

One of the benefits of having a unique identifier for each person is that you can list all the content or activity that person has created. This is a marked change from traditional message boards. At best, message boards allow for a search on a per-user basis; some show the last few posts made by a person.

Instead, most social networks or applications offer a date-based listing of all content the person has ever contributed to the site. This simple concept evolved from the blogging practice of listing authors' previous entries in reverse chronological order. The dates are not always prominent; sometimes it is a simple list containing entries with dates beside them. Figure 12-7 is an activity page from Last.fm.

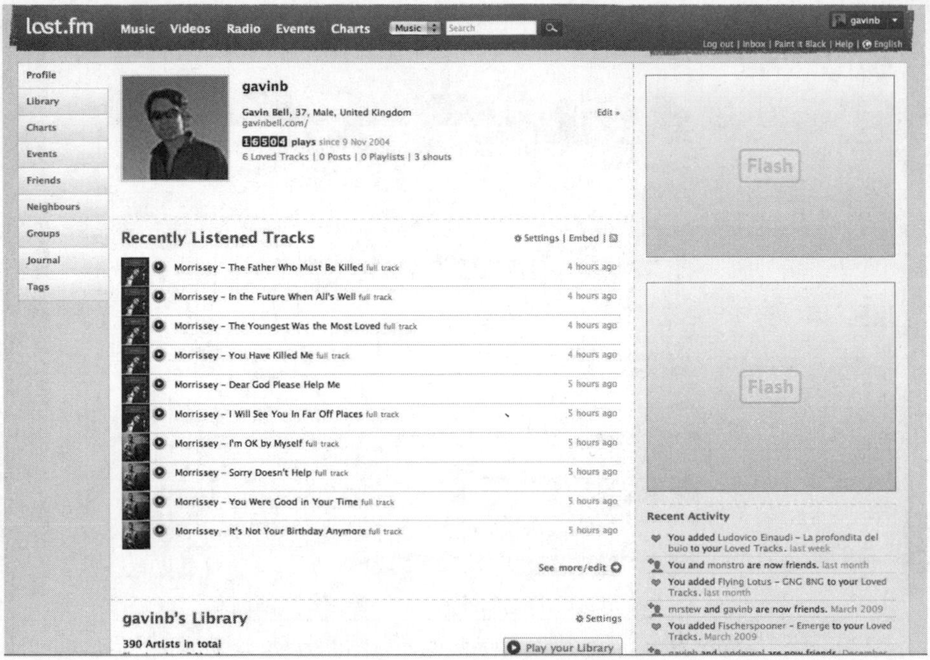

Figure 12-7. Last.fm personal activity page, showing recently listened to music

These pages contain all of the activity for a person under a unique username or screen name; often they have the person's real name on the profile, or referenced in the content. The profile page strongly represents the person; it shows both recent tracks listened to and recent activity in terms of loved tracks and connections with new people. There are separate pages for the person's library of artists, favorite tracks, and friends. Having a composite view as well helps to give a quick sense of the person. The next chapter is all about activity pages.

These profile pages and unique screen names are valuable. People are generally invisible on the Internet until you go looking for them. Over the past few years, there have been countless stories of companies hiring interns to investigate job candidates' presence on the Web. It is important that your audience is aware of what their profile offers their friends and the world.

Invisibility and Privacy

One aspect that most startles people when they start using social networks is the easy access they can give the rest of the world to search for them by name. Certainly a number of Nature Network scientists wondered how they became so visible on a Google search. If you have been using the Internet for a while, you have become accustomed to being visible and highly connected. However, explaining this visibility to your community can be hard. This is particularly a problem if you are already a major publisher and have a strong position on the Internet, as was the case with Nature Network.

It is important to ensure that your community is aware of what happens when they put content online, and that they have a good sense of what content is publicly visible. They will come to you first if they find their content being misused. (In Chapter 17, I will explain a strongly related topic: your API's use of their data.)

Good, clear privacy controls and straightforward communication regarding who can see what content on your site is essential to your community's peace of mind. There are great benefits from aggregation in terms of being able to find and follow people, but this means people and their activities are often publicly visible on the Internet in ways that were not available before. I'll pick up on this in Chapter 14 when I discuss making connections.

A final note on privacy: you should clearly indicate privacy states on your own site. On Twitter, you can see a padlock next to each private tweet. On Flickr, you can see a yellow badge indicating that the image is for friends or family only. However, it is important that this is carried through to remote clients. Twitterific and Tweetie, two popular Twitter clients, do not show the private status of a Twitter message in the same clear manner as the web-based Twitter interface, which can lead to inappropriate reuse of otherwise private content.

There are other ways to make the activity of your community private. Flickr, for instance, provides privacy controls to hide a user from a profile search so that the user can be browsed but not found from the search box. It is also possible to allow people to opt out from having their content indexed by search engines. A norobots directive is added to the HTML meta tags for Flickr's pages, which search engine robots will see and obey by omitting the page from their index.

Giving your community control over their visibility is important. Allowing users to hide themselves entirely is the easiest option. Allowing users more fine-grained control over their presence on the Internet is important, but more complex to implement. Last.fm lets its users hide their real-time track-by-track listing, showing only the aggregate counts of music that a user has listened to. Depending on the application you are creating, it will be appropriate to allow content-level hiding or activity hiding or entire profile hiding. Similarly, making sure your community understands what aspects of their behavior on your site are public is equally important.

Summary

Profile and activity pages are the core of making useful social software. You need to clearly inform your audience what the pages contain and give them tools to manage their representation of themselves on your site. It is their identity and their data, not yours. Make it secure, simple, and safe for people to sign up and easy to access when they forget things such as their username or password. Having unique validated identities means you have real, visible people inhabiting and interacting with one another on your site.

CHAPTER 13

Organizing Your Site for Navigation, Search, and Activity

Social applications create extra challenges for navigation design, as each person using the site has a unique personal view of the content. Within that unique context, you need to help people understand how information is arranged on your site so that they can find relevant people and content.

Three key pages usually vie to be regarded as the home page. These include the personal home page, which usually shows the member's recent updates to the site and those from friends. Then there is the more traditional home page for non-members. (Chapter 18 has several examples of these and discusses which style might be appropriate for your audience.) Finally, some sites need a non-personalized home page that allows the site owners to announce new features and content. The addition of tags and people acting as links also changes the overall navigational structure for a social application.

Once you let people inhabit your site, they need a different type of navigation from the classic lefthand navigation area pointing them to the content section. Your site has become less like a book and is less linear; you have an application that houses content, people, and tools and people move around within this new space in different and very personal ways. It is also not like a shop or product site. People will have a long-term engagement with the site (we hope), whereas shops are focused on making things easy to find and purchase and are very goal-driven in their navigation. As a result, we need to design a social application for social engagement.

This chapter is about letting the people on your site create navigation for themselves, while providing the framework they need to feel comfortable. Toward that end, we'll look at tagging, and we'll explore the differences between site home pages and personal home pages and how you can create them. Lastly, we'll explore the different kinds of activity pages you need to create to let your audience follow the interactions that are pertinent to them.

Understanding In-Page Navigation

Why does standard, hierarchical navigation fail on social sites? Standard lefthand navigation derives largely from the table of contents in a book or brochure, so when all the items of content are known in advance, it works well. However, when the structure of a site is based on less well-ordered information or the relevant information is personal to an individual, context becomes more important.

The key distinction is between content and activity. The kinds of community-oriented sites you are building are much more focused around activity, so the common lefthand navigation bar—which offers passive signposting—disappears and a more verb-oriented navigation takes over, reflecting the actions performed by the people on your site.

A catalog-based site, such as a product-oriented site for, say, bikes, will have a product page and some support pages. There might be 20 to 30 different types of bikes for sale, but there is an order and simplicity to the presentation. You can scale this approach up to a bigger shop, such as a department store or an online retailer such as Amazon, and it still hangs together. There is internal consistency in the information, even if there are millions of the product items.

However, if you move over to something such as Vox or Flickr, product-driven consistency evaporates. There are different kinds of content on these sites, and there are thousands of items of content at a time, or billions in the case of Flickr. In these cases, catalog approaches break down; there are just far too many items to enumerate or classify in one space. Therefore, classification becomes a pertinent issue with community-generated content. If you tried to go with a single ordering or taxonomy, who gets to define it? The content belongs to your audience, so can you realistically impose order on their content? Probably not; even if most of them would agree to a single taxonomy, it would be difficult to manage and evolve. Handling the issue of millions of items is more difficult on a site such as Flickr, as the object is always the same. There are billions of photos on Flickr; on Amazon, there are millions of books or CDs, but they all come with clear associated metadata, such as author or artist name.

Tagging Content

As we talked about briefly in the sidebar "Tags Create Navigation" on page 147, tagging is another approach to classifying content. Thomas Vander Wal coined the term *folksonomy* (*http://www.vanderwal.net/folksonomy.html*) to describe the kinds of emergent classification schemes social networks employ, by allowing freeform tags on content. The term comes from a concatenation of *folk* and *taxonomy*; it is loosely defined as a people-generated taxonomy. In a taxonomy, such as the Dewey Decimal System for library classification, there is a formal, fixed set of keywords in categories, which can evolve slowly over time. In a folksonomy, the keywords are known as tags, and there is no overt classification. Meaning emerges simply from frequency of usage. The items tagged "swan" define the term by being tagged. They tend to evolve more rapidly than a taxonomy, but they are also messy. The items tagged "turkey" will include both birds and the country.

A tag is just a word on an item of content. The word means something to the person who is labeling it. People apply tags largely for their own benefit to allow them to retrieve their content later. Other people's tags will hopefully translate well for you, but you might not understand the context. For instance, the tag "red" can mean very different things on Cork'd (a site about wine) and Flickr. The same word can also encompass multiple meanings on the same site, too; the turkey example from earlier is a good one.

Most often, though, tags work well, as they solve several problems. They provide labels for content, which then offers a new means of navigation and search. They devolve the classification issue to the person best suited for labeling the content: the person who created it. Finally, the labels can be associated with each other to derive collective meaning about people, groups, and places (see Figure 13-1).

Figure 13-1. Flickr "kitten" tag

The Flickr tag page in Figure 13-1 shows the public pictures on Flickr that relate to the word *kitten*. By default, they are ordered by most recent, but they can also be sorted by interestingness, as discussed in Chapter 10. It is possible to see related terms so that you can easily explore a subject area. Using tools such as this, it is easy to spend a long time looking at content on Flickr, without having to go to a formal home page or think about a hierarchy.

Finally, it is possible to explore clusters of tags related to the word *turkey*, as shown in Figure 13-2. These are automatically generated groupings of tags based on frequency

Figure 13-2. Flickr "turkey" tag cluster

of usage. Using these clusters, it is possible to separate pictures of Turkey the country from turkey the type of bird.

Another significant difference between people-led sites and content-led sites is the amount of context-led navigation on them. The tags provide in-page navigation to discover related content. If I tag something "tiger," then (depending on the site design) clicking on the tag will lead you to more of my things tagged "tiger" or more of everyone's things tagged "tiger." Often, both are available, as shown in Figure 13-3. Providing navigation with a sitewide scope and a local scope is difficult but important to achieve. If you click on a tag, e.g., "tiger" in Figure 13-3, you will be shown other tiger pictures that person has taken. Clicking on the globe icon takes you to pictures by everyone with that tag, as the pop-up label explains.

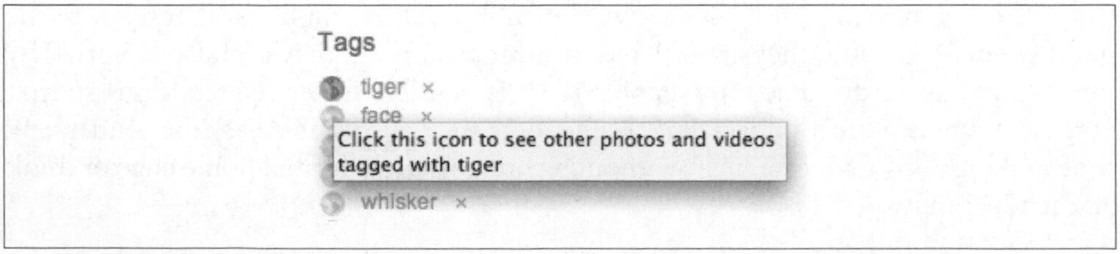

> Tags
>
> 🌐 tiger ×
> 🌐 face ×
> ┌───┐
> │ Click this icon to see other photos and videos │
> │ tagged with tiger   │
> └───┘
> 🌐 whisker ×

Figure 13-3. Flickr tag navigation

In addition to tags, there are the links to someone's profile page, her recent content, and, potentially, location-related information. Combined, these offer a wealth of possibilities for context-based navigation. This kind of rich context is impossible to represent in a static hierarchical navigation system. In addition, you can provide jumping-off points such as personal profiles, tag pages, and geographic location pages.

Tags and other contextual information split up the amorphous mass of content into reasonably meaningful chunks, but what about the people? Providing a means for people to find one another and then to keep track of the content they create engenders two separate problems to solve. The first one is a search problem, and the second one is much more complex, as we will see later. There is a third related problem that is simple to state—provide the ability to search the content—but is hard to implement well. Chapter 16 looks at search for content.

Searching for People

Searching for people is a problem that seems easy to solve, but when you have lots of people on your site, it scales badly; for instance, Twitter removed people search capability for months because it had such a negative impact on site performance. So, it can be tricky to get right. The basics are deciding on what you will let people search and who you will let search. First name and last name are obvious candidates on what to search, plus the screen name or username people have chosen. There is an underlying privacy issue involved with searches, however—do you let people search by email address? Searching by email domain is a bad idea, because it can give too much information regarding a company's participation on an application, or it can allow speculative search for people. If you decide to allow searching by email address, you should allow only whole email addresses as the search term: searching for all the "@gmail" addresses on a site might allow for email address harvesting, which you want to avoid. Email addresses should never be returned as search results. That makes it far too easy for spammers to gather them.

A second factor concerns what you show in terms of search results. What information on a person's profile page does the person regard as private (an issue we looked at in Chapter 12)? What sort of information you host for people will have a bearing on the answer to that question. Figures 13-4 through 13-7 show screen shots of people search results on Flickr, Last.fm, and Facebook. The most sensitive information is location (see Figure 13-7), which Dopplr manages in a discreet manner, showing next location but not time frame.

Flickr shows basic account statistics on the search results page, but shows all public information on the person's photo and profile pages. You can make photos private on Flickr, so you are not giving everything away. Some of the profile elements can have individual settings, too; email addresses can be set to friends only, for example.

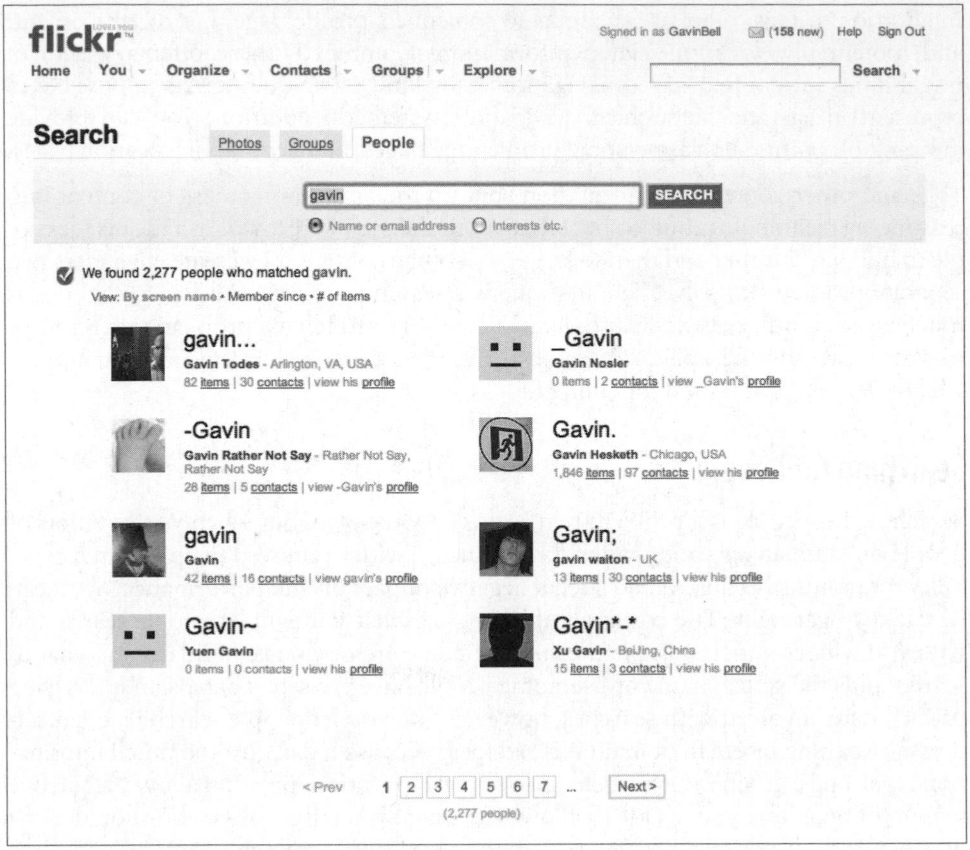

Figure 13-4. Flickr search results for "Gavin"

Facebook allows people to decide how much of their profile information should be available in a public search, which gives them some degree of privacy from inquisitive employers and old friends.

Last.fm is probably the most public of the sites. On this site, your music listening habits are publicly available to anyone who wants to look, though you can hide the real-time display of what you are listening to.

Dopplr provides a simple list of matching people's names and their main country of residence. One of the underlying beliefs of the Dopplr developers is that you should know the people you are intending to make a connection with, so providing a minimal public profile suits the approach of the site.

LinkedIn actually charges for its people search feature; on LinkedIn, you can find many people, but only if you pay for an account can you contact someone whom you do not know via a specific internal email for LinkedIn, called *InMail*. This account also provides more detailed results and more means to search for people.

Figure 13-5. Facebook search results for "Gavin"

If the information on your site is sensitive, you will want to have a slightly guarded approach to search capability, even going as far as making people register before they can search on the site. Deciding what profile elements are public and which you allow member control over is an important task. A search feature helps people find one another, which is good. However, you want to ensure that the people who are found in the search results are aware of and happy with the level of disclosure about themselves that your site allows. Good communication with your members is especially important if you change the scope of privacy on your search tools.

Connecting People Through Content

Profile pages can act as connectors to other content in that reading a comment or seeing an image in a search and clicking on the link for the person who left the comment or image will usually take you to that person's profile page. Sometimes it will take you to the person's main content or update page (Flickr and Twitter do this). Regardless, you

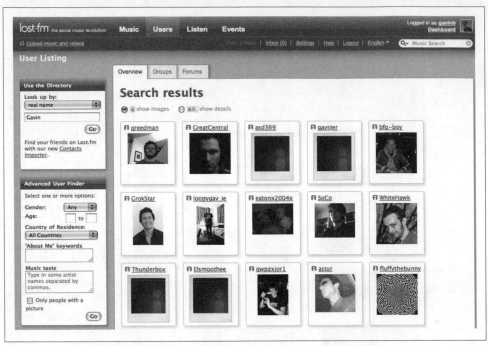

Figure 13-6. Last.fm search results for "Gavin"

have moved from the objects you were looking at to focus on a new person. Choosing something on the person's profile will take you in a related, but perhaps different, direction. This kind of pivot through a social application is quite common. In this way, content can be seen as a means of connecting people.

Each person's update page shows his recent updates on the system, be it places visited, comments made, or songs listened to. Update pages act as dedicated search results for individual people.

Providing Activity Pages

Social applications use three core types of pages to define people:

Profile page
> This is often a static page that represents a person. It may abstract some content updates from the update page (discussed next), or it may simply be a biography page. Blogger and Flickr have static profile pages. Last.fm has a mixed page type.

Update page
> This shows a person's most recently contributed content. Virtually every site has one of these pages. They form a primary focal point for their social objects. If the

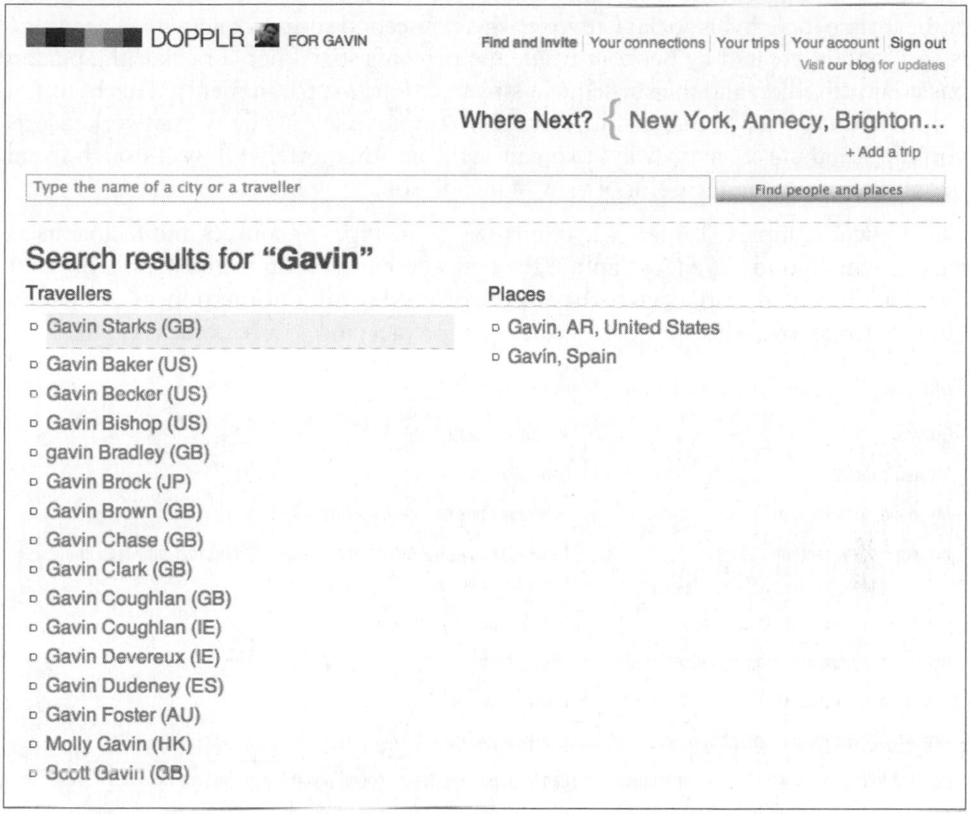

Figure 13-7. Dopplr search results for "Gavin"

people on your site generate a series of social objects, this is the page where these objects are gathered.

Activity page

This tracks the contributions of others so that you can get a sense of what is happening on the social application. Dopplr's Journal page and Flickr's Activity page are extensions of this concept. Flickr's Your Contacts page is a good example of pure updates from other pages. Some applications do not readily support this kind of page. For example, a "collected music your friends have listened to" page for Last.fm would be hard to make contextually meaningful.

The profile and update pages are pretty straightforward in terms of how they operate. Activity pages, however, are unique to each person, and probably have the most variance in terms of their form and behavior. They allow the people on your site to keep tabs on one another. A first attempt to create an activity page would lead to a simple page showing the recent activity from anyone the person has marked as a contact. This is where many sites start.

However, what about the comments on content that a person has created that do not come from people in his social network? This is a second source of activity. Then there is the content created by people outside the person's social network that the person has commented on and the subsequent stream of follow-up comments. This becomes a third source. Finally, there is the content from everyone outside the network. So, as you can see, there are many ways to organize the information that flows through social networks, even from the point of view of one person.

This topic is complex. Table 13-1 summarizes some types of sources and recipients as well as which kinds of pages capture the new content flowing to the people on your site. There are many variations to the norm in displaying this information, as companies attempt to discover the right balance between privacy, disclosure, and server load.

Table 13-1. Degrees of privacy in site content sources

Source	Public or private
My new content	Generally public
My friends' new content	Generally a private view for an individual
Everyone's new content	Generally public, but often not available as a bulk real-time feed, though this is an area of growth
Comments on my content	Generally private, but not on blogs
Replies to my comments on my friends' content	Generally private
Favorite activity by me	Often private; public on Flickr
Favorite activity on my content by others	Generally private
Content from groups of which I'm a member	Can be public or private depending on the group type
Responses to group activities	Unique private feed of public content

Merging some of these content types together into a composite page type is becoming more popular. Following an approach where each content type gets a page of its own can lead to a very unclear organization with many pages each having irregular updates. Consolidating all the external activity into a single page makes the page easier for other members to check. Aggregated activity pages can end up with a large amount of rapidly changing information on them. Tools to filter and control them are important; this is covered later in the chapter.

Determining Activity Page Content

Once you have mapped out the potential pages you want to build, then you need to determine how to limit the amount of content that appears on the page. No one wants to see all comments ever left for her by people in her network. The choice is basically between content posted during a specific time frame or a maximum number of entries per page. I encourage you to consider time frames. I think they are easier for most people to relate to and they do a better job of handling the uneven rate at which events can happen, such as sudden flurries of activity.

Let's look at a possible scenario.

Joe goes on holiday for a week and comes back. His network has been really productive and there are hundreds of new things for him to look at. The network activity page for Joe should not show everything. Pagination is a sensible option for handling these update pages, allowing 50 to a page and any additional updates on further pages. However, this is still a big database query to run and cache, so it is worth exploring a bit more.

Every person in Joe's network will be generating new items at varying rates, all of which will be new for Joe since his last visit. You do not want to mark every item in the database as seen or not seen by each person, though a last-viewed timestamp is useful. So, how do you manage to show Joe only the important new stuff? Curtailing the volume by use of pagination makes sense, but it does not respect the level of importance of the new items. There are different solutions to this problem, depending on the rate of content generation within your community, and all of them are based on some form of filtering. It is difficult to second-guess exactly what Joe would think is interesting if he had time to look at every update, so we need to rely on some heuristics. The following examples are how some real-world sites have addressed the issue of new content updates.

LinkedIn has a slow rate of new content, so it shows everything. Each update is also of high value; it is a connection between people you know or a job change for someone to whom you are connected.

Flickr has a rapid rate of new pictures arriving, so it gives a range of options to stem the tide. You can choose to see five at a time from a person, or just one at a time. You can also select from friends only or from friends and contacts. If someone has taken a lot of pictures, looking at his photo page will show you all the images that he has taken, organized in reverse chronological order. This works well for Flickr, because people might upload more than 100 pictures at a time. In terms of comments, Flickr combines favorites, tagging, and replies onto one page, but it collapses the replies to the last 10 on any photo.

Nature Network shows all activity from everyone in your network, but limits the view to the previous two weeks. This design decision was based on community scale and relative importance of the content. The Nature Network community is smaller than the Flickr, LinkedIn, and Facebook communities, so it can still show everything. Also, the updates are more likely to have a bearing on what someone does in her career, because the discussion is about science. Over time, Nature Network might give options to drop some of the content types, such as replies to a forum topic, but it would retain published papers, therefore keeping the higher-value content visible. Collapsing multiple replies into threads is a possibility, such as listing an update as "Simon Collins and 27 others replied to this topic." All the detailed replies are not displayed, so other information can be seen.

Facebook takes an interesting approach. On Facebook, you can vary the kinds of content you get in its news feed from personal updates to group memberships and new photos. However, you get only a sample of the activity from your friends. This sampling allows for the social grace of *plausible deniability*: just because you updated your Facebook page doesn't mean all your friends will see it. One way to describe Facebook's approach is *lossy*, in that you do not get every update from every friend.

The Facebook feed is not the same as a direct communication, and therefore the feed can be easily overlooked (sometimes deliberately). This can be helpful in tightly knit social spaces, as it avoids the small-town feeling that 100% communication would promote. The updates are there if you wish to visit each person's page, allowing you to see exactly what a close friend is up to, if you want to. In most social relationships, this flexibility is sensible. This sampling of updates also scales well, as it does not retrieve every single update. Facebook relaunched with a real-time update interface in spring 2009, taking the approach that Twitter has taken, but this results in high volumes of updates.

Filtering Activity Lists and the Past

Filtering content based on strength of relationship, usually denoted by a friend or contact, is common and effective, but many sites now offer only a single level of relationship. More advanced approaches can be based on coincidence of mutual friends—for example, two or three friends commenting on the same picture is arguably more interesting than one friend posting an image. However, these kinds of analysis can become expensive to generate when you have a large number of people, large contact lists, and/or high rates of new content production.

Another aspect to think about is the previous kinds of activity streams. Three months ago is a reasonable time frame to consider. Should the default view be the same as the view of today or yesterday? Filtering this data so that the significant events from the person's account and from her friends show up rather than every single event seems to be a reasonable approach. You also need to decide how far back you will show activity. Will you show activity from the launch of your site until the present day, or back to some limit determined by the size of the cache you are willing to maintain?

Maintaining 100% of anything is a big commitment. You will need to find a balance in terms of value to your community and cost to your company. Twitter search goes back only a few months, and the stream of your updates does not go back to the start of your involvement on the site. At the time of this writing, about 75% (3,200–4,200) of my updates are visible for me (which equates to about 20 months' worth of my updates). Flickr can show all your pictures from day one on your photostream. The relaunched home page (in September 2008) shows all the social interaction you participated in right back to the beginning of your involvement on the site. These kinds of 100% delivery promises are substantial in terms of servers and engineering. Promising to deliver the last 50 of something is quite a different offer from promising users everything they have ever done on a site. Kellan Elliot-McCrea, a Flickr engineer, gives a good explanation of the technical implications of implementing activity feeds at *http://laugh ingmeme.org/2009/03/18/streams-affordances-facebook-and-rounding-errors/*.

Using Replies to Create Conversations

Getting direct feedback on your content is satisfying. Having someone leave comments for you can brighten your day. Similarly, if you leave a comment on someone else's content it is beneficial to be able to see whether he or someone else has responded to your comment. Tracking these two streams of replies on your content and replies to your comments can happen on different pages. The streams are focused on different original sources of content, one being "your stuff" and the other "their stuff," so keeping them separate can make the interface work and language used to describe the func-tionality easier.

Some sites keep these two reply types on separate pages, while others mix them together as a single conversation. Flickr changed from separate pages to a unified activity page in September 2008. The Webmonkey article at *http://www.webmonkey.com/blog/Flickr _Home_Page_Update_Exposes__Hidden__Social_Features* gives a good overview of the changes.

In the remainder of this section, we'll look at Flickr (Figure 13-8), Nature Network (Figure 13-9), and Dopplr (Figure 13-10) as examples of how to manage these social relationships. Not just comments fall onto these pages. Rather, any sort of interaction will appear. In the case of Flickr, this includes comments, tags, and favorites for your photos. For Nature Network, it includes replies to the topics you raised on the site. Dopplr consolidates activity onto a journal page for documenting social interactions around traveling. The Dopplr journal page works because the rate of activity on the site is slow enough; people generally travel only a couple of times per month, at most.

Flickr includes the replies to your comments on other people's photo pages. Also, you can track responses to your comments. Allowing this view of comments encourages conversation around the photos, though you can also mute updates for photos for which you are no longer interested in seeing additional comments. Certainly, I have seen many conversations continued in this manner. It will also show favorites marked on your photos and tags other people applied to your photos. There is no separate page for tags or favorites from others; they are integrated into this single view.

On Nature Network, the two key response-led pages are the replies page that lists subsequent responses on any forum post on which you have previously left a comment, and a separate page that lists replies to any topic that you initiated on a forum. Keeping these pages separate made sense when considering the degree of involvement for the person viewing the page, in that if you initiate a topic, you have a different role than if

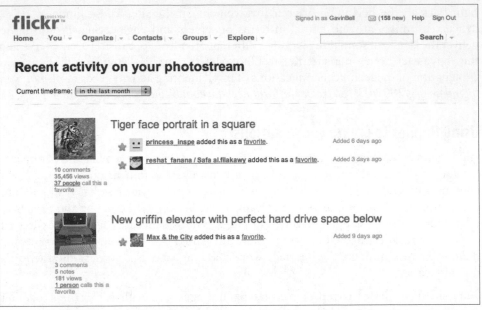

Figure 13-8. Flickr activity page, showing the version with activity for the owner of the account only

you make a comment on an existing topic. Nature Network is unlike the other two examples in that it comprises several different types of content, from events to message boards. It is an example of federated social software, whereby a series of applications integrate with a social network core: there is an events application, blogging provided by Movable Type, and the message board software.

The Dopplr travel journal page comprises a list of relevant activity for you on the site. Dopplr doesn't support conversations, but it shows *coincidences*, which are times when two or more people who you know are in the same place. This allows you to broker introductions. The journal page will also show you new people who have shared travel details with you.

Twitter used to have a "with others" page that was a combined activity page showing the activity from the people you follow, which was publicly available to anyone who looked at the page. (People who are hiding their activity are not shown on this view. The page showed only the Twitter messages from people with public profiles and those who you had permission to follow.) This "with others" page is a tricky concept to follow. Two people on Twitter will follow a different set of people. Being able to see the messages that another person is reading can help you to understand a comment made in reference to a message from someone you do not follow. However, there is a privacy concern here, as not everyone who the other person is following will have allowed you to see her messages on Twitter.

This sharing of output from other people on your activity page allows your followers to dip into the conversation you were seeing and understand the context of one of your

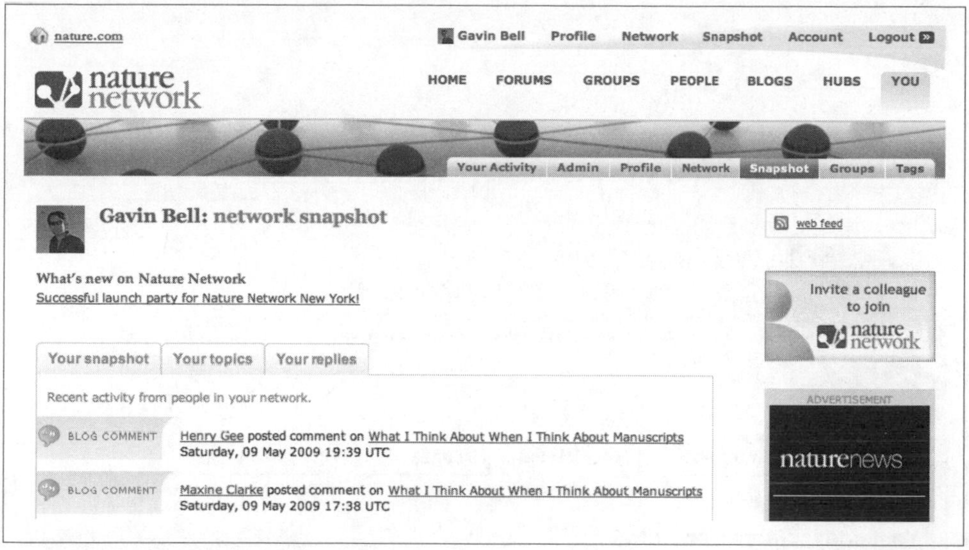

Figure 13-9. Nature Network snapshot page

comments. This collection of tweets is unique to every person and will show you private tweets from the people who you follow, as each view of these communities is unique, too. However, it is a great way to follow up on the conversations that other people are engaged in. (Note that as of this writing, this feature has been removed to help resolve some of the performance issues associated with generating all of these unique views. We will look at the caching and scaling issues these kinds of features generate in Chapter 16.)

Activity pages allow a person to see what her friends are doing on the site, what other people are saying about her stuff, and what people are saying to them via replies. Separating out these three different strands of content gives a person a choice in how she interacts with the site. The activity page will be a difficult page to get right, as there are many ways to implement it. You should expect to revisit this page every few months as your site grows and your community behavior changes.

Allowing for Content Initiation Versus Content Follow-Up

You can draw a distinction between the initiation of new content and a response to existing content. During the life of your social application, the relative value of these two activities will vary. In an application's early deployment, it is important to bring a group of people together; later it can be important to provide new content in which to engage these groups. Response-based content is important, but if the large number of responses drowns out the smaller amount of new content, it can be difficult for people to expand the scope of the site. A high volume of content from a small group of friends and early adopters can seem like a success, but it is important to continually bring in

Figure 13-10. Dopplr journal page, with some content made anonymous

and encourage new people. Conversely, too much new content can make the site feel empty and quiet. Retaining a flexible approach to feature development and the ability to change will make it easier to find the right balance.

Providing for Email Updates

Allowing people to get updates via email from others they know on your site as well as from your company is an important feature. The most important aspect of this is to ensure that the recipient of the email has complete and obvious control over whether she is sent that email. This is not only a privacy matter, but also a matter of simply being respectful of people's time. No one wants to deal with reading and deleting unwanted messages. The legal position in your country may also restrict your ability to send email to individuals. Remembering that a person's email address is not your property and that you do not have the right to send email to that address will keep you on the right side of the law.

Email updates should be meaningful, appropriate, and timely. That's simple to say, but tough to implement well. On any site there are several types of content you will want to send by email, from new content posted on the site, to replies to items, to the inevitable follower requests. Some of these updates should be sent in near-real time, while others can be sent as daily or weekly summaries. Often, these updates are all sent in real time, because it is the easiest case to write software to support. The single daily journal type of update used by Dopplr and FriendFeed works well, though the Friend-Feed update email can become huge. The daily journal update can still be preferable to receiving everything hourly or in real time.

A practice that is not helpful, but unfortunately is very widespread, is the "X sent you a message, click here to see it" pattern. The intention in this case is that the reader will click the link in the email to see the update, which will bring the reader back onto the site and he will then explore the rest of the site. I believe this irritates more people than it brings back to the site. If you are using this pattern, consider how you would react to a voicemail from me saying, "Hi, give me a call, thanks Gavin," rather than a real message. Given the current shifts to tools such as the iPhone and email on mobile devices, it is better to send the entire message and gain the additional traffic through better communication.

Creating RSS Feeds

RSS feeds should be simple to create from any page. Essentially, they should be a mirror of the content on the page. If you are struggling to determine what content should go into an RSS feed, it is a good indication that you have a page that is trying to solve too many problems. In early mockups of the activity page feature on Nature Network, a single page provided both the replies directed to you and the updates from the community. When creating the RSS feed, we realized that deciding how to segment the information for the feed was not the issue. Rather, separating the types of content on the page into multiple pages was the issue. As a result, generating an RSS feed that represents a composite view of activity on the site for a person is now common practice. A decision-making site that explores collective intelligence ideas generates a single RSS feed for all activity on the site relevant to that person.

RSS has become an expected feature on the new "Web 2.0" website, so making these feeds simple to create is essential. Why? It is nearly impossible to determine what people will want to follow on your site. For instance, they might be interested in a tag or a person or the replies to a particular topic. So, simplifying the process to create an RSS feed allows for greater flexibility when reacting to the dynamic interests of the visitors to your site.

Some RSS feeds contain private information. Ensuring that this stays private requires some thought. A traditional username and password approach can work here, but it makes the feeds much harder to work with. The username and password need to be set or entered to access them by the user on RSS reading applications or sites. A more common approach is to generate a random string for the URL and obfuscate the access method. For instance, a URL such as */profile/matt/updates.rss* would be easy to guess, whereas */profile/od4qubd5avdxzl5lgbf6h.rss* is impossible to guess, but also easy to cut and paste into an RSS reader. The privacy is then up to the individual; he needs to ensure that the URL does not appear in a public space, because that will give anyone access to his private information.

Who Stole My Home Page?

When designing a new web application, most people are tempted to start with the home page. Quickly, though, you will realize that once a person has an account, the type of content that is appropriate for the home page changes. You have a decision to make: do you keep a valid home page for your members, or do you make the home page become their page?

On Flickr, Dopplr, and other sites, you can no longer access the normal home page once you have an account, as you are automatically sent to your profile page instead. Often, though, there is a necessity to show content other than your own or that from your social network. To solve this problem, Flickr has created a section for its site, called Explore, which provides a means of browsing interesting content on the site. On the Dopplr site, meanwhile, given its focus on private relationships, aggregate trips are not public, so there is no shared public experience. In this case, information about cities surfaces when you add a trip to a new place, and these city pages act as focal points on the site, much in the same way a traditional home page might.

Many sites opt for the "replace the home page" pattern, but sometimes it makes sense to keep a home page as a separate entity. Nature Network kept its home page, because it offers a place to show content outside a person's set of contacts (also known as the *local graph* of the person's social network). It also offers a space to show content from editorial teams. Mixing editorial and social content on the same site is not that common. Nature Network has editorial content for each of the hubs on the site. By not replacing the home page, it provides an obvious place for people to go to find out what else is happening on the site. Instead of making the member's home page the same URL as the site's home page, Nature Network opted for a unique *url/me*, which delivers personal content to every person.

Regardless of how you choose to map the content on your site, you still need to offer two home pages: the personal home page and the general home page. As noted earlier, the personal page is where people get other users' updates. The general home page is where you find out about interesting stuff people outside your immediate social network are sharing.

The default home page for non-members of your site needs to draw people in and encourage them to sign up. In some cases, such as Digg or Delicious, the home page acts as the list for popular content, too. The main purpose of the default page is arguably advertising; some designs promote this heavily with the equivalent of a big arrow pointing to the sign-up box. In many cases, the aim is to clearly and succinctly explain what your site does and why people should sign up.

Finally, you may want to have a place to discuss what you are doing to the site. Running your own blog about your product gives you a place to talk about new features and interesting activity. All the sites mentioned in this chapter run a blog at *blog.domain*.com, often hosted with a separate company (frequently, WordPress or Tumblr). Running the blog separately means you have a place to notify your users when the site will come back up if you are offline for a time or in case of other problems.

Providing for Site Navigation

You will need to provide navigation to other sections of your site, too. You can't rely only on context-led page navigation. Typically, social applications have a horizontal navigation bar at the top of the page, providing key navigation. Often, there is a deep navigation map at the base of the page. Placing frequently used navigation buttons at the top of the page and less used tools at the bottom leaves more space at the top of the page for content. In addition, removing the typical lefthand navigation bar shifts the emphasis from the navigation and branding to the content from the people on the site. We read English from left to right, so a page layout with a navigation menu on the left and ads or other content on the right can give the community content a slightly hemmed-in feeling.

The rise of blogging in the past five years has promoted experimentation in designing clear, simple navigational structures for site. Blogs tend to focus on a time- and category-based design with a clear link to a simple underlying URL structure. There is much to learn from this work. Clearly indicating the content that is core to your site and showing the tools to manage this content is important. Your site navigation needs to be thought through entirely from the point of view of the people using the site. This might seem obvious, but once inside a project, it is easy to lose site of that point and pay attention to the impulse behind "that awesome feature that took months, which has to be included in the navigation."

The three examples shown in Figure 13-11 demonstrate the following common navigational layouts for websites:

Traditional website
> The standard layout has a branding space at the top, content navigation on the left, ad space on the right, and the copyright on the bottom. This layout is very common on many content and product-led websites.

Blog
> The content is usually prominent on the left, with the navigation and ads on the right. The footer is used for copyright and some navigation.

Social application

A social network site has the key navigation at the top, alongside some branding. At the bottom of the page is deeper site navigation. (Many blogs use this pattern, too.) It is also used on sites such as Apple.com. Today, pages can be quite long because, unlike during the infancy of websites, people are willing to scroll web pages. Amazon pages, for instance, are typically 8,000 pixels or more deep, and people happily scroll to the customer reviews at the bottom of the page (see *Designing for the Social Web* [New Riders], by Joshua Porter for more on this topic).

Finding a space for advertisements in the middle of the design can be a challenge. If this is the pattern you want to follow for your business model, consider adding advertisements on the right; the popular skyscraper format works well in that regard.

Figure 13-11 shows these three typical layouts.

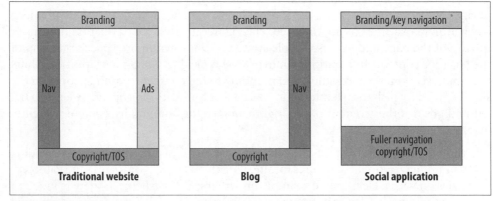

Figure 13-11. Screen areas for navigation branding and advertising versus actual content

Visually distinguishing the areas to which you can navigate is also important. Highlighting the different sections of a site is typically done via tabs. Frequently, there are two levels of tabs: one top-level set of tabs for the core sections and another set tied to the page content. Many sites also add JavaScript-based drop-down menus that offer options related to the main section. See the Flickr example in Figure 13-12 and the Vimeo example in Figure 13-13 for implementation of such elements.

Figure 13-12. Flickr menu structure, which uses drop-down menus on the top menu with triangles to show the presence of the menu; the links under "Your photostream" are simple links

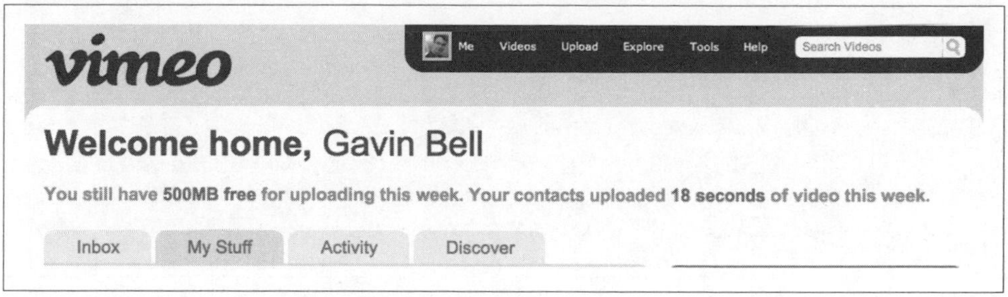

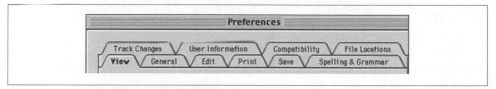

Figure 13-13. Vimeo menu structure, in which the drop-down menus are automated by a mouse rollover on the upper menu; the lower set of tabs is simple links

Tabs have had a mixed history in terms of usability, largely coming from double-layered tabs common in older Microsoft applications. They can be frustrating to use, as the tab ordering changes when you click on a rear tab. As you can see in Figure 13-14, using a closely placed double set of tabs makes it unclear which tab relates to the panel contents.

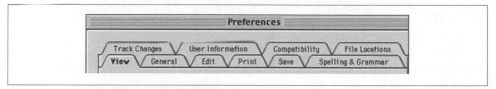

Figure 13-14. The double tab layer from Microsoft Word 98, taken from http://www.atpm.com/4.06/page8.shtml by Michael Tsai (used with permission)

If they are made visually distinctive, however, tabs can be an effective interface on the Web. A clear visual hierarchy will help people locate which section of the site and subsection they are looking at. Both the Flickr and Vimeo sites, for instance, use white-space to separate the tab blocks and then position each menu bar close to the relevant content. Making sure your navigation system is easy to use is important.

Site footers are a good place to offer a comprehensive set of navigational links. These are increasingly replacing the sitemap page. Usually these footers group sets of pages according to themes, such as a personal page, site help, developer tools, or general information about the company. Figure 13-15 shows the site footer for Last.fm.

Creating Page Titles

The <title> tag in HTML is often forgotten when designing a page. This tag rarely appears on page mockups. This lack of thought can lead to every page simply bearing your site's title, rather than a meaningful page title. These titles are important because they are what a search engine will display as the main entry on a search results page.

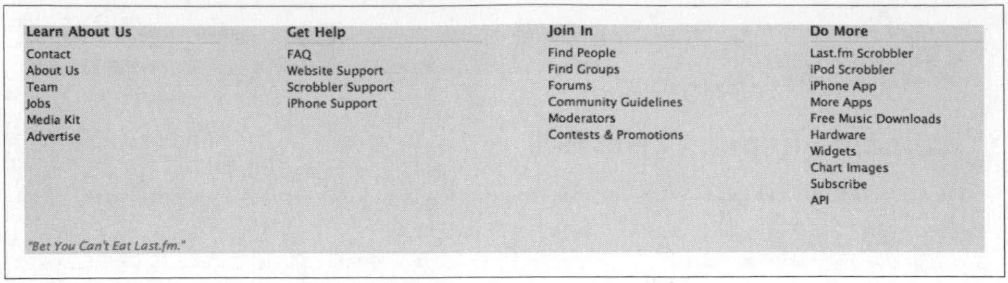

Figure 13-15. Site footer for Last.fm

The format of the titles, and what these titles should comprise, can take several forms. Let's look at a few:

Company—section—subsection—article title
> This used to be a very common pattern, but it means you have to read all the way to the end of the title to find out what the article is about. Also, a browser might truncate the end of the title.

Article title—subsection—section—company
> Reversing the previous format is another approach, but this means it can be hard for people to find your content in a menu of open windows.

Company—article title in subsection—section
> A better compromise, which is gaining popularity, is to place the company name at the beginning of the title and then put the most relevant piece of information next.

Nature Network took a very person-centric approach to this issue by displaying, for example, "Gavin Bell's profile on Nature Network" or "Constructing a complete model of consciousness from Brain Physiology, Cognition and Consciousness forum on Nature Network." This sentence-like structure for titles is a change from the punctuation characters, often used as separators on many sites. (This is probably an internationalization headache in hindsight, given the complexity of prepositions in Italian and other languages.)

The goal for a page title is twofold. First, it needs to be easy to locate on a web browser menu, so it should be short and informative, with the site name on the left. Probably more important is the fact that it is the label for a page on a search engine, so the leftmost place is where you will want to have the unique content-led information. Short product names are very helpful, as you can have both the product name and the content on the left. The key message is to drop the internal levels—for example, photo title on Flickr and artist on Last.fm.

Summary

A site requires some navigation structure to allow people to find their way around the content. On a social application, much of this navigation will come from your community. They will create the content, tag it, and generate the conversation around it. Your job is to create a simple structure that can hold this content and support the ongoing community interaction around it. Capabilities to search for people and tag content are important in initiating these conversations. The role of the activity page is to provide the heartbeat of the site for an individual because she will discover her social interactions with others through this page. It is important that activity pages are not seen only as web pages. Notification can be through an email or RSS feed, connecting the person back to her community.

CHAPTER 14

Making Connections

You are in the midst of planning your shiny new community or social network site, and you've got your social objects all laid out. It's time to look past the objects, and ask what binds your community together.

Social contact is a strong way to bring people together; letting people form relationships online is a natural extension of how we behave in face-to-face communications. However, when we are on the Internet, we need to be more explicit in how we denote these relationships. We end up with a more formal identification of relationships than happens face to face. Online relationships are either present or not present. Face-to-face relationships can be more fluid, changing over time.

Virtually every social software application allows you to create online relationships by marking someone as a contact and adding him to your social network for that website. The language might vary slightly, and there are different types of relationships that you can create, but the basic concept of a list of people who you have an identifiable relationship with is valid. Chapter 13 touched on how a profile page should include links to support adding people to your network to create the connections for your relationships. It's time to start building those links.

Choosing the Correct Relationship Model for Your Social Application

You need to determine how social relationships are formed for your site. There are several different ways you can let this occur, and the one you choose will depend on the nature of your audience. The simplest and most common model, suitable for most kinds of social networks, is the *add and notify* model. Adding a person to your network lets you follow his updates on your update page. The person is sent an email saying that you have added him to your network of contacts. Table 14-1 shows some relationship models, a description of how they work, and examples of sites that use them.

Table 14-1. Social online relationship models

Model	Description	Examples
Add and notify, also known as asymmetric follow	Everyone is free to add anyone to their network. Notifications are sent informing them of the addition.	Flickr, Twitter, and most social networks
Add and confirm	Each request must be approved. The person who is to be added to the requester's network needs to agree to be added.	Not very widely used; suitable for very formal applications
Add, confirm, and link back, also known as symmetric follow	This is a formal approach. It is a two-way addition: on confirmation, the requester is added to the requested person's network, and the requested person is added to the requester's network.	LinkedIn, Facebook

The first model, commonly known as *asymmetric follow*, is far and away the dominant one for social applications. The number of followers and the number of people a person follows do not need to be symmetric. If you are unsure which model to choose, consider the add and notify model. It is lightweight to implement, and easy for users to understand. Importantly, there are differences for the teenage market; here, a full two-way symmetric approach is recommended. This way, the teenagers have a clear idea of who they are interacting with and have given each person explicit permission to interact with them.

A more symmetrical model can be effective, as exemplified by the success of this type of model on both LinkedIn and Facebook. If the expected size of your social network per person is likely to be in the low hundreds, the symmetric model is a good one. If you want to allow for tens or hundreds of thousands of followers, as Twitter does, making the relationship confirmation-based and/or reciprocal will *not* work.

Not every site is like Twitter. Examine the needs of your community and subject area to see how their current relationships operate and what your social object requires for interaction.

The add and notify model describes only the simple relationship between two people, but many sites offer a means to make some relationships more important than others. A notification step is important on sites where there is a degree of value in the link between two people. If it enables something or allows access to a new means of communication, a confirmation stage may be required. If Twitter had, for example, set the ability to send a direct message as a capability of following, it would likely require a confirmation step. As it stands now on Twitter, following allows the person you are following to send you a message. The notification step is also a chance for the recipient to say no to the request, by blocking the addition.

Often, these two levels of a relationship are known as *friend* and *contact*. I suggest that two levels are enough to handle virtually every situation. If you want to offer more control, you should look at groups, which I will cover in "Administering Groups" on page 264. Two levels allow you to differentiate between people who are close friends and people who are acquaintances. This distinction is important for certain kinds of content, such as photos of your children you might not wish to share with everybody. While there are only two levels of explicit relationship, there is often a third, implicit group comprising the people who are not logged in to the site. Allowing two levels of relationship means there are five states of visibility in which an item of content can exist, as shown in Table 14-2.

Table 14-2. Content visibility based on two-level relationships

State	Visibility	Notes
Private	Visible only to the creator	Useful for drafts
Friends	Visible only to friends of the creator	Common for personal content
Friends and contacts	Visible to friends and contacts	Common for people who wish some level of privacy for all content
Anyone whose network I'm in (fans)	Visible to the creator's friends and contacts, plus anyone who has the creator in her social network	Allows content to be displayed just to members of the site who the creator has a personal contact with; not widely used
Everyone	Visible to anyone on the Internet who looks at the site	Can be limited to anyone who can access the site, by requiring a site login

A social application can set expectations for who you will connect with. For a dating site, this will be (almost) exclusively people you do not know. On most social networks, it tends to be people you know or have met. On Flickr, it might also be people whose photography you like. For Dopplr, the expectation is that you have some sort of working or personal relationship with the person with whom you are connecting. Making a decision early on as to who will connect and their expectations is an important aspect in application design.

Nature Network uses a simple add and notify model. We could have gone for a more controlled model, allowing only mutual two-way relationships, but we felt this would make senior scientists less likely to join and make those who are less senior unlikely to request to follow leading scientists. We could have extended the *fan-based model*, where the relationship is one-way, and created more notification tools supporting broadcast of publication or content to groups of people, but we respect the privacy of our professional scientists and don't want to allow others to intrude on their time unduly. Focus groups didn't show great interest in being obligated to follow dozens of other scientists as part of a two-way symmetric pattern.

Some social software services attract people who gain thousands of followers. Some of these people are already famous and use the services as a broadcast device. Some of them do engage in conversation, while others just follow back a small subset of their followers. They will cause you scaling problems, but they are not a concern otherwise. Famous people tend to have many more followers than they follow.

Creating the Language of Connections

The language that describes the process of adding relationships can be tricky to get right. The most basic version of it is as follows. You can alter the following words to suit the kind of site that you have, but these basic relationships and actions are a fundamental part of how social applications work:

Add

Makes the person part of your social network, and can be subject to confirmation.

Friend

Confers a special level of relationship and allows certain privileges for the person as to the content he can see or activities he can perform.

Contact

Describes a person in a social network with a normal level of relationship.

Fan

Describes the person who has a one-way relationship to a person on a social network. John is a fan of Mary; Mary has no relationship with John.

Follow

Describes what happens after the person is added. John follows Mary on that social network. This can be one-way or two-way: if Mary added John, they would follow one another.

Block

Ends the ability of someone to follow you; this can sometimes be reversed.

Blocking Relationships

Sadly, it is also necessary to provide tools to allow the ending of relationships. There are a variety of reasons why someone would want to do this, but some of the most common are spam and an unpleasant interaction. This capability is more common on sites where commenting on the content created by individuals is the main activity. A good example of this is Flickr. Blocking removes a person from your social network and stops her from being able to add you back to her network. In the case of Flickr, it also removes any comments the person has left and removes any of your photos from her favorites list. Essentially, you vanish from the site in terms of that person's profile. This practice is not foolproof, because the blocked person can create a new account, but it is an effective tool. Chapter 15 covers the challenges of dealing with bad behavior in "Extreme Measures: Banning Users and Removing Posts" on page 280, but let me leave you with the shortest guideline for good behavior. It comes from Flickr's Heather Champ, and it sums up a lot of the issues in dealing with people who are behaving badly: "Don't be that guy, you know that guy."

Another group comprises spammers. Generally, spammers do not engage in conversation; they simply add contact after contact hoping to promote the URLs they are entering on the site. This happens on most sites, from Flickr to Twitter to Digg, and so on. Usually, you can separate the genuinely high-volume people from the spammers by looking at the follower-to-fan ratio. Spammers generally follow many, many more people than follow them. Looking at the block functionality will also highlight these people to you as they will be blocked by a large number of your members. Building good administration systems to notify you when you have new spammers is important for maintaining the health of your community.

Information Brokers

A recent trend in social web applications has been to drop the classification of contacts as a *friend* or a *contact*. The focus of Dopplr, for example, is on sharing trips. This sharing of information rather than rating of a relationship between two people allows Dopplr to step back slightly and take an information-broker-based relationship rather than one focused on getting people to visit the website for *dopplr.com*. Visitors may not be interested in Dopplr per se but in where a certain person is going. Arguably, Twitter is doing the same, but less explicitly. In each case, there is no huge call to visit the website, and the majority of regularly used functionality is available via an API. This change in emphasis from actually visiting the website to being able to effectively use the site via other tools and programs means the functionality of Dopplr needs to work when removed from the supporting context of the website. The emphasis shifts to the information that Dopplr can provide rather than a specific web-based user interface element.

The location-sharing application Fire Eagle will take updates from you as to your whereabouts and will release this to approved client applications. The carbon-tracking system AMEE (*http://www.amee.com*) will take values corresponding to energy usage and can release this information to approved clients. These are two more extreme examples of this trend. They both dispense with the social network entirely, relying on providing a high-quality data service to other social web applications. Think about whether the product you are planning can work in this manner. Information broker applications such as these are going to be a fascinating area to watch over the next few years. Moving from a person-centric view of a social application to one that includes software as well as people will allow for more varieties of integration between social applications.

Notifications and Invitations

Generally, it is a good idea to send email when a relationship is created. If you have a confirmation model, this is obligatory; however, a change of status (from contact to friend) generally does not merit another email.

Social networks have something of a *tell no bad news* culture. It is very uncommon to receive an email saying that someone removed you from his social network. I do not know how this behavior became common practice, but it seems to be a good one to stick with. However, it can lead to unfulfilled expectations. For example, say, Kevin gets an email saying that famous actor MattD is following him. Later that week MattD drops Kevin as a contact and so Kevin's chatter on the social network loosely aimed at MattD goes unheard and Kevin is disappointed that MattD never replies. Is the silence better than Kevin receiving an email saying MattD has dropped him?

Invites and Add As Follower Requests

In general, a service will notify a person that there is an invite or an add as follower request for him. Usually, these invites don't expire. If you have an add and notify system, the inviter will automatically get the updates from the invitee on his update pages. If you have a confirmation-based system, the recipient must confirm the request.

An example invitation email follows. Ideally, you can make this conditional so that it changes depending on whether the invitee is reciprocating and adding the inviter. You might not want to include all the elements in the example, but a link to the person's profile and one to the Add link are important.

From: ScreenNameB via ServiceName *<servicename@servicename.com>*

Subject: [servicename] ScreenNameB is following you.

Hello <ScreenNameA>

ScreenNameB added you; you might want to reciprocate.

OR

ScreenNameB added you in return; you are both connected.

Perhaps ScreenNameB already knows you or just wants to follow your updates. You can reciprocate if you like.

This is their profile: *http://...*

This is their content: *http://...*

These are their contacts: *http://...*

If you have a confirmation-based system, you will need the following lines, too.

Click this link to add them to your network: *http://...*

Adding ScreenNameB means that they will automatically be able to see your updates.

Manage this notification using this link: *http://...*

Thanks,

Service Name - *http://serviceName.com*

Disclaimer

Given the potential for abuse by spammers, you need to think carefully about whether to allow the initial add-as-a-contact message to contain anything personal, certainly think about whether to include any content they have directly provided, even a link to another site. Many networks, such as LinkedIn, Facebook, and Nature Network, do allow a message to be sent. Others, such as SlideShare, Flickr, and Twitter, do not. If you do allow a message to be sent along with the invite, make sure there is a simple process to complain about the message content, should it be spam.

 Links in email should never do something automatically when clicked. A link such as *http://network.nature.com/friendships/new/aa1024* should always go to a web page with a POST-based confirmation button. Tools such as the Google Web Accelerator (*http://webaccelerator .google.com/*) will automatically follow all links in an email, and as much email is read using webmail interfaces such as Gmail, this can lead to unintended results. However, the Google Web Accelerator will not follow POST-based web form links.

Secure and Personal Invites

Security is a huge consideration; only the invitee should be able to access the link to an invite. You should not store the email address of the invited person. You can, however, store an encrypted hash of the address to which the invitation was sent so that you can determine whether the person is creating the account with the right email address.

It can be beneficial to allow multiple email addresses to be associated with a single account on your system. You will need to allow people to change their email addresses, and allow them to have more than one active email address for an account. For example, Simon invites Sarah to join ServiceB via her work email address. Sarah has already signed up for ServiceB, but using her personal email address. If you allow multiple email addresses to be associated, Sarah can associate her work email address as a non-primary address with ServiceB and accept Simon's invite.

Pending Invites

One area that gets poor attention in social application design is the period after an invite has been sent, but before it is accepted. Too many systems rely on email messages as the sole token of the invite; there is no reminder or memory on the website. Once an invite has been sent, there should be two places to find it. The first is a page that is part of the sender's profile for sent invites, each invite showing its acceptance status. On the recipients' page there should also be an element of their profile page showing unprocessed invites so that they can return to process invites after receiving them. Both LinkedIn and Facebook support this kind of reminding functionality well. However, all sites where there is a conditional aspect to invites should offer a history for invites.LinkedIn and Facebook support this kind of reminding functionality well. However, all sites where there is a conditional aspect to invites should offer a history for invites.

Spam

What counts as spam from your own service and what does not can be confusing to define as a best practice. Generally, if someone has signed up for a service, it is OK to send her emails connected with her use of the service. Sending her emails announcing a new service from your company is probably not OK, unless you obtained permission to do so. Sending emails about other companies in your group or third parties is definitely not recommended unless you have obtained an opt-in declaration from your members. The exact legal position in your country may impose additional requirements.

So, sending weekly updates, occasional reminders about your service, contact additions, and similar emails is okay, but make sure you offer your members the means to stop these emails. The email address belongs to them, so they should be able to control what arrives in their inbox from your company.

Social Network Portability

The following question came from the early adopters of the Web, the kinds of people who try out several new web applications every month: "Because I have already established who I know and like, can I please just tell you who they are in one action?"

If you are creating a new website, you will want it to grow quickly, and one great way to do that is to allow your members to import all of their existing friends at once. If your potential new members must re-create their friends list inside your new application, they will quickly become tired of the process. This concept of moving your friends around as an entity came about in 2007 under various titles. *Social graph*, *social network portability*, and *contact importing* all referred to largely the same thing.

Each person's social network added to your pot can mean more people on your site; making it easy for people to bring their friends to you is a good thing.

Social Graph

Social graph is a term that emerged in 2007 (see Brad Fitzpatrick's article at *http://bradfitz.com/social-graph-problem/*) to describe the set of friends and contacts that a person has across multiple websites. The mathematical term *graph* describes the broader relationships as opposed to the term *network* that had come to mean a set of relationships on a single site. It is a useful concept, but it can be misinterpreted if taken too simplistically. It does not mean you will want to import a single address book of people onto every site you visit. It is finer-grained than that. Rather, a site you are joining should be able to query a list of preexisting friends and tell you which of these people are already members of the new site. Google produced a Social Graph API product (*http://code.google.com/apis/socialgraph/*) for this purpose, which allows an application to query who is already connected to a person and produce a set of people who might be relevant to her.

The Future of Online Identity

I gave a talk titled "What is your provenance?" about the wider area of what being connected on the Internet means. The first time, I gave it at the XTech conference in May 2007. Subsequently, I gave the same talk at Google and it is available on Google Video (*http://video.google.com/videoplay?docid=-8663100900373306094*). The talk—and Brad Fitzpatrick's article at *http://bradfitz.com/social-graph-problem/*—give an overview of what a connected online identity will mean in the future. The work of Chris Messina, Kevin Marks, and others on the Open Social stack consisting of OpenID, OAuth, Portable Contacts, and Activity Streams is bringing this into reality. See Chapters 16 and 17 for more discussion on these areas.

Importing Friends by the Book

The main advantage that social network portability gives is to make the process of adding new people to a new application much easier. There are three main techniques for importing: scanning for microformatted content using the hCard and XFN `rel="me"` formats, querying an API for a person's contacts, and requesting webmail address book contacts. The last of these is the most widespread, and in later 2007 and early 2008, it was widely deployed using the "give me your password" antipattern. (An *antipattern* is a negative pattern, a common way of doing something that implements something in a poor or harmful way.)

Microformats turn human-readable information into something a computer can parse. hCard is a standard representation of business-card-like contact details. XFN is the cumbersomely named XHTML Friends Network, which is a means of marking up a list of people in terms of your relationship with them. The `rel="me"` version defines the author of the page and the items he owns (see *http://microformats.org* for more information).

Matt Biddulph from Dopplr has been implementing non-password-based mechanisms to access webmail address books and similar tools (see *http://code.google.com/p/identity -matcher/*). His plug-in—written as a gem module in the scripting language Ruby—contains the code to access Gmail, Windows Live, and Twitter, as well as make hCard-based queries, all without having to enter the password for the webmail provider on the requesting site (which is the heart of the antipattern). Biddulph has encapsulated the details of making the address book requests so that as a developer you simply need to ask which service the person uses and you get back a list of contacts.

Address books have been hard-to-access data objects on the Internet. Each application offers a different way to manage contacts, but importing them became much easier in

2008. Now, Yahoo!, AOL, Google, and Microsoft all offer a means to import an address book stored on these email systems. The Portable Contacts, based on open public standards, aims to offer a standard, simple approach to implementing an address book. It looks like promising (see *http://wiki.portablecontacts.net/*).

Another good example of using existing accounts to provide contact information is Get Satisfaction. Its profile creation page encourages you to give the username of an account on another system. It then simply takes the publicly available details from that site: location, avatar image, a website URL, and first and last names. The technique mainly relies on the other sites having implemented an hCard wrapper for these details on a profile page, because this is simple to do and so common. The elegance lies in that the technical aspects of hCard, for example, need never be mentioned to the potential new member. She simply gives her Flickr username and magic seemingly happens. In Figure 14-1, I entered "gavinbell" in the panel on the right and clicked the "Get flickr profile" button; my image appeared on the left automatically.

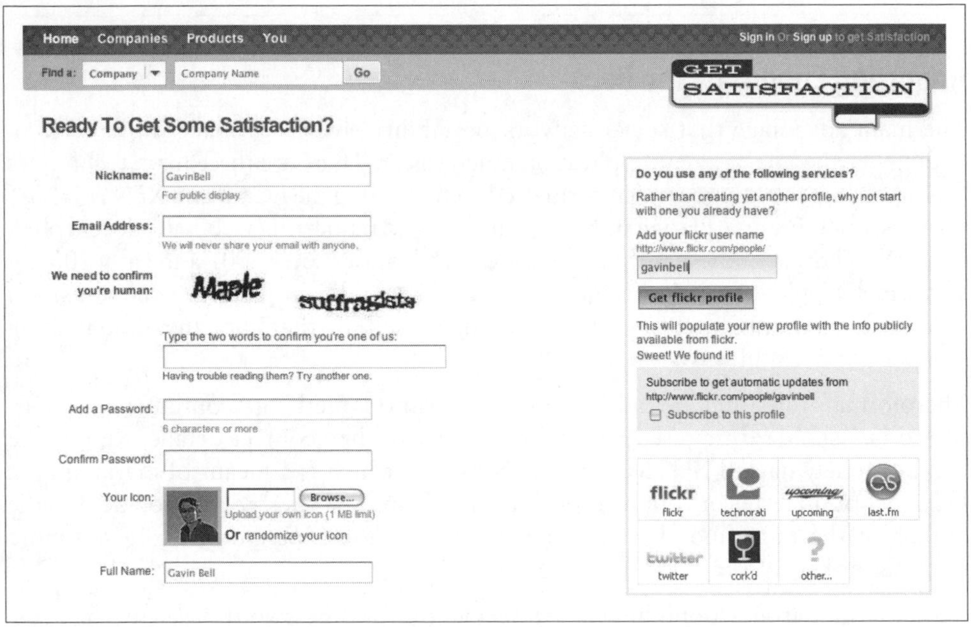

Figure 14-1. Get Satisfaction, showing profile creation using hCard data from existing profiles

This capability makes it easy to move profile information from one place to another, but it relies on people being trustworthy. It would be trivial to enter someone else's Flickr identity and pretend to be him on another service, though this kind of impersonation is perhaps unlikely. Along these lines, monitoring the accesses to your site for scraping behavior is an important duty. Repeated accesses should really come via a proper API in which the actual content requested is delivered without the rest of the screen clutter. The usage can also be tracked to an individual or company with an API.

Spamming, Antipatterns, and Phishing

Spamming contact lists is a very rude thing to do. After importing your address book entries, some sites will then email all of those people on your behalf inviting them to join the service you just did. A range of companies from Plaxo to Stumbleupon to Quechup have all fallen foul of this, either intentionally or accidentally. Plaxo did apologize,[*] which is the right way to deal with this situation, and it is now actively working on open web tools. Stumbleupon, on the other hand, confuses users with an interface that causes people with large address books to inadvertently send everyone an invite rather than just existing members.[†]

> In September 2007, many articles discussed the wave of unsolicited email that Quechup sent on behalf of its new users (*http://www.oreilly net.com/xml/blog/2007/09/quechup_another_social_network.html*). As Jennifer Golbeck points out, the ability to retrieve a list of contacts does not give a company the right to send unsolicited email seemingly on your behalf. Pete Cashmore notes at *http://mashable.com/2007/09/02/quechup/* that Quechup went wrong when it took users permission to access their contacts as implicit permission to email those contacts.
>
> If you are going to send emails on behalf of a member, make sure the member is an active participant on your site first and get his explicit permission before you send the email. Otherwise, you are spamming.

Importing contacts rarely requires a simple bulk import of everyone from an address book. For example, say, you have an account on Flickr and you join Cork'd, a site about wine, it is unlikely that all of your photography friends will be wine drinkers. This is one of those situations where the content is not owned by your company; it belongs to the person who imported it. You need the person's permission each time you use her information.

A better way to import friends is to let people select who they care about from their own contact lists. Spokeo, as shown in Figure 14-2, takes a very explicit approach to getting your contact details. It asks you to use your username and password for your webmail provider as the mechanism of sign-up, and asks its potential users to give up the password for their email to a third-party company. Thus, the password antipattern continues. Jeremy Keith describes it well at *http://adactio.com/journal/1357*:

> Allowing users to import contact lists from other services is a useful feature. But the means have to justify the ends. Empowering the user to import data through an authentication layer like OAuth is the correct way to export data. On the other hand, asking users to input their email address and password from a third-party site like GMail or Yahoo! Mail is completely unacceptable. Here's why:

---

[*] *http://blog.plaxo.com/archives/2006/03/an_apology.html*

[†] *http://www.insideview.ie/irisheyes/2008/02/stumbleupon-pro.html*

It teaches people how to be phished.

I don't know how much clearer I can make this: the end result of exporting data is desirable; teaching users to hand over their passwords to any site that asks for them is not. There is no excuse for asking for a third-party password on your website. You're doing it wrong. That authentication must happen on the third-party site.

Figure 14-2. Spokeo implementing the password antipattern

Webmail address books are too tempting a place for some people; they feel they can use them for their own marketing purposes. As Jeremy Keith notes, this encourages *phishing (http://en.wikipedia.org/wiki/Phishing)*. You are being phished when you enter your personal details on a site that pretends to be the proper site or pretends to act on behalf of the proper site. Commonly associated with fake emails from PayPal or a bank, clicking on a link in these fake emails takes you to a site where you enter your actual account details. The criminals behind the operation then use your details to empty your account.

Address Books, the OAuth Way

You should require that a user only enter his password for an account on the site for which he created it. By checking the URL in the address bar in his browser, a person who thinks he's entering, for instance, his Twitter password on the Twitter site can confirm that the site really is *twitter.com*. If the user has a Gmail account, he should only enter the password for it on the Gmail interface.

Token-based authentication systems such as OAuth provide a mechanism for third-party data access, letting you work from a single login while avoiding a basic problem.

In the case of Gmail, for instance, giving a third-party company your Google account details (password) lets the company access any of the other services you have on Google. In fact, this has actually been used as a potential hack (for more information, see *http://www.codinghorror.com/blog/archives/001072.html*).

OAuth implementations are becoming more common. For instance, FriendFeed recently implemented OAuth-based sign-up using Twitter as the address book provider. The user experience flow starts on the FriendFeed site, shown in Figure 14-3. Clicking the Twitter button, shown in Figure 14-3, takes you to a login page on the Twitter site, shown in Figure 14-4. Once you enter your username and password there, you are presented with an authentication page, as shown in Figure 14-5, where you grant FriendFeed access to the data associated with the Twitter account with which you have just logged in. Clicking Allow takes you back to the FriendFeed site and its normal account creation page, but with the data from Twitter already available, such as contacts and user profile information. All the authentication and approval happens on the Twitter site, not the FriendFeed site.

Figure 14-3. FriendFeed account creation via Twitter

![Twitter sign-in page]

Figure 14-4. Twitter sign-in for FriendFeed account creation

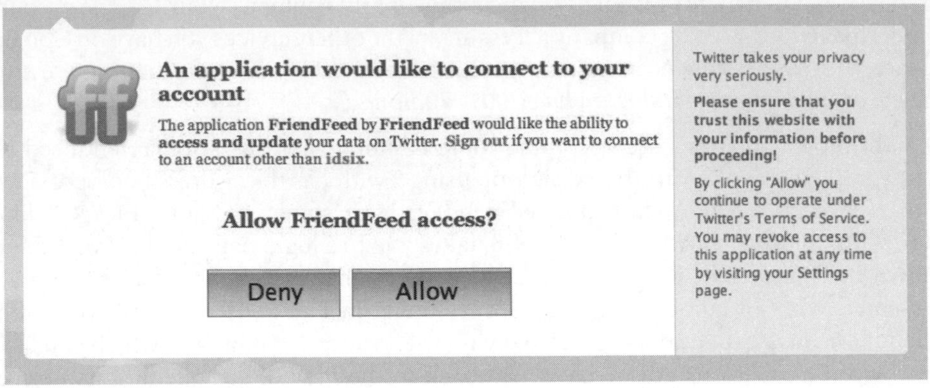

Figure 14-5. Granting FriendFeed access to the data associated with the Twitter idsix account

Creating a Common Social Stack for the Web

Social network portability is a fast-moving topic. At the time of this writing, in May 2009, there has been some great activity in the release of password-less but authenticated access to address books held by major webmail providers. However, more progress is to come in this area. OAuth provides a simple means of accessing third-party data, but it is not yet the accepted standard. That standard is coming with Portable Contacts.

A block of useful social technologies is being developed out in the open: OpenID, OAuth, microformats, and Portable Contacts. XRDS is another one of these technologies (*http://www.hueniverse.com/hueniverse/2008/07/beginners-guide.html*). Designed to support resource discovery, XRDS allows services to interoperate in a more automatic fashion, because these XRDS profiles act as a simple mechanism for determining what each service offers. Service discovery is obvious on a single application; XRDS defines how two different services can handle access control, for example.

Activity Streams is one of the newest technologies, and it is aimed at allowing easy exchange of activity event streams between different social applications; *http://activity strea.ms/* hosts the evolving specification.

Adoption and understanding of technologies such as OpenID and OAuth is progressing in the developer community. The OAuth-based flow was not possible in early 2008—a year later and it is possible. The general Internet population is very familiar with the idea that identity means an email address and a password. Using URLs to represent people as OpenID does, or giving data access to one site on another site, will take longer. However, OpenID and OAuth are the best mechanisms for providing common identity and access to data between multiple applications.

Ideally, you should never ask for a password for a service you do not control. Put pressure on the other service provider to implement OAuth, and you can get the data with a clean conscience.

Changing Relationships over Time

Our social network changes over time. We make new friends, we change jobs, we move, etc. All of these events change who we care about and who is physically close to us. However, social applications do not efficiently handle these changes; there is no ability to forget in this digital world. People who have large contact lists are likely to have people on them who they have forgotten they added, or no longer have enough of a context to remember why they added them. The networks in our social applications are only capable of growing, it seems, and they are binary in nature: relationships are either present or not. This area offers a lot to explore, particularly as people often complain about how much content they are presented with.

To help prune all of this, applications could show the people you look at a lot, or the people who update a lot and you skip over. By analyzing consumption behavior over time, it should be possible to identify those people who you are less interested in and suggest these accounts for pruning. However, we tend to not offer these tools for fear of offending. A small step in the right direction comes from the Mac OS X desktop RSS news reader, NetNewsWire, which has a Dinosaurs feature (shown in Figure 14-6) for detecting feeds that have not been updated in a set time period. Filtering tools such as one this are becoming essential in managing user experiences on the Web; they help us to determine which content to pay attention to.

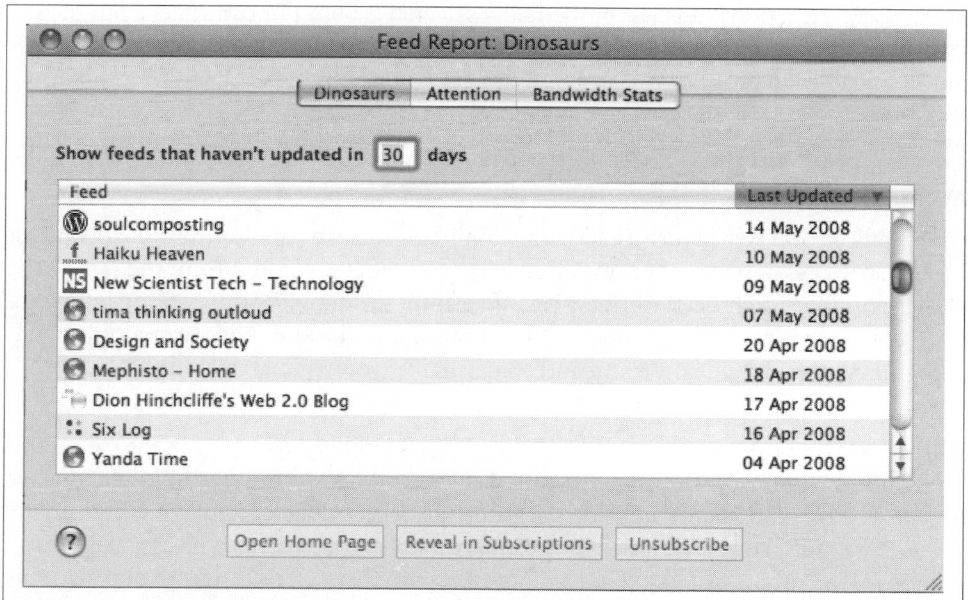

Figure 14-6. NetNewsWire Dinosaurs feature showing feeds that have not been updated recently; social applications should consider features such as this to help with filtering and management

Administering Groups

A common request within social applications is to create some form of group to let people self-associate in a smaller throng than the entire site. Creating groups is generally a good idea, but it does increase the complexity of your product in ways that are easy to underestimate. Adding groups means there are now some potentially semiprivate areas on your site. Certainly, there are now areas where some people have permission to do some things and other people do not. The other aspect to consider is that it is something else for people to get invited to join. So, this means more administration for your members to deal with.

Public or Private?

There are two schools of thought on groups. The dominant one represents groups as a public entity. The other type of group is a private selection of people created by a single individual, such as a private email mailing list.

Most groups in social software are of the public type. They are set up by a single individual, and they set the criteria for membership. Commonly this will be an open group that is publicly visible to other people on the site. Other common variants are the public group with approved membership, and the private invite-based group.

The second type of group is more personal and more recognizable in terms of how we act in social situations. It is the individually selected group. For example, from the list of people I know, I select people who I'd like to have in a group I create. Everyone is automatically a member of this group, but I control who is a member; you can't apply to join.

Private types of groups will become more prevalent as the need for semiprivacy on the Web increases.

The public group (see Figure 14-7) is the dominant social entity for multiple people to have a shared experience. This experience is one that is separated from the rest of the activity on the site. It need not be a private group; the activity simply happening in a different place is enough to separate it from the rest of the site. A close analogy would be a public bar with a main room and some smaller rooms upstairs; all the rooms are in the pub, but the rooms upstairs offer a separate experience from the rest of the place.

This dominant position of the public social group is unlikely to change in the near term. Typically, groups are publicly listed on a website and people are free to join and leave at will. The tools and content inside the group are often publicly visible too, but usually for reading only. To contribute to the group, you need to join. This type of group allows people to find others of a like mind and interact with them. This type of group also acts as a badge showing an affiliation with a particular subject area or activity, even if the individual rarely contributes to the group.

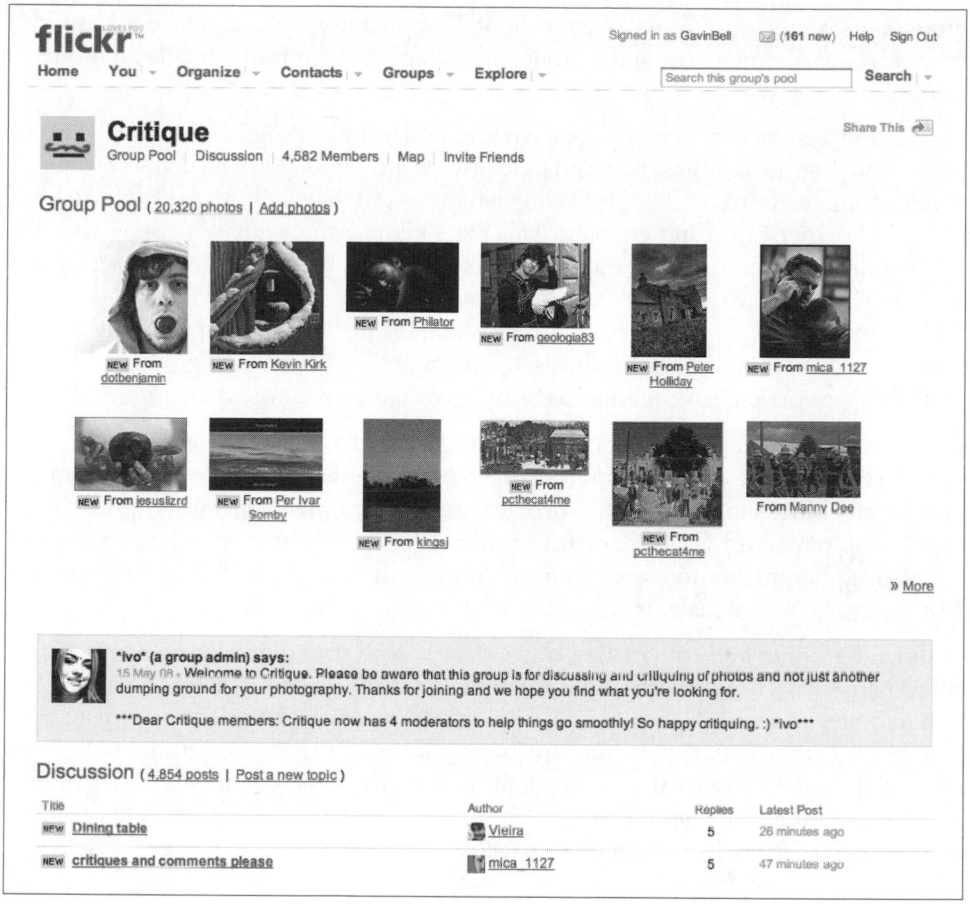

Figure 14-7. Flickr Critique group, a typical public group in a social application

Groups must have a means for members to talk to one another, frequently offered as a message board. Boards present a flat playing field for all members to participate. Anyone can initiate a topic, and anyone can respond.

Regulating Group Creation

On some sites, such as Flickr and Nature Network, anyone can create and administer a group. This approach does entail risks because you are delegating aspects of your site management to individuals you will probably not know, but it also means the site can grow faster. There are two main roles in a group: administrator, or owner, and moderator. You can see these roles in action in Figure 14-7. The administrator is defining the purpose of the group and has four moderators who help to manage the group.

The administrator owns the group, typically setting the title and purpose of the group. The administrator can also shut down the group and appoint other administrators or moderators. Larger groups will want to appoint moderators who can help manage the conversations and disputes in the group. See Chapter 15 for more details on moderation.

Public groups sometimes encourage a range of odd or less desirable behaviors. Two of these behaviors are *land grabbing* and its relative, *copycatting*. Both behaviors are about seeing groups as territory. People like to own things, so they will create groups to have a sense of ownership. Land grabbers will create many groups and will aspire to mark an area of the subject matter the site covers as theirs. They may do this with good intentions, but they often overreach and leave dormant groups that they do not have time to run. Copycats see successful groups and create mimic groups hoping for the same sort of success. On Flickr, this is a popular activity; dozens of groups are based on the images people have marked as favorites or ratios of views to favorites.

Early in the life of Nature Network, we had a student identified as a land grabber, who decided to create dozens of groups covering most areas of science. We had deliberately not put any blocks in place to stop people from creating lots of groups, but we didn't expect one person to create so many groups. We got in touch with him and asked whether he had meant to create so many groups, then worked with him to find out which ones he was actually interested in running.

Both land-grabber and copycatting behaviors can lead to multiple groups for a single subject area. This is not necessarily a bad thing, as many groups will not thrive because they require more effort than people expect. However, it can lead to confusion for people who are new to the site and are looking for, say, the Physics group, only to be presented with 35 groups all claiming to be about physics. For your site, you will find a happy medium, but you will need tools to manage and observe what is happening; see Chapter 16 for help with some management tools.

Summary

Relationships and creating connections for them are a key aspect of a social site. There are several different mechanisms, so you need to choose the most appropriate one for your audience. Privacy is an important element; being careful to ensure that people understand what is private is important. A common language is evolving to describe the terms and concepts for managing relationships, but you need to pick terms that make sense for your community.

The communication around relationship management generally means lots of emails being sent. There are good examples to learn from and good practices to follow. In addition, people are becoming overwhelmed with the amount of email that social web applications can generate, so we explored the future of social networking portability and some antipatterns to avoid. Be sure you understand the issues raised by including groups on your site, particularly the increased complexity and need for communication tools inside the group.

CHAPTER 15

Managing Communities

You want your members to have helpful, friendly interactions on your site—an experience they'll enjoy and want to have again. Unfortunately, that won't always happen, and not necessarily because you built your site incorrectly. The anonymity offered by the Internet gives some people the liberty to behave badly. Hiding behind a screen name makes some people feel like they can act with impunity. There are lots of names for the people who behave badly on the Internet: for instance, spammers, porn and drug merchants, trolls, griefers, and troublemakers. Some of them are trying to sell something, while others are just out to cause problems.

However, there are some ways to mitigate the worst of these problems, and your community can help you. Although community management and moderation approaches deserve a book of their own, this chapter will provide an overview of some of the key issues.

Social Behavior in the Real World

On most social forums, there are some people you know, some you might have invited, some you get to know, and a large number you don't know at all. There are many places in the real world with the same characteristics. Bars and restaurants, for instance, are independent commercial endeavors to which you can become a regular visitor, but they are not someone's personal home. They have staff members who run the place, and there are expected modes of interaction. A bar or café is probably the best fit to a message board or social network because bars and cafés support groups involved in conversations.

Three broad roles are worth discussing in this regard. For every café or bar, there is an owner, some staff members, and customers. On a website, there is a host or publisher, some people who help run the site, and readers who use the site. The important aspect of a bar is not really the décor or the beer—it is the ambiance. Are people dealt with in a friendly and attentive manner? Is the place clean and tidy? Are troublemakers dealt with quietly and discretely? It is based on these interactions that people decide whether they'll frequent the place, and the social interaction among the customers is shaped by these interactions. Make the staffing too obvious and people feel uncomfortable; make the staffing too lax and people will be poorly, served or perhaps hassled by someone they did not come to meet.

Like most analogies, this one falls apart if you push it too far (e.g., what is the "beer" that is being sold on most message boards?). However, the social framework of both places is similar. The role of the staff is to make sure the place is friendly and well maintained. In terms of social relationships, the staff's role is to deal with complaints, requests, and bad behavior among visitors.

The analogies in terms of human behavior for the Web are that the design of a site helps to make sense of the place. Features might be a reason to visit, but if visitors are ignored or other people are rude to them, they won't return. This analogy can be extended across much of the site and to different roles. There can be more than just three roles, and the degree to which you involve your community can be more complex than in a bar, but it helps to bring warmth and life into something that is essentially just code showing words and pictures.

Negative behaviors in a bar or café are the overt commercial activity analogous to spam: handing out fliers, begging, and selling illicit DVDs, for instance. These are much easier to deal with than arguments between customers.

Starting Up and Managing a Community

Starting a café or a bar is really hard work, and maintaining one is even more difficult. The same is true of communities on the Web. They require that you invest a lot of your time to draw the community together and get people to interact. Once your community is up and running, you need to take time to engage with them and understand their desires and interests.

Thinking of a website launch as similar to the launch of a real-world place is helpful. You would not open a café and then ignore it. Nevertheless, the idea of a site launch being the end of the project is very common, especially among broadcasters and advertising agencies. It stems from old media working habits. TV companies have a wrap party when a program is complete, but the program will be broadcast weeks or months later with a different team responsible for scheduling and promotion. With advertising agencies, the time lag is not the issue, but such agencies are used to dealing with one-way media. There is often no space for interaction with the audience, just a one-way message.

Launching a social web application comprises about 40% of the effort involved; the rest is comprised of encouraging people to use and continue to use the site, in addition to continued software development. In Chapter 6, I recommended that you allocate community management as part of people's work roles. Whether this involves everyone or a few individuals depends on the size of your company and the potential community.

Actually using your product and talking to people who use it online is the core part of the community manager's job. It is essential that you build a solid personal relationship with the people on your site. The staff members for most successful social web applications have a very visible public profile; they are part of the community. Even if you are not a startup site, you should emulate this behavior as much as possible so that you can find the people who really care about your product and support them, their desires, and their interests.

Most people want to live a life without lots of conflict. Your main challenge will be to get the people visiting your site to contribute. But once there, they might get into heated debates with other people on the site, so some clear and simple community guidelines can help everyone determine when people overstep boundaries. Generally, these are libel and personal attacks. I'll cover libel later in the chapter, as it is a specific subcase.

Trolls and Other Degenerates

Trolling or *griefing* occurs when people deliberately attempt to spoil the enjoyment of a site at the expense of others. (*Griefing* is a term from the online game world; *trolling* comes from Usenet and message boards.) Trolls start conversations with the intent to generate an emotional response and derail the normal conversations on a forum. "Don't feed the trolls" is a common expression referring to a simple approach to community management: don't give undue attention to those who are seeking to provoke it (see Figure 15-1). Generally, trolls do not care much about your site or the topic, they are simply getting involved to bait people. Given the lack of normal face-to-face cues on the Internet, people tend to misread the intention of a comment and respond more directly than they would if they were in front of the person. Trolls understand this and seed conversations that they know will get a reaction. Once the troll has instigated a verbal war, he will either leave the site, amused at the disruption he caused, or continue to add further provocation.

Figure 15-1. Don't feed the trolls (image from http://xkcd.com/493/ used with permission)

The article at *http://www.wired.com/gaming/virtualworlds/magazine/16-02/mf_goons* gives good insight into the reasons behind people griefing others on virtual games. Similar dynamics are at work in trolling:

> Broadly speaking, a griefer is an online version of the spoilsport—someone who takes pleasure in shattering the world of play itself. Not that griefers don't like online games. It's just that what they most enjoy about those games is making other players not enjoy them…. Their work is complete when the victims log off in a huff.

Unfortunately, being a troll is in the eye of the beholder. On an emotive issue, someone from the other side might seem to be a troll to you, but from his point of view he is behaving appropriately. A recent and detailed article and interview with a renowned troll (see *http://www.nytimes.com/2008/08/03/magazine/03trolls-t.html*) paints a similar picture for why trolls hassle and upset people on the Internet.

Troll is a pejorative term and often used to color other people's reactions to a new voice or a contentious point of view that disagrees with the commonly held view of the community. Another reason that you need to be involved with your community: to determine the difference between minority viewpoints and people just stirring the pot for a reaction.

A common expression in community circles is "Don't feed the trolls." Ignoring them can be an effective way to deal with trolls, as they are essentially attention seekers. Blatant trolls are easy to identify; they are against the core belief of the site and have simple baits. However, there are many more sophisticated trolls who can formulate a decent argument. Sometimes, they use sock puppets—additional accounts—to augment their arguments. Sock puppets can be easy to identify and ban, as they tend to agree only with the viewpoint of the troll and comment only on threads where the troll is active, but identifying them requires good management tools. Going to the effort of maintaining multiple, seemingly real, identities is a lot of work, but it does happen. A more likely situation you will need to deal with is argumentative regulars or difficult (usually misunderstood) newcomers coming to your site and causing trouble.

Separating Communities

To allow some normal conversations to continue on Usenet, many contentious groups create a subgroup for advocacy. For instance, the comp.sys.mac.advocacy group was created so that comparisons between the Macintosh and other computing platforms would not drown out other conversations. The website *http://www.newsdemon.com/newsgroup-info/comp.sys.mac.advocacy* has the original charter from 1992:

> The existence of *.advocacy sub-groups is a recent innovation in netnews. There are currently 5 or 6 *.advocacy newsgroups and they have had a mixed success. In most cases they *have* succeeded in limiting the appearance of comparative articles in the other groups of a hierarchy where they appear.

In 1992 lots of people were predicting the demise of the Mac, so encouraging people to discuss the future of Apple in one place meant that people who actually were using Macs could discuss their interest in peace.

Splitting a group can be beneficial when there is the potential for the noise of repeated arguments, or for a particularly noisy faction to drown out normal conversation. A parallel approach on the early version of the Flickr site was that rather than having a single feedback forum, there were two forums: a FlickrIdeas forum and a FlickrBugs forum. Separating negative feedback from ideas gives people a space to complain and allows the team to make constructive responses without having to talk about promised new features in the same breath. Mixing feature requests and bug filing makes for untidy product development; separating them makes it is easier to differentiate between bugs that are being reported and features that are being requested.

The now closed BBC Science discussion boards took a similar approach, separating the discussion of evolution from the main science conversations. This allowed the people who wanted to discuss science to skip past the creationism versus evolution arguments. If you take this approach, you need to ensure that you engage with the new community you have created; otherwise, they will come back to the rest of the site, negating your desire to give them a separate space.

Encouraging Good Behavior

Unfortunately, trolls and spammers are part of the Internet landscape and are unlikely to pack up and go home, so encouraging them to move on to another site is (sadly) the answer. One basic idea is to give weight to the online identity that everyone has on your site. The more information an identity has about someone, the easier it is to determine whether he starts arguments all the time or plays nicely.

This approach is slanted against newcomers, but it is an accurate reflection of how the real world operates. People in general do not get full access to a community the moment they walk through the door; respect and trust are earned. That being said, you do not need to implement all of these restrictions on day one; a wait-and-see approach is often best.

Authenticating Through Profile Pages

Much of the trolling that occurs on the Internet happens because people can hide or pretend to be someone else. Often, the identity they have is transient and flimsy; for instance, their last three posts or no link to an external site. By making detailed profile pages that show a summary of the contributions a person has made, you can give others in the community a sense of who that person is in real life. See Chapter 12 for more detail on profile pages.

There is an obvious privacy concern here: no one wants to feel that their every action on the site is being monitored. So, you need to strike a balance. Listing every comment or reply that an individual makes might be going too far; listing the areas of the site to which she contributes on a regular basis might be enough. This would mean that you can determine whether the person is a regular for that topic area, so others can know whether to trust her viewpoint.

In terms of data analysis, you should definitely capture a lot more data about your community than you actually display on the site. You want to be able to see how often someone replies to and starts topics. Chapter 16 discusses the kinds of admin systems you will need to create.

Even without these tracking tools, a simple biography profile page showing real name, photograph, and location gives people a place to give their identity further credence, if they wish to do so. The people who contribute without supplying any personal information will have less face validity on the forum. People can make stuff up or not provide what's requested, but having a profile page at least stops people from claiming one identity one minute and another identity on a different board later in the day:

> The serious ones would give credible information; the jerks hiding behind anonymity would be exposed for what they are.[*]

—Timothy Garton Ash

Rating Posts and People

A very popular technique on some sites allows people to rate the content of people's posts and then indirectly rate the people making them. Slashdot provided an early example of this method, with its *karma points*. A karma point was an earned token that allowed a longer-term member to bless the postings of a newer user with a "+5, insightful" rating, or negatively rate a member downward. Readers could then set a floor above which they would read the comments on a thread, typically zero or higher. This meant that most idiotic posts were filtered out of view. It was a manual approach and it generated a whole new repertoire of low-value postings of "Mod this up" or "KP please," but it represents a good early approach to community management.

The mechanism for allocating these points varies among sites, but the aim is to allow filtering of content. Either the post itself is rated or the person making the post is rated. The kinds of ratings vary, too. The most common practice now is to rate the content. This is usually offered as a single positive action, such as "like," "was helpful," or "favorite." Only providing the means for positive feedback encourages a happier community feeling, as people are not looking for content to be negative about. On the other hand, Amazon allows positive and negative ratings of reviews, which seems to work well for it.

---

[*] *http://www.guardian.co.uk/commentisfree/2006/jul/13/comment.mainsection*

The goal of rating is to let the best content float to the surface so that someone reading the site can see the best reply or best review of an item easily. Conversational threads on community software can become very long, so some summary tools help a lot.

Another affordance ratings offer is when they are aggregated onto a person's profile. Yelp, the restaurant review site, is a good example of this type of aggregation. Profile pages include a rating summary so that you can see whether the profile owner tends to rate high or low; the number of posts and replies the person has made is also available there. In this way, you get to see how helpful or knowledgeable he is. Trolls generally post a lot and don't get marked as being helpful very often. You can develop a complex algorithm for determining the most helpful people on a site, but frequently a simple count is enough to give people a sense of what a person is like. Figure 15-2 shows a profile from Get Satisfaction, which gives a brief summary of this person's contributions to the site.

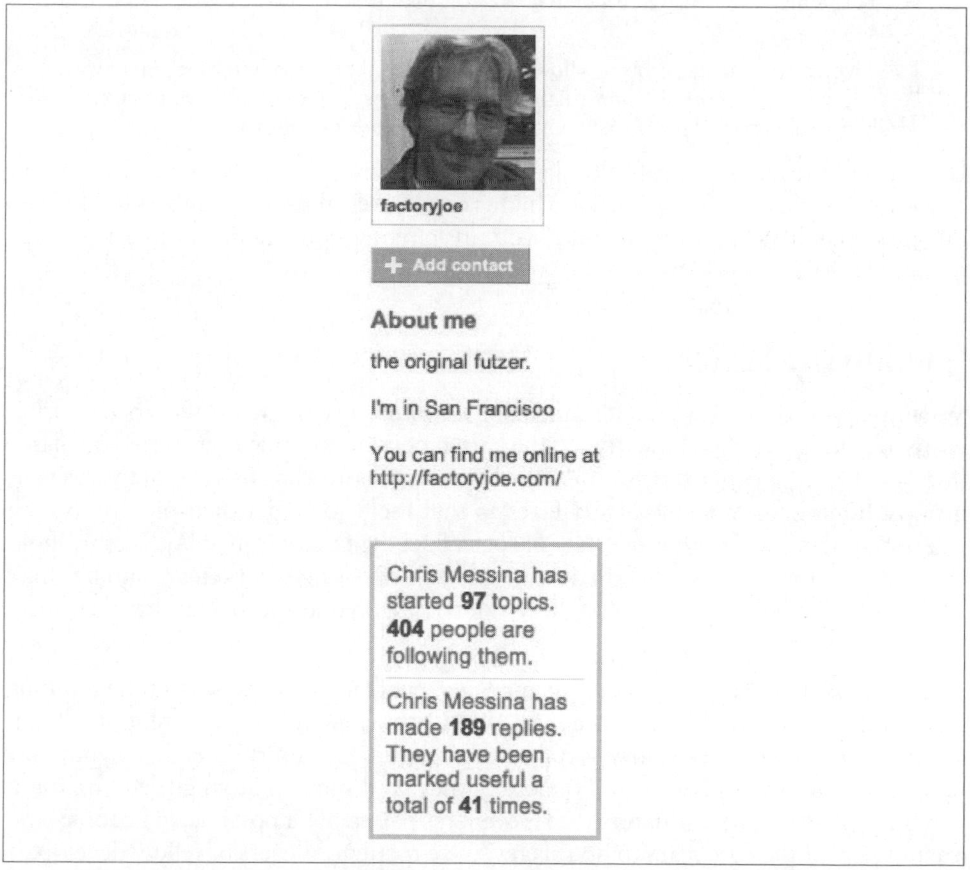

Figure 15-2. Chris Messina's profile from Get Satisfaction, showing the "marked as useful" functionality (used with permission)

A cautionary tale on points-based systems for members comes from Ben Brown, formerly of Consumating (*http://benbrown.com/says/2007/10/29/i-love-my-chicken-wire -mommy/*):

> The primary problem with Consumating points was that they did not actually give incentive to the members to do anything valuable. What we wanted people to do was write interesting posts, and then invite their friends to comment upon them. However, posting things to the site earned you nothing and inviting your friends earned you [a] similar amount of nothing. Even voting on and ranking content for us earned you nothing. The only way for a member to earn points was for another member to vote on one of their posts. We had essentially short-circuited our rewards system by handing over all of the power to the whims of our fickle members.
>
> Members without any pre-existing friends on the site had little chance to earn points unless they literally campaigned for them in the comments, encouraging point whoring. Members with lots of friends on the site sat in unimpeachable positions on the scoreboards, encouraging elitism. People became stressed out that they were not earning enough points, and became frustrated because they had no direct control over their scores.
>
> Even worse was our decision to allow negative votes that actually took points away. Anyone who joined the site immediately opened themselves to cavalcades of negative feedback from existing members whose goal was to protect their own ranking.

Directly linking points to profiles and making the controls for those points obvious and accessible can be harmful to your site. In this case, the established members could keep out new members. Be very careful if you are ranking your members in an obvious manner.

Gaming the System

Whenever you create a system for managing a community, someone will try to work it to his advantage. Earlier, I mentioned the karma point requesting that started on Slashdot. On Flickr, people started posting their pictures to dozens of loosely relevant groups, hoping for more views and faves so that they would get their pictures on the interestingness list. Another example of social hacking comes from eBay. Its threshold of 10 sales before some set of functionality is enabled is often worked around by small groups of people buying and selling low-value items to one another so that they seem to be legitimate.

Whenever planning a new community management feature, spend some time thinking through how you would try to break it. What behaviors are you unintentionally encouraging by creating some new social rules for your community? Analyzing your new feature for these flaws before you build it is time well spent. You might end up inadvertently creating a new situation that is even less palatable. If possible, get people who are not part of the core team to do this review; experienced users or fellow developers are good candidates. When making something new, it is hard to think like a bad guy as well as design for the well-behaved members, too.

Membership by Invitation or Selection

The famous Brainstorms community (*http://www.rheingold.com/community.html*), run by Howard Rheingold, operates on an invite-only basis. Once in, you need to be an actively contributing member for two weeks; otherwise, you get shown the door. Many other private mailing lists operate in this manner. Some even go as far as to allow blackballing of new members—any member can object to a new member joining without having to explain her reasoning. These measures are not necessary for many communities, but they are an effective tool for keeping out spammers and trolls.

Invite-only is widely used in setting up sites. The invite-only beta remains popular, and has a lot of advantages going for it—namely, that you get already-connected communities of people to join the site. (Chapter 18 explores launching in more depth.) Within Nature Network, private invite-only groups exist and are invisible until you are invited to join them. They are widely used as private spaces for reviewing published academic papers. Normally, the participants would not comment on these papers in public, so the private forum keeps their opinions safe from other scientists.

Search engines make everything on the Internet discoverable. Many communities may not want their activities to be quite this public. A place where all the participants are known and the conversation is hidden from the rest of the site can be regarded as private. This differs from the common type of Internet group, where common interest draws people together, rather than defined membership listings. Private groups place more demands on the person who is running the group and are harder to manage from a site perspective. If an argument breaks out among members of a private group, it is appropriate to bring this to the site moderator's attention, as he is unlikely to be a member of the group.

Some sites use external memberships as a means of controlling access to a site. For example, Sermo (*http://sermo.com*) is a site for doctors where they can discuss medical matters without comprising patient confidentiality. Members must be practicing MDs in the U.S. This type of site creates an automatic community, but it requires just as much work to encourage people to participate. Any site where the content should be available to only certain individuals should consider making areas private.

Access can be via payment or via a username and password with associated privileges. The challenge then becomes making sure only the right people get in. The Internet is rife with free password sites, and if you make the target too tempting, you will attract scammers.

Rewarding Good Behavior

Some sites open their functionality or even their membership on a good-behavior basis. If you are a good, active citizen on a site for a certain time period, you can use additional functionality of the site. A good example of this might be the ability to send personal messages directly to other members, or become a group host or help manage the community.

Earned privileges can be an effective way to encourage spammers to go away. A lot of spam is entirely automated, so having to participate on your site is a lot of work for a spammer. This technique is less effective with trolls, as their reward is not financial. In fact, making it hard to get in can increase their joy of spoiling the fun for those select few already inside.

One area worth looking at is any form of direct personal messaging. Some sites, such as Facebook and LinkedIn, make personal messaging available only when a two-way relationship is already in place. On Twitter, you can direct-message anyone who follows you, but simply following someone does not mean that you can direct-message her. Others, such as Nature Network, allow direct messaging on the decision of the recipient; she can opt-in to allow other people to send messages to her, a capability that is turned off by default. In both cases, the ability for a new person to send personal messages could be further controlled on the basis of previous behavior.

Helping the Community Manage Itself

Taking on the entire community management for a busy site is a big undertaking. Companies such as Yahoo! and the BBC spend large amounts of money running their sites, often using external companies to handle moderation. Sometimes this is necessary, but increasingly other approaches are proving to be more (cost-) effective.

Probably the most important thing you can do is to get the community to help you run the site, using the administrative tools you create for them. For example, I set up a running group on Flickr, then stopped running as often and so my support for the group dropped off, too. Feeling bad about that, I looked to see who was active and found someone who was starting conversations and posting lots of photos. I contacted him, asked whether he wanted to help run the group, he accepted, and I made him an admin.

Flickr supports this flexible approach to group management, as virtually all the groups are run by their members. Anyone can create a group and anyone can then create further admins and moderators of the group. There are two benefits to getting the community involved in running things: your costs drop and the members start to feel that it is their community. Keeping this sense of involvement is important. Some companies cannot accommodate Flickr-style moderation; often their editorial needs require them to retain control of the moderation process. Many newspapers fall into this category. In these cases, you can still get the community to help with moderation by flagging issues for editorial attention.

There are many approaches to community management, from empowering some people to help manage the community to allowing everyone to rate the content of everyone else. There are also a range of semiautomatic posting approaches based on analysis of comment frequency and the content of comments. In the next section, we'll look at some of these tools.

Moderating a Community

There are many models for how moderation should work on a site, and new ones are appearing frequently. The problems remain the same: keep people friendly, stop trouble as soon as possible, and allow people to feel involved. Online conversations can get heated quickly, given the partial attention they are frequently given compared to a face-to-face conversation. The limited text-only medium also means people say things that they intend as innocuous, but can be misread easily.

Allowing limited edits after posting is one good way of smoothing things over. Offering a grace period of 15 minutes means corrections can be made and hasty sentences revised, as in the example in Figure 15-3. On a fast-moving board you may find that the 15-minute window means there are already responses to the post. In this case, it is important to timestamp the comment to show that it was edited. A *belt and braces* approach would be to version the comment in question so that the previous comment can still be read. Few sites need that level of content management, but the automatic timestamping can be helpful.

gavin replied less than a minute ago — Delete or Edit (for 15 minutes) — Inappropriate?

@Fraser thanks for the feedback on batch uploading, it makes sense.

Figure 15-3. Allowing a 15-minute grace period for editing posts (this element is taken from Get Satisfaction)

Moderation is the process of dealing with a situation in which someone is upset or irritated. It generally involves at least two people, and the situation can range from mild factual inaccuracies to hate speech or libel. There needs to be a means for raising the moderation request, a means of notifying the appropriate person of the request, and a means of responding to it. There are dozens of ways to do this, especially around the triggering of the moderation request.

A simple system allows for any member to raise a moderation request on any comment left by another member. More complex systems might require multiple people to request moderation, or allow only people of a certain level or seniority to request it. Some systems have the moderators reading and acting on posts, essentially acting as both users and moderators.

Once the moderation request has been raised, it needs to be communicated to the people who are responsible for handling moderation for that section of the site. Typically, this is done through email, but it could be an SMS message, or an IM, or even a dedicated web application.

Handling the moderation is the next step. Again, a simple approach is one in which the moderator decides whether the comment is inappropriate, and if she decides it is, the comment from the original author will be modified in some manner. Simply removing the comment entirely will disrupt the conversation flow on the site, so replacing it is usually the best approach. A "this comment has been removed by the moderators" note is effective. Another approach is that of *disemvoweling*, from Teresa Nielsen Hayden, moderator at Making Light and Boing Boing. Disemvoweling removes all the vowels from a comment left by a person (see *http://en.wikipedia.org/wiki/Disemvoweling*). It is still possible to read the comment; it just requires a bit more effort, so many people will pass over it and move on. It can be an effective means of silencing, but not censoring. Moving arguing commentators to a *naughty room* can also be very effective. Sometimes people want to have an argument, so giving them a space to take it outside is sometimes the best approach to handling this kind of energy. Usually everyone else would rather get on with a productive discussion; the arguing pair can be safely moved elsewhere.

Some sites make the moderation response process more collective, requiring that another person agree with the suggested moderation action. This makes moderation more of a community act, resulting in less potential for partial moderation. It can be an effective approach when the moderators are also active users of the site. The politics of moderation could fill many pages. Starting with a simple system and developing it alongside your community will help you create one that works well. It can be easy to fall into a *them and us* model, and difficult to get out of. Most members of your site are not out to get you, but keeping the jerks at bay can be tiring work, particularly if their attacks on the moderators become personal.

Some companies run quite strict forums. Apple, for instance, is notorious for shutting down conversations on its forums that become too critical or noisy. Issues are rarely acknowledged, but Apple does pay some attention to the forums and fixes are forthcoming for problems. See the article at *http://www.guardian.co.uk/technology/blog/2007/dec/21/applecensorshipatissueoni* for some examples.

On Wikipedia, moderation and page locking are a high art. The "talk" page for any article often comprises a long-running debate over the content. Some pages become a battleground between the whitewashers, who want to force an issue in a particular direction, and the neutral-point-of-view editors. For instance, the George W. Bush page is sometimes fully locked (see *http://en.wikipedia.org/wiki/Wikipedia:Protection_policy*). Most organizations will not have the passions that ride behind Apple and Wikipedia, but these examples are helpful in anticipating the kinds of issues your company (commercial or non-commercial) might have to deal with.

Intervention and Course Correction

A major part of community management is ensuring that people get along with one another. Some of the work can feel like that of a counselor or social worker, in that you're dealing with arguments between individuals, or you're ensuring that one group is not actively upsetting another. Tools that allow rapid bursts of activity are helpful in this regard. Arguments tend to be fast-paced. Using direct emails to intervene and arbitrate is a very effective mechanism. People can forget that the site is run by other people and that the rest of the community comprises people too, so a gentle personal reminder can bring them back to more reasonable ground.

The other main job of a moderator (or host) is to encourage conversation and bring it back on topic for that board. Sometimes simply intervening and commenting on a thread can help to direct it back on topic. Other useful techniques are *locking*, *pinning*, and *splitting*. Locking or closing a topic when an issue is no longer productively being discussed can be one approach to stopping a conversation that is overly negative. Pinning usually means making the conversation one of the first topics visible on the message board. This is very helpful for frequently asked questions or announcements. Splitting can take an otherwise useful conversation that is buried inside another topic and make it one in its own right. For example, say that in an arts forum, John posts about theatre ticket availability; 15 posts later, Jane comments about public transportation closures for the evening in question. The main topic of the thread then becomes public transportation. This might be a good candidate to split and move to the travel forum rather than keeping it in the arts forum.

Community management is the positive side of moderation, though not everyone will agree with the community managers. The community managers are the public face of the site (see "Community Managers" on page 75). Their actions and opinions help to shape how the site will evolve and what types of community interactions will be encouraged. They are a critical part of the site, more important than how the software gets built or chosen; but often this role is understaffed or the person or people in this role are not given the tools require to do the job properly. Meg Pickard, head of Social Media Development at the *Guardian*, has drawn up some guidelines for running communities that are a good starting place for your own community; see *http://www.guardian.co.uk/talkpolicy*.

Premoderation and Libel

Some companies decide that vetting everything is the safe approach. While this does mean that only content you have approved will be on the site, it is a very slow way to get a conversation going. Opening hours and vetting are appropriate for forums aimed at children, however; for a good example, see the BBC CBBC message board, aimed at kids 15 and younger (*http://www.bbc.co.uk/cbbc/mb/*).

Online conversations can get heated and move very quickly. There are countless examples of heated conversations happening while the editorial staff looked the other way. The *LA Times* wikitorial is a famous example. The Internet operates 24 hours a day, even if your team or staff members do not. This can lead some companies to think that having the opening hours for the community coincide with their working hours is appropriate. If you do this, though, you will miss some of your best discussions.

According to U.S. and UK law, premoderating or vetting a board means you become the publisher of the content and so you take on the legal responsibility for libel. Libel law is complex and varies from country to country, so make sure you get legal advice on how the law pertains to your country. Understanding the position in the United States is important, as libel claimants can file claims in any country you have offices in and settlements tend to be higher in the U.S.

Extreme Measures: Banning Users and Removing Posts

Sometimes things get out of hand and it is tempting to reach for the *ban* button. Simple, outright, permanent banning of people encourages them to come right back again under a different name. However, if you have profiles, the amount of work involved in creating a new profile will discourage banned people from popping up again. A better approach is to give a *timeout*, a ban for a few days. Bans from certain sections of the site can work well, too. You want to retain the person as a member of your community in most cases, but ensure that he is aware you think his behavior is out of line. Banning should never be the immediate response, except for porn, spammers, or other extreme examples.

Too frequently, a ban or removal of a post will make the moderation seem harsh, and the community will feel like they are being watched and may drift elsewhere. It is important, then, to have a clear set of house rules and ensure that your own team sticks to them. If you are changing policy, make the changes clear, too.

Competing commercial needs can cause conflict in terms of policy setting. If you do not allow advertising or items for sale, handling manufacturers and vendors on your forums might become tricky; encouraging them to have a voice without giving them a free storefront is a challenge. Working with your commercial partners and getting them to understand the balance between community involvement and your needs for advertising income is important. Handling criticism of commercial partners from the community is also necessary.

Banning should be your last resort, and you should use it only when the situation has become unworkable for everyone concerned. Those banned should pose a real problem to the entire community, disrupting the positive experience; you should never ban someone simply because he does not agree with you. Repeated breaking of community guidelines and a failure to respond to approaches for reasonable behavior are the basic guidelines upon which to make this kind of decision. There is no other choice for some kinds of users:

> However, we've come to the conclusion that sometimes there is simply not a way to deal with a member of the community who insists on constantly and consistently harassing other community members.[†]

Good moderation is an active process, one that evolves and changes as the site community develops. As such, it is also necessary to be responsive to the wider community that your group is part of: the phrase "no man is an island" is just as true for Internet-based social software. Community management at Flickr is a good case in point:

> Heather Champ doesn't just guard the pool and blow the occasional whistle; it's a far more delicate, and revealing, dance that keeps the user population here happy, healthy and growing.[‡]

Heather Champ is Flickr's Director of Community. In the article from which the preceding quote was taken, she describes the daily process of reviewing and deciding which communities to work with and which to act against. Finding a balance between benefiting the individual and the community at the same time is the goal, and it requires an active approach to community management.

Absent Landlords Lead to Weak Communities

Community management is a full-time job. Someone needs to be encouraging people and reining them in all the time. The time it takes to do this can be hard to carve out of a busy job. Supporting community management is a bigger undertaking than many people realize. As a result, often you find sites with minimal management in place.

Building good communities requires more work than the setup does. If your own staff will manage the site, you need to factor this into their working hours. If you are relying on the community to help you manage the site, you need to give them tools for managing their groups and forums. These tools need to be clear and simple to use for the tasks that require urgent attention. Good guidelines on how to run communities and coaching early on for new community managers can have a huge impact on whether they succeed or fail. So few people are willing to start things on the Internet that those who are willing need your help to keep them at it.

Filtering and Automation

Repetitive, low-value posting can be a very negative influence. One-word or one-phrase comments such as "Lame" and "First post" create a very juvenile atmosphere. Slashdot

---

† *http://blog.getsatisfaction.com/2008/05/20/the-ban-hammer/*

‡ *http:///www.sfgate.com/cgi-bin/article.cgi?f=/g/a/2008/09/29/onthejob.DTL*

famously suffers from this kind of behavior. It is quite widespread, though, and the web comic XKCD's message board developed a novel tool to deter "me too" comments.

The tool ROBOT9000 (*http://blag.xkcd.com/2008/01/14/robot9000-and-xkcd-signal -attacking-noise-in-chat/*) analyzes past conversations on a message board and allows only the posts that are unique. So, you can have one occurrence of "Lame," for instance, but it cannot appear again. Offenders get a time-based ban that lengthens with each repeated occurrence. This sort of intelligent filter can be a real help in forcing people to use their brains and not their fingers first.

Get Satisfaction is trying to solve a similar problem: that of asking the same questions repeatedly. On the site, new topics are filtered and matched against previous topics. Before a person can submit her new topic, she is shown the matching previous problems. This appeals to basic human nature: people want answers quickly. They often think their situation is unique, and quickly ask a question without searching the forums first. By using their question as a detailed search query, you ensure that any good candidate topics are likely to be found. Get Satisfaction gains a happy new user, as she found her answer, and the company in question avoids having the same issue dealt with in dozens of repeat postings.

Filtering topics and replies is a relatively recent development, but many sites could improve with this intelligent matching approach. Matt Gemmell made a similar argument recently in his blog, *http://mattgemmell.com/2008/12/08/what-have-you-tried*. The post is aimed at Cocoa developers and the increasing numbers of so-called programmers who do no research and just ask for code to be written or modified. He makes the argument that problem solving should be part a developer's mindset.

Encouraging your members to research and think before starting new conversations will make for a better community experience all around. Photography sites, for instance, are filled with questions about which lens is best, and hi-fi sites with questions about which amplifier and speakers to buy. The problem is widespread and filtering offers an approach to solving it that gets around the general laziness of most people, who will not formulate a detailed query but will happily write a new topic in the hope of an answer.

Balancing Anonymity and Pseudo-Anonymity

I touched on this topic earlier in the book, but the choice you make in terms of how much you want your participants to tell the truth about who they are will have a direct bearing on the kind of community you create. Few sites allow fully anonymous commenting, where the site owner does not know who is commenting. Most require an account of some form to be created with email validation. Thus, all commenting is pseudo-anonymous, rather than anonymous. The participants can hide their identity from the others on the site, but you, as the site owner, should be able to get in contact with them if the need arises.

You'll need to allow for screen names, as all the John Smiths in the world cannot be guaranteed the username "JohnSmith." However, encouraging the use of real names means it is easier to create a community where people know one another and can find friends. The popular practice of linking to profiles on other sites is making an anonymous profile on the Internet harder to maintain. For the majority of forums, encouraging the use of real names as screen names is a good baseline. However, there are many situations in which people will not wish to be seen online discussing sensitive issues, or they will worry about being caught wasting employers' time on the Internet, so you cannot mandate the use of real names on your site. The larger the role you allow for pseudo-anonymous usage of your site, the more opportunity people have for mischief. This is fine for some sites, but if you want long-term, more serious discussions to evolve, allowing people to use their real names will help. This can be based on profile information, if names are too sensitive. Describing someone as "late 30s, lives in London, and develops web applications" describes me and many of my friends, but it gives a better sense of who I am than simply "zzgavin."

Summary

Once the initial site is complete, community management will account for more of the budget and will define the site more than any feature. Striking a balance between people, editorial, and technology is important; you need all three of these elements pulling together for a system to work well. Once the site is live, the community managers and the users of the site are the main people who will give direction and opinion regarding how the site should be developing. They are key to its future, as they are the people who are there. However, the noisiest people are not necessarily the people to build for. Your community managers will help to find the middle space between the new people you have not met yet and the keen regulars.

Managing the conversations on your site can be a difficult task: situations will get out of hand, and people will get upset. Some of your users will likely hate you, and will tell you this loudly. Developing a well-understood set of community guidelines and a good set of tools to track and manage the traffic on the site will help keep this in check. Taking time for a regular meeting of the community and product managers is also a helpful activity, giving time to review how you and the community are interacting.

CHAPTER 16

Writing the Application

A complex system that works is invariably found to have evolved from a simple system that worked. The inverse proposition also appears to be true: A complex system designed from scratch never works and cannot be made to work. You have to start over, beginning with a working simple system.[*]

—John Gall

This chapter and the following one are the main technical chapters in this book. That being said, this chapter is not aimed only at developers; you will not find a lot of code here. This chapter offers advice on how to create applications and integrate the design and product management aspects of building an application with the code-writing aspects.

I'm going to make a few assumptions about your experience first: you use validating HTML and probably have a preference for HTML, XHTML, or HTML5; you use CSS to present the visual aspects of your site and JavaScript to handle the behavior of your application in the browser; and you understand the benefits of unobtrusive JavaScript so that your site degrades gracefully and works well without JavaScript. If my assumptions are incorrect, Jeffrey Zeldman's *Designing with Web Standards* (Peachpit Press) and Jeremy Keith's *Bulletproof Ajax* (New Riders) are important reading first.

I'm also not recommending any particular language; recent social web applications have come in everything from Lisp to Scala to PHP, Ruby, and Python; there are even some C applications. Pick the one you feel comfortable developing with and concentrate on writing clean, understandable code.

If you come from a Java background, you might be more familiar with books such as *Enterprise Integration Patterns* by Gregor Hohpe and Bobby Woolf or *Patterns of Enterprise Application Architecture* by Mark Fowler (both published by Addison-Wesley

---

[*] *http://en.wikipedia.org/wiki/Gall's_law*

Professional). This chapter won't go into the depths that those books do, but as web applications grow from being scripts talking to locally hosted SQL databases to multiserver distributed applications, a lot of the material in those books becomes relevant.

So, what is in this chapter? I'll show how social applications differ in architecture, development approaches, design, and deployment from other applications. We'll also look at some important recent open web protocols and frameworks. The internal admin systems and collective intelligence you can glean from these social applications will round out the chapter, with space to look at the environmental impact of your application for good measure.

Small Is Good: A Reprise

Simple systems are easier to relate to, and are more likely to work than complex systems. They do need to have certain capabilities to support extension into greater complexity, however. From the start, design your systems with the expectation of adding to them. This means you need to think about how elements might integrate rather than building closed systems. Starting small means you can more easily test whether your approach to something is correct. However, it is too easy to find your plans for a small thing growing like a weed, with additional functionality being added and clouding the initial focus. Larger teams and companies suffer from this in particular; there are too many opinions and vested interests to support.

One main content type and two to three activities to do should be enough for launch. One of these activities must be the primary one and the others should act in a supporting role. You can add more capabilities later. Keeping your focus on one small product is not easy. Remember Steve Jobs's quote about product focus, "I am as proud of the things we have not done as I am of the things we have done."[†] You need to be just as prepared to set limits and not pursue every interesting idea.

Designing an API and expecting further development to come from the API is a good approach to deflecting the desire for a big application. A good example of a site that still feels small is Flickr; there are many things to do on Flickr, but the focus of the application is still people and photographs.

How Social Applications Differ from Web Applications

There are key differences between a regular website and a social web application. Much of the content on a social application belongs to the people who use the site, as opposed to the site owners on a regular website. This ownership aspect is probably the most significant difference.

---

† *http://money.cnn.com/galleries/2008/fortune/0803/gallery.jobsqna.fortune/6.html*

In a social web application, other people's identities are strongly linked to the content they have contributed, and both their identity and this content are strongly linked to your site. Other people are an explicit part of your website. Social web applications are no longer a simple case of your content, your servers, your databases, and your software. Other people are involved. You can't easily talk with these other people and explain things to them. In addition, they have rights; the content belongs to them. You need to respect their needs and try to do the right thing with their data. The data remains theirs, which is easy to forget.

The structure of this data is also different. It is not a simple table of inventory to show on a page. It is highly interlinked and frequently polymorphic. A tag belongs to a piece of content, yet the tag was placed by a person. Depending on your application, this same tag could have been placed by multiple people on the same item of content. The tag itself might be a member of various tag clusters, which help to refine its meaning. Functionality can be polymorphic, too; a commenting service can exist on events or on articles.

Then there is your community; a good social application will be a close fit for your community's needs, but any one of them will be unable to articulate what the community actually wants, let alone how to build it. They can describe what they personally want, but abstracting this across the thousands of people on your site is difficult. Yet they are there on your site, at arm's reach as a user of your service. Given the relationships that are prevalent on social applications, you are likely to interact with a good number of users on a daily basis on your site. The scope for staff-to-member interaction on most other types of sites is low.

Drawing on this relationship between your community and your site is a strength. Carefully listening to the community will help you figure out what they want, and this should lead to your site being a success. Your community should shape what you build, not specify what you build. Certainly, you should hold off on building a large and complex site before unveiling it as a completed entity.

One other aspect that affects social web applications is the rapidly evolving swirl of protocols, APIs, and frameworks. Over little more than a year from early 2008 and into 2009, there has been much activity in open social web technologies. OpenID, OAuth, Portable Contacts, Open Social, Activity Streams, and the many Connect services have all progressed in leaps and bounds. This alone makes fixed, multiquarter development plans fragile at best.

Agile Methodologies

Agile approaches to working with lean software such as XP and Scrum are popular ways of delivering social applications. Planning a month at a time with an actively maintained product backlist is a good development structure for social applications. A *product backlist* is a simple list of all the ideas you've had for your product, good and bad. On a monthly basis, you assess what is relevant and put that forward for the next month's release. This approach comes from Scrum, and the intention is to slow the pace of bright ideas interrupting already planned work, but to still have a place to capture them.

Planning even quarterly releases means you will be creating the application your community wanted four to five months earlier, given the time required to plan and agree on functionality.

The Agile Manifesto‡ is a good approach to social application development (see *http://agilemanifesto.org/*) and makes the following recommendations. The italic items are valued over the items on the righthand side:

> *Individuals and interactions* over processes and tools
>
> *Working software* over comprehensive documentation
>
> *Customer collaboration* over contract negotiation
>
> *Responding to change* over following a plan

The end-to-end prototyping approach encouraged within agile methodologies is also a good approach to discovering how things might work on your site. Making a working version of the first element of your problem in your application means you have a working version. Building each component completely, one at a time, means you get a working application only at the end of the process.

Understanding the balance between prototyping and designing the user interface is important. The interface is key, but this does not mean you have to craft the perfect interface and then graft it onto finished server-side code. The user interface is merely one layer; it does not specify the system architecture. It should be possible to have overlapping streams of work determining both the user experience and the technical implementation on a new application and on larger features. Before we discuss these considerations, I want to jump ahead and address how to deploy new versions of your applications to your thriving community.

Deployment and Version Control

Retaining flexibility is important when deploying and managing version control. There are many schools of thought on how version launches should be handled. Some people adhere to infrequent and major releases, as is done in desktop software development. But the majority of web application developers I've spoken with prefer a more open source model of "release early and often."

This works differently on varying teams. For instance, some teams insist on making sure the trunk is always deployable, even down to having a 15-minute warning prior

---

‡ *The Agile Manifesto* is property of ©2001 Kent Beck, Mike Beedle, Arie van Bennekum, Alistair Cockburn, Ward Cunningham, Martin Fowler, James Grenning, Jim Highsmith, Andrew Hunt, Ron Jeffries, Jon Kern, Brian Marick, Robert C. Martin, Steve Mellor, Ken Schwaber, Jeff Sutherland, and Dave Thomas.

to deployment (the *trunk* is the current, in-development version of your application; it is where all the check-ins of code get merged). Flickr and Last.fm, which both deploy frequently, use IRC as a live communications medium for logging all deployment and configuration activity. (See *http://www.slideshare.net/jallspaw/operational-efficiency-hacks-web20-expo2009* and look specifically at slides 111 through 124. Also see "Infrastructure and Web Operations" on page 294.) Multiple deploys per day are possible; even 50 per day in some environments supported by techniques such as continuous integration, which we'll discuss later.

Many teams over the past few years have moved from CVS (Concurrent Versions System, one of the original version control systems) to Subversion and, more recently, to distributed tools. Popular approaches to retaining flexibility revolve around the concept of *branching*. There are three main options, each of which has advantages:

- Developing each new feature in a new branch gives a clear separation of where the new stuff is being created, but makes multiple features hard to develop.
- Developing in the trunk and deploying from the trunk wraps features in *conditionals*. This gets more complex as the size of the team grows.
- Developing in the trunk and branching for a deployment retains the conditionality of the previous approach, but gives clarity on what makes the cut for release and what doesn't. This is probably the most popular approach used with tools such as Subversion.

Distributed version control tools, such as Mercurial and Git, are in vogue as of early 2009. Compared to centralized version controls tools, systems such as Git make simple commits more difficult, but they make previously complex tasks such as merging and branching much easier. This means experiments are much easier to carry out, which keeps a deployable trunk. Distributed version control works better with the less office-centric nature of working environments. Every developer has a complete working repository of the code and can make his own changes, then selectively merge these changes into the common version. This selectivity provides freedom and allows for private experimentation.

Understanding your version control system is essential. The product management team needs to understand the system's potential and its constraints; the development team needs to understand the possibilities. This is regardless of the choice of version control tool, be it SVN, Git, or some other option.

If you have a simple deployment approach, you have the three tiers with something similar to the following setup:

Developer's machine
    This is the local checked-out instance of code being worked on by individual developers.

Dev

> This is the current checked-in and deployed version of unreleased code for deployment. Initial testing happens here. This server is also the first integration point for code from each developer. An automated build server may create these deploys.

Staging

> Once past the dev tests, the unreleased code is deployed against (a snapshot of) production data.

Public beta

> If necessary, you can put new code on separate servers that selected users have limited access to for testing (see the next section for more on this).

Live

> This is the current released code and live data. It is publicly visible.

This is a fine model, but it allows for only one possible view of the code to the public. To give alpha users access to unreleased code, they need to see either the staging server or the public beta server and work against a snapshot copy of live data.

Testing Live Is Possible, but Use Conditionality

An improved version of deployment management allows for different types of users on the site. A filter for alpha-feature users allows two sets of code to coexist on the live deployed site. This requires some thought in terms of database setup, perhaps making copies of tables or writing data twice—to duplicate tables—during migration periods. A further wrinkle on this results from making different features available to different types of users. For example, there might be a core feature set, a specific set of alpha features, and a special need-to-know set of new features. To enable this approach, you need to be able to support tagged releases and assign the tags to people. Conditional logic then determines which code runs for which group of people.

Conditionality, like the tagged release setup, gives a much more human approach to developing features. It is more complex to code for, but it makes rapid deployment feasible. The internal conversation turns from deploying a feature in a specific public release at the end of the month, to deploying it for Matt, Paul, and Tom to see what they think now. You get a much more rapid turnaround in terms of feature deployment and bug fixing. Alongside these micro deployments, you also can make more standard feature-led releases. To achieve these releases, you simply ensure that all the conditional features are either tested and then made available for all, or are removed. This means you can keep all the development in the trunk and deploy regularly, even several times per day.

Working in this manner is best with small teams in the same room or, at least, in the same building. Teams that know one another well can work in this manner, too. However, this technique will not work as well with large teams that communicate through project managers, as it is very likely that information will get distorted as its passed from person to person—each adding a layer of interpretation so that, for example, once a developer's question about parameters for visualization of a rating system gets passed through several non-technical managers, it has turned into one about visualization for user profiles. There is unintentional loss of clarity as the information is passed from person to person, due to an incomplete understanding of the query and development systems.

The essence of this approach involves easy, regular communication. Everyone on the team should *know* the state of the current development build and what is going to happen next. An analogy about a home renovation is appropriate here: the carpenter, the plumber, and the plasterer need to coordinate to ensure that the underfloor (radiant) heating system is fitted correctly. They also need to know what the plans are for the electrical work so that they leave space for this work.

Test-Driven Development

Another step toward a more fluid style of development comes from testing properly. Regular, small deployments are recommended, but if they aren't carefully planned, they can turn into "firefighting." However, with the right discipline and tools, it can be a fantastic development approach. Reliable test support for your project is essential. Tests need to be fine-grained and comprehensive.

This is not the same as quality assurance (QA), which is usually done by people, perhaps supported by automated tools. Testing here is entirely automated and integrated into the build process. QA typically will test an entire section of an application when it is ready. In this kind of automated testing, testing occurs at the level of individual function calls.

Approaches such as test-driven development (TDD) are very useful. Test-first development encourages an approach whereby the test is written first and run to show that it fails. The code is written to make the test pass, and then the code is refactored, or tidied up. Taking small steps here is the right approach. Tests should be fine-grained; a single test per feature is not enough, but this level of test coverage is what you often get from tests written after the main code for the application has been written. TDD gives you these fine-grained tests as part of the developer workflow.

The developer should understand the application she is building and the new requirements for the feature. (See Kent Beck's book *Test-Driven Development: By Example* [Addison-Wesley Professional] for more.) The key aspect is that the tests are written before the application code, rather than in response to the code. This tends to produce applications with less code and less debugging required. The code needs to support the tests. Reverting to a prechange version and rewriting based on a version control system becomes more appealing than debugging. The key contribution from non-developer members of the team is a set of well-written use cases, including error condition behaviors.

Meanwhile, newer approaches such as behavior-driven development (BDD) add a deeper context to the testing approach of test-driven development. BDD helps developers see why a feature is being created. Unlike test-driven development, BDD adds a layer in front of the development process. As such, some people might think it complicates development. However, advocates of BDD suggest that this is simply a change to how requirements are drawn up, and the focus on why a feature is being created outweighs the potential additional work involved. Defining desired behaviors and supporting them with tests can give everyone a more complete picture of what is happening. The language used in BDD is also much more similar to the business language used by the rest of the team, so it creates a shared vocabulary, which springs from the story-like approach to defining behaviors.

Support for both test- and behavior-driven development exists in every mainstream language. On the projects I've read about and worked on, both approaches have been a great help; such tests are definitely not wasted programmer time.

Automated Builds Make Management Easier

The next step in getting to an easier deployment is an automated one step-build process. There should be a simple script or even a web interface that allows checkout from version control, runs any appropriate checks, and then deploys. Rollback should be just as simple so that in case of a problem, a newly deployed release can be reverted. This is becoming much more common, but older projects, particularly ones which have components in multiple languages, often require several manual steps before reaching the deployment stage. Automation is good; humans make mistakes, particularly under pressure, so automating this drudgery is a great idea.

Continuous Integration (CI) (*http://martinfowler.com/articles/continuousIntegration .html*)—another tool for supporting flexible development—runs your tests every time something is checked into source control. With CI, integration stops being a scary prospect and becomes a regular activity. See *http://confluence.public.thoughtworks.org/ display/CC/CI+Feature+Matrix* for a list of current CI tools. Daily integration of builds can be a way to work up to a Continuous Integration process, if you have an existing project.

Applying Developer Tools to Social Applications

So, how do all these techniques apply to social software? The ability to rapidly deploy features to see whether they are liked and then to either move forward with them or drop them depends on reliable code; BDD and TDD will help deliver this. CI, meanwhile, will help keep your project just a few hours away from deployment. You still need to keep a firm handle on how the whole user experience will manifest itself as it matures, but with these tools, you should have a firm base from which to work. Most people like to feel you are paying attention to them; being able to rapidly iterate your application shows that you care about your community. Having to tell your users that a bug that occurred in April won't be fixed until the July build says a lot to them about your approach to community management.

Making Use of Flexible Development with Your Community

There are a variety of ways to use flexible development, one of which is to randomly sample users. Twitter, for instance, sampled a percentage of its users with its new search interface in the first quarter of 2009. Based on the feedback, it altered the user interface for the search product it got when it acquired Summize (*http://blog.twitter.com/2009/04/discovery-engine-is-coming.html*). Sampling up to 2% or 3% of your users can be a very effective way to find out how a large group of people will use a new feature without giving everyone access to it. Many other companies use public betas for testing new features.

Another useful approach is to use a private group or groups. Many sites have a private "Friend of X" type of group whose members get access to features a few days ahead of the main release. On Dopplr, for example, there are different private groups for different features. Some are trip-related, some are early users, and some are based on accepted invites. Each of these private test groups is more focused than a single alpha testing group. Groups such as this contain people who are not immediate friends, so there is some distance that allows for a more critical assessment.

That being said, enabling conditional access on your application requires five things:

- A group of people who you'd like to test the new feature
- A new feature to test
- A means of adding the conditional logic into your application
- Some criteria for determining success or value
- A mechanism for offering feedback on the new feature

You will need to select a specific group of people to test the new feature. This can be a regular test group or a special group you've formed just to test this feature. The criteria for choosing these people should be clear. The likelihood of the group to use the feature once it is deployed should be high on your list of criteria (different features will have different requirements). As for the second bullet point, obviously you need a new feature to test, and it should be functioning, but a few rough edges can be acceptable.

Then you'll need to make the feature available to the people you have chosen. Conditional application logic on your live site is becoming the most popular approach to doing this. There are two reasons behind this. First, it may seem more complex to have conditionality on your live site, but having a separate set of hardware and operations management is also complex. Second, it means the testing will be happening as part of the person's normal use of the site, rather than pretend use on a test server.

Finally, you'll need to obtain some feedback. Decide how you will determine success for the features before you plan your feedback mechanisms. It might be that the feature is simply faster, or that more of something is done. Using contact lists as an example, you might implement access to external address books as a feature. Having implemented this feature, you might look for an increase in the rate of new people being invited and generally improved feedback on the contact management section. Obviously, each feature will have unique criteria. You can gather qualitative feedback from your testers via email or on a private forum, but often some quantitative data is most helpful. For this you will need to determine a baseline measurement for the feature. A baseline would normally consist of counts related to the feature being developed. In the address book example, the rate of invites per user of the site per month might be one measure for a baseline. Then, note how this changes for your group of testers.

Lots of companies take this approach to testing. For instance, in early 2009, 37signals wrote a blog post about how it used A/B testing on five different versions of a page, and monitored which version got the greatest number of orders (for more information on this, see *http://www.37signals.com/svn/posts/1711-design-decisions-the-new-back pack-marketing-site*).

Infrastructure and Web Operations

Now that your code is deployable, you now will need something on which to deploy it. Early on, you can probably use a single server for everything. Many hosting accounts will put the database as localhost on the same machine and rely on RAID for live backups, with regular external backups. This does leave you vulnerable to spiky loads from the network effect, however.

I'll cover scaling in "Scaling and Messaging Architectures" on page 309, but for now, it's important to know that there is a lot to look at in terms of a good monitoring infrastructure. Ganglia (*http://ganglia.info/*) is becoming a favorite for monitoring cluster environments, and Nagios (*http://www.nagios.org/*) is good for other services and general installations. Monitoring your servers is a great idea. From simply making sure your service is up to live analysis of throughput and cache efficiency, there is a lot to observe and improve. Hosting web applications costs money. Using monitoring, you can ensure that you are spending less money, as well as ready in case of downtime.

There are some interesting graphs of web operations activity (no, really) on the Flickr group WebOps Visualizations page (*http://www.flickr.com/groups/webopsviz/*); this group is turning into a great place for analysis of odd behaviors for web ops staff. The group was set up by John Allspaw, operations manager at Flickr. He also wrote *The Art of Capacity Planning (http://oreilly.com/catalog/9780596518578/)* (O'Reilly).

Good operations management is key to getting successful social software sites to work well. There are many strands to this—the software build process I discussed is one of them—but the main area is monitoring and managing the servers running your site.

Managing Operations

Good operations management has six main aspects. Paying attention to all six will help ensure your site's success. As your site grows, there will be many more areas to manage, but these are good to start with:

Run multiple web servers with a reverse proxy, even if you have a single server
Using multiple web servers to run your applications means you can restart some of them with new versions of software, leave others alone to try out different features, or simply do rolling restarts to deploy code without any downtime. Try using HAProxy (*http://haproxy.1wt.eu*) or Nginx (*http://nginx.net*) as a proxy and load balancer; I'll discuss this further later in the chapter.

Use deployment management tools to manage your servers
If you have more than one server, Puppet (*http://reductivelabs.com/*) or Chef (*http://wiki.opscode.com/display/chef/Home*) will help you to manage the whole life cycle as well as different types of service. Tools such as these can create new servers and upgrade operating systems, which can help you immensely; as I said earlier, humans make mistakes, but tested scripts do not. This should get rid of a lot of false bugs.

Make sure you control the libraries and software versions you use
Countless hours are lost due to live and staging environments having different libraries installed. Tools such as Capistrano (*http://www.capify.org/*) will manage this for you. Versions are available for a variety of languages; for example, Fabric (*http://www.nongnu.org/fab/*) is available for Python. No software should be deployed to live without requiring environment changes as well.

Avoid single points of failure, or at least know about them
Sometimes these are unavoidable due to the cost or sheer size of a data set, but a single point of failure will come and bite you when you least expect it—you can count on that. A master database is an obvious single point of failure. There is one place that your data is written to; however, there will be other points of failure in hardware, software, and even people.

Use caching, as it helps immensely
There is a lot of content on a social application, but given the many ways that content is reused, coupled with privacy issues, whole pages are hard to cache. Memcached (see "Cache, Then Shard" on page 316) is the dominant tool for content fragment caching, but many frameworks offer their own tools, which can be easier to start with.

Have a documented backup procedure and test your backups
Avoid the sad tale of ma.gnolia (*http://factoryjoe.com/blog/2009/02/16/what-really -happened-at-magnolia-and-lessons-learned/*). Filesystem corruption had insidiously crept into the ma.gnolia backups, and although the live system kept going for a while, eventually the database became corrupt and the backups failed. The backups had not been tested. However, given that ma.gnolia started in 2005 when

good scalable hosting environments didn't really exist, the real story is about the difficulties of a small team doing it all, from operation management to development and customer support. Migrating from the initial hosting environment to a distributed system is a significant challenge for a small team.

Designing Social Applications

So far we've looked at the automation and management of applications, but not at actual code implementation; let's do that now. The behavioral aspect of an application is embodied in the application code, be it JavaScript and Ajax or a Ruby controller. This level of design— the design of the interaction—is as much a part of the detail that makes an application work as the elegance of the typography:

> Most people make the mistake of thinking design is what it looks like. That's not what we think design is. It's not just what it looks like and feels like. Design is how it works.§

> —Steve Jobs on the iPod

Steve Jobs was talking about a physical object, but one which also had a desktop application and, in time, an online component, too. Most social applications do not have a physical component, though external sensors are changing that. However, the expression "design is how it works" is also true for social applications. The behavior is the important aspect that needs to be captured. What an application looks like is important, but not as important as how it works.

Using Prototypes, Not Pictures

In Chapter 7, I recommended the use of prototypes rather than sticking with flat Photoshop mockups. I'll reiterate that here: the sooner you can get a sense of how something really works, the sooner you will understand whether your approach will really work. In larger companies, the traditional model of a set of signed-off Photoshop documents being a deliverable to a team of developers to turn into HTML and CSS still persists. Often, this is the last glimpse the non-development team has of the product, until all of the HTML, CSS, and application code is written. Thus, something non-interactive is being used to lead the design of something interactive; can you see a problem with this?

Tools such as PolyPage, a JQuery plug-in, make dynamic page states possible (see *http://24ways.org/2008/easier-page-states-for-wireframes* for background information and *http://github.com/andykent/polypage/tree/master* to download it). Using PolyPage makes it possible to mimic the logged-in and logged-out behavior of a page. Using event handlers allows you to hide content for an even better sense of mock behavior.

---

§ *http://www.wired.com/gadgets/mac/commentary/cultofmac/2006/10/71956*

One real advantage of using tools such as PolyPage and hand-built HTML is that the code can often define the conditional logic the application code will need to use. The designers and developers will therefore be thinking along the same lines. "Logged in and has admin rights" means one view, while "not logged in" means another. This is much better than a flat JPEG and several pages of text describing changes to represent a single page. Tools that automatically generate code for you miss out on this level of documentation, as they tend to care more about the position of elements on the page in terms of code generation. Application logic is much more helpful when simply documenting in the actual prototype.

Assisting Developers with Use Cases

A frequent request from developers is a *use case*. This helps them to understand the whole picture of the application rather than simply implementing a feature. Being able to see how a new feature fits into the existing site behavior and data storage needs means developers can make sensible refactoring decisions, rather than bolting another feature onto the existing system. Keeping the amount of code in your application small is a real benefit. Code requires maintenance, so the more code you have, the more time you will spend managing the older code. Think of gardening: to get a rose to flower, sometimes you need to prune out the older woody growth.

Use cases are also a fundamental part of the behavior-driven development approach and are required for prototyping. The alternative is a feature-led development approach—for instance, we need feature *X*; asking for feature *X* and not planning out the situations in which it will be used is lazy product management. The result likely will not be what you expected. Each role or actor in the application needs to be assessed and have his interaction with the new feature properly articulated. These roles include non-members, members, admins, and if necessary, members who don't qualify for using the feature. A use case also allows an opportunity to check the behavior with external users of your product prior to development.

Designing in Good Behaviors

You want your site to fail gracefully. Your site should continue to work well when the CSS fails to load, relying on good, basic HTML structure to keep running. It should work well without images, too, as this is how blind people and search engines will perceive it. As such, accessibility is a good trait to build into your site. Toward that end, unobtrusive JavaScript takes the approach of layering additional behaviors on top of a working site, such as implementing on-page editing in a new layer, as opposed to going to a new page. The underlying HTML links and forms can do the job perfectly well. Working from the jazzy version down to the accessible version simply never happens, as it is too much work to reimplement most of the behavior. Accessibility is not a tick list, it is a basic approach. Jeremy Keith's excellent article on how to keep behavior separate from content (*http://www.alistapart.com/articles/behavioralseparation*) gives a clear introduction to this (see). His book, *Bulletproof Ajax*, is also a good guide to the approach.

Another good design element is to provide useful error pages. A 404 error page should not just say "Not Found"; it should offer a basic sitemap and provide search functionality. Likewise, a 500 error page should describe how the error occurred, if appropriate. In addition, a feedback form that goes directly to the development team can actually be a real help in the early stages of a site's growth. Giving your community the ability to recover from errors and not feel like they have done something wrong is a humane and encouraging approach, which fits well with a community application.

Your App Has Its Own Point of View

Just because your application can accommodate a particular feature doesn't mean you should include it; and if you have concerns about including the feature, take them seriously. Applications should not be like Swiss army knives; they should have a focus. Throughout this book, I have mentioned some examples of natural extension: video added to Flickr, events added to Last.fm, and the small list of applications added to LinkedIn.

The way Flickr chose to handle adding video to its site is worth looking at further. The Flickr team wanted to add video in such a way that the rest of the application was not disrupted by a medium that could have very different viewing characteristics. Limiting video clips to 90 seconds meant the rapid browsing (flicking) experience you can have with physical photos was not pushed aside by the more time-demanding linear video viewing experience.

How Code Review Helps Reduce Problems

There should be a house style for implementing a feature, from application code to visual styling. In terms of code, there should be established conventions for naming variables, a comment style, and a preference for packaging modules. All of these should be set in place before copious amounts of code are written. A familiar structure is a huge help when returning to debug something months after the code was written. Enforcing this is particularly important with new hires; ideally they should work directly with the main team for a few months. In addition, freelancers, if used, need to appreciate that they are creating something that has an existing set of behaviors and they must respect this way of doing things.

Code review entails another developer checking your code to ensure that it makes sense to her before it is committed to the repository. This process can help to maintain coding standards and ensures that no one is writing code on her own, and thus introducing a human single point of failure. For instance, Twitter uses *http://www.review-board .org/* to review code, but there are many other tools out there.

Digg also feels strongly about code review: "Digg doesn't allow a single line of code to be pushed to production unless it has been peer reviewed; thus enforcing their coding standards."[||]

Code reviews help build a clearer picture of what is and is not appropriate for the application you are building. It also helps to transfer knowledge around your team. People external to the team may think they are a waste of time, but their advantages lie in ongoing support of the product. Design review is a common practice; similarly, code review should be a standard, too.

The practice of using lead development teams and a QA team to find bugs is one that is less common on strong social software teams. Developers know their own code and should fix their own bugs. A policy of fixing bugs before creating new features will also encourage a stable product. Otherwise, it is like building higher and higher on an unstable foundation.

The Power and Responsibility of Naming

The topic of URLs has cropped up a few times in this book, especially in Chapter 11. Since 1996, Tim Berners-Lee has been saying not to include current technological details in your URLs. There is no need for anyone to know you are running Perl or to know the folder structure of your application. URLs have been defined by Tim Berners-Lee, Roy Fielding, and Larry Masinter in RFC 3986 (see *http://tools.ietf.org/html/rfc3986*).

The task is instead to define the names you want to have for your objects and people and services, and then to map these to the scripts or code modules that comprise your application. An approach that is too "bare metal" leads to fragility. The following is a brittle URL:

> *specific-server.service.com/cgi-bin/subfolder/scriptname.cgi?param1=17&content= etc*

These next examples are good persistent URLs:

> *service.com/profile/profilename*
> *service.com/objecttype/objectid/verb/qualifier*

You need to address four key aspects in URL design:

Ownership
> Most objects in a social application are owned by someone, and the owner should be identified in the URL hierarchy; for example, */zzgavin/places/*.

|| *https://twitter.com/daveman692/statuses/1245472774*

Object reference

> The next aspect is the social object on your site, be it photographs, trips, places, or music. These can have meaningful names if the namespace for them is small enough. Generally, they will have a unique key referencing the object. This should be something resilient to database provider changes and something you can recalculate in case of software changes.

Action

> These are the tasks that someone on your site can perform; e.g., add, delete, or search for something. There are two often-used styles: make the verbs have a common URL, such as */trip/add/id*, or make the verbs an extension of the private space for a user, such as */profileid/add/*. These URLs represent unique personal actions, like adding someone to a profile or joining a group, and are unlikely to be shared with other people. They should also be close to your API in terms of their design.

Qualifier

> Clusters or tags combine terms that refine a search space. They refer to a non-specific group of objects. For instance, the photos on Flickr tagged "sunflower" will change over time, but the concept will stay the same. Qualifiers, objects, and people are frequently used in concert. For instance, */photos/gavinbell/tags/london* refers to my photos of London, and */photos/tags/london* refers to everyone's pictures of London.
>
> In the Ruby on Rails framework, there is good support for mapping resources and code. The routing functions define URL paths and map these to controller actions and parameters. Similar approaches exist in other frameworks.

One aspect of URL design that sometimes throws people off is aggregation views, especially private home pages. If your site design supports a main home page and a personal home page, the private view often uses */me* for mapping. The */me* URL invokes the aggregation view for the person who is logged in. For instance, Twitter uses */home* for this page. The controller or module invoked by this page determines what to include on this page. There is no need to include noise such as user ID, active modules, last visited time, or chosen template style in these kinds of URLs. Furthermore, you should store all of this information in a database so that you can simply retrieve it and, if necessary, cache it. You can take a similar approach for any news-type page: the request to access the page and the logged-in person's identity (which can be determined by a session cookie) are all that you need.

Your aim should be to have the simplest URL structure you can devise, ideally one that has a sentence-like structure so that people can understand it. Giving something a URL with unintelligible codes and code-level directives on what templates to include says you care more about your developers than you do the people on your site.

Being RESTful

Much time is spent in developer circles arguing over Roy T. Fielding's PhD dissertation, "Architectural Styles and the Design of Network-based Software Architectures" (*http: //www.ics.uci.edu/~fielding/pubs/dissertation/top.htm*), which defines the REST (REpresentational State Transfer) approach. It is not closely tied to HTTP, though HTTP is a good example of REST. (Fielding also cowrote the HTTP specification.)

REST implies a focus on resources or, in our case, social objects. To do things with these resources, you make URL-based queries on them with as many URL paths as needed per the number of resources or nouns. The REST approach sets out some criteria for being RESTful. The model is client/server-based and it is stateless in operation, in that state is not maintained from one transaction to the next. RESTful systems support caching and layering, because each transaction knows only about the resource it needs to operate on and the action it needs to perform. The representation of the resource must be understandable by the system processing the transaction. The representation and action are encoded in the URLs for your web application. REST is not specific to web applications. The principles can be applied to other systems, but we will explore REST in the context of web applications for the rest of the book.

Unlike REST, Remote Procedure Calls (RPCs) are verb-based. There will be a single RPC endpoint for your application, and you pass it the equivalent of a function call and some parameters. Compare this with REST where the resources and actions are spread across the URL space for the application. The Atom Publishing Protocol (*http: //www.atomenabled.org/developers/protocol/*) is a good example of a pure RESTful protocol; so is Amazon's S3 storage service (*http://aws.amazon.com/s3/*).

Some great APIs on the Web are largely RPC-based. Flickr is a good example. Confusion comes when developers try to offer an RPC- and a REST-based approach from a common code base. This is still a current area of development and discussion, with Roy Fielding helping to clarify what he intended in his article at *http://roy.gbiv.com/untangled/2008/rest-apis-must-be-hypertext-driven*.

Why is this important? RESTful approaches make it easier to build new applications against existing object stores (your application). REST is largely self-documenting, so there is less complexity with it. RPC is like building a semiprivate application on top of the Web; REST is like extending the Web. Given that social applications are moving the Web into the hands of the people who use it, REST is a good fit. The Web is made of things (my photos are part of Flickr, for instance), so "take this thing and do something" is a better match than the service-based approach of RPC. The *do something* can be as simple as view it, or as powerful as delete it.

Leonard Richardson and Sam Ruby wrote a good book on the subject: *RESTful Web Services* (*http://oreilly.com/catalog/9780596529260/*) (O'Reilly). We'll look more at REST in Chapter 17.

Beyond the Web Interface, Please

The Web is not the only interface to think about. Email is perfectly good for sending and receiving information. Instant Messaging (IM) interfaces such as AIM, Jabber, and Twitter also work well as input and for IM output interfaces. Mobile platforms have risen strongly on the back of the success of the iPhone and other Internet first phones. The old approaches of templates embedded in code make this multiplatform delivery very hard to achieve. CSS and HTML are examples of separating content from styling, and recent approaches using JavaScript separate behavior from content.

The Model-View-Controller (MVC) paradigm harks back many years to the language Smalltalk, which was created at Xerox PARC in the 1970s. The paradigm separates the primary aspects of an application into three layers concerned with behavior, activity, and data representation. MVC has had a new lease of life on the Web through the success of the Ruby on Rails development framework. MVC separates content from behavior and display.

The MVC approach suits social applications very well, given the potential for multiple interfaces to access content. Separating behavior from content modeling simplifies the code structure. It is arguably the dominant paradigm for building web applications today. MVC also underlies the Cocoa framework for Mac OS X and iPhone application development. Developing applications in this manner allows the Model layer to persist across implementations, with the View layer changing depending on the type of device. An example might be a web application that has an iPhone application interface.

 If you want to abstract the data even further from the view, you should explore the material on creating APIs in Chapter 17.

i18n, L10n, and Their Friend, UTF-8

This book is written in English, so I'm going to take a guess and say that the primary interface of your application will be in English. If not, stick with me through the next couple of sentences and try not to smirk (too much). English, be it American or British, Australian or even Canadian, has a big hidden problem: it is all too easy to be lax at representing information. English can be represented in 7-bit ASCII. In the 1980s, modem companies even tried to squeeze more speed out of telephone lines by packing eight 7-bit encoded characters into seven 8-bit bytes. This issue plagues development languages as the core string-handling libraries are often based on English. When other languages are processed, odd results happen. There are ways to fix these problems, and they are not that difficult. A computer language can take 10–20 years to mature and evolve, so these early ASCII-only issues are still around for some languages.

First, store and present all your content as UTF-8, or UTF-16 if you need to deal with non-Roman character sets. Second, ensure that you completely understand which character encoding is being used in all your libraries, web servers, and development languages. Third, do not try to launch in more than one language. See Joel Spolsky's useful article on Unicode (*http://www.joelonsoftware.com/articles/Unicode.html*) for a thorough understanding of the relationships between character sets, encodings, display glyphs, and the Web. No, really, go and read it. As Joel says, it is not that difficult, and you'll feel better about the rest of the world.

There are several common abbreviations for the process of running an application in multiple languages. Globalization (g11n) sums up the processes of internationalization (i18n) and the subsequent localization (L10n). The process of making your application international-ready is represented by the i18n work. This work can start as soon as you do; developing processes, such as ensuring that you use UTF-8, is good housekeeping. Focus on building an awesome application for one country or region first. The community should drive your planning, and they will let you know when they need a version in a specific language.

The key is to introduce as many i18n practices as you can where they don't significantly slow you down. Start extracting/marking up strings when you have only 10 templates. Then introduce the markup to support these strings as language variants as a standard part of your development approach early on, if you have time to do this kind of work. It will save a huge amount of work if you ever do localize. However, if doing this means you need to stop work on other features for a month to think about i18n prior to launch, maybe launch first and see what the community demand turns out to be.

The process of i18n involves finding all the developer- and user-facing strings in your application and replacing them with a reference to the appropriate language version. This means you will have libraries of en_us and en_uk or pt_br (Brazilian Portuguese) for your application (creating these language libraries is not something to deal with prior to launch, get your product out there first). Both Flickr and Movable Type use this approach, as does Apple for its Cocoa framework. The L10n work then concerns making the application local to a country and language.

 Simon Batistoni from Flickr has a couple of good presentations on the internationalization of Flickr; see *http://hitherto.net/talk_files/Ni_Hao_Monde.pdf* and *http://hitherto.net/talk_files/sxsw_2008_flickr_intl.pdf*.

Here is a short checklist of g11n issues to consider:

- Use international-friendly functions for things such as date formatting (e.g., use "strftime," not "date" in PHP).

- Handle time zones for your users, as not everything happens in GMT. Also consider daylight saving time or summertime hour changes, because they happen at different times of the year in different countries.

- Do not hardcode currency amounts into your template. Also, do not assume a single currency or payment system will be used.

- Be aware that languages vary in their compactness. English is quite a compact language in terms of space taken to express the same meaning. German, by comparison, takes more space and has long compound nouns. Arabic languages flow from right to left, and so on. Each of these points affects screen layouts.

- Remember that translation costs money and time; once you have localized, you need to consider how you launch new features, ideally in each language at the same time. However, this means you are extending the launch process. Launching separately makes maintenance much harder and compromises the user experience.

Running your product in other languages will give you access to other markets, but this benefit comes with a cost. Do pay attention to the aforementioned concerns so that you can localize easily later on, but don't compromise your initial application development and launch. You need a successful business first to be in a position to support other languages.

Bug Tracking and Issue Management

A critical aspect of the application life cycle is your ability to document problems and resolve them. Typically, these are called *bugs*, but a bug is a fickle thing. A developer saying "It works on my machine" but other people finding the bug is probably a sign of inconsistent development environments across different machines. To know where this inconsistency lies, you need to be able to accurately re-create the development environment. This means everything from the operating system version to installed modules for each language to web server parameters and proxies.

After establishing a good environment, you can find real bugs, of which there are several different types. The real skill is in determining what is going wrong and prioritizing the fix. The following list shows some common classes of bugs:

Crashers
Some sort of input or behavior makes your application crash. Having a good stack trace is invaluable in being able to determine what went wrong. Ruby on Rails does this quite well compared to, say, Perl. Dumping the stack trace into an email and sending it to the development team is more helpful than appending a one-line entry to the web server error log.

Browser incompatibilities
You can decide which of these you will fix. Supporting Safari 3, Firefox 3, and only Internet Explorer 7 (IE7) and later is becoming much more common. Your

community access statistics will help determine whether this is an option. The cost of supporting the non-standards–based behavior of IE6 can be significant.

Privacy breaches

Hopefully, you won't have one of these. Maintaining the security of private user data from credit card details and passwords to private posts is important. It is a trust situation. Testing for security flaws is hard, as it requires a nasty mindset. If you do have a privacy breach, apologize to the affected user first. For more information, see "Handling Security" on page 307.

Non-standard behavior complaints

These are a simpler class of bugs. A calendar file that doesn't work properly with a specific calendar application is a good example. You might be following the specification document, but the external client application doesn't, so you have to choose whether or not to support it.

The previous classes of bugs are pretty clear-cut: the application either doesn't work or it does. Virtually everything beyond this is a variant on a feature change or a matter of opinion. Software applications are complex entities and humans are inconsistent beings, which make for misunderstandings and confusion, even on close-knit teams. "Determining When a Bug Is a Bug" on page 379 will take another look at how this works over the life cycle of your application.

Tracking Tools

Software teams can have their momentum rapidly depleted by lots of bug fixing, particularly if it is all across the application. Each change will require a context switch to rethink how the code was designed the last time and what has happened since. A context switch is expensive in terms of time. Reacquainting oneself with old code is seen as a non-task by non-developers.

Minimizing context switching will mean your software development team is more productive. Issue management software (*bug tracking* as it is often called) helps tremendously. This is an obvious idea, and as such dozens of products are available to solve this problem for you.

Being able to link the issue tracker to the application project management tool and the code repository is a very useful capability. The ability to raise an issue, have it assigned to a feature set, and tie it into a code release gives a lot of transparency to the development process. Questions such as "Does the widget branch resolve issues 235 and 452 with the current deploy 1.2?" should be discoverable from a web interface, not from code analysis.

There are more mature tools with good user interfaces for centralized code repositories. Subversion support in particular is quite strong with tools such as JIRA, FogBugz, and Trac (*http://trac.edgewall.org/*). Web-based bug tracking systems such as Lighthouse (*http://www.lighthouseapp.com/*) are also popular; these tend to be combined with repository hosting accounts. The move to distributed code repositories residing on Mercurial or Git creates complicated issue tracking despite bringing its own advantages, but TicGit (*http://wiki.github.com/schacon/ticgit*) seems like a promising candidate for Git-based repositories.

Prioritizing Issues

There are different ways to figure out what to deal with and what to leave in the tracker. Of course, a simple system is much easier than a complex one, but complex systems can evolve accidentally. A priority system of 1, 2, and 3 can be used to manage work. However, a common weakness with numeric ratings is that everything ends up bunched up as a 1.

Another approach is to use the MoSCoW approach from the Dynamic Systems Development Method, another agile software development method. This gives tasks a rating from *Must*, through *Should*, down to *Could* (if there is time), and finally to *Will not* (this time, but *Would like* in the future). This approach works well with some teams as the levels are more understandable than a simple numeric rating. Which model you use will depend on your team.

A further popular approach is to use urgent, important, and routine as your labels. *Urgent* is used only for crashing bugs; all other work stops until the problem is fixed. *Important* is reserved for main new features and bugs that you need to deal with. Everything else is *Routine*. This model puts clean code ahead of new functionality, which should mean a more stable and bug-free system. However, this can be hard to achieve in many companies, where new stuff trumps bugs, as new stuff is shinier. A policy of "the feature isn't complete until there are no bugs logged" can be effective, but communicating that "a feature launched but is not done" also has its complexities.

No application will have a clean sheet for every feature; sometimes you need to be able to mark something as "won't fix" and move on. Balancing the need to fix or extend old features with the need to create new ones is a real challenge when building web applications. Just as with web browser support, there are decisions to be made about how much to invest in any feature. Applications need to be seen as a complete ecology; you need to tend to all of them equally, which can mean leaving known issues while you work on something else.

Differentiating Bugs from Feature Requests

Being able to determine whether the reporter of a bug is saying "this doesn't work for me" or "I don't like how this works" is a key developer skill. Feature requests masquerading as bug requests snarl application development, particularly if the bugs get priority in your workflow. Development methodologies that enforce one-month-at-a-time planning approaches mitigate these requests to some degree. Your community will be both a huge help and a demanding bunch. They can be helpful in verifying bugs as a general issue and clarifying misconceptions in how something really works. They'll also pound you with their ideas about how something should work and how it is a tiny change and will make your application/service the most useful product. These will primarily be about issues of new functionality that you do not offer, requests to bring back something you've stopped doing, or usability issues. Usability issues are worth paying attention to, as they can point out something you've misunderstood.

Depending on your market position and audience, you might want to have a public road map (such as Vimeo) or a public bug tracker (such as Six Apart with Movable Type and Twitter with its API). This is particularly relevant if you have a large developer community. The ability for a developer to raise a ticket and annotate a bug, ideally with an isolated test case, can be invaluable. Virtually all open source applications have these as public assets for the community. Commercial endeavors are obviously more careful around this, hence the frequent split between the API, which is shared, and the application, which is semiprivate. The more pressing bugs for a social application are around the API and security, so sharing these can be helpful.

Handling Security

The topic of security could be a whole book in itself—several, in fact. Security is hard to do well; most frameworks and tools are set up to make things easy to hook up and implement, with security left as an afterthought. This might sound surprising, but switching to look at your site from the outside is hard. There are already enough context switches from the user point of view, to the developer using your API, and to your own company point of view. Taking on the viewpoint of a hacker trying to break your site is tricky.

However, it is important, particularly early on when your code is small. Alex Payne from Twitter describes the position well:

> I suggested to the team that we do a full internal security audit. Stop all work, context switch to Bad Guy Mode, find issues, fix them. I wish I could say that we've done that audit in its entirety, but the demands of a growing product supported by a tiny team overshadowed its priority.#

In 2009, there was password hash compromise on the music service Spotify (*http://www .spotify.com/blog/archives/2009/03/04/spotify-security-notice/*). The password hashes for Spotify were reverse-engineered so that someone could attempt to guess your password if he knew your username. Security across your API, and in this case the access protocol from a desktop application, is just as important as security on your own site. This API was not public, but it did not stop people from trying to access it.

Beyond hacking account access, many other attacks can happen as well. For instance, Chapter 12 looked at password management. In addition, people can try to redirect your community to a misleading site or trick them into deleting content—so-called

---

#*http://al3x.net/2009/01/12/the-thing-about-security.html*

clickjacking. SQL injection attacks are also common. The approach here is to escape every item of content you receive, and to unescape only the content you really want to display. *Whitelisting*, whereby you create a list of the HTML that you will allow, is the only approach that you can feel comfortable with; filtering is doomed, given the cleverness and amount of free time people are willing to spend carrying out these kinds of attacks. The MySpace worm relied on combining and executing composed JavaScript—for example, "inne"+"rHTML." The hack relies on executing JavaScript so that the strings are combined to form the HTML word "innerHTML," which can then allow for executable code, where normally the string `innerHTML` would be filtered out. This kind of combination attack is almost impossible to filter out. (See *http://namb .la/popular/tech.html* for the technical details of the MySpace worm.)

 Escaping means not treating the input text as entered. For example, an angle bracket will not be represented as an angle bracket when used as an HTML entity, and will be escaped to `&#x3008` or represented as `u"\u3008"` in Python. This means it will not be parsed as HTML code.

Cross-site scripting attacks will use any editable field as a potential weakness for launching an attack. For instance, the CSS fields of the Twitter profile have been used to create a self-propagating worm (*http://dcortesi.com/2009/04/11/twitter-stalkdaily -worm-postmortem/*). The Twitter attack, like the MySpace attack, shows the severity of the network effect on social applications. They can spread very rapidly. The worm had a heavy performance impact on MySpace, in particular.

Simon Willison gives a good summary of website security at *http://simonwillison.net/ 2008/talks/head-horror/*. Particular techniques to note include ensuring that you know the source of form submissions, that you use a token that is generated on your site for logged-in users, and that you process forms only if this unique token per user is passed along with the form. Finally, make sure the token is secure.

Site security is painstaking work, but making it part of the regular deployment cycle will help you avoid the horror of a vast security audit at some future point, right after you've been hacked. Unfortunately, most companies leave security until then, as they are too busy making the service thrive. Simply making your service available is a lot of work, especially if you have high growth rates, but security is still important. It would be wise to make sure that your entire development team has a good understanding of the current security threats that exist on the Web. Securing your site is the responsibility of all of your developers, from those on the client-side to those working on the API and database code.

Rapid User Interfaces

A responsive interface is important in many areas of the Web; on a social application, where someone might view dozens of pages in a session, it is a requirement. Social

---

applications do a lot, though. The web page is a resource in terms of REST. It may be laden with microformats, plus there is the actual content and the actions the viewer can take with this content. These pages are complex, and so are the mechanisms used to generate them. Performance to the user is critical, so "queue everything else" is an approach that came into the mainstream in late 2008 and early 2009. Rapid page delivery matters, too, as "Making Your Code Green and Fast" on page 325 shows. The behaviors triggered by your application matter, as well. First let's look at how we create new functionality.

Rapid Prototyping

Much of this book has focused on the visual user interface to the application, as this is the primary aspect for the majority of your audience. Getting to that stage means making the interface, but also making the code that implements the functionality.

Using the programming language console for code-level prototyping is a very flexible way of approaching prototyping. It works well for scripting languages such as Python and Ruby; compiled languages do not have this option, however. Being able to build up your objects and then extend their behavior is akin to developing the API first. It is a cheap way to experiment with possible options rather than waiting until there is a user interface in place. You are more likely to make rapid discoveries in this kind of environment, and then you can take these back to the product development cycle as a "we could also do this" offering, often within a day or two of proposing the idea.

Scaling and Messaging Architectures

Network effects make social software hard to scale up in a simple manner. Features such as asymmetric following mean one person's activity can result in thousands of updates flowing through your systems. Privacy can make cache strategies inefficient, too.

The common asymmetric follow model of social relationships can create harsh scaling issues. If @stephenfry updates Twitter, nearly 400,000 people get his update. That is a lot of activity to manage, much more than a single individual can normally create on a site such as eBay, Amazon, or a news site. Privacy makes this asymmetry even more complicated. As we discussed in Chapter 8 discussed, privacy affects search, updates to river of news flows, tagging, and other features. It is also hard on caching.

Figure 16-1 shows two visualizations of *following* in a social network. Supporting asymmetric follows will allow for a more connected network. The black node on the left has three connections, all two-way. On the right, it has 11 connections, but again only 3 of them are two-way. Scaling is a more significant problem on the right.

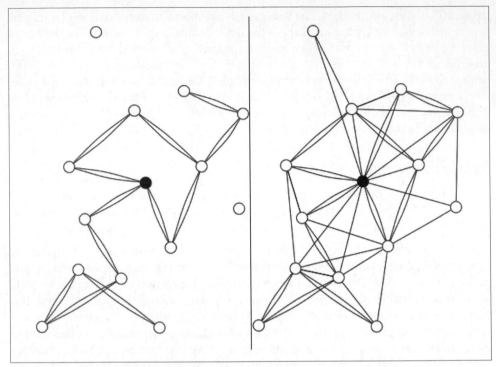

Figure 16-1. Symmetric and asymmetric following patterns in a social application; the symmetric pattern on the left allows only two-way symmetric relationships and the asymmetric pattern on the right allows asymmetric relationships

On the left is a purely symmetric follow arrangement; on the right is the same pattern with one-way or asymmetric follows allowed. The asymmetric version shows a much richer level of connections per node. The network is more highly connected.

Earlier in this chapter, I mentioned *Enterprise Integration Patterns*; it has a fantastic array of messaging patterns that you can study and apply to your application. It is common now to see a social application as a series of interacting applications rather than as a single monolithic block of code. The book describes 65 different patterns for letting applications operate in a message-passing manner.

A simple approach to application design is to do the minimum amount you need to get control back to the person who requested the page, and then do the rest of the updates asynchronously via a queue of tasks. Queues are really at the heart of making your application more parallel, and less single-path and linear in nature. You still need to process the queue, and if it fills faster than you can process it, you have gained nothing. Most social applications, however, do have a quieter period. At some point, it will be nighttime for your application; commonly this will be when it is daytime across the Pacific, as the population density here is much lower than elsewhere on Earth.

Ajax Helps with Scaling

Earlier approaches to web development stem largely from older Common Gateway Interface (CGI)-based ideas of web servers invoking server applications to perform a task and return some output. Typically, these applications pull data from a database, find an appropriate template, generate an entirely new HTML page, and return this page to the user.

We have moved beyond this to a world of `XMLHttpRequest`-based applications, which return packets of data to client-side applications that then show this update to the reader. *Just* the data rather than an entire newly rendered page is sent over the wire. Moving a small packet of data rather than a whole page makes for better interaction styles. This reduction in turnaround time for user interactions leads to Ajax-powered applications placing much higher response time requirements on your applications. People have a natural tendency to relax if a whole-page refresh is taking place. If a single element is changing, they expect immediacy, like they would get from a desktop application. However, given that the volume of data being moved is smaller, it means an overall easing of scaling issues. Moving a few hundred bytes of data requires less effort than a full-page download.

Queuing Non-Visible Updates

Ajax helps with page interactions, but much of what you need to do in a social application is not visible. When someone uploads a piece of content to a site, the primary activity is to show her that the content has arrived. It is not necessary to update the followers' pages, any tag pages, and so on. All of these activities can be safely queued and done within a short time from the time of upload. Assessing what can be taken out of the direct user-driven activity loop is a first step in making your applications more scalable using queuing. Figure 16-2 illustrates the linear *do everything* model and the queuing model. Each segment with an arrowhead represents a specific application task; the Queued model returns control to the the user much sooner. The following section illustrates some examples of application-based queuing.

In the figure, each arrow represents a task that follows the user event. In the queued model, four tasks are queued for later processing and control returns to the user sooner.

Real Time Versus Near Time

The queuing stage in web development determines which processes must happen in real time when a user submits a request to a web application and which processes must happen soon afterward. The closest analogy is the SQL transaction: what can happen outside the transaction that the HTTP request triggers?

In social applications, everything outside the remit of the `XMLHttpRequest` is in near time. The only thing that needs to happen in real time is ensuring that the data sent by the

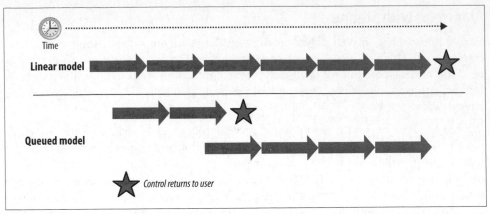

Figure 16-2. Queued versus linear approaches for processing events following a user interaction with the site

web browser is stored appropriately, and that the person on the other end sees her information updated. Everything else—from implied updates, to logging, to marking caches as dirty—can happen asynchronously. This means your users receive responses much more rapidly. An example might help clarify this idea.

When Twitter was in the early phase of development (with 50,000 users or so) Evan Williams, the CEO, had 1,500 followers, and they were sending a lot of updates over SMS or text messages. Twitter was constructed to send all the SMS messages and then return the Twitter user an "all done" message, but this was taking more than 40 seconds, so Twitter implemented a queuing system that guaranteed the sending of the SMS, but outside of the HTTP request loop.

At Nature, we use TheSchwartz queuing system, supplied as part of Movable Type, to queue updates to an internal search service; pass new comments to our in-house social application, Nature Network; and deal with failure situations for registration against the main internal identity management system. The loose coupling that comes from queues, and the ability to easily retry after a failure, makes queuing very attractive, at the cost of another system to manage.

Going back to Twitter, its developers initially thought it was going to be a microblogging service, so the choice of Rails as a Content Management System (CMS) solution was appropriate. However, when people started using Twitter as a real-time conversation service, the original platform choice was no longer appropriate. If Twitter had used another framework to get to market, would it have arrived too late? We will never know, but each framework has its costs and benefits; there is no perfect language or framework. Twitter's recent migration to Scala for the underlying messaging infrastructure is a better fit in terms of real-time requirements. For an interesting technical review of Twitter's move from Ruby to Scala, see *http://www.artima.com/scalazine/articles/twitter_on_scala.html*.

Polling Versus Pushing

One common argument concerns the direction in which updates should flow. Many aspects of the Internet operate in a polling model: a service checks to see whether there is an update for it, perhaps pulling over an RSS or Atom feed. This is fine for small numbers of feeds, but when one service is polling for hundreds of feeds, it becomes inefficient for both parties. Using a queue to push content over HTTP to a remote interface is an attractive alternative. The recipient application does not waste time checking for content when there is none, but it does need to be able to respond to the incoming push content, as this will come from an external agent. This model is very appropriate for activity stream updates from internal applications or with partner applications.

Publish/subscribe (pubsub) is a common implementation of this model. It allows a publisher to announce updates to subscribers as they happen; subscribers do not poll for activity. (See *Enterprise Integration Patterns* for more about this pattern.) The Pub-SubHubbub protocol (*http://pubsubhubbub.googlecode.com/svn/trunk/pubsubhubbub -core-0.1.html*) is an open source approach to pubsub over HTTP, which allows for push-based content delivery over the Internet.

For internal queuing, products such as Apache ActiveMQ (*http://activemq.apache .org/*) and RabbitMQ (*http://www.rabbitmq.com/*) allow for private message queuing between known applications. They are not really appropriate for largescale public API usage, but they are invaluable for private use. Using one of these products means that you will have another platform to maintain, but the benefits of these queuing stores are worth it. One issue to be aware of is queue failure. Some of these products support in-memory queues only, so items will be lost in case of power failure.

XMPP Messaging

An option for Internet-based messaging is Extensible Messaging and Presence Protocol (XMPP; *http://xmpp.org/about/*), which is an Internet-wide messaging system.[*] The full specification is quite complex, and creating a server for it can be a lot of work. However, much of the client side of XMPP has been neatly encapsulated in the form of language modules—for example, Jabber::Simple for Ruby, Smack for Java, and many others.

The argument in favor of XMPP is that implementing to a shared messaging system is less work than writing an interface for each application separately. Each application has one outbound and one inbound interface. The outbound interface sends all updates to a central server or linked servers, and the inbound interface subscribes to certain updates from one of these servers. This is particularly relevant when some of the consumers of the messages are not on your network.

---

[*] For more information on XMPP, check out these sources: *http://www.slideshare.net/rabble/beyond-rest -building-data-services-with-xmpp-pubsub* and *http://www.loiclemeur.com/english/2008/12/xmpp-pubsub -aka.html*.

Outbound updates contain Atom-formatted content about who created the update, how it was created, the actual content, and any tags or media files associated with the content. Inbound subscriptions would receive content matching certain subscribed actions or subscribed tags, or from certain people. Atom is a data format (*http://tools .ietf.org/html/rfc4287*) that was developed to address some of the weaknesses of RSS. XMPP forms the basis of the Google Wave, a new communications platform launched in 2009, that Google proposed as an open extension to the XMPP protocol (see *http:// www.waveprotocol.org* for details of its implementation).

Using Atom or RSS feeds to subscribe to these kinds of activities is CPU-intensive. The sending application has to send one message once, as opposed to generating separate dynamic feeds for every requesting application. At some point, it is impossible to generate the RSS fast enough to ensure a 100% complete feed. XMPP supports a 100% delivery approach to content, so it will retry in case of failure. The basic HTTP protocol supports no such thing, though PubSubHubbub aims to.

An asynchronous model of intra-application communication will take less time to maintain and use less energy. For instance, Twitter's power bill dropped once it adopted queuing. Dopplr, meanwhile, is built on an asynchronous architecture to allow it to scale efficiently. Whether you choose internal message queuing, a PubSubHubbub approach, or XMPP will depend on your developer audience and product needs.

External Processing: Scaling on the Fly and by the Batch

If you take the queuing approach to handling some aspects of your community interaction, you will end up with some queued updates that you can handle in batches. Sending out notification emails or SMS messages about activity is a good example. Processing statistics is another one, and we'll look at that in this section.

Processing individual access statistics for a person is not work that your main web server(s) should be doing. Having servers spinning simply to process this kind of background task seems like a waste of money, too. Services such as Amazon EC2 (Elastic Compute Cloud) and others give you a spare set of servers to use as you need. Batch processing data sets and processing additional load at peak times is a perfect usage.

 The overview at *http://agiletesting.blogspot.com/2009/04/experiences-de ploying-large-scale.html* is a great firsthand account of using EC2 to deal with scaling.

You can use batch processing only if you have already designed in parallel stages, as described earlier. You need to have broken out of the user interaction loop to have something to process. If everything is expected to happen in real time only, you can only use these services as additional web servers under a round-robin proxy, which is fine, but they are not designed to be used continuously in this manner based on the service-level agreement (SLA) from Amazon. When you have only a single box at a hosting company, it might seem foolish to spend time designing for a multisystem architecture. However, even single servers have multiple CPU cores, so designing for parallel steps makes sense, even at the algorithm level.

One service that can immediately make use of multiple cores is Hadoop, an open source implementation of the Google Map Reduce data processing architecture. Hadoop relies on multiple machines and multiple cores to distribute processing of data in parallel. Hadoop is being used for a map generation toolkit called Maps from Scratch (*http://www.mapsfromscratch.com/*), put together by Stamen Design. Even more useful to social software applications is the Apache Lucene project Mahout, which builds a machine learning engine on top of a Hadoop cluster using content stored in Lucene. Machine learning involves processing large volumes of information by a computer to train an algorithm or discover patterns. In "Machine Learning and Big Data Sets," I will cover machine learning in greater detail. Services such as Amazon Elastic Cloud, as its Hadoop product is called, are cost-prohibitive to own, but renting time on them is feasible. Hadoop is a distributed computing platform based on an approach called map/reduce. The basic concept is to break hard problems down into small parallel steps (the map phase) and then combine all the subanswers (the reduce phase) to produce the final answer. Many search and filtering problems are very suitable for this approach.

Performance Testing

Scaling is an interesting area, but how do you know whether you are using what you have effectively? Testing with high loads without real data is difficult. You can fake connection load testing using tools such as Apache Bench, but generating large amounts of pretend-community-generated content is a real challenge. Performance testers need to be careful in this area; it is too easy to generate spurious results based on mock data. However, timing each subsystem and finding the hotspots is time well spent, as single points of failure will generally make themselves known when you have high loads and can be difficult to predict. Much of the scaling technology relies on doing as much as possible in memory, so any process that eats up memory can be a problem.

Languages Don't Scale

It is what you do with languages that counts, but you should also pick the language that suits your application area. Many factors contribute to language choice: developer familiarity, library availability, ease of prototyping, and ease of deployment all need to be factored in. Choosing which scripting language to use is always difficult. The Yahoo! home page is written in PHP, for example; it would be faster in C, but much harder to change. The infrastructure you place around your applications is generally much more relevant. Pick a poor caching approach, and it won't matter which language you choose.

Cache, Then Shard

The simplest approach to development is a single application deployment talking to a local database on a single Apache instance with no caching. There are millions of applications like this in the world. Most installs of blogging or message board software get along quite happily like this, for example. Adding memcached and a reverse proxy can help a lot, even on the same hardware. It also becomes easier to move to multiple machines with services such as this. All of this is focused on the delivery of content beyond your database and avoiding hitting the database for frequently accessed content.

Products such as memcached (*http://www.danga.com/memcached/*) are almost a default now on large social applications, delivering regularly accessed content straight from memory without troubling your database. In many cases, these products will cache application-generated fragments, thereby saving your application servers, too.

At some point, you are likely to run up against the limitations of your database server. Multiple slaves and a master database for writing is a common scaling option. Clients read from the slaves and write to the master. At this level of scaling, you probably have several application servers, multiple web servers handling incoming connections, and your database master/slave setup, plus machines for memcached and monitoring. You can go a very long way with this approach, as most accesses are reads, not writes.

Eventually, though, you'll hit the limits of your writable master. This is quite a hard limit; prior to this all scaling involves relatively small-scale changes to how an application can retrieve an item of content. To help avoid this hard limit, check the cache before checking the database. You will also need to change the basic application logic because content needs to be stored in different places. A single machine can no longer hold all relationships. You can split up the database, but not across joins.

Sharding the database is the next approach. Sharding works by spreading the writes across multiple servers; in effect, horizontally scaling the master write server. For instance, instead of keeping all the user records in a single table, you keep records A–M on one database and N–Z on a second database. Now your application logic needs to know which database to write to on the basis of the account in question. You can split things up further, by also sharding content types.

Latency is another issue that can affect your data systems. Once you have multiple geographic data centers, the time between when a write occurs and when the written data becomes available can be long enough that a page refresh will show the discontinuity. Latency is really outside the scope of this book, but the systems that Facebook and others are developing to manage this issue are interesting to read about, and many of them are being released as open source products.

For more information on database scaling approaches, see Cal Henderson's book, *Building Scalable Web Sites* (*http://oreilly.com/catalog/9780596102357/*) (O'Reilly).

Fast and Light Data Storage

Much of the data that we store in our databases does not need to be in a relational store. A simple key/value storage product might suffice for some activities. These are blazingly fast in comparison to a relational database such as MySQL, and they are very well suited to gathering data for processing later. Products such as Tokyo Cabinet (*http://tokyoca binet.sourceforge.net/*) can store 1 million records in less than one second. Architecting your application so that you can use a key/value storage product such as this makes a lot of sense in terms of scaling. If your data is generally retrieved by primary keys with few joins, this is a definite possibility. Richard Jones from Last.fm wrote a good review of current 2009 options, available at *http://www.metabrew.com/article/anti-rdbms-a-list -of-distributed-key-value-stores/*.

Implementing Search

As discussed in Chapter 13, Search is critical to your site, and it is also a system that you will change and replace over time as your needs grow and the content in your site settles down. Providing for a simple, direct query on some MySQL table fields is often good enough for the first few months. Note that the default minimum search string length on MySQL is four characters, so you might want to change this.

Why does search not stay as originally designed? It is hard to predict what sort of content you will get on your site, even if you know the kind of content you want to acquire. Which metadata aspects are the ones that your community will care about? In terms of search design, I'll assume that you know the context of a search match. You can determine who wrote the item of content and whether this content is an event, a comment, or a photo description. Make sure you use this contextual information. Returning search results that show contextual information such as ownership and that enrich the display with the photo or date of the event are much more meaningful and useful than simple plain-text lists.

Search volume will determine when to replace your simple query on MySQL (or similar) with a dedicated search product, perhaps based on Lucene (*http://lucene.apache.org/*) or one of that family, such as Solr. You should have enough search traffic to warrant the extra effort that maintaining a separate archive of content and another application requires. Perhaps the search traffic is impacting the efficiency of the main database, or your API traffic is growing and needs access to a separate server.

A lot of the focus in social web applications is on the browsing experience, but many aspects of it are search-driven. In fact, much of your API is a search product. There is, however, a difference between searching by person and searching by tags and content. Search by person on your application should present an interface for activity based on the relationships between the searcher and the person returned in the search results. In this regard, you should show any relationship present between people and offer a means to create a relationship. This activity based on the context model should sound familiar from Chapter 7. You can extend this to other metadata-rich aspects of your application as well (e.g., place). The aim is to turn search results pages into something that recognizes the person who is searching and offers her contextually relevant activities to perform.

Identity and Management of User Data

There are three common models to account creation: register with an email address; use another site to provide an identity (e.g., Twitter provides identities to several applications); and use OpenID, which is a more recent option. Each of these has strengths and weaknesses.

Using an email and password is by far the most common approach. Almost everyone on the Internet has an email address and is capable of verifying an account by clicking on a link in an email. However, this approach has disadvantages too: your users will have to remember another password for all of the various accounts they have on the Web, or their security will be compromised if they use the same password everywhere.

Creating a secure password is a difficult task. Implementing a green-amber-red grading system with corresponding weak-fair-strong indications for the strength of a password helps a lot. Simple alphanumeric passwords are much easier to remember, but passwords with only letters and numbers and no punctuation characters are less secure Checking passwords against a dictionary is also useful; words that appear in a dictionary are easier to guess, and hackers can easily work through a list of these.

Also, ensuring that your login system does not allow repeated automated guesses at passwords is a good idea. Allowing only 3 tries and then enforcing a 10-minute wait will mean a possible 432 tries per day, which is plenty. Allowing 1 per second equals 86,400 attempts per day (which would be two days to try the entire Oxford English Dictionary). So, passwords that are dictionary words do weaken security, but there are things you can do to mitigate this.

Using another site to provide verification of identity (proxying) is also a good approach, especially if you are a satellite of a larger site. An example of using another source for managing identity is Foodfeed, which takes identity from Twitter. FriendFeed also has started using this approach using OAuth, as we discussed in Chapter 13.

The most recent approach to identity management is OpenID (*http://openid.net/*), an open protocol. With OpenID, a single digital identity can be used across multiple sites on the Internet, as opposed to creating a new, different identity at each site. Individuals can obtain an OpenID from many sources (most large Internet companies offer them). We'll talk more about OpenID in the following section.

OpenID for Identity

OpenID turns identity into a web-addressable resource. Instead of an email, you obtain a URL that represents you. The majority of identities come from large existing companies such as AOL, Yahoo!, and Six Apart. You log in to the host site and use this identity to access other sites on the Internet. One password and one common profile are intended to make life simpler. Many people will choose to have more than one OpenID, perhaps separating their work and personal lives.

Use of OpenID does not mean an account is not created; it merely changes the credentials used to access a site. As site owner, you can request further details, such as an avatar image via Attribute Exchange (*http://openid.net/specs/openid-attribute-exchange -1_0.html*). Attribute Exchange allows a service to which someone has just logged in to request additional profile details from the OpenID provider, enabling richer profiles on the Internet.

Using the term *OpenID* as a brand to prompt the user does not help with registration, as it is largely unfamiliar. Saying "Use your OpenID to log in" will be meaningful only to the small community who care about the ability to use OpenID. However, saying "Use your Yahoo! ID or your LiveJournal or WordPress identity to access this site" will help dramatically. Keep the OpenID name around for fellow developers who are familiar with such things, but for the majority of people, use the branding they are already familiar with. "Log in with Gmail" is a direction users understand. The Google OpenID and OAuth hybrid have shown fantastic success rates (for more information, go to *http: //www.readwriteweb.com/archives/comcast_property_sees_92_success_rate_openid .php*).

 For technical details on Google's use of the OpenID and OAuth hybrid, see *https://sites.google.com/site/oauthgoog/UXFedLogin*.

The next phase in OpenID support might come from web browser companies. Supporting OpenID in the browser would be a tremendous advantage (*http://radar.oreilly .com/2008/12/getting-openid-into-the-browse.html*). An individual would be able to log into her browser and access existing services and create accounts to new services without having to think about the technical details involved.

What to Ask for on Registration

Account creation is the first step in a person's relationship with you, so don't put a multipage form in his way. Grab the minimum amount of information he needs to participate in your community—usually login details, a nickname or real name, and password reminder details. Once he becomes a more active user, you can prompt him to provide more information.

This gradual registration model will feel completely familiar to people who regularly use the Web and explore new sites. But for people on marketing and advertising teams, it is very scary. The idea that you let an opportunity pass to collect information is hard for them to appreciate, so build prompts into your application that allow people to fill in further details, or link some features to other sections of your application with more complete information. For many sites, this will not be necessary, but in the more professional areas of social software, a wealth of actively maintained profiles means the site can continue growing. For instance, the LinkedIn approach of showing the percentage a profile is complete is a nice visual approach to encouraging completion, while avoiding irritating prompts.

When a User Chooses to Leave

There are many reasons why people will just stop using your service, but they'll usually only delete their accounts if they are annoyed with you. They might also be accounts that you have chosen to delete as a result of moderating content.

Deleted accounts need to be handled carefully. Retaining the integrity of conversations is important, as we explored in Chapter 15. Simply deleting every trace of a person damages previous conversations. Here are some guidelines to help you handle the process when users leave your site or delete their accounts:

- Make it easy for the person to find the "Delete my account" link. Don't make it an elaborate four- or five-stage process involving a phone call. Gain explicit confirmation that the person wants to delete his account. However, two "Are you sure?" prompts are a good idea.

- Make it easy for him to get a file containing all of his content—defining "all" is slightly complex, however. Certainly, all the primary content he contributed is valid, and his contacts on the site are definitely a good idea, but every reply he posted on a message board probably doesn't need to be included.

- Retain his comments on other people's content, as removing them would disrupt the remaining conversation threads.

- Annotate and unlink his avatar. Adding "[deleted]" makes it clear that the person is no longer an active member.

- Decide whether account deletion is final. Some sites treat deletion as a lapsed subscription, but most sites consider the delete action final.

- Decide whether to make the identifier available to another user after a specified period of time (e.g., six months or a year). Many sites issue identifiers once and do not allow reuse, whereas some sites let active users claim dormant or deleted accounts. There are arguments on both sides, but regardless of which approach you take, have a clear, consistent policy.

Admin Users

Many sites create admin accounts as an extension of the normal user account model. These are special users with additional powers. This model is very common and has its benefits: there is a single pool of users, and it is simple to promote people to give them extra powers. A more secure approach is to separate user accounts from staff accounts so that every person has a normal user account, allowing admin staff to use the site in exactly the same way the community does. The staff members who run the site get an extra account that uses a separate authentication system, perhaps linked to your company authentication system. This account gives them access to administration powers beyond those available to normal users of the site.

This two-account system makes it easier for your staff to contribute and be social on the site, without the big badge of "STAFF" following them around. It also makes it much easier to deal with staff members leaving and new people joining the company. Any staff activity will come from the staff account. It is better to flag the content contributed by staff members than to have the staff flag associated with a person and then be associated with the content. The connection is that staff content has been created, not that Jane is a staff member and she created some content.

The most common place for this to be visible is on any discussion forums, particularly company-run forums for problems, ideas, and discussion of your product. It needs to be clear to your own staff and to people reading contributions when people are acting as staff members. This is important because some of your new employees will come from your community. If you simply allow them to use their existing community account and flag it as a staff account now that they are employees, you need to deal with their previous activity on the site. Using a separate staff account makes this much clearer.

Finally, separating staff and user accounts makes them less prone to a dictionary or other automated attack. The authentication endpoint for staff accounts will be different from the normal one and not available over an API. Also, you can add hardware tokens such as the common RSA key fobs to secure these accounts even further if you wish.

 Make sure your staff accounts are secure. Twitter had a dictionary attack on a staff member's account; see *http://blog.wired.com/27bstroke6/ 2009/01/professed-twitt.html* for details.

Accessing Content via OAuth

Identity is managed via OpenID or email address and password, as noted earlier, but what about access to the content associated with an identity? The photos or microblog posts are the content in these services. These social objects are the reason for the services to exist. Simple identity is not really that interesting on its own. The content is the exciting part. OAuth is the protocol that gives fine-grained access to content for third-party applications.

The strongest advantage to OAuth is that it avoids the password antipattern. There is no point at which the third party can impersonate you. The identity credentials that OAuth grants are permission-based to the service, not whole-identity-based. Explicit read and write permissions are granted. The permission to read photos or to write photos is at stake; global account access to the photos is never granted. With OAuth, you give a third party permission to read and/or update content on your behalf, but not to impersonate you. Also, this permission is held as a detail in your account with each service. It is possible to see which third-party applications have access to which data for a service.

Figure 16-3 shows that I have granted the Dopplr and Fireball applications read and write access to my data within Fire Eagle. Compare this to a system based on email and passwords. You will have no indication of which services have access to your data, and any one of them could impersonate you because they hold the full identity credentials for the Twitter or Dopplr account, and they use the same password for API and personal account access. Also, when you change the password on your account—say, you forget it—all of these services are locked out. OAuth resolves all of these problems.

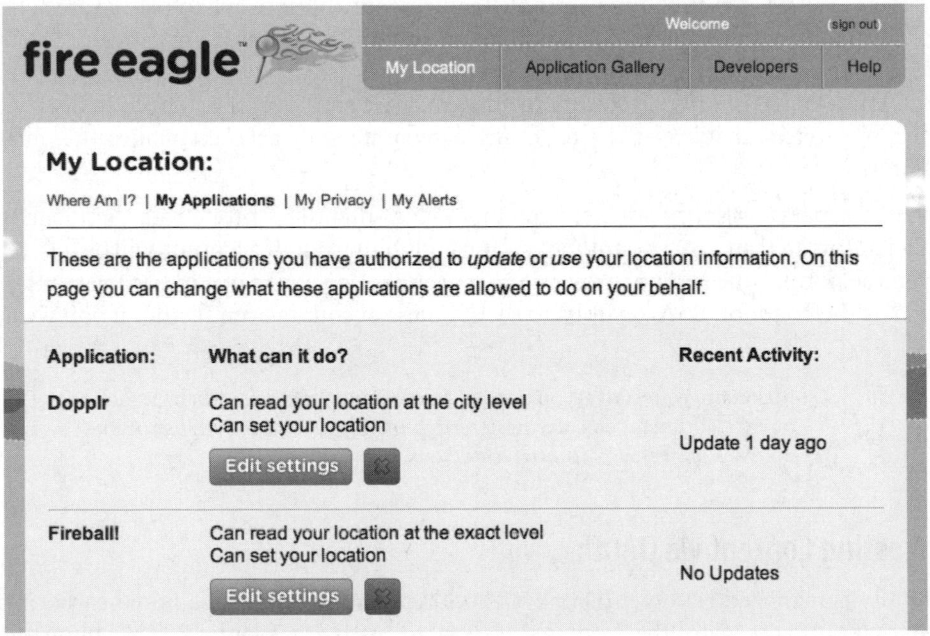

Figure 16-3. Fire Eagle showing applications that have been granted access and the level of access granted

The cost is an additional step in the sign-up process for external applications. OAuth mandates that permission to access content is issued only on the service website. For instance, I need to be logged in to Fire Eagle to give Dopplr access to my content. This is commonly called *token-based authentication*.

This is not a completely new idea. Since it launched, Flickr has used a similar model for accessing photos. Similarly, the Movable Type blogging system has used a separate API password since version 3, for both the XML-RPC and the AtomPub interfaces. The edit profile page for Movable Type, shown in Figure 16-4, shows the normal account password and, below it, the reveal link for the API password. (I've obscured my email address and username.)

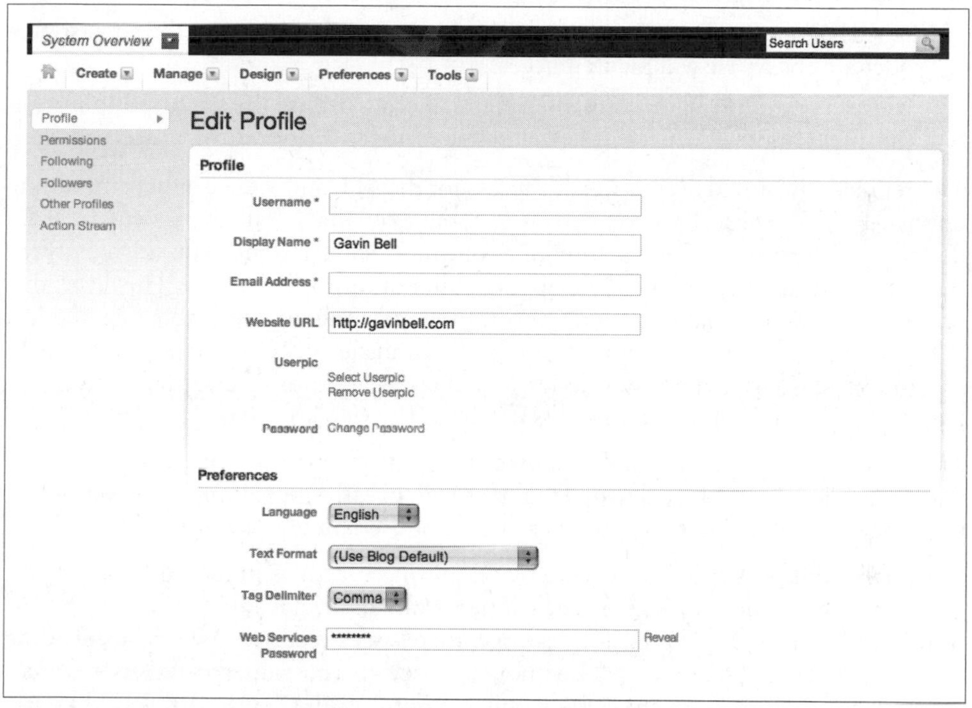

Figure 16-4. Moveable Type Pro Edit Profile page showing the separate web services password at the bottom

OAuth uses the following flow:

1. The OAuth service requests access to account information using its consumer key and a consumer secret. These are generic, but they initiate the request. The OAuth service responds with an OAuth token and a token secret, also known as a *request token*.

2. OAuth takes the user to the service, where she may need to sign in. The user can authorize your application's access to her data.

3. The user grants access, which takes her back to your site with an access token. This can be used to get content.

The flow for desktop applications and from the iPhone is not quite as smooth. The iPhone is helped by the application's ability to define specific application URLs—for example, *tweetie://*, which will launch the named application. Check out *http://fireeagle .yahoo.net/developer/documentation/oauth_best_practice* for good advice on creating mobile OAuth implementations.

Hiding the service-based authorization is not a good idea. From the desktop, the process is similar, but it requires an extra step:

1. The user launches the desktop application.
2. He clicks on the "Request permission" link, which takes him to the service provider's website. He will log in if necessary.
3. The user grants permission and then manually goes back to the desktop application and clicks another link there. This last click fetches the new OAuth access token.

Twitter recently moved over to OAuth access for the API, and there is much grumbling on the API mailing list about the perceived complexity that entailed, particularly from desktop application developers. It requires one more step, and the gains are mainly for the security of the person using the application, not for the developer. However, this process is about as complex as email verification when signing up with a new service. When a website sends out a verification email, for instance, often the person needs to switch applications and go to a desktop mail application to receive the appropriate email. He clicks on this link and is taken back to the web browser.

The conversations on Simon Willison's short post at *http://simonwillison.net/2009/Jan/ 2/adactio/* show some of the debate around OAuth in early 2009. It is not a silver bullet, but it does make a lot of sense to use it instead of username/password.

OAuth makes the Web a more secure place, putting control is in the right place: with the user of the service. It also stops developers from taking advantage of having access to full credentials. On Twitter, for example, there was a recurrent practice of sending a Twitter message about the service without the user's permission, so other users would see "X is using third-party application Y; try it out." With OAuth, this would be impossible unless you had explicitly given permission to send Twitter messages. For much more technical detail on OAuth , see *http://www.slideshare.net/kellan/advanced-oauth -wrangling*.

Federation

It is possible that the social web will end up with a larger number of federated instances as opposed to the single dominant player approach we have at the moment. Facebook may be the largest social network, but it is far from the only one. Increasing specialization and the desire for interoperability will encourage federation.

The mobile or cell phone market is a good example of what might happen. At first, it was hard to place a call from one network to another. Consumer demand led to this becoming much easier. Now it is not even noted as an issue—any mobile phone in the world can call any other phone.

In terms of identity management, the various Facebook Connect or Google Connect services are the start of a trend toward interoperability. I think this will move toward activity-based interoperability, too. Tools such as ma.gnolia's planned M2 (*http://wiki .ma.gnolia.org/M2-Product-Charter*) for bookmark sharing, and Identi.ca (based on a proposed open microblogging protocol), show that there is at least a developer desire for federated systems. Similarly, the Adium (*http://www.adiumx.com/*) IM client federates the various IM protocols.

Google bought Jaiku and has made the application both open source (*http://jaikido .blogspot.com/blog/2009/03/jaikuengine-is-now-open-source.html*) and a model for a federated microblogging and activity aggregation. Jyri Engeström wrote about it at the time:

> For a while now, many in the microblogging community have been wondering how to add contacts and exchange updates and comments across services.
>
> For instance, some of my friends are on Jaiku, others are on Twitter, and a third group use FriendFeed. How could I follow everyone without having to deal with creating and managing an account on all three?[†]

Federation of services on the Internet is a real issue. However, it does not have a firm specification yet, such as OAuth. It is also a more complex problem, with both hard technical and commercial problems to solve. How do we take the Internet and make it service-agnostic and still retain commercial value in services that are largely free to use? There is a parallel between microblogging now and the early mobile phone networks. Initially, it was only possible to make a call on the same service, as now it is only possible to message within Twitter. This was resolved for mobile phone network operators by accounting incoming and outgoing minutes and SMS messages. Financial settlements resolved any discrepancies. For a federated microblogging future, there are no minutes to charge for or handsets to sell, as in the telecommunications world.

Making Your Code Green and Fast

Running web applications uses energy, that much should be obvious. Reducing the amount of energy your application uses should lower your hosting bill and reduce the environmental impact of your company. This is more of an issue at a larger scale, but unless you start thinking about the average costs per person for a page display early in the development of your application, you will have a lot of refactoring to do later. This may not seem like a major issue at first glance, but it was a significant enough issue for

---

† *http://www.zengestrom.com/blog/2008/12/foreign-friends-from-a-servicecentric-to-an-objectcentric -social-web.html*

Google that it designed its own server to reduce the cost per search. Much social software has the same low revenue per click. Building your own server farm is out of most people's league; however, there is lots of potential to reduce costs in other ways. Some analysis from Google on the environmental impact of search requests shows that about 0.2g of CO_2 is produced per request. The energy required to produce a glass of orange juice is equal to roughly 1,000 search requests in terms of its impact:

> Early on, there was an emphasis on the dollar per (search) query, Hoelzle said. We were forced to focus. Revenue per query is very low.[‡]
>
> —Urs Hoelzle, Google's vice president of operations

Fortunately, reducing energy usage also overlaps with creating a user experience that feels quick and responsive. Steve Souders's book *High Performance Web Sites* (*http://oreilly.com/catalog/9780596529307/*) (O'Reilly) gives 14 guidelines for making sites feel faster. You can find an overview of the guidelines on the Yahoo! developer website (*http://developer.yahoo.com/performance/rules.html*). These guidelines rest on the principle that concentrating on purely optimizing backend application code resulting in HTML generation is a flawed approach. It represents only a tiny fraction of the time taken for a page to become visible (see Figure 16-5, which shows the tiny amount of time it takes for HTML to download compared to the time it takes for the page components to download). Ensuring that content is cached appropriately and that you are minimizing the number of files that must be downloaded per page are primary ideas in this approach.

The YSlow Firefox plug-in (*http://developer.yahoo.com/yslow/*) that Steve Souders created while at Yahoo! is an essential tool in making your pages more energy-efficient and faster to display. The queuing approaches also help. Doing as much as possible asynchronously in a queue means that control returns to the user more quickly. It is then possible to batch-process some of the remaining tasks. Propagation of updates is a task that needs to run immediately; otherwise, you will fall behind with the constant flow of updates. But overview statistics or non-user aggregation processes are not needed in real time, so they can be run overnight during quiet times. Another, more widely used approach is Amazon's EC2. Why run your own additional servers when you can rent time on someone else's? This approach is particularly suitable for batch processes, but it can also work as part of a round-robin server group for peak loads. The aim here is to level off your own power consumption and reduce the number of machines you have running idle, and, of course, lowered energy usage means less cost per user, which helps with profitability.

‡ *http://news.cnet.com/8301-1001_3-10209580-92.html*

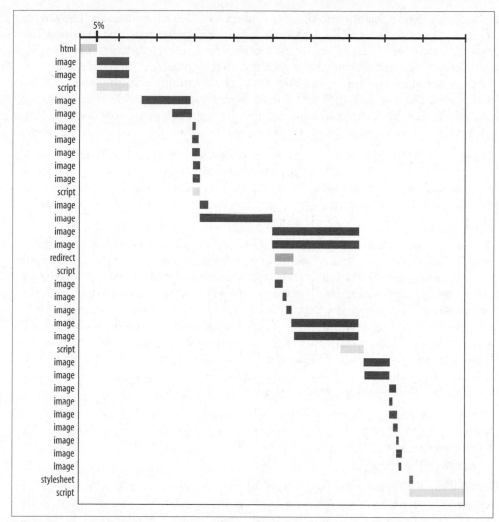

Figure 16-5. Downloading http://www.yahoo.com in Internet Explorer (from Steve Souders, used with permission)

Building Admin Tools and Gleaning Collective Intelligence

Without a good set of administration tools you will have no idea what is happening on your site. I don't just mean site statistics tools such as Google Analytics, though some kind of statistics tool is essential. I mean the tools to manage and monitor activity on your site in terms of the core social activity, not just page impressions. You need tools to determine the rate of new sign-ups, creation of objects, and status of members. You also need tools to block and ban, as discussed in Chapter 15.

Too often these tools are left to the scraps of time available post-launch. The ongoing quest for more features or the inevitable bug fixing diverts time and attention from making good tools that your community never sees, and even though it *may never see them*, they are *essential for running a good site*, so their presence is important. Be aware that you can skew community behavior simply by counting something and displaying it in public. These analysis tools can also encourage you to value what you are counting and miss other changes in your community behavior that you are not counting. If you count it, you will tend to value it; be careful that you do not get led by the numbers.

There are different styles for these tools. Some sites use a single portal that gives access to everything; others use a private page behind every object on the site (e.g., */person/ zzgavin/<admin>* or *photo/asdaq3r/<admin>*). Some simply add an admin data layer on top of the usual view of the page. Appending "admin" to the URL is enough, as long as you have permission to see admin pages.

A mixture of approaches works. A complex view, such as an events listing, can benefit from having admin tools layered on top of it to delete content, rather than re-create the view. Supporting hackable URLs for admin access to people and content means you do not need to create a search interface to (re)find the item to do the admin task. Yet, often a summary interface is what you need to get a sense of what is happening on the site. On top of this, you will want the operations interfaces to monitor performances and systems. It is rare to see admin applications; they tend to be private and obviously full of personal data. Do not design a detailed admin application prior to getting some real data into your system. You can build the wrong thing too easily. Build an admin interface section by section based on growth.

The design patterns for these kinds of administration systems are quite opaque and hidden, because they deal with company confidential data, so they are rarely public. Some basic patterns do exist.

An overlay system on top of the social objects and profile pages, as noted earlier, combined with a summary stats page is a good start. Much of your admin work will be focused on people, so a tool that can pull up detailed data about a user will be very useful. Time using site, any payment information, number of contacts, counts of activity by content type, and actions are helpful to give a sense of overall activity. People will come to your attention for what they have recently done, so showing a sample of their recent sitewide activity will be helpful. Any explicit moderation activity should be clearly called out. Overall summary data about the general behavior of your application can be essential in understanding what is changing on your site. The next two sections outline the sort of data analysis tools you will need to create to do this well.

Social Network Analysis

There are many questions to ask in terms of what statistics to collect—what kinds of data to collect for users and objects, what tools to use to track and visualize the data, and so on. Capturing data early for use much later is an important trick. Timestamping your activities is also important. Knowing when something happened, be it a tagging or a comment, means you can see when it happened a second time, rather than just knowing you have two tags for an object.

Many social network analysis tools are available. These tools need data for analysis in the form of lists of friends and, in many cases, time data around friendship formation. This information is useful in modeling what sorts of relationships you have on your site. Discovering that you have 10% of your community at a low level of activity ("follow a few people," "post irregularly," "came via a previous promotion") means you can develop functionality to encourage them to participate more. Without the metadata it would be harder to see this constituency.

Machine Learning and Big Data Sets

How do you determine what you need to capture to explore the overall community behavior? The seemingly magical side of your applications comes from machine learning, which is a form of artificial intelligence. Learning algorithms are applied to large volumes of data, and they can be trained to make predictions or find patterns in the data. Toby Segaran's *Programming Collective Intelligence (http://oreilly.com/catalog/9780596529321/)* (O'Reilly) takes relatively simple machine learning techniques and shows how to create tools such as a recommendation engine, a price comparison tool, and various clustering tools. Many of these tools are starting to be used within social applications.

Collecting all of this data means you know a lot about your community. Given the right tools, you can use the data to find out even more and then create a space to explore it. Flickr did this with its interestingness feature a few years ago. Recommendations from music services such as Last.fm and Spotify can also be very appealing. Look at Toby Segaran's book for a very readable and useful guide to machine learning.

Machine learning can be very CPU-intensive once you have enough data to make it useful. So, running these processes on services such as EC2 is a good match. This is exactly the kind of batch process you might run daily or weekly. This kind of machine learning analysis—primarily for recommendations or log analysis—is becoming very common. Large-scale users of Hadoop include Facebook with 1.3 petabytes of data, Last.fm with 85 terabytes, and Yahoo!, which has 10,000 machines running Hadoop.§ A good platform for exploring machine learning is the Mahout product that runs on top of a Hadoop cluster. Mahout has implemented several core machine learning algorithms, and Hadoop provides a computational environment in which to run these processes. In addition, Amazon provides its Elastic Map Reduce service, which, like EC2, allows for intermittent access.

§ *http://wikis.sun.com/download/attachments/38208497/Hadoop-Primer.pdf*

Reputation Systems

The means by which you maintain a list of who is interesting and relevant to each person on your site is a difficult problem, but one that can be informed by machine learning tools. Getting beyond simply collecting social objects and listing them in collections is a good aim for social applications. Reputation and recommendation systems are an important aspect of this work. However, there is a great potential for these to turn into a game, which can have an unhealthy aspect because people will try to stay at the top of any list that you make. At the time of this writing, Bryce Glass and Randy Farmer were in the process of writing *Building Reputation Systems* (*http://buildingreputation .com*), which reviews approaches to creating and maintaining reputation profiles in depth. They are defining a grammar for referencing how reputation systems operate, which looks to be a very useful approach.

Summary

You have spent time building a site that is small and good. It feels coherent and makes sense to the product team. Now is the time to get your friends in to kick the tires a bit and see what they think. This soft-launch private alpha phase is really important. It is a second chance to see whether the site makes sense to more than the development team. You no doubt have already shown it to a few people, but the reaction of a few dozen people coming in via IM or email will give you a stronger sense of whether the site makes sense without you beside them. Don't be afraid of cutting features if the feedback is strongly negative on some of it.

Mostly, the feedback will be about wording and positioning, but among this will be a sense of what they think you have made. This is an important aspect to listen for in private alpha feedback. Hopefully what they think and what you think will be closely aligned; if not, look again at how you are portraying your main functionality.

Good social applications do a few things well. They offer a well-supported API and have a polished, coherent user interface. Support for the primary social objects is of utmost importance, and the community features are obvious and clear. Assess your development plans and make sure you can see how you will create something that people will love.

CHAPTER 17

Building APIs, Integration, and the Rest of the Web

No man is an island, entire of itself.

—John Donne, Meditation XVII

"We need to be on the Web" was the cry of the 1990s. Some smart companies realized there was more to this than choosing a hosting provider and whether to use Microsoft IIS or Apache. For example, Google and Amazon are deeply enmeshed with the Internet, with links to their services and pages on many pages other than their own. Having a website is a good start to engaging with your community, but intentionally limiting a website to just pages consumable by humans misses out on the real potential of the Web. Today, a website is more than a brochure; it is a data repository with multiple interfaces to the content. Facebook and other closed sites have gradually opened up over the past year. For instance, the *New York Times* has gone from having a registration barrier to having a real-time API for its content. Being merely on the Internet is no longer enough.

"On the Internet" Versus "In the Internet"

So far this book has mainly focused on creating your own application. In this chapter, we will look at how to integrate your application with the other services your company might own and with the rest of the Internet. Much of this additional functionality comes from what are commonly called *application programming interfaces*. These APIs are the machine-facing interfaces for your application. Other software will depend on them. They can be arguably more important than your user interface on your website. APIs can do many things for your product; one of the most noticeable is spread awareness of your product and links to it across the Internet.

Google's AdSense ads are seemingly everywhere. Many sites use Google Search to provide search services. Similarly, many people link to Amazon's pages as their first point of reference for a book. Both of these examples do have a financial motivation behind the linking practice, but regardless they have widespread coverage on the Internet for Amazon and Google far from their own sites. The API-led services that both companies offer show the value in allowing some of your content to be reused by others. Amazon was probably the first widely used web API.

Social applications such as Twitter and Flickr have detailed public APIs, and as such their API usage dwarfs the normal HTML page accesses for these companies. In March 2009, Twitter's traffic was 10% to 20% web-driven and the rest was API-driven.* Recently, the *Guardian* newspaper built a range of API and data services (*http://www .guardian.co.uk/open-platform/*) with which it aims to broaden its online reach. Matt McAlister (head of the Guardian Developer Network) described this mission to build API and data services as "weaving the *Guardian* into the fabric of the Web." This is a good description of what an API and a liberal policy on content reuse can offer. While the *Guardian*'s offering is not social software, much of what it offers will be included in other social applications, showing that content publishers can also have a hand in the social web through their own content. The *Guardian* also has an active community on its site, but unlike the *New York Times* (*http://developer.nytimes.com/*), the former is not making the user-contributed content available via its APIs. Both stances are appropriate choices, however.

Making Your Place Within the Internet

Once you grasp that your site is part of the connected whole of the Internet (something I hope you did much earlier in this book), then you need to see which pieces of your site can connect to others on the Internet. This covers both outgoing and incoming uses. Common areas for incoming uses are the contacts APIs mentioned earlier in Chapter 14. Automating the process of allowing people to bring and find their friends on a new site helps to increase your membership and makes the site more useful for these new members.

This integration has a wider footprint than you might initially imagine. It spreads into the choice of external data sets upon which you build your application. Choosing the Yahoo! WOE (Where on Earth) identifiers for geographic locations will make any future linkup with Flickr or Upcoming much easier. Other sites use people's Twitter IDs as a means of jumpstarting the identity framework for their own applications; for example, *http://zzgavin.foodfeed.us/* and *http://www.fluidinfo.com/terry/2009/01/24/flu iddb-domain-names-available-early-and-free-for-twitter-users/*.

---

* These figures come from notes (*http://gojko.net/2009/03/16/qcon-london-2009-upgrading-twitter-without -service-disruptions/*) on a presentation by Evan Weaver from Twitter (*http://blog.evanweaver.com/articles/ 2009/03/13/qcon-presentation/*).

A final example is using the hCard provided through the microformat on another site to simplify the new account creation process on your site. The Get Satisfaction example from Figure 14-1 illustrated this concept.

By building on the behaviors and data formats commonly used on the Internet, you are working with the its affordances rather than against them. The hub-and-spoke model commonly used as a simple model of how the Internet works becomes more tightly interlinked if everyone uses these approaches. (In case the hub-and-spoke model is new to you, here's a quick primer. If you are only linked, you are a spoke; if you link to other people, you can become a hub. The model is simplistic, as it usually looks at only a small subset of the Web; the reality has many more hubs than are typically drawn.)

Why an API?

Earlier I said an API is a software interface to your site. Why would you make one of these? To answer this question, I'll give you an example. How would you get an image posted to Flickr onto a blog you run without an API?

Without an API, you would need to manually find the right size image and either copy it to your blog server and create the HTML to link to it, or figure out the HTML to link to the image hosted on Flickr's servers. This might be easy for most people reading this book, but it's much harder for the majority of people who use Flickr and have a blog.

Happily, Flickr is able to use the common weblog API services that virtually all blog software implements to support the simple process of selecting an image and the blog to post it to, as shown in Figure 17-1.

Taking this a step further, many people write blog posts in a desktop application. Figure 17-2 shows the Media Manager tool from MarsEdit. Without a photo access API from Flickr, it would be hard to take an image you own on Flickr and post it to your blog from the desktop application.

In these examples, the APIs provide ease of use for the end user of your product, but there is a layer above this for people who are making other products based on your tools. The APIs that the author of MarsEdit uses to find the images is the one that this chapter is about.

There are, in fact, several different types of APIs that you might create:

- One that allows end users to access your product through an alternative interface
- One that might be commercially privileged
- One that is aimed purely at developers for testing their applications
- One that allows a developer to build her own application
- One that might allow another service partner to integrate with your products

Before deciding which type of API to create, you need to think about who you are making an API for and which activities you are supporting by creating one.

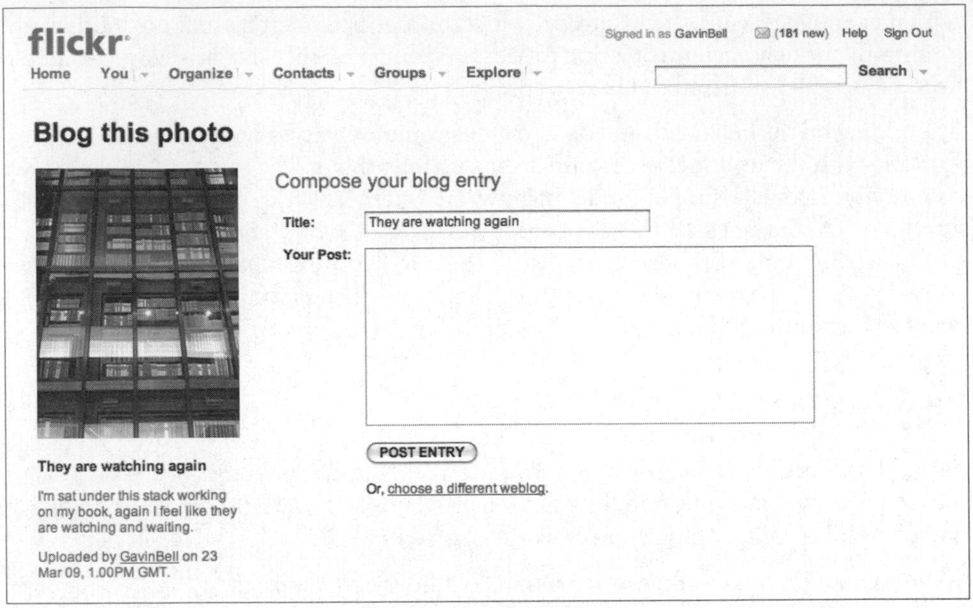

Figure 17-1. The Flickr "Blog this photo" posting service

Exposing Your Content to Search from the Internet

One of the most useful ways to make an API is to wrap an API layer around your content search services. While I was writing this chapter, I received a Twitter message showing that my tweet mentioning the British Library had been included in a blog post.[†] Perhaps this is a trivial example, but without the API to make the aggregation simple, the inclusion would never have happened. Content search available from outside your own website is a very powerful tool for increasing your audience and making your content much more useful to other people. However, there are significant issues in terms of how you make this content available, particularly if you have a high rate of new content creation. We'll look at these issues later in this chapter.

Running Services, Not Sites

An API is the first step toward your company being able to run services and not just sites. Along with this comes a need for good terms of service and a potential model for revenue sharing, or at least an understanding that such a model might be implemented. Either the content is yours, or it belongs to your community members and as the site owner it is your responsibility to encourage respect for their wishes. For instance, Flickr allows individuals to license their content under the Creative Commons licenses in addition to the default of All Rights Reserved, which gives users a greater degree of

[†] *http://looceefir.wordpress.com/2009/03/24/aggregating-british-library-tweets/*

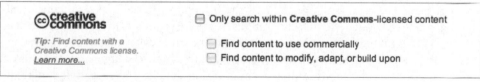

Figure 17-2. MarsEdit Media Manager showing its easy access to images hosted on Flickr

freedom in expressing the kinds of reuse they want to allow. Flickr echoes this in its search interface (see Figure 17-3) and in its APIs (*http://www.flickr.com/services/api/ flickr.photos.licenses.getInfo.html*).

creative commons

Tip: Find content with a Creative Commons license.
Learn more...

☐ Only search within **Creative Commons**-licensed content

☐ Find content to use commercially
☐ Find content to modify, adapt, or build upon

Figure 17-3. Creative Commons search options from the Flickr advanced search page

Being Open Is Good

Being more open than your competitors is one approach to gaining an advantage over their products. Imagine Amazon with a restrictive use policy concerning its ASIN identifiers. (These are the product identifiers that Amazon uses, and they are part of each URL for a product.) Until recently, the changing URLs of many newspapers made even linking to their content difficult, as the link would break after a few days once the content moved into the paid archive area. An API can be a company strategy; let others embrace and extend your application or your content. The BBC, for instance, has been taking the latter approach with its program information, and recently it rebuilt its identity management system around OpenSocial as opposed to the closed source bespoke (custom-made) code that was there (*http://www.bbc.co.uk/ontologies/pro grammes/2009-02-20.shtml*). Having people build applications or reuse content against your services gives your company more opportunities to be seen.

Arguing for Your API Internally

Creating an application with an API will allow you to integrate it with others, as we looked at previously. However, you will need to consider other kinds of integration. For instance, if you are an already existing company, there will be many software systems—from registration to payment management to content production—to consider. Social software is often the first new thing these older applications will have to integrate with. If you are not an existing company, there are different issues to consider. First, let's look at big companies.

If your company is large enough, you might have multiple social web applications in parallel development or with different teams. Many books have decried the simplistic approach of making a website that matches your organizational chart, including *Information Architecture for the World Wide Web*, Third Edition (*http://oreilly.com/cata log/9780596527341/*) by Peter Morville and Louis Rosenfeld (O'Reilly). Making web applications that treat your audience as a collective whole is just as important here. There is not a separate audience for the news site and for the discussion board for features, so users trying to access the news site and the discussion board should have the same log-in details. This will mean cutting across departmental boundaries, and probably some arguing will result.

A hard-line approach is sometimes necessary. There should be a single identity for any single organization. Yahoo!, Google, and the BBC do it. Just like people continually claim to need "advanced" search capabilities, there are groups who will argue the need for a special login for their application. With the possible exception of short-lived experiments, a single public identity should be workable for every organization. Internal tools can have separate or additional authentication details, which in fact, can be desirable for security reasons.

Implementing User Management and Open Single Sign-On

Identity management is not the only place where integration can be a headache, but it is the most common, as social applications require identity. Failing to offer a single identity leaves your customers with the following problem: which one of my "megacorp" identities do I use to log in? Which profile is associated with this message board? This can result in a bad user experience and one that can make people leave. In particular, asking people to create another account when they already have one will cause irritation.

Why does this occur? Many frameworks and all off-the-shelf social software have a user database at their core. For instance, if you install MediaWiki to run a wiki, and a few months later you want to create a blog using WordPress, each application will want to manage its identity separately. This is in addition to the email reminder service you probably already have. OpenID solves a lot of these issues, but in 2009 this problem still persists. Therefore, deciding what your hub application will be is important. Nature Network started in 2005, and a strong intention has been to create the single public-facing identity hub for it. Over the past few years, both Yahoo! and Google have integrated their identity management systems on the majority of their applications.

The open stack of OpenID and OAuth is a good starting point for building an identity management framework. OAuth is probably the more useful of these if you need to choose where to focus your efforts. OpenID has great potential and the gentle masking of it, as "Use your Yahoo!, Flickr, Gmail, or AOL identity to log in," will help greatly. OAuth is more widely useful in the context of API usage. Dozens of Flickr applications have been granted access to my Flickr account via a very similar mechanism to OAuth, yet I have one Flickr account. By enabling OAuth, you create a secure means of allowing access to the content hosted on your site for your community. Another option is to base your application on a product such as OpenSocial, where a lot of this behavior is built-in. OpenSocial also supports OAuth and OpenID (see *http://opensocial.org*).

Integrating Other Services

Many other aspects of your site might need to integrate with internal systems. Payment services are a common centralized activity. Building yet another financial management system will not make you popular with the accounting department, though. Therefore, you should pass people over to the money-taking service, but make sure you can skin it to make it feel like it's a part of your own property. Sending people out to another service that looks different from your own can be unsettling. At least maintain your own site branding, if possible. Many magazine subscription services, for example, frequently use a centralized subscription payment service and fulfillment operation, but they at least retain the magazine brand.

Lightweight Integration Works Best

If you are integrating with a third party, you might need to design an API for them. They will have a data source or service that you want to use, but perhaps have never integrated with another website. Keep it lightweight and simple. Use XML over HTTP and avoid the heavier end of service integration, like Simple Object Access Protocol (SOAP) and the web services (*http://www.w3.org/TR/ws-arch/*) protocols, unless you absolutely have to. Flickr and Google have offered SOAP access for web services in the past, but found that the usage figures for SOAP are much lower than for simple RPC or REST APIs.

Avoiding Data Migration Headaches

Data migration between different systems is a huge headache. Writing and testing import and export code and keeping both systems live during the handover are best avoided. But how? In 2009, Twitter is in the midst of migrating to OAuth from email and password authentication. Flickr is still using its internal OAuth-like system and has not yet moved to a pure OAuth approach. Customer support is one of the primary aspects that needs attention in a move such as this. With thousands or millions of active users, there will be some people who have problems. Moving everyone using Twitter's external applications means hundreds of thousands of people will have to reset credentials for perhaps two to three applications each. Picking the right technology for public-facing authentication is difficult, and changing it is troublesome.

What about other forms of data migration? Public-facing authentication is a difficult problem, but other areas are difficult to migrate, too. For instance, changing your reference geographic data set would require a lot of work. Staying with publicly available or common data sets means you are likely to have other people working on the same problems. Migrating a user system where email verification was not initially implemented to one where email validation is the default will involve jumping through quite a few hoops. People move and lose access to email accounts more often than you might expect.

Researching this area carefully and taking advice from the developer community is the only feasible approach. Working with the ongoing standards process to ensure that you are doing the right thing also helps.

If you do need to migrate data, you need to test and test again. Having a long period when you are running both systems during migration is possible, though some systems are best migrated quickly. Changing log-in credentials is a good example (refer back to the discussion of the long migration of Flickr users to the Yahoo! identity systems in Chapter 6). The key step is to stop new sign-ups through the system to be replaced, and then briskly setting up a migration system with a well-briefed customer service team to handle any problems.

Avoiding Duplication

Companies with multiple products accessing the same data can end up with identifier duplication. Projects can act as silos, and information does not always pass between them as easily as you might want. Time is also a factor. Sometimes the same content will get identifiers from different phases of a production process. When putting content on the Web, it is advisable to have a single canonical representation of your objects. It is quite common to have multiple identifiers pointing at the same object. The quest for a single identifier for everything is a lost cause. Accept that there will be multiple identifiers in any large system and create the means to translate between them.

Email Notifications: Managing Your Output from Multiple Applications

Regardless of the scale of your operation, people like email updates, but they can quickly get frustrated with them, too. Sending email to your customers is not a right; in fact, in many countries, people have a right not to receive email sent by you. Giving a simple means for your community to control which emails they receive from you is a good idea. Consolidating content to be sent into a single email also tends to be appreciated. Sending an email every time something happens on the site can get bothersome. A good alternative is to use a queuing system. Park all the updates and then send them when they are ready for that person in the intervals the person wishes: as they happen, daily, weekly, or never. Finally, separating service-related emails from announcements and event notifications is polite. If you have multiple applications, consider managing the overall email volume that your customers receive from you. A simple logging application that notes when a person has been sent email can be helpful for knowing whether a marketing email will be appreciated. Many social applications opt to never send third-party emails, while some make it an option; tracking what you send makes this a safer practice.

Making an API the Core of the Application

An API can be seen as an optional extra on top of your application, or it can be seen as how you should make applications. Building your own features on top of the same API calls as your external third-party developers means you are writing less code and consolidating testing. Note that these APIs do not have to run on the same servers; they just need to use the same code. This also does not mean you are given wholesale access to your application code, but rather that you are selectively sharing some of the calls you use to create your own features.

The other approach is to create a separate set of code to comprise your API. This is usually made after the main application code and needs to be kept in sync with how it evolves. There are security advantages to this approach. For instance, you know exactly what developers have access to. Also, they are less likely to reverse-engineer an undocumented call, and it is easier to set up on a separate server group, as it is essentially a separate application. The weakness is that it might never happen: the additional work required to create an API needs to fight it out for time and money from bug fixes and new features.

Handling People and Objects, the Stuff of Social Applications

Social applications are made of two basic ingredients: the people who use your applications and the content they contribute to your service. Pretty much everything else is built on top of these two aspects. If you have private accounts, authentication will be required to access them. Frequently, these objects are gathered into collections via aggregation points such as tags, place, or time—for instance, all posts with red as a tag, or all photos in London, or all articles from March 2009. People are also accessed via containers; for example, all followers of person ID 6. Many API calls are basically a search with parameters—give me this kind of object matching this value. Write-based API calls are obviously a bit different, but much of your traffic will be read-based API calls.

Generally, people will want to create complementary activities to your main application—remote access from the desktop or a mobile device or widget is a common product. The Scout service, shown in Figure 17-4, finds out which of your images have made it into the Explore section of Flickr; this is a simple extension of a core Flickr service, purely based on API reads. An API call to read content seems like a duplication of the website, but an API read can deliver just the item of content and not the surrounding images, CSS, and JavaScript. This makes it a much less intensive service to provide and encourages people not to just screen-scrape your site.

 Screen scraping is an old and much used technique that predates widespread API availability and microformats. Screen-scraping programs would be written to download and interpret the HTML on a website, and then extract the relevant content. Screen scrapers are error-prone, and a small change in the format of the HTML pages will generally break the screen scraper. The technique is still commonly used to read data from legacy mainframe systems, however.

Designing an API

How do you go about designing an API? The first step is to decide what content and behaviors you want to make available. Generally, read and write access to your primary social object will comprise this initial step. Access to the friends and followers of your community members is also popular. Offering a type of search will allow a huge range of applications to be created. The Hunch application, shown in Figure 17-5, lists a range of applications the Hunch team would like to see created to run alongside Hunch; this is a great approach.

Next you need to decide what sort of applications you would like people to create. Purely client-side applications can be created via a JavaScript API. If you want to allow fuller web applications, you will need to create a server-side API. If you have a server-side API, you will need to decide on OAuth versus email and password security (hopefully, you'll choose OAuth). Expect the first few products that people build on your API to be wrappers for their favorite language. If you provide PHP, someone will create a Ruby wrapper, and so on.

Finally, you need to decide on an architectural style and response format. Prototyping an application while designing the API helps to ensure you are making something that

Figure 17-4. Scout service tracking the Flickr Explore pages and showing which of your pictures made the top 500 for any given day (http://bighugelabs.com/flickr/scout.php)

works and that you are not depending on some internal knowledge or access. Let's take a look at some architectural styles.

RPC

The Remote Procedure Call (RPC) is historically the most common approach to API design. It usually has a single URL or endpoint, and each API call is passed along with the parameters as a POST or GET request. The interaction is verb-focused: do this or do that. Essentially, each API call is running a program on another machine. It often implies use of other services such as SOAP and the web services specifications, which increase the complexity of implementation.

REST

REST (REpresentational State Transfer) is becoming more popular as a style. Your entire site acts as the API; this is the closest thing to making your code and API overlap. The interaction is resource- or noun-focused, and actions are reflected in the verbs

API Ideas

This is a list of applications we would like to see that could be developed using our API in the future.

- iPhone App
- Live flash visualization of topics that people are playing right now, a la digg Labs
- Flash visualization of live activity in my community
- Widget that shows off your answers to Teach Hunch About You for your blog/website
- Auto-publish your Teach Hunch About You answers, favorites, and plays to Twitter, Facebook
- Badge trophy case
- Facebook nemesis detector
- Hunch Zeitgeist... e.g. this week people are Hunching recession topics
- Predict your answer to Teach Hunch About You questions
- Individual Hunch topics like ("What should I wear today?") wired into iGoogle
- Factoids widget that shows off random correlations
- IM bot that lets you play a topic in a chat window
- Flash graph for users clustered by similarity
- Flash proximity graphs for people in your various taste neighborhoods, e.g. Sense-of-Humor neighborhood, Personality neighborhood
- Voice activiated 1800-find-a-bar
- Bookmarklet for adding any item on a webpage to Hunch

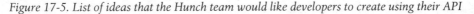

Figure 17-5. List of ideas that the Hunch team would like developers to create using their API

present in the HTTP specification. Pure REST APIs are uncommon, but frameworks such as Ruby on Rails version 2 and later are making them substantially easier to create. Viewing an object is as simple as doing a GET, such as on `/person/id`; creating an object uses a POST, such as on `/person`.

XMPP

XMPP has become popular recently for high-volume services. It is obviously not based on HTTP, and handles guarantee delivery situations very well. Fire Eagle, Yahoo!'s location-sharing service, is one of the better known implementations of XMPP. XMPP requires a separate set of software to maintain, but it relieves your web servers of handling this traffic. If you have a range of third-party applications polling for user updates, this is something to consider. See "API and Scaling Issues" on page 350 for more information.

Response Formats

An API call implies a response. XML is a common default for this response, but JavaScript Object Notation (JSON) is probably more popular (see *http://json.org*), as it is easier to work with than firing up a whole XML parser for a few hundred bytes of content. There are other options, including SOAP, should you wish, and some APIs even return serialized PHP. XML and JSON are probably the most popular response formats.

Comparing Social APIs

Three products that have had a good number of applications built with them are Tumblr (the microblogging service), Flickr, and Twitter. Between them they represent a good cross-section of social web application API approaches.

Tumblr

Tumblr (*http://www.tumblr.com/api*) has an API that is largely focused on making updates easy from external applications. There are just four calls, and the style is REST-like: a POST call to **/api/write**, a GET call to **/api/read**, a call for authentication, and a call to create a session. These calls are sufficient to create Mac OS X dashboard widgets and iPhone applications, and they allow integration with other social services such as Ping.fm and desktop applications such as MarsEdit. There is no access to the social network in Tumblr, but the API is clean and easy to understand.

Flickr

Flickr (*http://www.tumblr.com/api*) is the oldest of these three applications and has a mature API that offers a rich set of functionality. Flickr offers several modes of operation. The basic one is remote photo upload, but this includes a huge range of functionality for placing a photo in sets and groups, plus tagging and geotagging. In addition, there are sets of API calls for accessing the social graph of each person. There is also a group of API calls for remote viewing of photos, including the ability to mark something as a favorite and to comment. There are API calls for accessing the geographic aspect of Flickr, and there are tools for searching for photographs and people on Flickr.

Enough functionality is provided to almost completely replicate Flickr on a client application. Based on this comprehensive API, myriad Flickr applications and Flickr photographs are embedded in many services, from Upcoming to Last.fm and many blog posts.

Flickr's API is essentially RPC in nature, offering a single endpoint for data access and passing parameters to make each query. The RPC version expects to receive an XML data packet, and the REST version expects the appropriate GET or POST as parameters.

The Flickr API offers a wide variety of response formats. Compfight, for one, provides a rapid visual search (see Figure 17-6) for Flickr, based on its API (*http://compfight.com*).

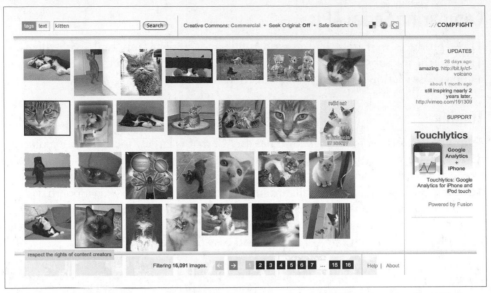

Figure 17-6. Compfight kitten search based on the Flickr API and displaying images from Flickr

Twitter

The Twitter API (*http://apiwiki.twitter.com/*) is currently a two-part offering. The main API is focused on people and content uploads or viewing; a separate search API is offered as a result of an acquisition of another company in 2008. There are many applications for Twitter. The majority of the activity on Twitter's servers is API-driven. Many people visit the site perhaps weekly, while they use Twitter several times per day (or hour). The API is very complete as a result.

Content posting, social network management, and timeline management are all included. It is possible to use Twitter for days at a time without visiting the site. A good example (see Figure 17-7) of a full-featured client is Tweetie (*http://www.atebits.com/tweetie-iphone/*). This client supports search and the ability to follow and unfollow from within the application. Part of the huge rise in Twitter's popularity comes from the availability of clients such as Tweetie.

The API in Twitter is largely REST-like and highly detailed; in addition, developer community management is clear and well documented. A wiki with documentation and a changelog, plus an active mailing list, support the developer community well.

One tactic that Twitter took with its applications was to allow each client to say who created the message (see Figure 17-8). The text "twitterrific" is displayed on the Twitter website, and it links through to the site where someone can download Twitterific. This makes it very easy for new products to get exposure to people on Twitter.

Figure 17-7. Tweetie, a fully featured iPhone application for Twitter

Figure 17-8. Twitter message source, indicating which Twitter client application posted the message

In Figure 17-8, Twitter displays the names of external applications that send messages to Twitter, giving rapid exposure to new Twitter clients.

Reviewing the APIs

The APIs generally have three sections to them: data about people, data about objects, and search facilities. None of the APIs allows for remote account creation. Twitter is considering this, but only for formal, trusted partners. Account creation should really happen on your own site.

Simple APIs such as Tumblr are appropriate starting points and may be all you require. Flickr's API shows the degree to which Flickr has also become a photographic and, arguably, geographic service on the Web. Finally, Twitter, through its API, has successfully gotten itself in many people's pockets on a daily basis.

One aspect that Apple has handled very well with the iPhone SDK release was the creation of the App Store. Giving developers a visible marketplace rapidly increased adoption of new applications. Twitter took a slightly different approach. It provided a link to the source for each application that sent messages to Twitter. Each new application had to be added to an approved list by Twitter first.

Writable APIs

Creating a writable API means two things. You need to authenticate that the developer has the permission from the person using the application to upload the content. This is the previously mentioned OAuth versus password and email choice of account management.

Another, subtler aspect of this is that data written to one place can take time to appear back on the website, particularly if a queuing system is being used. You need to decide how important this latency is for your community. You can fake the immediacy of a text update quite easily using a combination of `XMLHTTPRequest` and DOM manipulation. The viewing person will see the update and generally assume that everyone else has done so as well. The fact that it is being queued for processing is immaterial. With larger items of content, such as photographs, videos, and presentations, your community will get the idea that the service needs to do something with the content before they see it. Solving this problem becomes increasingly more difficult in distributed systems.

Extending and Fine-Tuning Your API

Determining what to send about an object is an important decision. One of the reasons to have an API is to reduce the amount of data you need to send, but send too little and you will encourage multiple requests per operation from third-party developers. Flickr sends a small amount of data per interaction, but allows selective requesting of licensing information, geographic data, or ownership information. These extras[‡] are a clean way to extend an API. They avoid a pattern whereby the developer requests a range of objects and then, photo by photo, all the other information about each one, only to use 3 of 26 pieces of information, discarding the rest.

Wrapping API Calls

Frequently the exact implementation details of your own application will be masked by an API wrapper, allowing easy integration into your language of choice. All the external developers need to care about is the API wrapper, leaving you free to work on the underlying code. Encouraging creation of these wrappers will help build a good developer community. Even better, you can create the first few yourself. Listing these

‡ *http://code.flickr.com/blog/2008/08/19/standard-photos-response-apis-for-civilized-age/*

wrappers as part of your API documentation will probably encourage people to create more applications. Make sure the listing is kept up-to-date, though: seeing a wrapper for your favorite language, and then finding a dormant project that doesn't work with the current API, just leads to frustration.

Using API Alternatives

You might not need to create an API for every aspect of your site. A combination of microformats and RSS/Atom feeds will create a read-only API. Many applications now bristle with feeds for all sorts of objects. A photo can have a feed of comments. A tag will have recently tagged objects. A person will have her recently contributed content. Feeds such as these are an easy way to place content outside your site and elsewhere on the Web. They might end up combined in a Yahoo! Pipes or similar mashup or simply in an RSS reader so that someone can keep tabs on activity on your site. Yahoo! Pipes is a highly configurable product for processing data that is available in RSS form. It is possible to integrate this data with Yahoo! software such as search products. It can also be used as a basic scripting tool for processing web feeds.

Microformats (*http://microformats.org/*) also allow content reuse, but in a more specialized manner. They wrap people, places, and dates. Other applications can take this content and reuse it, knowing that it is a person and not the result of an unstable screen-scraping process. Finally, taking date-based data and offering an iCalendar (*.ics*) file (*http://tools.ietf.org/html/rfc2445*) of the events means the content that is important to a person on your site can appear in his calendar. Dopplr and Upcoming amongst others are avid providers of these kinds of calendar files.

Using HTML Badges

Not everyone is capable of putting content in the form of RSS or microformats to good use. By creating web badges, you can make it easier for people to take a piece of your site with them. Web badges commonly allow people to put their photos or planned travels or recent messages on their own site or social network page. Flickr, Twitter, and Dopplr all offer them, along with companies such as SlideShare, which allows embedding of presentations. It is a remarkably effective method of allowing non-developers to reuse individual content.

Interoperability Is Harder with Snowflake APIs

Building an API is a lot of work. Usually there will be something else on which to base at least some of the work, which helps a lot with interoperability. Too often, though, people decide that their problem is unique and create a specialized, or *snowflake*, API (*http://www.dehora.net/journal/2009/01/09/snowflake-apis/*). When you use a snowflake API, you create extra work for all of the developers who want to use your application. The classic example of this was access to address book contacts on a webmail system. Every provider did it in a slightly different manner, making interoperability impossible, but now the Portable Contacts specification standardizes the process of accessing contacts. Before you create a wholly new approach to a problem, first check to see whether there is a related approach in a common standard. Your developer community will thank you.

Sticking with Standards

There are many useful standards on the Internet for building applications, particularly social applications. In this chapter, we've already discussed OpenID, OAuth, microformats, RSS, Atom, XMPP, and even XML. We've looked at OpenID and OAuth in length, so now let's check out some of the other standards.

The Portable Contacts (*http://portablecontacts.net/*) specification shows how to simply build a common means of access to address book information or contacts. Currently, this is done via bespoke APIs for contact access or screen scraping for hCard microformatted data, if you are lucky.

AtomPub (*http://www.ietf.org/rfc/rfc5023*) is a protocol for accessing and editing webbased resources. It is formally ratified by the Internet Engineering Task Force (IETF), is heavily influenced by the REST architectural style, and supports Unicode by default.

Activity Streams (*http://activitystrea.ms/*) is a draft specification that is looking to formalize the updates that flow from social applications. This looks like a promising way to move forward for social network federation.

Standardizing APIs

In the microblogging community, numerous products compete with Twitter. The Identica/Laconica (*http://laconi.ca/trac/*) project, among others, mimics the Twitter API so that many clients simply need to have their root API URL changed and they will work. Six Apart took a similar approach when it launched its TypePad AntiSpam (*http://antispam.typepad.com/*) competitor to the Automattic product Akismet (*http://akismet.com/*). In both cases, the APIs are plug-in replacements. So, changing services is trivial and uptake is much easier.

Using OpenSocial

Facebook's application platform attracted a lot of attention, but it is limited to Facebook users only. An alternative approach to Facebook's application platform comes from Google. It created an open source alternative platform called OpenSocial (*http://code.google.com/apis/opensocial/docs/*). One of the more popular implementations of OpenSocial is Shindig (*http://incubator.apache.org/shindig/*), which is an Apache Incubator project with implementations in Java and PHP. Using Shindig, you implement a container so that other applications can be placed inside it. Then you can create whatever application you like, with this space left ready for others to come and use.

OpenSocial has two parts. The first is a specification for JavaScript-based Gadgets or Widgets. The second, more interesting, aspect is a mechanism for applications to gain access to the host's underlying social network. LinkedIn used this recently to allow Huddle (*http://www.huddle.net*), a collaboration tools provider, and SlideShare (*http://slideshare.net*) to create applications that can be embedded on a person's profile page. In the case of LinkedIn and Huddle, the contacts of the LinkedIn user become available within the Huddle application (*http://www.linkedin.com/static?key=application_direc tory*).

OpenSocial offers a lot to a company that is creating a new social application from scratch. It standardizes the mechanisms for accessing information about people, handling activities, and storing data persistently. It also allows application developers to quickly build applications to work on your platform; they do not have another new API to learn. As such, it is a good starting point for creating a social application.

Creating a Standard

Most of these standards have not come from large companies deciding that this was the way things should be done. For instance, OAuth came from a group of developers trying to solve a problem. It is possible to create a standard such as OAuth, but it takes lots of time and effort. Start with a common problem and find like-minded people to help solve it. There are plenty of emerging areas from federation to providing real-time services upon which to focus your efforts. Tools such as Google Code and GitHub combined with a mailing list and a wiki make it easy to get these initiatives started.

Managing the Developer Community

Flickr communicates regularly with its developer community via its blog and a mailing list. Like many social application companies, many of its developers have quite a public persona. This visibility translates into a stronger sense of community on Flickr's site than that of a company with closed development cycles.

Key tools for maintaining good communication with a community of developers include mailing lists, a technical blog, a Twitter account, and a status page. Ideally, there should be an issue tracker and potentially an immediate road map for new features. Tools such as a public issue tracker are very valuable to developers who depend on your product. Twitter uses Google Code services for the tracker it offers (*http://code .google.com/p/twitter-api/updates/list*). Vimeo offers a public road map for its product (*http://www.vimeo.com/roadmap*). These tools sit alongside a comprehensive set of documentation and the companies' willingness to be open and admit mistakes.

Another good example is the build.lastfm.com service from Last.fm. This is a showcase for third-party applications that people have created for Last.fm. From the build.lastfm.com service, there are links to the documentation and mailing lists so that you can create your own applications. These sorts of marketplaces are important because they can create a sense of activity around your applications. They also make your developer community feel valued, and thus likely to make more applications for your API, rather than moving on to another application.

API and Scaling Issues

APIs place unique demands on your servers. Normally, you will have your own peer-reviewed, well-tested code running on your hardware. By releasing an API, you are letting anyone run code against your hardware. Given that social application APIs are tempting places for amateur developers to try out their skills, this could be a recipe for high server loads and problems.

The solution is the *developer key*. To make a call, each developer must pass in a developer key. This key is tracked and allowed a certain number of requests per day or per hour. Going over this limit returns a 400 error code that should tell the developer to back off a bit in terms of request rate. This throttling approach is quite widespread on social applications. Another option is to provide a refilling bucket approach rather than a fixed limit—perhaps 5,000 requests in a rolling 24 hours, but no more than 250 per hour. These limits can be reviewed once it is clear that the developer is producing a serious application and can respect the rate limiter.

Allowing Integration

Once you create an API, you are allowing people to integrate your content with their own. There are two aspects to this. The first is which rights you grant the developers in terms of using your content. This is more of a concern if you are a publisher. The second thing you need to think of is the individuals who have contributed content to your site. Now that you have these external developers using your service, you need to consider how this changes the user experience for non-developer users of your service. The Flickr examples from Chapter 8 are worth reviewing in terms of third-party rights management.

Running the API on your main site servers can work, but if you are expecting irregular or potentially high loads, it is advisable to have server capacity just for the API. The simplest approach is to poll an RSS feed. This will work fine for infrequently used feeds, but even this can be a strain if thousands of feeds are in use. Generation of these feeds as needed and a good caching policy will help, combined with monitoring IP and user account or developer key usage.

For the majority of applications, the combination of a developer key and monitoring, combined with approaches such as the Flickr Extras extensions mentioned earlier, will allow you to manage traffic levels on your APIs quite well. An emerging area in 2009 is the publication/subscribe (pubsub) model. XMPP is one such approach, which we discussed in Chapter 16. XMPP is an interesting protocol, but it suffers somewhat, as it is a different protocol from the rest of the Web, which runs on HTTP. It means you need to run a different set of servers and encourage your developers to work on this protocol that is likely new to them.

A new approach is PubSubHubbub, which offers decentralized pubsub, but running over HTTP. It is an extension to the Atom standards, which we discussed in Chapter 16. The following quote comes from the initial definition for PubSubHubbub:

> We offer this spec in hopes that it fills a need or at least advances the state of the discussion in the pubsub space. Polling sucks. We think a decentralized pubsub layer is a fundamental, missing layer in the Internet architecture today and its existence, more than just enabling the obvious lower latency feed readers, would enable many cool applications, most of which we can't even imagine. But we're looking forward to decentralized social networking.§

This approach removes the constant polling for new content that RSS implies. When new content is generated by an application, it notifies its local hub, which then tells any subscribers via the callback HTTP address they have supplied. This is an interesting way to develop applications that can push content to interested parties rather than relying on constant checks for non-existent new content (*http://pubsubhubbub.appspot .com/*).

Real Time Versus Near Time for APIs

Twitter offers a real-time feed to selected partners. This includes every Twitter message sent being passed to these external systems as it happens. This feed used to run on XMPP, but it has moved over to a Scala-powered solution. A key aspect of the real-time feed for Twitter is that it provides the content as a complete service to other companies on which they can build products on top of. These so-called *fire hoses* of data place a heavy load on both parties in terms of service availability. Many other applications need up-to-the-minute search-based results, but not a complete fire hose.

Two other approaches come from the *New York Times* and Flickr (again). Neither company offers a complete feed of its real-time data creation. The *New York Times* offers The Times Newswire API (*http://developer.nytimes.com/docs/times_newswire _api/*), which provides news stories over the past 24 hours. This is a lot of content, but it is not at the scale of the full Twitter feed.

Flickr offers a real-time service, but not a complete feed. It wraps the service in a light-hearted presentational style with "notional pandas," which look at the new Flickr photos and (algorithmically) select the ones they like:

---

§ PubSubHubbub Core 0.1, Working Draft, *http://pubsubhubbub.googlecode.com/svn/trunk/ pubsubhubbub-core-0.1.html*

Ling Ling and Hsing Hsing both return photos they are currently interested in, both have slightly different tastes in photos depending on their mood. The (currently) third Panda Wang Wang returns photos that have recently been geotagged, not quite real time but close.‖

This approach delivers photos that provide a good taste of what is on Flickr, but not the complete content. It is also possible, of course, to get the feed for any one individual. Flickr could offer an unfiltered public feed, but has deliberately chosen not to offer that as part of its API. The fully real-time model implies delivering all your content, which is a heavy architectural undertaking; check whether a search- or sample-based approach might suffice.

APIs Can Be Restrictive

An API is a private interface to your application's content. It will restrict, sometimes intentionally, what is possible with the content. The API is generally designed in the interests of the company creating it and its immediate business partners, and, of course, the community using the application. The developers are in there, too, but probably not at the top of the list. When using an API, it can be frustrating to know that a piece of data or particular function call is in use on the site but is not available to external developers.

Association of small amounts of data against larger applications is best done in the main application database, but the ownership and access structures of large relational databases make this impossible. An alternative approach is FluidDB (*http://www.fluidinfo.com/*), which proposes a flat model of content and attributes. Anyone can assign attributes on any item of content in the database. There is no longer any need for an API; the entire system has a single general API. This approach looks to be interesting for a range of problems where a wiki might be a good choice but more appropriate structure is needed.

Not Just Your Own API

While you're creating your own API for external use on other aspects of your site, you might well be using someone else's API. This free functionality from others can be fantastic. There are excellent free services on the Internet for performing many tasks that might be hard to implement or that rely on restricted, large, or private data sets. How do you manage all of these external dependencies on others' APIs? You can use a similar model as for scaling. Make sure all the external services are wrapped in an asynchronous connection, outside the direct user feedback loop. Offline processing, if at all possible, is the best approach. If you are using JavaScript APIs, ensure that there is a fallback position and that you can do something if that map is not available. One

---

‖ *http://code.flickr.com/blog/2009/03/03/panda-tuesday-the-history-of-the-panda-new-apis-explore-and -you/*

further point about JavaScript: make sure you do not overload your pages with included JavaScript, and be sure to track and monitor the size of the pages you are actually delivering.

Create an API?

A social application without even a minimal API has unfulfilled potential. Giving external applications access to your site will keep your community in contact with the people on your site. Allowing access to metadata will surprise you with the kinds of applications developers will build with your content. Many decisions need to be made to create an API for your application, but whether to have one should not be in question. A thriving developer community is the sign of a healthy social application.

Summary

Defining your API should be one of the first technical steps in creating your application. An API is too expensive and awkward to add after launch, so planning your own API in parallel with your development is the right approach. Basing your API on common standards and behaviors will make it much more likely that other developers will take to your new API because it will be familiar to them. This new developer community needs your support. Do this well, and they will reward you with increased exposure and plenty of new functionality, as well as bringing new people to your application.

CHAPTER 18

Launching, Marketing, and Evolving Social Applications

You need to introduce your application to people you do not know, and you need to listen to them tell you what they really want from it. Once you launch, the focus will be on making people aware of your application, refining the functionality you offer, and adding new functionality.

Loving and Hating the Home Page

Home pages are hard work; I've deliberately avoided talking about them too much until this chapter because I think there is too much focus on them. In some instances, they are the first place that new people will come to, but much of your first arrivals' experiences will come via a search result or from a link to someone's content or profile page. The idea that people enter a social software site through the home page and that it therefore acts as a front door is largely dead and buried.

In fact, there are two versions of the home page, as we looked at in Chapter 13. One is the personalized version for people with an account, and the other is for people who have never visited your site before and ended up on it when a search engine result led them to an internal page. These people do not have the social context that a link from someone's personal page would bring, so in this case, the home page is very much a marketing exercise. You have a brief period to capture their attention and get them to read more or click the sign-up button. As Figures 18-1 through 18-4 show, different sites take different approaches to designing this type of home page.

Figure 18-1. Dopplr home page

Figure 18-2. Flickr home page

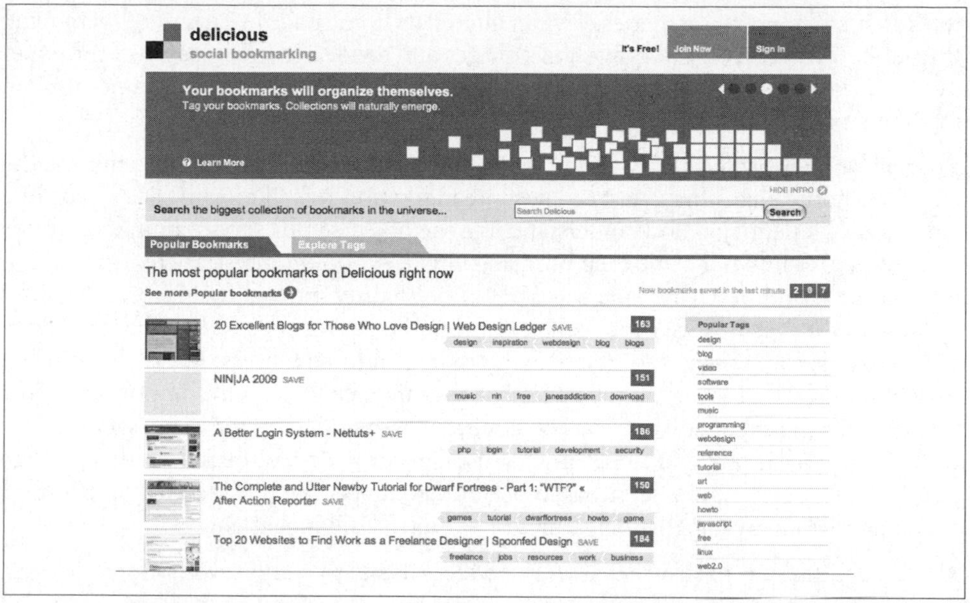

Figure 18-3. Delicious home page

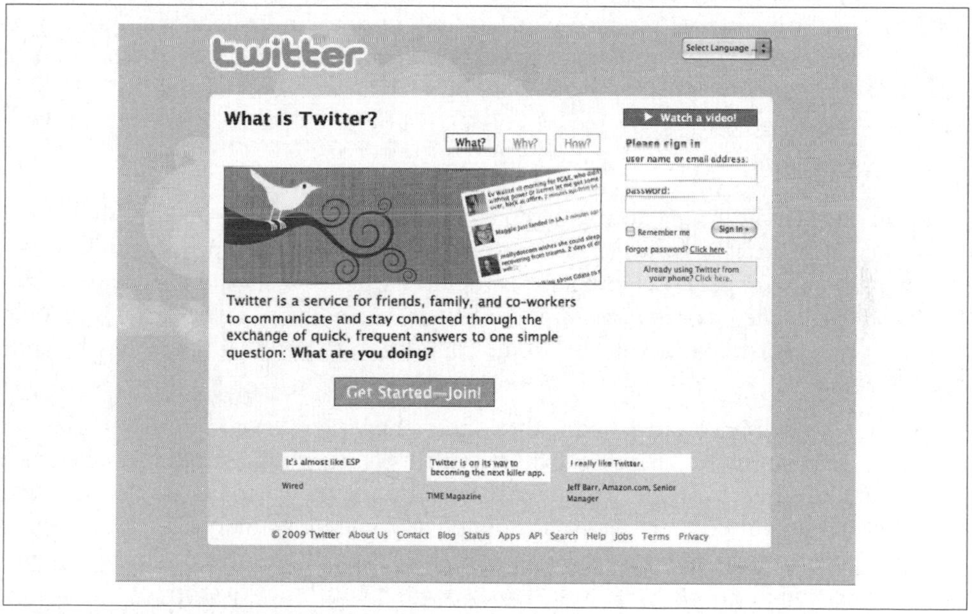

Figure 18-4. Twitter home page

The Delicious home page is the most functional of the four examples, showing recent popular content. Both Flickr and Dopplr show elements of their contributed content: Dopplr shows popular cities and a quote, and Flickr shows a striking photo and explains the different supported activities. Twitter altered its home page in early 2009, removing the public Twitter feed and now shows quotes and a video to give a sense of the experience. Twitter is also the only one not to offer the option to search its content from the home page.

Your home page can be highly functional , offering an experience similar to the one the Delicious home page offers, or it can be more marketing-led, like Twitter's. Which one you choose depends on how understandable the objects your service hinges upon are when they are shown outside their normal context. A bookmark is easy to understand, whereas a stream of Twitter messages could be slightly more difficult to understand because of the lack of social connection to the authors. Dopplr and Flickr both choose to show range of content and functionality to appeal to new users. Flickr also offers a tour, but it is much lower on the page. The prominence of search is important. Most people, with the exception of geeks, do not immediately sign up for a new service; they want to explore it first and find out what it might provide for them. Offering a range of ways to understand the service is important. Some people will search, some rely on quotes, and some want a list of features or a tour to convince them.

A final suggestion is to ensure that your service is useful to people even before they sign up. Much of Flickr, Dopplr, and Delicious makes sense to people who have not logged in because travel information, photos, and bookmarks have utility of their own, whereas the nature of Twitter makes it a harder service to understand without experiencing it. No doubt Twitter will find ways to give a sample of its content, perhaps using the favoriting function and creating something such as *http://favrd.com/*.

Your Site Launch

Your market will influence how you approach your launch. Some may see launching as an endpoint, but it is far from it. This is the time when you allow people you've never met to come and experience your site for the first time. You should make sure to see this fresh *out-of-the-box experience* prior to launching, and you can because the people you are likely to ask to test will have some connection to you (e.g., they may be your friends).

Without your helping hand to guide them, these new people will figure out whether your site makes sense to them and will tell other people about it. Now is when you need to make sure your team is still together and ready to welcome people. Respond to any immediate misunderstandings about what your site actually does by changing the brief text on the home page or giving some better examples. Do not start trying to change functionality; hold your course and see what continues to crop up.

The Soft-Launch Approach

Following the advice in Chapter 16 about a soft-launch approach, you should have knocked the rough edges off your application and should now be ready to show it to strangers. If you have a social application that works with an existing community—say, a Twitter or Flickr application—you might want to limit the number of people who come to you on launch day so that you don't have to deal with scaling issues in a panic on day one.

There is a real trade-off to explore here. Having 10,000 people sign up on day one sounds fantastic, but if your application crashes or times out a lot, most of them will never come back. On the other hand, allowing people to give an email address to get an invite in a few days will capture most of those 10,000 people, but it will also give you a chance to slowly add new people. The first few days in public might make you want to change the user interface of some elements or rewrite some aspect of your application. A strong "like it, but" response to a feature can provoke this kind of change. Grappling with scale issues and feedback on the application's functionality at the same time is not a good position to be in—what you really want is sustained growth based on word-of-mouth from happy users.

The Hard-Launch Approach

The other approach is a hard launch whereby all visitors are welcome and the launch includes marketing, PR, and a big push. This can work, but you need to be confident that your application has been checked by enough external people so that the "like it, but" crowd is small in number. When doing a big launch, you must be ready with scaling options, and a flexible hosting company can be a great help with this. Owning the hardware to scale to a level you'll not sustain for maybe a year is foolish economics. Many applications have a huge spike on day one and then hopefully a rapid growth back to this spike level over the coming weeks if they are lucky or months if they are less lucky. Services such as Amazon EC2 can be invaluable for handling these sorts of bursty loads.

Your Product Name

One thing you need to do regardless of which launch approach you take is decide on a name. Obviously, it has to be a free domain name unencumbered by trademarks. More than that, it needs to be a good name. Two-syllable names work really well, particularly ones that can be turned into verbs easily. *Flickring* and *tweeting* roll easily off the tongue and help to cement a person's relationship with the site. An easy-to-form collective noun is a harder nut to crack, but *Flickr-inos* and *Dopplr-istas* do exist. However, being able to generalize a product name can weaken its trademark value; hence you now hear people "Hoover-ing" with a Dyson. Because of this, Google is resisting the use of *googling* as a verb, but in the short term hearing people *Flickring* pictures communicates a lot.

Now that you have a plan and a name, you need a community, which we will discuss next.

A Friendly Invitation

The common *invite your friends* approach works for both hard and soft launches. For a hard launch, it simply grows numbers and provides a social context for the new people who are arriving, which I'll explore later in the chapter. For a soft-launch approach, the number of invites a user is allowed to send becomes a parameter you can tinker with to bring in more or less people to your site. The most famous example of this is probably the Google Gmail invites, which when launched became very desirable. This is simple economics: restricting the supply of something that is in demand makes its effective price/desirability rise. The flipside of this is a slow-moving application where you increase the number of invites a user can use when he failed to give away the ones he already had. Careful monitoring of the number of sent versus accepted invites and the number of unsent invites is a key marketing metric. Those people who are successfully inviting people to your application are worth encouraging, but don't give out invites to people who already have plenty. It can make you look foolish or desperate.

Invites can give you a certain level of desirability, they can provide a social context, and they can help with scaling issues. You can also give out invites to a waiting list of applicants for your site. These invites are less powerful because they all come from you, but they do help with scaling issues and somewhat with desirability.

A last point about invites: people forget, so a polite reminder a week or so after sending an invite to those who have not accepted can be quite effective. However, you should do this only for invites that the individual has requested. For invites sent by your users to potential new members, allow them to send the reminder; it is more likely to be effective. If you send the reminder on their behalf, it can be seen as unsolicited and spam-like.

Financing Your Site

Keep in mind this simple but extremely important formula:

> Community != Money, unfortunately[*]

Launching and refining are useful topics to discuss, but servers and staff members need to be paid for. Taking new types of social objects online will bring traffic. Take Flickr and YouTube, for example. Given the 2009 downturn in the advertising market, which looks likely to persist for a while, the old business plan standby of "advertising supported" is looking less realistic. However, there are a variety of means of garnering income for your site.

A popular approach is to offer a paid membership for extra features, while making sure to retain enough functionality to keep the free users' attention. Many sites successfully charge a few dollars per month or $20 per year for a pro membership.

---

[*] In case you aren't a programmer, != means not equal to.

An ad-supported plan can work well if you have good representation from a particular niche group (more so if that niche is well heeled). Using text ads, like Google AdSense, can work well if there is enough of a context for the matching algorithm to find relevance. On many sites, such as Twitter, there is just not enough text to support this kind of model. Many sites aim text ads at free users and remove them from paid accounts, which seems to be a popular model.

Affiliate sell-through of products might be a successful approach, depending on your content. Balancing the ads and the content that is leading the sales against the community content can become a concern, however. Any paying users are likely to resent the ads appearing on their pages, yet they are the ones most likely to have enough interest to buy the advertised products. Offering a *support this site* store can be an effective and non-intrusive way for this to work. Dopplr, for example, has a shop selling travel products and a partnership with a hotel chain. Partnerships can work in a variety of ways, but the social application needs to have a large community for it to even be relevant for discussion.

Lastly, sponsorship can be a good model, as long as the sponsor is not too direct about site functionality. The sponsorship is usually for a fixed period of time, and the functionality remains, so make sure whatever you make with them is something useful and is not too closely tied to the sponsor's brand so that you can reuse it later or cleanly dispense with it.

Offering Premium and Freemium Models

Offering a service for free and upselling to a paid, premium model is becoming a popular tactic.† Many sites are either moving from fully paid services to offering a free version or creating a paid offering on top of an existing free product. For instance, Twitter announced in March 2009 that it would be implementing paid accounts for companies (at the time of this writing, there is little additional detail on this). Flickr offered paid accounts within a few months of its launch to cover costs, and after Yahoo! purchased it, it retained this model, though at a reduced yearly rate.

Upselling models can suffer from overly keen salespeople. For example, it alleged that Yelp, the restaurant review site, alters the presentation of favorable reviews on the basis of whether the premium listing is taken (see *http://www.eastbayexpress.com/gyrobase/ yelp_and_the_business_of_extortion_2_0/Content?oid=927491&showFullText=true*). Given the opaqueness of the Yelp review listing model and the liberal terms and conditions Yelp operates under, it is easy for these kinds of accusations to be thrown around. Yelp is by no means the only company to be accused of this.

---

† Chris Anderson has a list of business models based on making your service free at *http://www.longtail.com/ the_long_tail/2009/03/terrific-survey-of-free-business-models-online.html*.

Marketing

Some Internet developers think of marketing as a dirty activity, or something that they just couldn't do themselves. This is a pity, as there are great opportunities for marketing social applications. Beyond letting your community use their content to add a badge to their site, there are other opportunities to make announcements or create a buzz. Simple breakthrough numbers, such as your first 1,000 or 10,000 users, can be a cause for celebration. If you have a flexible development model, you can time releases for particular events, while shipping out the minor updates and bug fixes. Naming these releases and announcing them to your community with a coherent message helps the community to understand what you are doing and that you are working hard to improve the product. The naming can be up to you. For instance, Dopplr names its releases after the city in which the announcement will be made, and given that Dopplr is about travel, this makes a lot of sense.

"Eat your own dog food" is a common expression—it means use your own tools to do things. If you are not actively using your own product, people might think that you lack faith in it. Using your product will also help you figure out what does and doesn't work. Moreover, producing content using your own tools is a great way to show your users what is possible.

Taking stock of what your community has been creating is important; it gives you a chance to see how people are using your tools and what they are making with them. For instance, the Flickr blog is filled almost daily with lovely pictures from the photographers who use it. They are actively curating the site and finding these images. With Dopplr, the content is largely private and much less visual. The annual view of someone's travels was something the Dopplr team made to show activity. Each report is a private view of what you have been up to in the past year. In order to provide an example of what the report looks like with the public, the team created one for Barack Obama, showing where he had traveled during his presidential campaign. The annual report, shown in Figure 18-5, launched shortly before the inauguration and was picked up by various newspapers because of its timely relevance. This is a great example of how to generate marketing for your product.[‡]

Achieving and Managing Critical Mass

Achieving critical mass means becoming the default application for a group of people for an activity. Social applications can (and need to) achieve a certain critical mass. Of course, the exact size varies depending on the domain and subject. For instance, Sermo (http://sermo.com) arguably has critical mass in the medical space in the United States, as its users comprise many of the medical practitioners there. Sermo also

---

[‡] See   http://blog.dopplr.com/2009/01/15/dopplr-presents-the-personal-annual-report-2008-freshly-generated -for-you-and-barack-obama/.

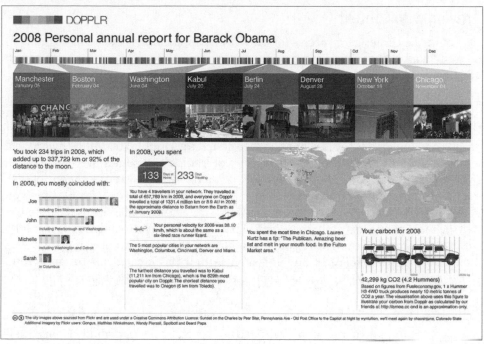

Figure 18-5. Dopplr annual report on Barack Obama

provides a private space for physicians to get help with clinical cases. Twitter has millions of people using it, many times the number of Sermo, but it took that sort of scale for an application to have such a broad appeal. Some might argue that Twitter doesn't yet have critical mass; certainly it is smaller than Facebook.

Flickr achieved critical mass for Internet-aware photographers and became the default "friending" application for a year or so. Then Facebook and Twitter came along and supplanted its position. In the meantime, Flickr stayed true to its photography roots and did not try to compete with Facebook on being the friend application. Critical mass can be a two-edged sword in that respect. When Flickr ceded the friending application crown it had worn lightly, a vibrant photography application and community was still in existence.

Achieving widespread use within a community is great, but it needs to be the community you want, and you need to be creating the functionality that your community wants. Time will tell whether the Facebook community warms to the real-time news feed that Facebook released in early 2009.

Arriving with Context

One of the key criteria for success for many social applications beyond basic utility for an individual is that her friends use the application. New members who arrive with context from friends are more likely to stick with your application.

Dopplr ran for several months as an invite-only application. This meant new members already knew someone who was an active member of the site. Dopplr's seed group was the common "friends of the founders" group, which mainly included active travelers to international conferences. The team then added the Dopplr 100 (*http://www.dopplr .com/100*), which was a hand-selected group of leading companies in technology, industry, design, advertising, and publishing. If you had an email address at one of these companies, you could get an invite. Dopplr then connected you with people from your company. Friendly competition between rivals such as IBM and Sun ensued as to who had the most members.§ Prior to launching publicly, Dopplr also did rounds for NGOs (*http://www.dopplr.com/ngo100*) and for mobile telecommunications companies (*http: //www.dopplr.com/mobile25*). Subsequently, Dopplr has created invites and groups based on conferences (*http://www.dopplr.com/group/future-of-web-apps-expo-london -2008/public*).

Maintaining context is really important to Dopplr, arguably more so than for some other applications, as many people will not travel several times per month. Contextually meaningful content can be a very useful tool elsewhere, helping to avoid the blank page devoid of updates as the person is connected to no one on the site.

Twitter has added a Suggested Users feature, shown in Figure 18-6 (*http://blog.twitter .com/2009/03/suggested-users.html*). When people join, it suggests to them popular people to follow so that they can get a sense of what Twitter is all about. This approach can lead to a lot of competition and suspicion about how to get on this special list, as these lists can generate a lot of followers for those included on them.

FriendFeed has an interesting way of showing new people: if someone you follow marks something as liked on FriendFeed, it will appear in your feed, as shown in Figure 18-7. This bleed-through of content from one person to another helps build social context among groups of friends using the service.

---

§ *http://www.redmonk.com/jgovernor/2007/10/18/now-its-a-game-an-ibm-vs-sun-game-dopplr-meets -cagefightr/*

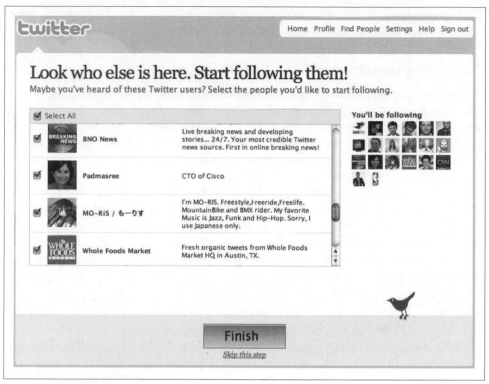

Figure 18-6. Suggested users from Twitter

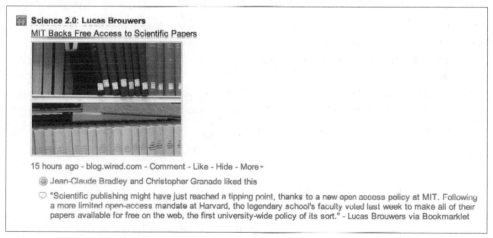

Figure 18-7. FriendFeed bleed-through favorites, showing an item from someone I do not follow; the favorites come from people I do follow

Wesabe, the personal finance application, is a good example of another class of applications that relies on the private contributions of others to make the data more useful.

These applications still benefit from the fact that friends are using the application, but they are not sharing explicitly public information with one another.

Considering Contact Import APIs and Their Importance

The previous section showed the importance of social context, but you can accept only one invite to a new service. So, what about the rest of your social circle? Back in Chapter 14, we looked at contact-importing APIs as a means of bringing these other people to your application. In terms of launch, there are two key needs. The first, the top priority, is to connect people to their friends already on the site—this is more important than bringing in new people. They need to see social value in using your application before they will put in the effort, and their friends use of the application is a strong endorsement. You should allow users to send invites to friends who are not already members, but most people will want to kick the tires first before inviting friends to something they've not experienced. Most people do not recommend a restaurant, film, or book without having eaten at, watched, or read it first. So, we should not expect social software to be any different.

This *finding already active friends first* approach doesn't preclude importing address books of contacts from other services, just that the next action should be to show those people active on the service, rather than listing contacts for a bulk invite. The purpose of contact import is to help your members find their friends, not increase your site numbers. It'll do that as well—just don't make that the blatant goal.

Using Tools and Services for Launch and Support

There is now a whole ecosystem of products and tools that you can use to support your new application's launch. For instance, you can use Get Satisfaction to provide support. A Twitter account gives you a space to talk about your product and gain informal feedback. A blog, ideally not hosted on your hardware, gives you a place to make announcements and to put the inevitable "we are down" status messages. Having a dedicated *status.service.com* site is a great idea, but a separate blog is enough early on.

For developers, a wiki with API details, perhaps separate technical blogs, and a mailing list will enable your developer community to talk with you and one another.

Nurturing the First Few Hundred Users

Your first few hundred sign-ups are an important subcommunity; this will be the group of people closest to you personally and most likely the ones to try things out for you. Think of them as a post-launch user-testing community. You can give them access to new features a day or two ahead of launching them to the whole community. They might feel a bit special, and you'll get some useful feedback. Dopplr uses a range of metrics to determine whether someone should be an alpha tester for a certain feature. For example, some metrics include the first 1,000 people, the people with the most trips, and those who successfully invited the most new users in the beta period. Each of these metrics can be used to test different types of new functionality.

Encouraging Your Community

The best way to get new people to sign up is through a recommendation from a friend. It will cost you nothing. If you provide the means for people to take the content they have placed on your site and you let them put it on their websites, blogs, or Facebook pages, many more people will know of your existence. I think many people's first experience of SlideShare was seeing an embedded presentation (see Figure 18-8).

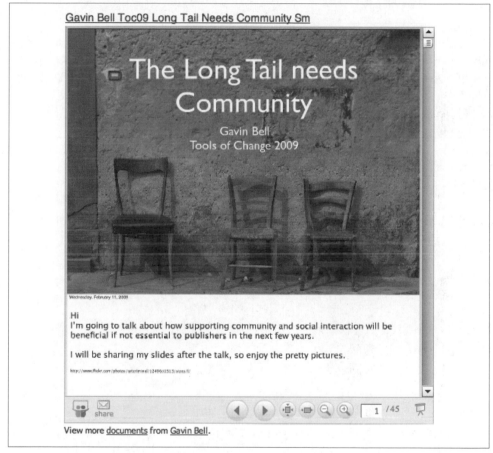

Figure 18-8. Gavin Bell's Tools of Change slides as an embeddable widget from SlideShare, allowing placement on a blog and spreading awareness of SlideShare

Encouraging your community to run face-to-face meet-ups can be effective. The Flickr meet-ups in particular are quite fun. They work as an effective hook for the discussion when there is less of an obvious connection between the members. For example, LinkedIn or Twitter can be less self-perpetuating.

Speaking at conferences and barcamps can encourage some new people to join your site, but the technical community there is small compared to the general population, so you should do it more to encourage developers and perhaps get some publicity for a release.

 A *barcamp* is a type of conference called an *unconference*. It has no set speaker list—the attendees are the speakers, and everyone has an opportunity to speak. They tend to be one- or two-day events, often on weekends.

The language and iconography that you use on your site can also deliver a level of unexpected personal connection. Your application can have personality. For instance, Flickr is sometimes down for a "massage," and Twitter has its famous fail whale (see Figure 18-9).[||] The fail whale humanizes the page and deflects some of the community irritation when Twitter is down.

Figure 18-9. The fail whale from Twitter's maintenance page

[||] *http://www.readwriteweb.com/archives/the_story_of_the_fail_whale.php*

Evolving Your Site

The real work starts after you launch your site. A constant process of evaluation of new ideas and iteration of features starts. Sometimes this happens very quickly. For example, when Hunch, a new machine-learning-driven collective knowledge site, launched there was no site-wide discussion space. A couple of weeks after the launch, a new Workshop feature (*http://www.hunch.com/teach/workshop/*) was added that allowed users to ask questions and get feedback.

 Evolution is natural; no social application is ever finished. Once you stop working on your site and developing new things, you have given up.

Remaining in Beta

In 2006 and 2007, it was common to have a "beta" badge on your site to show that it was not the final product and that the software was still evolving. Most sites have dispensed with such a badge. (Flickr had a humorous gamma badge for a few months.) The badges may be gone, but the concept of being in perpetual beta is not. These kinds of applications are never finished—they are more like services than finished products. It is not something that you can shrinkwrap and sell for a few quarters before starting work on version 2. Monthly release cycles and a full-time staff are now a realistic expectation for many projects. *Tweetmeme*, which aggregates URLs quoted from Twitter and archives the content, started as a £500 experiment and is now consuming £10,000 per month, with a staff of four and lots of server space and bandwidth. Getting to version 1 and going public is the easy part; sustaining the application and the community is the hard part.

Balancing Feature Requests and Issue Management

Balancing new development with bug fixes is a major challenge. In Twitter's case, its rapid growth meant any development was all about making it stable and not about new features. The fact that a broad API was in place meant third parties were about to create dozens of applications to provide the additional functionality Twitter had not provided. Without an API, would Twitter have seen continued success? That's hard to tell, but without an API, it would probably have a smaller active user community.

Your application will always have a long list of bugs, from minor deprecated browser bugs to major features that will require an overhaul to correct. How do you figure out whether to fix the bugs or make new stuff? Get this wrong and you end up with the sophisticated development approach called *fire fighting*, lots of hectic activity and little progress. Small teams help; there should never be only one person who knows how something works. One-month-at-a-time development plans that include bug fixing are a good approach. Picking a main theme for each build so that you are not touching every aspect of the application every month is also helpful.

Balancing new development with bug fixes is largely about planning and communication. Ensuring that everyone, or at least everyone's manager, is in agreement about what needs to be built and fixed each month will lessen the unexpected. One of the best ways to introduce inconsistency is to change your mind in terms of functionality late or leave planning a feature to the last minute. Software development takes time; the later the planning runs, the less time there is to implement the feature and test it. Bugs occur when people are forgetful or don't understand the implications of their decisions.

Social applications are complex, as they are highly interconnected. That tag you left on your friend's photo might appear in a dozen other views on the site. Unless this is understood and documented, changing the behavior of the tag could be error-prone; see "Determining When a Bug Is a Bug" on page 379 for more on this.

Adding Functionality

Soon after you have built and launched your application, your community will request extra functionality. You will have more ideas, too. Retaining focus is essential at this point. You still need to be able to describe what your application does in a couple of sentences, but the temptation to cater to new groups will be powerful. Well-defined, purposeful applications are better than ones that try to do too much. Even large companies such as Google and Yahoo! offer a range of applications that do a single job well, rather than a single monolithic application. In particular with social networking, tools offering everything including the kitchen sink can seem like a good idea, but staying small and focused provides a less complex and easier-to-understand user experience.

Twitter is well known for being the social application without a business model. It is (sensibly, I think) taking its time to see how its community and developers are using its application. The early shift from a microblogging application into a real-time communications channel changed the needs it had for its software and gave it a different set of content to work with. Many successful applications start out with a small feature set and evolve it to fit the needs of their community. Dopplr started with trips and social interactions and is developing into places. Flickr started with real-time conversations around photography and added comments and locations.

Build Something New or Refine the Old?

Hopefully, you have built a relatively small application that offers your community two or three useful things they can do. You now have a choice to make: do you extend the functionality of the existing tools, or do you make a whole new feature? Refining what you have is more difficult, but often it is the correct option. Staying your course when all around you everyone is making helpful suggestions, sometimes quite forcefully, is difficult. Twitter resisted the addition of groups to its product, and Flickr held out against the constant early demands for print services, so it can be done.

You might also have internal pressures in a larger company to exhibit visible signs that you are doing something with the funds you have. Throwing up a new section or new piece of functionality is an easier internal sell than refining your existing product. Refining can be seen as admitting you did it incorrectly in the first place. A lot of what we do in life has a date when the event is 100% complete, such as attending a concert, making a sale, or getting married, but social applications don't. They need constant refinement, like a relationship.

Having the conviction to say this is a first draft or a pilot and sticking with the need to revise is hard, but good user experiences come from a well-honed interface, not a collection of loosely linked-together first passes at functionality. However, some companies are often keen to see a launch as an endpoint and reallocate the staff elsewhere. Fight against this instinct as hard as you can. Earlier in the book, I mentioned that you get to launch about 40% of your budget; much of the remaining 60% should be for refinement and extending functionality, not building new features. Find out the areas of your application that are misunderstood or clumsy from user testing, log analysis, or A/B testing, and improve them so that you have a firm foundation to build upon.

Adding new functionality too early will increase the complexity of your product and decrease the likelihood of new people being able to easily understand what you are offering. Social applications are not like shopping malls—bigger is not better.

Adding Functionality After Refining

You can't spend all your time just refining the site you launched; at some point you will want to add something new. Every site will add features as it grows. How you choose what to build next is often a difficult decision, as choosing one thing almost always means not building something else. The best kind of new functionality will be constantly drawing attention to itself by its absence, while something that a devoted minority are clamoring for might be a dead end.

Natural extension of your product is what to look for; something that works well with the existing social objects and interactions that people on your site are contributing. For Flickr, the extension to geocode pictures worked well for two reasons. People were trying to geocode their pictures using word-based tags; for example, "London". The Flickr community was also worldwide, so coverage would be good. Compared to, say, printing, where Flickr had to find a third-party company in the countries in which it had a following, adding geocoding was a much more natural extension.

If you are adding new functionality that will result in your community having to generate a new type of content, you should pause for thought. Asking for more attention from your community can fail; it is better to build on the existing social object relationships than extend to another entirely different object type. It can work, but the right conditions need to exist to support the extension.

Adding events is a common request on many sites, but if you are supporting photography, events are less fundamental (core) than supporting music. Extending this example, Last.fm is a better place to add events than Flickr is, even though both have external events and people take photos of music concerts. Listening to music at concerts is closer to the activity of listening to music and it maps onto the artists that make the music. Meeting up to take some photos is a complementary activity, not a core activity for Flickr, even if it is notionally supported by Flickr. The music social object is strongly connected to the artist, so the experiences are linked. The same is not true for photography; hence the call for event support as an object in Last.fm is much stronger.

You should watch your site for people making use of your tools in ways that you did not expect. This can be a sign of several things: that you have a potential subcommunity, that you need to build features to make that behavior easier, or that something on your site is hard to understand or not obvious.

Orkut, the social network Google bought a few years ago, took off in Brazil, partly from a minor feature on the site that depicted the size of country membership in direct proportion to the size of the country flag. Brazilians took this as a challenge to make their flag the biggest, and certainly larger than the U.S. flag. Orkut responded by hiring a product manager who could speak Brazilian Portuguese so that Orkut could understand its new largest community.

An interesting approach to product management is the public development road map from Vimeo (*http://www.vimeo.com/roadmap*). Public road maps are a common feature in open source projects; particularly ones hosted using the Subversion repository, web-based project management tool, Trac, which has a built-in road map feature. However, exposing your future feature list for an application that is not open source is uncommon. Many other companies will talk about future developments in their blog; some companies will not mention any future projects. Your community will likely have a sense of your future projects. Communicating your next plans is a balance between overpromising and giving ideas away to the competition. It can reduce the amount of noisy feedback you get from your community. They will certainly have strong opinions on what you should be doing next.

Watching for What Your Community Demands

Something to bear in mind is that your most avid users are not the ones for which you should create new features. If you follow them too closely, you risk building increasingly specialized functionality that will not benefit the majority of your community. An often-related idea is that you should listen to customer feedback and ignore it. You don't literally ignore it, but neither do you slavishly follow it. You can be led into this approach when your site is small; if a few of the noisier people on the site start publicly asking for certain features, you rush to implement X, Y, and Z features in an effort to meet their needs. Often, what they are asking for are small changes, but these small changes can soak up design and development time, so be careful about saying yes too early.

Understanding what they are asking for can be difficult. A recent essay by Matt Gemmell, a Mac OS X and iPhone developer, described the sorts of things clients asked him for. His MGTwitterEngine library drives most of the Twitter clients on the iPhone and on Mac OS X. The user and developer communities for Twitter applications and social web applications are similar; they are not filled with unintelligent people. These people want something, but they might find it difficult to request it in the language that is spoken inside your company:

> However, in this industry in particular, there's a tendency to talk about our clients in (shall we say) unsympathetic terms. There's often a knowledge gap between ourselves and our clients (which is presumably partly why the client is using our services in the first place), and there's a sort of world-weary and slightly mean-spirited habit of char-acterizing clients as stupid because of how that knowledge-gap manifests itself.#

Gemmell's essay expands on this theme and explores half a dozen types of common requests and what they might really be asking for. Can you just add another of those? Can you make that configurable? Can it do X when Y occurs? These are some of the questions he addresses.

On Nature Network, we built the *snapshot*, a personalized activity tracker that dis-played the recent activity of each person's social network. This generated a lot of activity on the blogs with people replying to one another's blog posts. At face value this looked good, as there were busy blogs. However, this activity masked the fact that the forums were quieter than we expected them to be for the level of activity on the blogs. After analyzing what was happening, we noticed that the opportunities for someone to see new topics on the forums were limited to looking at the page for that forum and to that topic appearing in a member's snapshot of the network. So, we altered the site navi-gation to make it easier to discover new topics on the forums.

Observing the lack of something expected led us to assess how people were using the application and to discover that we needed to change something simple, the navigation, to make something more obvious. The second aspect is that communities of different sizes need different navigation and tools. Early on, tools to bring people together are useful; later tools to broaden what they can see are more appropriate.

Listening is a lot harder than it sounds. Paying attention to what your colleagues in your company say; or to what your investors say; or to what peers say; or even your own intuition is a lot easier. Audience feedback is a quiet background murmur. You need to learn to hear it. You need to pick out the significant strands of conversation and turn them into product ideas, rather than taking the well-meant suggestions at face value. Your members are expressing a need for themselves, something they want your

#*http://mattgemmell.com/2009/04/29/client-requests*

application to do. It is your job to determine what to create in response, something that takes your business in the direction you want to go, but also something that meets their needs.

Bear in mind, though, that your community will erroneously estimate how long something will take. Generally, it is assumed that only the user interface needs to change, and that can't take longer than a few days or a couple of weeks, at most. For more stories on estimation errors, see the 37signals essay at *http://www.37signals.com/svn/ archives2/revealing_hidden_assumptions_in_estimation.php*.

A key difference between social web application development and more general web application development is the closeness of the audience. On many successful social web applications, the developers and designers are active members of the site. They will get direct feedback and requests, plus they benefit from any feature addition.

If you and your team are active users of the site you are creating, you will see any awkwardness and clumsy implementations firsthand. Obviously, this is not possible for every site, but the ideal situation is that you and the rest of your team are an active part of the community you are creating.

Delicious and Boolean search

The bookmarking application Delicious listened to its community, who were requesting a Boolean search tool (*http://www.mail-archive.com/ydn-delicious@yahoogroups .com/msg00485.html*). They wanted the ability to combine tags so that they could make compound queries by altering the URL—for example, *spring -season* to search for the word *spring*, but not include any results matching the word *season*. This would help someone looking for the Java framework or a metal spring. The team at Delicious spent several weeks developing this feature and launched it to discover lower-than-expected usage rates. A section of their community had identified something that was missing from the site that they thought they would need, but in reality it was not a feature they would use on a regular basis. Much of the functionality has subsequently been wrapped into tag bundles, leaving the "ruby+gem" syntax behind. Following your early community too closely can result in creating functionality that is simply a bright idea, not a genuinely useful feature.

Flickr printing and video

Another two examples come from Flickr. There was strong demand from the community to support printing of pictures early in the life of the website. More recently, some of the community has requested video and others have argued passionately against it. In both cases, the Flickr team listened and did deliver both printing and video, but not as a simple bolt-on feature. For printing, they tested multiple suppliers and sourced a supplier who could provide good prints and could offer the service worldwide, not just in the United States.

For video, they spent a long time working out how to add video to the site without disrupting the current user experience. Video can be a very dominant medium, but Flickr has a strong community around sharing photography and engaging in conversation around that photography. The time-based nature of video disrupts this flow, so when the Flickr team added video, they limited the length to 90 seconds. They called these videos *long photos*. This allows video to be added to the site, but to retain the current interaction patterns.

Twitter and @replies

Listening to your community can drive new functionality. On Twitter, the initial approach to messaging was one-way only; there was no concept of a reply to another message. Members of the community started to use the common message board convention of using an @ symbol and a username to signify that the message was a public reply directed at a particular person. Twitter noticed this and incorporated parsing new messages for an @ symbol and adding the "in reply to username" text as metadata on the message.

Keeping Up with the Competition (or Not)

Something that people will always bring to you is "Site X does Y, why can't your site do this too?" There are two answers to this. The first is that you should retain your focus on what you do well. The second is remembering that you are part of the wider Internet. Being "on" the Internet is a poor substitute for being "part of" the Internet. Your site does not need to do everything, nor should you try to do everything. Partner up with other providers, or use "free" services such as Yahoo! or Google Groups, to run mailing lists.

Small pieces loosely joined was the clarion call of the early 2000s in terms of building web applications. The portal strategies of the late 1990s had led to huge sites offering every feature the developers could imagine. Examine your space, pick the task or audience you are going to support, and build tools to cater to that task or group.

Product comparison matrices can be very useful to help direct your focus. They help to determine how your product is different and meaningful to the audience you are catering to. There is no magic to them: a simple spreadsheet of features, a list of competitors, plus some time is all you need. Their main weakness is that they can turn into a list of the new features you need to build. Rather than a way of differentiating, they become a parity tracking tool to keep up with the Joneses. In some circumstances, you do need to offer a broad range, but this is rarely in actual features; more often it is in terms of support. For a photography application supporting new RAW file formats it is definitely a parity service. Adding new ways to manage your photos just because site X already has that feature might just be a form of "catch-up" and may not provide distinctive value for your product. Ensuring you have a unique product is more important than becoming a "me too" product.

Supporting open standards is generally a good idea. Facebook added OpenID as an authentication mechanism in May 2009, easily becoming the largest relying party overnight.* Google followed Yahoo! SearchMonkey by indexing microformatted content and making this part of its returned search results. In all three cases, these companies watched these standards evolve, and in some cases they helped out. When the standards had achieved sufficient adoption or maturity, they added them to their products.

Avoiding Feature-Led Development

Feature-led development, or *featuritis*, is a sad condition in which social web applications are afflicted with rapid feature additions and bloat. Often, this condition obscures the original shape of the web application. Usually the condition is terminal due to declining attention from the audience, but a harsh pruning may save the application. Humor aside, rapidly extending the feature set of a web application is not a good idea. You may understand where the product is heading and how the components link together, but you run the risk of alienating your initial audience and confusing newcomers to your site.

Featuritis is a common affliction when you have a development team and designers ready and waiting. Some of the agile methodologies almost encourage it—maintaining a backlog and the monthly cycle of pulling new features off the list and pushing them through the mill. Adding features to the site is not a bad thing per se, but it is important to keep a sense of perspective as to how your site is changing and why you are adding these features. It is important to understand how to turn these feature requests into useful tools for your community.

For every request, there are a range of questions you need to ask to determine how this functionality will meet the needs of the existing and any new community. Largely this is about understanding context; actions should not happen in a vacuum. Social network applications are full of interrelationships between people, tags, and groups. You need to determine how your new feature fits into this landscape.

An example will help to give this reasoning some context. A popular feature discussion for many publishers is "Can we add commenting...?" "Why add this feature" is the most basic question, but it is hard to answer if it's asked in such a blunt manner. The following questions can help you get to a better understanding of the need for commenting:

- Who is this for?
- What is the purpose?
- What is the longevity/time frame?
- What is out of scope?

* *http://developers.facebook.com/news.php?blog=1&story=246*

- What is the supporting workflow context?
- How will this enable community?
- What needs to change in the existing website?
- What are the dependencies?

Asking questions to understand the right context for creating new features is not about the software. Try to take it from "I want to implement commenting" to "With comments our members can do X and Y." This mistake of picking a feature or technology first is just the familiar retelling of a technology looking for a problem to solve. If you cannot justify how your existing community will use the functionality, you should not build it, regardless of any internal pressure to deliver feature X.

At the conference South by South West Interaction, held in Austin, Texas, in 2008, Michael Lopp from Apple described features for the sake of the feature as "I want a pony" features. Apple has pony meetings to get rid of these needless features: everyone wants a pony, but not everyone needs a pony. A *pony* is best described as an internally desired feature that can get delivered for political reasons, rather than for community benefit. Watch out for ponies, as they need a lot of looking after.

Encouraging Data-Supported Development

A good approach to building a new feature is to base it on data you have already collected or can obtain easily. Relying on your community to generate the data to support a new feature can work, but it is a slow approach. A few examples will help explain this more fully.

LinkedIn collected company information from people using the site for three to four years before it launched a company directory. By doing this, it had millions of data points, so it could deal with problems such as inconsistent names for a company. Also, when the feature launched, it was fleshed out; many of your previous companies suddenly became social objects. Compare this to launching the company feature two to three years earlier: someone would have to be the first person to create his company. Waiting was a hard thing to do, but it was probably the right thing in this case.

Flickr experienced a similar occurrence. It could have launched places when people started geocoding pictures, but it waited until it had hundreds of thousands of pictures to draw on. It used hand-tagged pictures, allowing some tags to be incorrect; for example, Reading in England got lots of pictures of books instead of the town called Reading (apparently it is quite a studious place). Making places visible certainly encouraged the activity. Recently, Flickr had more than 100 million geotagged photos and dispensed with the manual word matches on tagged photos, so the "Reading" tagged pictures would appear only if they had been placed on a map, too (*http://code .flickr.com/blog/2009/03/16/changelog-revision-of-the-places-page-also-neighbor hoods/*).

The final advantage of building on top of existing data is that you have something to experiment with and, more importantly, real sample data to test against. Building a feature that uses data that hasn't been collected yet is not recommended. It is far too hard to predict the data-entry patterns of thousands of people. Attempting this will lead to features that require a lot of maintenance.

Designing your system so that you can implicitly collect data on which you might want to create a new feature is a trick in itself. Tagging is a flexible way to collect this data. Adding optional fields for collecting data can also work. The LinkedIn approach of collecting workplace information as a natural part of the profile and then aggregating this into a new object, the company, is a good example.

Making Useful Products (Experience-Led)

My opinion is that people value small coherent feature sets and appreciate incremental changes to those features. Over the long term, you can take people a great distance using this approach, but lurching shifts in direction will irritate or confuse your community. In Chapter 7, we explored Experience Design and Activity Theory approaches to creating the initial product. Unsurprisingly, these approaches can be useful here, too. Rather than focusing on the level of the feature and how that feature behaves, look at the experiences or activities you are trying to support. Language can be clumsy in describing the difference between these ideas, so here is an example to clarify.

If you are creating a blogging application, the activities you are supporting are blog post creation, blog post management, and commenting management. These are the biggest high-level tasks that people come to your application to perform. The features are the *how* tasks: the details of the editor and the implementation of the comment registration system. If you make your product design decisions with respect to the high-level tasks, you will retain a coherency in your user experience. Getting stuck in the minutiae of *how* the registration system works can lead to losing sight of the overall purpose of the feature. Integrating new technology or arguments over support for a certain protocol is often the source of some of these issues.

Allied to this is how you package a release of your product. If you release a connected series of features as opposed to a set of small changes across the site, you have an easier story to tell your users. Remember that your web application is still a small part of someone's total experience. Assuming that a related product will be of interest or that an explicit connection to another service will be appreciated can fail. Someone might be on your blogging site to write about cookery, but that doesn't mean further cookery services will be welcome; this person might have her recipe management elsewhere.

Integrating with other third-party services definitely has two sides. Assuming too much technical experience—for example, that people will have a Flickr account for photographs—can make people feel excluded. So, make sure to provide a basic tool to do all the functionality on your site. On the other hand, trying to offer all the functionality that competitors do and not allowing any integration will also dissatisfy people. You need to understand the broader arc of their experience, as opposed to trying to take control or offer the sum total experience.

Determining When a Bug Is a Bug

You are probably thinking, what about bug fixes? How do they fit in with this holistic approach? You are right, they are an issue. Bug fixes by their very nature will occur across the entire site and can mean changes in how to implement features. There are three rough groupings for maintenance release work. There are bugs: things that are just plain broken, CSS or JavaScript issues with browsers, the wrong data on the page, and so on. There are also changes to how something works, or "improvements." And lastly, there are feature requests masquerading as bugs. The first group is easy: fix them and release them as quickly as you can.

The problem lies in the latter two classes. Separating the "this doesn't work for me" from "this should work like this" is a hard problem to solve. Bug databases are littered with bugs that turned into whole new features for the site, as something did not work right for someone. There is unfortunately no real cure for this, but communication and training can go a long way. Developers can sometimes see a way to solve something that does fix the issue at hand, but in fact adds a whole new piece of functionality. Editorial staff members often are not aware of the boundaries between changing how something looks on a page and how it is implemented behind the scenes, so a simple request implies a big change to the implementation of a feature.

Analysis and estimation are very helpful in forestalling unexpected feature development. Ideally, no decent-size bug, taking more than one day to fix, should be added to the planned release cycle until someone has had a chance to assess what might need to be changed and how long that might take. This pre-bug-fixing analysis does take time and can seem like wasted effort, but it helps to avoid piecemeal development, which can waste a lot of time and energy. Bug reports are a mine of useful information, but purely dealing with the surface symptoms can mask an underlying problem. A series of bug reports in a single area probably points to a feature that has been implemented incorrectly. If these are dispatched for fixing immediately, the overview of the problem gets lost.

An advantage that agile development practices offer is the fixed-month plan so that developers can plan out a big feature and organize their work accordingly. A disadvantage is that a fixed-month plan can mean a month between releases, and bug fixing getting low priority in that case. Entire books could be written on managing maintenance and feature development, as it is such a complex area. However, using the idea that something that does not work as planned should be fixed immediately is reasonable to understand the concept. It is contingent on good feature planning, adequate software test coverage, and feature testing with real data before deployment. In Chapter 16, we looked at how to attain regular deployment schedules using these ideas.

The second two classes of bugs are often a sign of disagreement in terms of how the application should be developed, particularly if they come from inside your team. They can also come from a mismatch between the product ideas and implementation. Moving briskly through each phase of feature development with the team in the same room is the ideal. The longer the time between feature development, design, and implementation, or the farther apart the teams sit, the more chance there is for misunderstanding to creep into the process. This is often realized in post-hoc bug fixes which change how the feature is implemented. Ideally, these changes are best captured as feature feedback combined with community feedback and result in a version 2 of that feature. One or two people saying something, even if they are internal staff members, is not usually enough to change a feature.

Staying Focused and Coherent

Web applications should make their core intentions obvious. They should have a personality and as such resist some feature additions or changes. To avoid this means to create software that lacks purpose. Creating this kind of focused software will attract some groups of people and repel others, but you are more likely to generate a bond with your community with this approach than if you use bland software. Compare Apple Pages with Microsoft Word. Pages sets out to create pretty, short documents with page layout at the core of the application. Word, with its long history, attempts to offer every possible feature for the office worker, along with a dozen other roles. The same is true of Keynote versus PowerPoint. Adding text-only posts to Flickr would radically change the application, though virtually all the tools are in place to support blogging on Flickr. Dopplr decided not to support trip itinerary management, focusing instead on the social aspects of travel.

The development and design company 37signals uses the term *opinionated software* to describe this approach. It helps a lot in deciding what your application should do next if you have a strong idea of what you set out to do:

> Some people argue software should be agnostic. They say it's arrogant for developers to limit features or ignore feature requests. They say software should always be as flexible as possible.

> We think that's bull…. The best software has a vision. The best software takes sides. When someone uses software, they're not just looking for features, they're looking for an approach. They're looking for a vision. Decide what your vision is and run with it.

> And remember, if they don't like your vision, there are plenty of other visions out there for people. Don't go chasing people you'll never make happy.[†]

On Nature Network, we decided not to support nesting of discussion threads on our message boards, as we wanted people to start new conversations, not change topic midway through an existing conversation. Our thinking was that a later member

---

† *Getting Real*, 37signals, (*http://gettingreal.37signals.com/ch04_Make_Opinionated_Software.php*)

searching for information would find less value in a topic that starts with the subject he is interested in, but then drifts off into talking about an unrelated conversation.

Planning for Redesigns and Refactoring

Inevitably, you will come to the point when you need to do a big visual redesign (a technical refactoring) or implement a major feature that touches your entire site. A good example is the Flickr localization project, which took many months to complete.[‡] However, Flickr remained an actively maintained site during the long development of the localization project. This is an important concept, as mentioned in Chapter 16; you should always be able to deploy your current trunk code so that you can roll out a bug fix or minor feature.

Refactoring and redesigns are healthy processes to go through for your application. They are a chance to fix early mistakes and reallocate screen space to a new behavior. Code refactoring is easier to manage, as only one layer of the application is generally changing.

A full redesign can be a time-consuming and exhausting experience, particularly if you have a large application with dozens of screens. The redesign of Nature Network from three columns to two columns (the sharp-eyed among you will have noticed this change in the pictures in this book) took several months to agree on and plan, and then another couple of months to implement. The most important driver in a redesign should be to improve the user experience, though branding changes are often a driver. The reason for the redesign of Nature Network was to increase the width of the main column of content from 550 pixels to 740 pixels. This greatly improved the readability of the longer stretches of text. Getting the basic grid for your site correct on the first attempt is a good idea.

Establishing the Rhythm of Your Evolving Application

Watching people come in, fill your product with their content, chatter, and interact is a lovely feeling. One of the most important lessons in building social applications is that the community will feel it is their application, too. The strong communities on Flickr and Twitter attest to this sense of bonding that their communities have with these applications. Creating this is hard; there is no easy answer or magic feature you can build. Keeping your application simple, dealing with troublemakers, and building features that your community really want are a good part of the process. The best word to describe it is a *relationship*. The individuals on your site are forming relationships with one another. Early on you will be involved in getting this moving; after a time it should be self-supporting. New members of the community are invited or drawn to the activity. Good luck with running your own community.

---

† *http://code.flickr.com/blog/2008/10/08/whats-in-a-resource/*

Summary

Getting ready for launch is stressful; launching can be a bit of a surprise, hopefully a good one. Be thoughtful when planning your launch. Make sure you've got feedback from people external to your team, because you will be too familiar with the product to have enough perspective to see how new people will perceive it. The home page and initial product presentation are important. They give a flavor of what awaits inside. Decide what the appropriate experience is for people who have not yet signed up. How much can they do without compromising privacy? Where is the value in the aggregated public data?

Post launch, the focus moves to iteration on your core feature set. Be careful about adding new features early on, and make sure your current application really works first.

I hope this book has helped you understand the problem you are trying to solve more clearly and enables you to start with that small, focused application for your community. Best of luck!

Index

We'd like to hear your suggestions for improving our indexes. Send email to *index@oreilly.com*.

Drupal social application, 22, 151, 152
Dublin core metadata, 206
dynamic pages
    shifting from static, 43
    visual design considerations, 39–46
Dynamic Systems Development Method, 306

E

80:20 rule, 57
eat your own dog food, 362
eBay site
    online financial transactions, 71
    profile pages, 110
economies of attention, 101
Economist (periodical), 58
editorial staff, 25
efficacy, sense of, 36
Elliot-McCrea, Kellan, 169, 181, 237
Ellison, Nicole, 139
email
    as interface, 302
    command-line interfaces and, 194
    commenting and, 170
    etiquette tips, 256
    filtering updates, 240
    group formation and, 145
    handling moderation, 277
    identity management and, 210, 214
    internal messaging systems and, 174
    intervention via, 279
    links to web pages, 255
    managing from multiple applications, 339
    OpenID differences, 211
    personal groups and, 196
    security and, 255
    spamming, 121, 210, 213, 229
    teenagers and, 126
    verification guidelines, 213
    verifying invitations, 198
email address harvesting, 229
encryption, 255
energy consumption, 182, 325
Engeström, Jyri, 46, 55, 156, 325
English Cut site, 22
Equity.org site, 184
error pages, 298
escaping, 308
event and conference management, 177
EXIF format, 199

experience arc, 37, 148
experimentation, 92–91
Extensible Messaging and Presence Protocol
    (XMPP), 313, 342, 351

F

Fabric tool, 295
Facebook Connect tool, 140, 151, 152, 153,
    325
Facebook site
    activity pages and, 236
    Activity Streams initiative, 101
    activity support, 139, 153
    add-as-a-contact messages, 255
    as centralized service, 140
    as social platform, 151
    authentication and, 376
    collecting data, 57
    critical mass and, 363
    displaying recent actions, 166
    evolution of, 125
    internal messaging systems, 173
    lifestreaming considerations, 138
    machine learning and, 329
    Mini-Feed feature, 72
    OpenSocial and, 348
    pending invitations, 255
    people searches, 229, 230
    personal messaging on, 276
    profile pages, 215
    reactions to change, 71
    relationship models, 250
    size of, 324
    teenage members, 126
failing faster, 92
fake friends, 176
Fake, Caterina, 18
fan-based model, 251
FAQs page, 147
Farmer, Randy, 330
faving (marking favorites), 130, 171–172, 252
featuritis, 376
federation, 139, 324
feedback
    collecting, 35
    community demands and, 373
FETHR service, 139
FFFFOUND! site
    architecture of participation, 163

linking web pages, 255
non-password-based access, 257
OpenSocial support, 152
security considerations, 260
site launch of, 360
spam and, 121
XMLHttpRequest object, 40
Google Maps, 315
Google OpenSocial framework, 151
Google Reader, 128, 130, 167, 171
Google Search, 331
Google Social Graph API, 201
Google Talk, 194
Google Video, 257
Google Wave, 314
Google Web Accelerator, 255
GPS services, 194, 202
Gracenote database, 63, 64, 184
Greenfield, Adam, 37
Grenning, James, 288
grid references, 202
griefing, 269
groups
    admin considerations, 145, 265
    advocacy subgroups, 271
    aggregation tools for, 150
    as FriendFeed rooms, 150, 151
    cohesion considerations, 164
    collaboration tools for, 150–151
    collective views, 196
    conversations in, 145–149, 196
    creating, 264
    data modeling and, 196–197
    defined, 196, 197
    development platforms, 151–152
    flexible development with, 293
    invitations to, 197
    invite-only, 275
    managing, 145, 265
    personal, 196
    privacy and, 197, 264, 275
    public, 196, 264, 266
    social contact information, 153
    supporting formation of, 144
    types of, 264–265
    white label social software, 152
Gruber, John, 170
Guardian (newspaper)
    API support, 332

commenting and, 59, 144, 170
community guidelines, 279
time implication example, 206
website presence, 58, 143

H

Hack Day site, 92
hackable URLs, 184, 203, 328
Hadoop service, 315, 329
Hansard transcripts, 188
HAProxy tool, 295
hashtags, 28, 75
hAtom microformat, 207
Haughey, Matt, 170, 181
Hayden-Teresa Nielsen, 278
hCard microformat, 191, 257–258, 333
HCI (human–computer interaction), 88
Henderson, Cal, 169, 316
Highsmith, Jim, 288
Hoelzle, Urs, 326
Hohpe, Gregor, 285
Holmes, Thomas, 70
home pages
    competition for, 225
    interaction design considerations, 86
    organizing, 242
    overview, 355–360
    private, 300
    profile pages as, 214
    versions of, 355
    visual design considerations, 47
Horowitz, Bradley, 58
hotel industry, 106
HTML
    frontend, 24, 48
    separating content from style, 302
    whitelisting, 308
hub-and-spoke model, 333
Huddle application, 152, 349
human–computer interaction (HCI), 88
Hunch application, 340
Hunt, Andrew, 288
Hunt, Tara, 36
hypertext information systems, 88

I

IATA (International Air Transport
    Association), 184

media types affecting, 53–58
patterns listed, 54
response to evolving needs, 62–66
Media Manager tool, 333
MediaWiki, 337
Mellor, Steve, 288
member-driven relationships, 11, 12
memcached technology, 198, 295, 316
memex, 88
Mercurial tool, 4, 289, 306
message boards
conversing in, 145–149
defined, 22
design considerations, 147
editing posts, 149
filtering on, 147, 282
group interaction via, 145, 265
interest-led communities and, 124
leeching behavior on, 146
making, 149
member-driven, 11
moderating, 149
naming influences perspective, 82
nested threads, 149
profile pages on, 148
search engine keyword analysis, 148
site planning considerations, 21
tagging content, 146, 149
text analysis of questions, 146
The Archers program, 19
trolling on, 269
vetting conversations, 279
messaging systems
internal, 173–175
rewarding good behavior, 275
scaling and, 309–317
Messina, Chris, 257, 273
metadata
data modeling and, 199
exploring groups, 196
GPS-derived values in, 194, 202
location, 201–205
search considerations, 317
video example, 193
MetaFilter.com site, 109
MGTwitterEngine library, 373
microblogs
attraction to, 100
content reuse and, 121

federated services, 139
lifestreaming considerations, 138
mobile phone networks and, 325
popularity of, 132
republishing and, 132
microformats
API support, 192
content reuse and, 347
defined, 257
development of, 262
screen scraping and, 340
Microsoft, 200, 258
Mint site, 71
MobileMe, 142
mockups
implementation considerations, 96
interaction design and, 86
site planning and, 31, 32
wireframes as, 83
Model-View-Controller (MVC) paradigm, 302
modeling data (see data modeling)
moderators
defined, 145
discussion forums, 59
focus groups, 83
for commenting, 144, 277
for communities, 277–278, 280
message boards and, 149
responsibilities, 279
monitoring systems, 294
Morville, Peter, 88, 336
MoSCoW approach, 306
Movable Type Motion platform, 152
Movable Type system
i18n approach, 303
OpenID support, 212
password support, 323
popularity of, 143
response to crises, 142
TheSchwartz queuing system, 312
Mozilla browser, 40
MVC (Model-View-Controller) paradigm, 302
My name is E application, 121
MySpace site
activity management, 139
evolution of, 125
handling security, 308
OpenSocial support, 152
teenage members, 126

Puppet tool, 295
pushing versus polling, 313

Q

QA (quality assurance), 291, 299
Qik application, 138
quality assurance (QA), 291, 299
Quechup (company), 259
queuing model, 311, 313

R

RabbitMQ, 313
Radiohead (band), 159
Rahe, Richard, 70
rapid iteration of code, 89
rapid prototyping, 309
rapid user interfaces, 308
rate of change (schema theory), 71
rating
    as social element, 60–62
    content, 172, 273
    posts and people, 272–274
RDF (Resource Description Framework), 206
real names
    identity management and, 210
    in people searches, 229
real time versus near time, 311, 351
real-time services, 4
ReCaptcha service, 218
recent actions, displaying, 165–168
recipe books, 105
refactoring code, 381
registration, account, 213, 319
Reichelt, Leisa, 83, 84
rel element, 181, 201, 257
relationships
    add and confirm model, 250
    add and notify model, 249, 251
    analyzing, 7–14
    as models of interaction, 93
    asymmetric follow model, 250
    attachment to community, 37
    behavior and interaction-based, 9–12
    blocking, 252
    building, 160
    changing over time, 263
    connecting to content, 200
    contributor-driven, 11, 13

creating and nurturing, 93
customer-service-driven, 10, 12
establishing, 109, 381
fan-based model, 251
Flickr levels supported, 116
information-broker-based, 253
language of connections, 252
managing, 14–20
member-driven, 11, 12
modeling, 200–201, 249–251
newspapers and, 58
persistent, 109
portability considerations, 256–258
pros and cons of, 12–14
publisher-driven, 10, 12
sending invitations, 253–256
sending notifications, 253–256
setting exposure levels, 115–119
social objects and, 156
symmetric follow model, 250
release stage, 34
releases
    interaction design considerations, 85
    product creation guidelines, 107
Remote Procedure Calls (see RPCs)
reputation systems, 330
reputation, sense of, 36
request tokens, 323
resistance to change, 69–73
Resource Description Framework (RDF), 206
response formats, 342
REST (REpresentational State Transfer)
    API support, 337, 341
    functionality, 301
    Tumblr support, 343
    Twitter support, 344
rev element, 181
RevCanonical application, 181
reverse chronological order
    in blogging, 141, 221
    marking favorites, 172
RFC 3986, 299
RFC 822, 207
RFID tag, 184
Rheingold, Howard, 275
Richardson, Leonard, 301
ripple effect, 90
river of news view
    defined, 132

U

About the Author

Gavin Bell has been playing around with the Web since 1993. He has worked in academia, designed multimedia CD-ROM applications, and worked in advertising. After a few years at the BBC advising how to create web applications and creating systems to represent TV and radio programs on the Web, he is now at the Nature Publishing Group, designing social software for scientists and speaking at conferences on the social web.

Gavin lives in London with his wife, Lucy, his sons, Oscar and Max, and their two cats. He is looking forward to regaining family weekends, seeing friends, and writing code to make social apps, rather than writing about them.

Colophon

The insects on the cover of *Building Social Web Applications* are garden spiders (*Argiope aurantia*). Found largely throughout the U.S., Canada, Mexico, and Central America, the garden spider is distinguished from other spiders by the yellow and black coloring on its abdomen. It is not poisonous.

Female garden spiders weave a very distinctive web. It is circular and can be as wide as two feet. At the center of the web is the stabilimentum, a conspicuous silk structure. Only garden spiders that are active in the daytime weave webs with stabilimenta. There are a variety of theories about the stabilimentum's purpose, including that it camouflages the spider in the center of the web; it traps prey; and it helps birds spot the web to avoid flying through it. Spiders usually spend the summer in one location and move in early fall.

When it is time to mate, males will build a small web nearby a female's and woo her by plucking strands on her web. Males must always be cautious when courting, as females are likely to attack them. Males die after mating, and females will sometimes eat their carcasses.

Females can produce as many as four sacs, each with 1,000 eggs inside. They suspend the sacs from the center of their webs because that is where they spend most of their time. They guard their eggs for as long as they can, but as the weather cools, they become weaker and usually die around the first frost. The young spiders emerge from the sac in spring.

The cover image is from Dover Pictorial Archive. The cover font is Adobe ITC Garamond. The text font is Linotype Birka; the heading font is Adobe Myriad Condensed; and the code font is LucasFont's TheSansMonoCondensed.

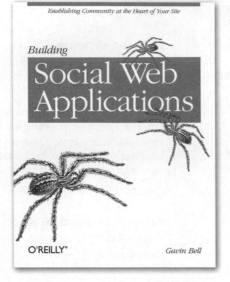